Rethinking the Acceptable Year

Rethinking the Acceptable Year

The Jubilee and the *Basileia* in Luke 4 and Beyond

CHRISTOPHER JAMES LUTHY

Foreword by Keith Dyer

WIPF & STOCK · Eugene, Oregon

RETHINKING THE ACCEPTABLE YEAR
The Jubilee and the *Basileia* in Luke 4 and Beyond

Copyright © 2019 Christopher James Luthy. All rights reserved. Except for brief quotations in critical publications or reviews, no part of this book may be reproduced in any manner without prior written permission from the publisher. Write: Permissions, Wipf and Stock Publishers, 199 W. 8th Ave., Suite 3, Eugene, OR 97401.

Wipf & Stock
An Imprint of Wipf and Stock Publishers
199 W. 8th Ave., Suite 3
Eugene, OR 97401

www.wipfandstock.com

PAPERBACK ISBN: 978-1-5326-8471-5
HARDCOVER ISBN: 978-1-5326-8472-2
EBOOK ISBN: 978-1-5326-8473-9

Manufactured in the U.S.A.   NOVEMBER 5, 2019

To Amy, with love and gratitude.

Contents

List of Tables | viii

Foreword by Keith Dyer | ix

Preface | xi

Acknowledgments | xiii

Abbreviations | xiv

Introduction | 1

1　*Basileia* of God and Jubilee Traditions in the Old Testament | 14

2　*Basileia* of God and Jubilee Traditions in Second Temple Literature | 45

3　The *Basileia* and Jubilee in Luke—Setting the Scene | 77

4　The *Basileia* Proclaimed, Explained, and Fulfilled—Isaiah 61 and Luke | 99

5　The Event at Nazareth—Luke 4:14–30 | 124

6　Beyond Nazareth—Other Themes and Passages in Luke with Suggested Jubilary Connections | 160

Conclusion | 186

Appendix 1—A History of Interpretation: The Jubilee in Luke-Acts | 193

Appendix 2—The Early Church and the Jubilee | 206

Bibliography | 215

Scripture Index | 233

List of Tables

Table 1 A Comparison between the text of 4Q521 and texts in Isaiah and Luke | 106

Table 2 Text and Translation of Isaiah 61:1–2a | 111

Table 3 Text and Translation of Luke 4:14–30 | 126

Table 4 A Comparison between Luke 4:18–19 and Isaiah 61:1–2a and 58:6 in the Septuagint | 133

Foreword

Questions about whether the Jubilee traditions have shaped the thinking of Jesus, or Luke, or both, have led to a persistent note of uncertainty in scholarly publications over recent decades. Sometimes the evidence and arguments in favor of the Jubilee have been used to sound a trumpet call to radical economic action and to tackling other social justice issues. Sometimes the calls have been muted by doubts about the clarity of the connections between the Jubilee and the Nazareth manifesto, for example. Even some scholars supportive of the economic and ethical campaigns inspired by the Jubilee texts have been skeptical that they were ever enacted historically or had any direct influence on the Jesus traditions. So despite the good work that has been done in clarifying the methods used for detecting and interpreting such traditions, a clear consensus over the afterlife of the Jubilee motifs in Jewish and Christian literature remains elusive.

On the other hand, the significance of the *basileia tou Theou* (kingdom of God) for Luke's retelling of the Jesus story has long been recognized, though the nature and timing of its implications continue to generate discussion. The relative importance of the *basileia* and the Jubilee in Luke's narrative, and whether there is any connection between them in Luke or in the older traditions, are areas that have not been adequately explored until now.

In this book Rev. Dr. Chris Luthy explores these issues and revisits these arguments with a focus on Luke's Gospel and its possible sources, encouraged by the availability of new textual evidence. This is not a polemic for or against the Jubilee or the *basileia* and their implications, but a dispassionate review of their significance for Luke's Gospel with a sideways glance at Acts. With great care and precision, Dr. Luthy systematically evaluates a wide range of texts thought to carry the vocabulary and imprint of the Jubilee and/or *basileia* traditions, and assesses the possibility that they have influenced the Lukan narrative and theology.

The conclusions he draws should not be interpreted as an attack on the Jubilee agendas for social justice and release from poverty, but as a strengthening of the foundations for, and understanding of, meaningful action and engagement today. The Luthy family themselves have been engaged in transformative ministry and mission in Queensland, Tasmania, and Indonesia over many years, and it is in these contexts that Chris has undertaken this research—sometimes under very difficult circumstances. Consequently, this book is not merely a theoretical discussion about the history of traditions, but a rigorous exploration, grounded in praxis, of the biblical and theological basis for the reality of God's dynamic reign and its implications for our world.

I commend it to your reading and active response.

—Keith Dyer

Associate Professor (New Testament)
Whitley College, University of Divinity
August, 2019

Preface

Before I met my wife, I had no interest whatsoever in the biblical Jubilee. I had undoubtedly heard of it, though I probably could not have explained what it was to anyone who might have asked. It was one those "Old Testament things" that held little interest for me (an ignorant and regrettable attitude).

My wife, however, had spent significant time in a missional context, in which she had been exposed to a number of articles and books which highlighted the importance of the Jubilee. Some of these even mentioned how important the Jubilee was in Jesus' ministry. After she shared some of this with me, my interest was piqued. I considered myself to be reasonably familiar with Jesus' message and ministry, and yet to learn that there were many who considered the Jubilee (which I knew barely anything about) to be an integral part of Jesus' message was quite confronting. This was particularly the case given that the "clearest" reference to the Jubilee in Luke's Gospel was in the Nazareth episode (Luke 4:16–30)—a programmatic passage that is vitally important if one is to rightly understand the Lukan Jesus' ministry. I felt the need to study further.

That journey became almost an obsession. I quickly gathered every book and journal article I could find which mentioned the Jubilee. I read and read and read. The overwhelming message I was reading was that in Luke's Gospel, and in particular the Nazareth episode, there were definite references to the biblical Jubilee which could shine light on Luke's two-part work. There were, however, several dissenting voices who were skeptical of such claims. Instead, they stated that the suggested Lukan Jubilee references had not yet been rigorously investigated. There were also different views as to how the Jubilee should be understood and different opinions as to what consituted a reference to the Jubilee (and, therefore, different opinions on the number of Jubilee references in Luke's work).

At the time, I was searching for a PhD topic, and so I decided to investigate the various suggested Lukan references to the Jubilee in order to definitively demonstrate their importance in Luke's work. I began studying the background to the Jubilee in the Old Testament and the Second Temple documents and analyzing the various suggested Lukan references. During this process, a surprising (and somewhat frustrating) thing occurred: I found myself agreeing more and more with those who doubted the presence of Jubilee images and allusions in Luke-Acts. In fact, I became more and more convinced that to import Jubilee thinking into Luke's work was to misread his message.

Eventually, my study concluded that every suggested allusion in Luke-Acts can be satisfactorily explained without reference to the Jubilee, and that many of the suggested allusions to the Jubilee are better explained as references to the *basileia* of God. This book is fundamentally a reproduction of that study. I remain thoroughly convinced of this study's conclusions and am hopeful that the reader will also find the thesis compelling.

I remember one of my first ever lecturers stating unequicovally that biblical studies research must be helpful to the church. His words have frequently come to mind during the course of this study. My hope is that in some way this study will prove to be helpful, particularly in regards to understanding the fulfillment of Jesus' proclamation of the acceptable year.

Acknowledgments

Living in North West Tasmania for much of this study made access to some materials difficult. I am therefore very grateful to Dr. Sharon Ringe, Dr. Donald Blosser, and Dr. Jacob Elias, who all graciously sent me a copy of their PhD dissertations, as well as Dr. David O'Brien, who sent me his insightful study on Jubilee interpretations. I am also indebted to Sue McQuay, who spent many hours editing the original manuscript. Thank you.

I also wish to acknowledge the continuous support of Dr. Keith Dyer, for his availability (oftentimes at short notice), his patience, the sharing of his knowledge and experience, and his genuine care. I am very grateful. Many thanks also to Dr. Mark Brett for his valuable comments and recommendations.

My family has been constantly amazing during the preparation of this manuscript. Thank you Josiah, Eliana, and Elijah for allowing your Daddy the time to study. To my wife, Amy, you truly are "a wife of noble character." Thank you for your motivation, prayers, and unwavering support. Without you, this study would not have been possible.

There are, of course, many others who have been an important part of the journey at different times and in different ways. I am grateful for all of you.

Soli Deo Gloria

Abbreviations

Hebrew Bible/Old Testament

Gen	Genesis	Song	Song of Songs
Exod	Exodus	Isa	Isaiah
Lev	Leviticus	Jer	Jeremiah
Num	Numbers	Lam	Lamentations
Deut	Deuteronomy	Ezek	Ezekiel
Josh	Joshua	Dan	Daniel
Judg	Judges	Hos	Hosea
Ruth	Ruth	Joel	Joel
1–2 Sam	1–2 Samuel	Amos	Amos
1–2 Kgs	1–2 Kings	Obad	Obadiah
1–2 Chr	1–2 Chronicles	Jonah	Jonah
Ezra	Ezra	Mic	Micah
Neh	Nehemiah	Nah	Nahum
Esth	Esther	Hab	Habakkuk
Job	Job	Zeph	Zephaniah
Ps/Pss	Psalms	Hag	Haggai
Prov	Proverbs	Zech	Zechariah
Eccl	Ecclesiastes	Mal	Malachi

New Testament

Matt	Matthew	1–2 Tim	1–2 Timothy
Mark	Mark	Titus	Titus
Luke	Luke	Phlm	Philemon
John	John	Heb	Hebrews
Acts	Acts	Jas	James
Rom	Romans	1–2 Pet	1–2 Peter
1–2 Cor	1–2 Corinthians	1–2 Thess	1–2 Thessalonians
Eph	Ephesians	1–2–3 John	1–2–3 John
Phil	Philippians	Jude	Jude
Col	Colossians	Rev	Revelation
Gal	Galatians		

Apocryphal/Deuterocanonical Books

Tob	Tobit	Sg Three	Song of the Three Young Men
Jdt	Judith	Sus	Susanna
Add Esth	Additions to Esther	Bar	Baruch
Wis	Wisdom of Solomon	Bel	Bel and the Dragon
Sir	Sirach/Ecclesiasticus	1–2 Macc	1–2 Maccabees
1–3 Esd	1–3 Esdras	3–4 Macc	3–4 Maccabees
Pr Man	Prayer of Manasseh		

Old Testament Pseudepigrapha

Jub.	Jubilees
Pss. Sol.	Psalms of Solomon
1 En.	1 Enoch (Ethiopic Apocalypse)
2 En.	2 Enoch (Slavonic Apocalypse)
3 En.	3 Enoch (Hebrew Apocalypse)
4 Ezra	4 Ezra
Vis. Ezra	Vision of Ezra
Apoc. Sedr.	Apocalypse of Sedrach

3 Bar.	3 Baruch (Greek Apocalypse)
T. Sim.	Testament of Simeon
T. Levi	Testament of Levi
T. 12 Patr	Testaments of the Twelve Patriarchs
T. Isaac	Testament of Isaac
T. Jac.	Testament of Jacob
T. Mos.	Testament of Moses
T. Benj.	Testament of Benjamin
T. Ab.	Testament of Abraham
T. Jos.	Testament of Joseph
Apocr. Ezek.	Apocryphon of Ezekiel
Apoc. Zeph.	Apocalypse of Zephaniah
Gk. Apoc. Ezra	Greek Apocalypse of Ezra
Apoc. El. (C)	Coptic Apocalypse of Elijah
Hist. Rech.	History of the Rechabites
Hel. Syn. Pr.	Hellenistic Synagogal Prayers
Odes Sol.	Odes of Solomon
Jos. Asen.	Joseph and Aseneth
LAB	Liber antiquitatum biblicarum
LAE	Life of Adam and Eve
Lad. Jac.	Ladder of Jacob
Jan. Jam.	Jannes and Jambres

Dead Sea Scrolls

1Q20 / 1Qap Gen^{ar}	Genesis Apocryphon
1Q28b / 1QSb	Rule of the Blessings
1QH^a	Hodayot^a or Thanksgiving Hymns^a
1QM	Milḥamah or War Scroll
1QS	Community Rule
CD	Cairo Genizah copy of the Damascus Document
4Q174 / 4QFlor	Florilegium, also Midrash on Eschatology
11Q13 / 11QMelch	Melchizedek

Mishnah

An *m.* denotes a tractate from the Mishnah.

ᶜAbod. Zar.	ᶜAbodah Zarah	Avodah Zarah
ʾAbot	ʾAbot	Avot
ᶜArak.	ᶜArakhin	Arakhin
Bek.	Bekorot	Bekhorot
Ber.	Berakot	Berakhot
Git.	Giṭṭin	Gittin
Qidd.	Qiddušin	Quiddushin
Roš Haš.	Roš Haššanah	Rosh HaShanah
Šabb.	Šabbat	Shabbat
Sanh.	Sanhedrin	Sanhedrin
Šeb.	Šebiᶜit	Shev'it
Soṭah	Soṭah	Sotah
Tamid	Tamid	Tamid
Yoma	Yoma (= Kippurim)	Yoma

Targums and Other Rabbinic Works

Tg. Ps.-J	Targum Pseudo-Jonathan
Tg. Isa.	Targum Isaiah
Rab.	Rabbah
Mek.	Mekhilta
Midr.	Midrash

Greek and Latin Works

Aristotle:
Poet.   *Poetics*
Josephus:
Ant.   *Jewish Antiquities*
Philo:

Abraham	On the Life of Abraham
Decalogue	On the Decalogue
Hypothetica	Hypothetica
Migration	On the Migration of Abraham
QG	Questions and Answers on Genesis
Sobriety	On Sobriety
Spec. Laws	On the Special Laws
Virtues	On the Virtues

Irenaeus:

Haer.	Heresies

Lucian:

Quom. Hist. conscr. sit	Quomodo Historia conscribenda sit (How to Write History)

Pliny the Younger:

Ep.	Epistulae

Suetonius:

Vit.	Vitellius

Early Christian Works

Apos. Con.	Apostolic Constitutions and Canons

Ambrose:

On the Decease	On the Decease of His Brother Saytrus

Augustine:

Expositions	Expositions on the Book of Psalms

John Chrysostom:

Hom. Matt.	Homilies on Matthew

Clement of Alexandria:

Strom.	Stromata (Miscellanies)

Hippolytus:

Fr. Ps.	Fragmenta in Psalmos
Schol. Matt.	Scholia in Matthaeum

Origen:

Princ.	De principiis (Peri archÆn)

Journals, Periodicals, Major Reference Works, and Series

AB	The Anchor Bible
ACCS	Ancient Christian Commentary on Scripture
ACNT	Augsburg Commentaries on the New Testament
AJPS	*Asian Journal of Pentecostal Studies*
AnBib	Analecta Biblica
ANF	*Ante-Nicene Fathers.* 10 vols. Edited by Alexander Roberts and James Donaldson. 1885–1887. Reprint, Peabody, MA: Hendrickson, 1994.
ANTC	Abingdon New Testament Commentaries
AUSS	*Andrews University Seminary Studies*
BBR	*Bulletin for Biblical Research*
BDAG	Walter Bauer, Frederick W. Danker, W. F. Arndt, and F. W. Gingrich. *Greek–English Lexicon of the New Testament and Other Early Christian Literature.* 3rd ed. Chicago: University of Chicago Press, 2000.
BDB	Francis Brown, S. R. Driver, and Charles A. Briggs. *Hebrew and English Lexicon of the Old Testament.* Oxford: Clarendon, 1907.
BECNT	Baker Exegetical Commentary on the New Testament
Belief	Belief: A Theological Commentary on the Bible
BETL	Bibliotheca ephemeridum theologicarum lovaniensium
BHT	Beiträge zur historischen Theologie
BibInt	Biblical Interpretation
BR	*Biblical Research*
BSac	*Bibliotheca Sacra*
BTB	*Biblical Theology Bulletin*
BTCB	Brazos Theological Commentary on the Bible
BThe	*Black Theology*
BTNT	Biblical Theology of the New Testament
CahRB	Cahiers de la Revue biblique
CBQ	*Catholic Biblical Quarterly*
CBC	Cornerstone Biblical Commentaries
CGTC	Cambridge Greek Testament Commentary
COQG	Christian Origins and the Question of God
CTM	*Concordia Theological Monthly*
CTR	*Criswell Theological Review*

CurBS	*Currents in Research: Biblical Studies*
DNTB	*Dictionary of New Testament Background*. Edited by Craig A. Evans and Stanley E. Porter. Downers Grove, IL: InterVarsity, 2000.
DSD	*Dead Sea Discoveries*
EBC	Expositor's Bible Commentary
EBS	Exploring the Bible Series
ECC	Eerdmans Critical Commentary
EKKNT	Evangelisch-katholischer Kommentar zum Neuen Testament
EUS	European University Studies
EvQ	*Evangelical Quarterly*
ExAud	*Ex Auditu*
FB	Forschung zur Bibel
FC	Fathers of the Church. Washington, DC: Catholic University of America Press, 1947–2013.
HNTC	Holman New Testament Commentary
HTKNT	Herders theologischer Kommentar zum Neuen Testament
ICC	International Critical Commentary
ICJ	*International Congregational Journal*
IRM	*International Review of Mission*
IRT	Issues in Religion and Theology
JAAR	*Journal of the American Academy of Religion*
JBL	*Journal of Biblical Literature*
JE	*The Jewish Encyclopedia*. 12 vols. Edited by Isidore Singer. New York: Funk & Wagnalls, 1925.
JETS	*Journal of the Evangelical Theological Society*
JJS	*Journal of Jewish Studies*
JPTSup	Journal of Pentecostal Theology Supplement Series
JSJ	*Journal for the Study of Judaism in the Persian, Hellenistic, and Roman Periods*
JSNT	*Journal for the Study of the New Testament*
JSNTSup	Journal for the Study of the New Testament: Supplement Series
JSOT	*Journal for the Study of the Old Testament*
JSOTSup	Journal for the Study of the Old Testament: Supplement Series
JSP	*Journal for the Study of the Pseudepigrapha*
JSPSup	Journal for the Study of the Pseudepigrapha: Supplement Series
KBANT	Kommentare und Beiträge zum Alten und Neuen Testament

KEK	Kritisch-exegetischer Kommentar über das Neue Testament
LCL	Loeb Classical Library
LNTS	Library of New Testament Studies
Missiology	*Missiology: An International Review*
MNTC	Moffatt New Testament Commentary
NAC	The New American Commentary
NCB	New Century Bible
NIB	The New Interpreter's Bible
NICNT	New International Commentary on the New Testament
NICOT	New International Commentary on the Old Testament
NIDNTTE	*New International Dictionary of New Testament Theology and Exegesis*. Edited by Moisés Silva. 2nd ed. 5 vols. Grand Rapids: Zondervan, 2014.
NIGTC	New International Greek Testament Commentary
NLCNT	New London Commentary on the New Testament
NovT	*Novum Testamentum*
NovTSup	Supplements to Novum Testamentum
NPNF1	*Nicene and Post-Nicene Fathers, Series 1*. 14 vols. Edited by Philip Schaff. 1886–1889. Reprint, Peabody, MA: Hendrickson, 1994.
NPNF2	*Nicene and Post-Nicene Fathers, Series 2*. 14 vols. Edited by Philip Schaff and Henry Wace. 1890–1900. Reprint, Peabody, MA: Hendrickson, 1994.
NTOA	Novum Testamentum et Orbis Antiquus
NTR	New Testament Readings
NTS	*New Testament Studies*
NTT	New Testament Theology
OTL	Old Testament Library
OTP	*The Old Testament Pseudepigrapha*. 2 vols. Edited by James H. Charlesworth. 2nd ed. Peabody, MA: Hendrickson, 2011.
Paideia	Paideia: Commentaries on the New Testament
PenNTC	Penguin New Testament Commentaries
PilNTC	Pillar New Testament Commentaries
PGNT	Phoenix Guides to the New Testament
ProEccl	*Pro Ecclesia*
Proof	*Prooftexts: A Journal of Jewish Literary History*
REC	Reformed Expository Commentary
ResQ	*Restoration Quarterly*

RGRW	Religions in the Graeco-Roman World
RJ	*Reformed Journal*
RTR	*Reformed Theological Review*
SBL	Society for Biblical Literature
SBLDS	Society of Biblical Literature Dissertation Series
SBLMS	Society of Biblical Literature Monograph Series
SBLSymS	Society of Biblical Literature Symposium Series
SBS	Stuttgarter Bibelstudien
SBT	Studies in Biblical Theology
SCJ	*Stone-Campbell Journal*
SCO	The Scrolls and Christian Origins
SDSSRL	Studies in the Dead Sea Scrolls and Related Literature
SHBC	Smith & Helwys Bible Commentary
SHS	Scripture and Hermeneutics Series
SJT	*Scottish Journal of Theology*
SJSJ	Supplements to the Journal for the Study of Judaism
SNTA	Studiorum Novi Testamenti Auxilia
SNTSMS	Society for New Testament Studies Monograph Series
SP	Sacra Pagina
StPatr	*Studia Patristica*
TBS	The Biblical Seminar
TCLit	Translations of Christian Literature
TDNT	*Theological Dictionary of the New Testament.* 10 vols. Edited by Gerhard Kittel and Gerhard Friedrich. Translated by Geoffrey W. Bromiley. Grand Rapids: Eerdmans, 1964–76.
TGST	Tesi Gregoriana Serie Teologia
THKNT	Theologischer Handkommentar zum Neuen Testament
TJ	*Trinity Journal*
TLNT	Theological Lexicon of the New Testament
TLOT	*Theological Lexicon of the Old Testament.* Edited by Ernst Jenni and Claus Westermann. Translated by Mark Biddle. 3 vols. Peabody, MA: Hendrickson, 1997.
TPINTC	TPI New Testament Commentaries
TynBul	*Tyndale Bulletin*
UBCS	Understanding the Bible Commentary Series
UBT	Understanding Biblical Themes
VT	*Vetus Testamentum*

VTSup	Supplements to Vetus Testamentum
WBC	Word Biblical Commentary
WesBC	Westminster Bible Companion
WBCS	Wesleyan Bible Commentary Series
WTJ	*Westminster Theological Journal*
WUNT	Wissenschaftliche Untersuchungen zum Neuen Testament
WW	*Word and World*
ZAW	*Zeitschrift für die Alttestamentliche Wissenschaft*
ZECNT	Zondervan Exegetical Commentary on the New Testament
ZNW	*Zeitschrift für die neutestamentliche Wissenschaft und die Kunde der älteren Kirche*

Other Abbreviations

BCE	Before Common Era
CE	Common Era
LXX	Septuagint
MT	Masoretic Text
Q	Quelle (source)
Repr.	Reprint
UBS	United Bible Societies

Introduction

Background and Overview of Literature

The biblical Jubilee has undergone a wide range of interpretations at various times and places throughout history. These interpretations have, at times, exercised a profound level of influence on Jews, Christians, and others, and its influence continues in the modern era. Since the 1950s in particular, there has been an increasing focus on the Jubilee, particularly in regard to how Jubilee practices and principles can be applied to current contexts.[1] This renewed interest has been accompanied by a significant body of research addressing the theological, historical, and socioeconomic aspects of the Jubilee in the Old Testament texts, Second Temple literature, and Qumran documents, and the New Testament texts. Of the New Testament texts, Luke-Acts is frequently cited as containing the most explicit Jubilee texts and motifs. In particular, Jesus' synagogue ministry in Nazareth (4:16–30) has attracted the most attention as a Jubilee text.[2] Moreover, since this text is often understood to be a programmatic description of Jesus' mission, it has also been argued that appreciating Jesus' proclamation of a Jubilee year is of critical importance if one is to properly understand Jesus' ministry throughout Luke's Gospel.[3]

The renewed focus on the Jubilee has seen many articles and monographs produced, which have explored what has sometimes been termed

---

1. See appendix 1.

2. Bruno, for example, states unequivocally that "the clearest reference to the Jubilee in the NT comes in Jesus' first synagogue sermon in Luke's Gospel." Bruno, "'Jesus is our Jubilee,'" 84.

3. Blosser, "Jesus and the Jubilee," 1. For the purposes of this study, "Luke" has been used to refer primarily to the text and implied author behind that text.

1

Lukan Jubilary theology.[4] Three of these works which overlap the present study are the studies by Robert Sloan, Donald Blosser, and Sharon Ringe. Each of these scholars was responding in part to the controversial work of John Howard Yoder, who helped popularize the view that Luke presented Jesus as proclaiming a Jubilee year in Luke 4:16–30 in order to restructure sociopolitical and economic relations among the people of God.[5] While Sloan, Blosser, and Ringe ultimately disagreed with Yoder's position, they all arrived at different conclusions.

Sloan's dissertation briefly investigated the provisions of the original Jubilee legislation.[6] He argued that the predominant use of the Jubilee legislation in Jewish literature was eschatological, though he only mentioned a few sections of the Pentateuch and 11QMelch to support his claims.[7] Sloan then examined Jesus' supposed proclamation of a Jubilee year in Luke 4:16–30 and determined that the theological basis of the pericope is the Jubilee year, which was "eschatologically interpreted and mediated through Is. 61, and as such applied by Jesus to himself."[8] He then explored other textual and thematic references to the Jubilee in Luke's Gospel, focusing largely on Luke's use of ἄφεσις and ἀφίημι, the Sermon on the Plain (6:20–38), and the Lord's Prayer (11:2–4).[9] He concluded that the notion of Jubilee has profoundly influenced the theological character of many Lukan words and themes.[10] Sloan also concluded that Luke's Gospel was largely shaped by the

---

4. See, for example, Sloan, *Favorable Year*; Blosser, "Jubilee"; Ringe, "Jubilee Proclamation"; Barker, "The Time is Fulfilled," 22–32; Bruno, "'Jesus is our Jubilee'"; and Hertig, "Jubilee Mission".

5. Yoder, *Politics*, 28–33. The sections pertaining to the Jubilee were largely based on André Trocmé's *Jesus and the Nonviolent Revolution*, first published in English in 1973.

6. Sloan, *Favorable Year*, 4–18.

7. Sloan briefly mentions that Daniel, Jubilees, the Qumran literature, and later Talmudic literature all mention the Jubilee, but he argues that it is not necessary to trace the historical development of the Jubilee theme through these works. He does, however, state unequivocally that it is "abundantly clear from the above-mentioned citations [that] their overall tendency [is] to give to the Levitical vision of Jubilee an increased eschatological flavor." Sloan, *Favorable Year*, 10–11, 168.

This blanket assessment, however, is clearly an oversimplification of the literature. If Sloan had analyzed the late Second Temple Jewish references to the Jubilee, he would probably have come to a different conclusion, which may have affected the outcome of his study.

8. Sloan, *Favorable Year*, 89.

9. Sloan also believes that all references to the "kingdom," "preaching the good news," and "the poor" throughout Luke's Gospel must be connected to the Jubilee, since he argues that Jesus' initial programmatic statement of mission (Luke 4:16–30) is a picture of the eschatological Jubilee. Sloan, *Favorable Year*, 118–46, 174.

10. Sloan, *Favorable Year*, 146.

image of the Jubilee, which was used as a metaphorical expression for the present and future eschatological salvation of God, which Jesus inaugurated and which will be consummated in the future.[11]

Blosser adopted a different approach. He spent nearly half of his dissertation surveying references to the Jubilee throughout the Old Testament and the intertestamental literature in order to understand how its meaning developed and how Jesus' audience might have understood the Nazareth proclamation.[12] He then examined Luke 4:14–30 in considerable detail by exploring both the historical occasion that Luke referred to and Luke's narrative purposes for including the account.[13] Blosser concluded that Luke intended to present the Jubilee as being a core theme of Luke 4:14–30.[14] He argued that the Jubilee was presented as a paradigm for obedience in the Kingdom of God.[15] He also argued that Luke intended that the Nazareth pericope have programmatic significance throughout his narrative; he found frequent references to the Jubilee throughout Luke's Gospel.[16] Finally, Blosser also argued that part of the reason why Luke wrote his account was so that the people of God might implement Jubilee principles and practices in their own lives.[17] Blosser therefore disagreed with Sloan's arguments about the future eschatological import of the Jubilee, instead viewing its chief significance as providing "a paradigm for the social and economic life of the community of believers in the new age (which was announced by Jesus that day at Nazareth)."[18]

Like Blosser, Ringe also gave considerable attention to the development in interpretation of the Jubilee throughout the Old Testament and late Second Temple Jewish literature.[19] She then used the Old Testament Jubilee references (with some conditions) as the main criteria for identifying

---

11. Sloan, *Favorable Year*, 162–67.
12. Blosser, "Jubilee," 1–63.
13. Blosser, "Jubilee," 64–116.
14. Blosser, "Jubilee," 99, 148.
15. Blosser, "Jubilee," 147–49.
16. In particular, Blosser identifies the Jubilee theme in Luke's Gospel in the Magnificat (1:46–55), the Sermon on the Plain (6:20–26 and 34–36), Jesus' answer to John the Baptist (7:18–23), the mission of the Twelve (9:1–6), the Lord's Prayer (11:1–4), Jesus' sermon about earthly possessions and heavenly treasures (12:22–34), the parable of the great banquet (14:12–24), the parable of the dishonest steward (16:1–9), the account of the rich man and Lazarus (16:19–31), Jesus' encounter with the rich ruler (18:18–30), and Jesus' encounter with Zaccheus (19:1–10). Blosser, "Jubilee," 133–43.
17. Blosser, "Jubilee," 149–53.
18. Blosser, "Jubilee," 150.
19. Ringe, "Jubilee Proclamation," 19–116.

allusions to the Jubilee in the Synoptic Gospels and Acts.[20] She was not primarily interested in whether or not the Synoptic authors intended to use Jubilee imagery; she was more concerned about the "phenomenon of Jubilee themes and motifs in the synoptic gospels, and of the implications and meaning of such themes and motifs in the picture of Jesus which the gospels present."[21] Indeed, Ringe noted that there is no clear evidence that either the Synoptic Gospel writers or Jesus intentionally presented a Jubilee program.[22] Despite this, however, she also argued that the Synoptic Gospels' collective picture of Jesus presents him as pronouncing a Jubilee message, even though he may not have been aware of it.[23] That is, Jesus' message and self-presentation included some themes (such as "good news to the poor" and "release") which were usually associated with Jubilee traditions, though he and the authors of the Gospels may not have made the connection with the Jubilee.[24] Finally, Ringe explored Jubilee references in Acts and concluded that there is little evidence of Jubilee themes outside of the sermon in Acts 10:34–43.[25] She therefore concluded that Jubilee themes were not significant for the early church's primary message about salvation and Christology, though they sometimes appeared in summaries of that message.[26]

Thus, Sloan, Blosser, and Ringe all arrived at very different conclusions. Sloan and Blosser both concluded that Luke intentionally presented Jesus as proclaiming a Jubilee year, whereas Ringe remained unconvinced that either the Synoptic authors or Jesus had a Jubilee program in mind. Sloan believed that Luke presented Jesus as proclaiming an eschatological Jubilee message which reflected the message of salvation.[27] Blosser, however, viewed Luke's presentation of Jesus' Jubilee announcement as being a paradigmatic expression of what obedience should look like for the people of God; it denotes that those things which oppress and dehumanize people (such as poverty, slavery, and loss of hope) should have no place in the kingdom of God.[28] Ringe concluded that Luke (and the other Synoptic authors) probably did not have a Jubilee program in mind, however she nonetheless argued that the Jubilee themes of "good news to the poor" and

---

20. Ringe, "Jubilee Proclamation," 118–20.
21. Ringe, "Jubilee Proclamation," 120.
22. Ringe, "Jubilee Proclamation," 264–65.
23. Ringe, "Jubilee Proclamation," 265.
24. Ringe, "Jubilee Proclamation," 292.
25. Ringe, "Jubilee Proclamation," 293.
26. Ringe, "Jubilee Proclamation," 294.
27. Sloan, *Favorable Year*, 162–67.
28. Blosser, "Jubilee," 149–50, 153.

"release"/"forgiveness" in Matthew, Mark, and Luke function as symbols and images of the Jubilee, which point to the significance of Jesus and his message.[29] All three scholars also evidently believed that 11QMelch gives important insights into how Jubilee motifs in Luke's Gospel should be understood, particularly in relation to the Isaianic quotation in Luke 4:16–30.[30]

Aside from these three dissertations, the subject of the Jubilee in the New Testament has been addressed in numerous other monographs, journal articles, and commentaries, particularly in relation to Luke 4:16–30.[31] The majority of these studies have concluded that Luke did indeed present Jesus as proclaiming a Jubilee year or that he employed Jubilee imagery to elucidate Jesus' ministry.[32] Indeed, as Bart Koet has noted, there is now "almost general consensus" that an allusion to the Jubilee exists in Luke's work.[33]

There are, however, some scholars who remain unconvinced that the author of Luke-Acts was concerned with the Jubilee. Jacob Elias's doctoral dissertation, a redaction-critical study of Luke 4:14–30, concludes that it was unlikely that Luke understood the new salvation era announced in Luke 4:18–19 in Jubilean terms, though it was possible that Jesus may have framed his ministry in Jubilean categories (though this is also unclear).[34] Similarly, in examining Luke 4:14–21, Robert Tannehill observed that while Isa 61:1–2 "develops themes from the Jubilee year, it is not so clear that the author of Luke-Acts was aware of the connection between this passage and the law of Jubilee."[35] This brief comment has influenced some other Lukan commentators also to question whether Luke was at all concerned with the Jubilee year.[36]

29. Ringe, "Jubilee Proclamation," 287–94.

30. Sloan, *Favorable Year*, 43–44; Blosser, "Jubilee," 49–50; and Ringe, "Jubilee Proclamation," 114.

31. For an overview of the literature related to the interpretation of the Jubilee, see appendix 1. For a comprehensive (though somewhat dated) survey of texts which address the Nazareth pericope, see Schreck, "Nazareth Pericope" 399–471.

32. Some of these studies include: Willoughby, "Concept of Jubilee," 41–55; Richard, "Now is the Time," 50–51; Sanders, "Sins," 84–92; Shin, *Ausrufung*; Hanks, *Third World*, 97–104; Massyngbaerde Ford, *My Enemy is My Guest*, 53–64; Green, *The Gospel of Luke* (NICNT), 209–13; Tiede, *Luke*, 106–07; Bovon, *Lukas*, 1:210–16; Strobel, "Ausrufung," 40–46; Sabourin, *St Luke*, 136–37; and Sanders, "Isaiah in Luke," 20–25.

33. Koet, *Five Studies*, 25.

34. Elias, "Beginning," 200.

35. Tannehill, *Narrative Unity*, 68.

36. See, for example, Stein, *Luke*, 157 and Garland, *Luke*, 200. Other scholars who have also come to this conclusion include Rodgers, "Luke 4:16–30," 81–82; Johnson, *Luke*, 81; Prior, *Jesus the Liberator*, 139–41; and Keck, *Luke*, 106.

The study that most explicitly argues against the presence of Jubilee allusions in Luke-Acts, however, is a journal article by David O'Brien which specifically addresses the differences between the early Jewish and early Christian interpretations of the Jubilee year.[37] O'Brien argues that it seems unlikely that early Christian interpreters (including Luke) would have made a connection between the Jubilee and Isaiah 61.[38] He also observes that there is no need to associate Luke's use of ἄφεσις with the Jubilee legislation.[39] The brevity of O'Brien's article, however, limited his examination of Luke 4:16–30, and Luke's wider two-part corpus was not addressed.

Objective of This Study

As the above literature overview demonstrates, there have been no recent monograph-length treatments that have questioned the assumption of Jubilary motifs in Luke's two-part corpus. While initial questions have been asked, the subject has not yet received adequate attention. Indeed, the majority of New Testament Jubilee research has presumed a Lukan Jubilee program and therefore has focused more on *how* Luke's supposed Jubilee program should be interpreted and applied.[40]

This study, therefore, initially commenced as an examination into the likelihood of Lukan references to the Jubilee. A pattern, however, soon emerged when many of the suggested Jubilee allusions were examined. In particular, it became clear that many of the passages in question were chiefly concerned with the *basileia* of God rather than the Jubilee.[41] This then prompted the question as to whether a connection in the tradition exists between the Jubilee and the *basileia* in the Old Testament and the Second Temple literature. After this was investigated and found to be lacking, the thesis for this study became clear: this study posits that most of the suggested references and allusions to the Jubilee in Luke-Acts are better explained as references to the βασιλεία τοῦ θεοῦ, and that there is no explicit relationship between the two concepts in first-century Jewish and Christian literature.[42]

37. O'Brien, "Comparison," 436–42.
38. O'Brien, "Comparison," 441–42.
39. O'Brien, "Comparison," 439–40.
40. For example, Lowell Noble argues that Jesus' Jubilee proclamation in Luke 4:16–19 supports the case for affordable housing. John Howard Yoder, however, argues that Jesus proclaimed a Jubilee year at Nazareth in order to support his wider message of radical Christian pacifism. Noble, "Ownership," 34–37 and Yoder, *Politics*, 60.
41. The term βασιλεία has frequently been transliterated throughout this study in order to avoid the anachronistic use of "kingdom."
42. There are, of course, differences in opinion as to when some documents were

This study will therefore reassess the evidence for the use of Jubilary language and motifs in the traditions behind Luke and the text itself, with some attention to Acts. It will focus on references to Isaiah 61 in Luke-Acts, and particularly the Nazareth episode (Luke 4:14–30), which is frequently identified as the clearest reference to the Jubilee in Luke's narrative.[43] This text is also often recognized as being programmatic in Luke's presentation of Jesus' ministry.[44] Indeed, Willoughby argues that its "significance for our general understanding of Lukan theology can hardly be overestimated."[45] Since this is the case, if it can be shown that it is unlikely that Luke presented a Jubilee program in the Nazareth episode, this will affect our overall understanding of the Lukan Jesus' ministry. It will also give grounds to question the presence of Jubilee motifs in the remainder of Luke's narrative, and affect the interpretation of later references to Luke 4:14–30 in Luke's narrative.[46] Based on this, it will also give grounds to question how one might understand the practical implications of the Jubilee in the twenty-first century (a topic which is particularly popular in missional circles).

This study explores therefore a clear and significant gap in the current Jubilee and Lukan literature. Significantly, it is also able to draw from some recently published historical evidence which has not been taken into account by many of the previous studies.[47]

---

written (the analysis of which falls outside the scope of this study). There may also be further writings yet to be discovered/published which may impact the findings of this study.

43. Bruno, "Jesus is our Jubilee," 84.

44. See, for example, Bock, *Theology*, 136; Rowe, *Early Narrative Christology*, 78–80; Tannehill, *Narrative Unity*, 62; Green, *The Gospel of Luke* (NICNT), 207; and Willoughby, "Concept of Jubilee," 42.

45. Willoughby, "Concept of Jubilee," 42.

46. Lukan texts which refer back to the Nazareth episode include Luke 7:22 and Acts 10:37–38.

47. In particular, the Dead Sea Scroll 4Q521 provides some significant insights into how Isa 61 might have been interpreted by first-century readers, however it was first published in 1992—after some of the more important New Testament Jubilee research was completed. Brooke, *Dead Sea Scrolls*, 79.

Similarly, the early church literature has also been largely ignored in Jubilee research. Aside from the present study, it is only O'Brien who has examined in detail the early church's interpretation of the Jubilee. O'Brien, "Comparison," 441–42.

There are, admittedly, difficulties in drawing definitive conclusions about Luke's work based on later Christian interpretations. Despite this, these later works provide some insight as to how the Jubilee was interpreted, as well as a gauge of how important the topic was. I have therefore included a survey of the early church's interpretation of the Jubilee (see appendix 2).

Structure and Approach

In order to achieve this objective, a number of key questions require answers, including the following:

1. What were the Jubilee traditions which are alleged to have influenced Luke?
2. How was the *basileia* of God understood in the first century?
3. Is there a relationship between the Jubilee traditions and the *basileia* traditions in the Old Testament and Second Temple literature?
4. How was Isaiah 61:1–2 understood in the first century? Was there a perceived relationship between this text and either the Jubilee or the *basileia* (or both)?
5. How consistent are the suggested references to the Jubilee in Luke-Acts with other explicit early Jubilee traditions?
6. If the suggested references do not align with how the Jubilee was understood in the first century, can the references be better explained in reference to the *basileia*?

With these questions in mind, the body of the study contains six chapters. In the first chapter, the focus is the development of Jubilee and *basileia* of God traditions throughout the Old Testament, with an accompanying examination of any semantic or literary relationship between the two sets of traditions. Luke's use of Old Testament texts is also briefly addressed. The following chapter largely follows this same format, with the focus instead turning to Second Temple literature. Thus, two chapters cover a study into the history of Jubilee and *basileia* of God interpretations from the Old Testament through to the Second Temple literature, as well as any possible relationship between the two concepts. This, in turn, aids in determining the likely way/s in which Luke (and his readership) would have viewed both the Jubilee and the *basileia*.

The third chapter addresses the more foundational subjects of the likely author and audience of Luke-Acts, before investigating the two Greek words which are of chief importance in discussions of the Jubilee in the New Testament: ἄφεσις and ἀφίημι. This study also explores the *basileia* of God in Luke-Acts, since it is argued that many suggested references to the Jubilee are, in fact, better understood as references to the *basileia*.

Of all the Old Testament texts cited or alluded to in the New Testament, it is Isaiah 61:1–2 which has by far received the most attention. For this reason, this text is the subject of the following chapter. Isaiah 61 traditions in the rabbinic literature, the Dead Sea Scrolls, and other sources are examined to determine likely ways in which the text was understood in the first century. Luke's use of Isaiah 61 is also examined in this context.

The final two chapters examine the suggested references to the Jubilee in Luke-Acts. The most frequently suggested Lukan reference to the Jubilee is Luke 4:14–30, and as such this text is examined in greater detail than the others. These chapters also include an examination of Lukan themes which bear some semblance to those of the Jubilee (in particular, the reversal of fortunes, debt cancellation, and the redistribution of property).

There are a number of methodological approaches employed in this study. The objective of the study lends itself to the historical-grammatical method, though within this wider methodology, a more specific approach was required to assess the suggested references to the Jubilee in New Testament texts. Indeed, the wider question of how one can determine and validate the presence of Old Testament quotations or allusions in the New Testament is itself difficult to answer. Part of the difficulty lies in the lack of clarity as to how Old Testament references should be classified. Porter, for example, lists fifteen terms which are regularly used to define different categories of Old Testament references in the New Testament (and admits his list is far from comprehensive).[48] Others simplify the classification to two categories of quotations and allusions.[49] While the specificity of a greater number of classifications affords some benefits, this study has limited the categorization of Old Testament texts to quotations and allusions.[50] Of these two categories, it is the determination of what constitutes an allusion which required a specific set of criteria.[51]

---

48. Porter, "The Use of the Old Testament," 80.

49. There are, of course, scholars with other classifications as well. The most notable other category is that of echo, which is viewed as distinct from allusion. Porter, for example, argues that "an allusion is concerned to bring an external person, place, or literary work into the contemporary text, whereas echo does not have the specificity of allusion but is reserved for language that is thematically related to a more general notion or concept." Porter, "Allusions and Echoes," 40.

Since there are some scholars that treat the two categories synonymously, there are differing definitions of echoes and allusions, and in many cases the distinction between the two categories is largely subjective, so this study will group allusions and echoes together.

50. Another area of dispute is the definition of the term "intertextuality." For some scholars, intertextuality is the term used to describe the procedure by which later biblical texts refer to earlier ones and how the meanings of both texts are therefore affected. The word is also used for a variety of other purposes, however, and has therefore been used sparingly in this study. For a brief but helpful discussion of the word and its uses, see Beale, *Handbook*, 39–40.

51. That is not to say that the identification and determination of quotations is an

Allusions can be defined as "an incomparable or unique parallel in wording, syntax, concept, or cluster of motifs in the same order or structure."[52] How they are identified, however, is a subject of much debate. In the past, the identification of an allusion was a largely arbitrary process. That is, there was no clear methodology to test whether or not a proposed allusion was valid or not. More recently, however, many scholars have adopted a more systematic approach. The most well-known is Richard Hays's methodology.[53] He has argued that the validity of an intertextual link can be assessed via the use of seven "tests" or criteria:[54]

1. Availability. This criterion assesses the accessibility of the writer and/or his audience to the proposed source text (be it Greek or Hebrew).

2. Volume. This examines how explicit or overt the allusion/echo is. That is, the degree of verbatim repetition or syntactical patterns and the relative weightiness of the section of Scripture being referred to.

---

easy task. Indeed, there are significant differences in opinion as to what constitutes a quotation. In fact, it was not until Dietrich-Alex Koch's study in 1986 that using a precise methodology for determining the presence of a quotation was popularized (he employed seven criteria). Since then there have been other proposals (most notably Christopher Stanley's), but as yet there is no firm consensus as to the criteria for identifying Old Testament quotations. Koch, *Die Schrift*, 11–23.

In relation to the determination of Old Testament quotations in Luke's work, there are again disagreements. Moyise and Fitzmyer have counted twenty-five quotations in Luke's Gospel, the *United Bible Society's Greek Version of the New Testament* lists twenty-seven quotations, and Charles Kimball argues there are thirty-three. Additionally, Luke did not employ a consistent introductory formula and, in many cases, did not use an explicit introduction at all. Moyise, *Old Testament in the New*, 45; Fitzmyer, cited in Pao and Schnabel, "Luke," 251; Aland et al., *Greek New Testament*, 901; and Kimball, *Jesus' Exposition*, 204–05.

52. Beale, *Handbook*, 31.

53. See Hays, *Echoes of Scripture in the Letters*, 25–32 and Hays, *The Conversion of the Imagination*, 34–45.

54. Hays, *Echoes of Scripture in the Letters*, 29–32 and Hays, *The Conversion of the Imagination*, 34–45. Hays restricts these criteria to 'hearing echoes,' which he differentiates from allusions. He argues that allusions can be thought of as being more obvious intertextual references, while echoes are more subtle, and may not have been intended by the author. Hays, *Echoes of Scripture in the Letters*, 29 and Hays, *Echoes of Scripture in the Gospels*, 10–11.

As Beale has noted, however, the distinction is not altogether helpful, since there are some scholars who treat echoes and allusions synonymously, and those who treat them separately often struggle to categorize them clearly, except insofar as saying that echoes are more subtle. Beale, *Handbook*, 32. Thus, for the purposes of this study, Hays's criteria will be applied to allusions, though the term "allusions" will encompass both what Hays would term "allusions" and "echoes."

3. Recurrence. That is, whether or not there are other references by the same author to the proposed allusion, and if there are, how often they occur.

4. Thematic Coherence. This criterion assesses how well the Old Testament echo/allusion fits with the argument that is being mounted in the surrounding text.

5. Historical Plausibility. That is, could the biblical author have intended the proposed meaning? Additionally, could the intended audience have understood the proposed meaning? In essence, this criterion emphasizes the historical situation of the bibilical author and his audience.

6. History of Interpretation. While the previous criterion assesses the biblical author's contemporary audience, this criterion assesses the subsequent history of interpretation of the passage in question (that is, whether the proposed allusion has been recognized by others throughout history).

7. Satisfaction. This refers to whether the proposed allusion makes sense in its immediate context and whether it illuminates the surrounding discourse, regardless of the previous six criteria.

Hays is quick to admit that these criteria are not foolproof, in the sense that there are only shades of certainty when the criteria are applied to particular texts.[55] Nevertheless, he argues that they have a cumulative effect; the more of them fall into place, the more one can be certain that an Old Testament allusion is in fact present.[56] Finally, Hays also makes room for some exceptional texts, whereby the above tests "fail to account for the spontaneous power of particular intertextual conjunctions."[57] That is, he argues there are texts which can have meanings other than what the author intended and that transcend the hermeneutical structures of biblical scholars.[58]

While the seven criteria Hays has proposed are frequently cited as a helpful starting point in the assessment of a possible allusion, there are some who have been critical of Hays's methodology.[59] Porter, for example,

---

55. Hays, *Echoes of Scripture in the Letters*, 32–33.
56. Hays, *Echoes of Scripture in the Letters*, 32.
57. Hays, *Echoes of Scripture in the Letters*, 32–33.
58. Hays, *Echoes of Scripture in the Letters*, 33.
59. For a survey and review of those who have responded to Hays's criteria, see Litwak, "Echoes of Scripture?" 260–88.

finds insufficiencies with each of the seven criteria.[60] Some of his criticisms hold weight. For example, Porter rightly recognizes that the final criterion, which Hays argues is the most important, lacks a precision of definition, and is in fact more concerned with the interpretation of an allusion.[61] In fact, by Hays's own admission the final four criteria are focused on the interpretation of allusions, which then leaves only three criteria which truly serve the purpose of identifying Old Testament allusions.[62] Others, such as Bates, find no real criticism of Hays's criteria, but instead argue that there are other criteria which should be added.[63] Bates argues in favor of what he calls a "diachronic intertextuality," whereby a text is informed not only by the sociohistorical discourse that precedes it, but also by other texts written contemporarily and afterwards.[64] It is difficult, however, to see Bates's contributions as little more than an expansion (albeit a helpful one) on Hays's sixth criterion, which addresses the history of interpretation. Beale, on the other hand, approves of Hays's criteria but notes that some of the criteria overlap so much they could be combined to reduce the list to five criteria.[65] In spite of these criticisms, however, there are many who agree that, when taken together, the cumulative effect serves to provide a sound and helpful approach to discern and discuss the presence of Old Testament allusions (or "echoes") in New Testament texts. Thus, Hays's criteria have been employed in the following chapters for the purpose of identifying and validating specific Old Testament allusions in Lukan texts.[66]

When applied to suggested Jubilary allusions in Luke-Acts, some of Hays's criteria can be examined once without the need to address them later in relation to specific texts. For example, with regard to the fifth criterion,

---

60. Porter, "Allusions and Echoes," 38–39. For a rebuttal of Porter's criticisms, see Lucas, "Assessing Stanley E. Porter's Objections," 93–111.

61. Porter, "Allusions and Echoes," 39.

62. Porter, "Allusions and Echoes," 39.

63. Bates, "Beyond Hays's Echoes," 269–71.

64. Bates, "Beyond Hays's Echoes," 271, 274.

65. In particular, Beale notes that the criteria "Availability" and "Historical Plausibility" could be combined, as could "Thematic Coherence" and "Satisfaction." Beale, *Handbook*, 35.

66. Admittedly, Hays originally developed his criteria for Pauline works. There seems to be no reason, however, why the criteria could not equally well be applied to Luke-Acts. The methodology employed in this study is therefore markedly different from that employed in some other studies. In Ringe's study, for example, she argues that allusions to the Jubilee (which she refers to as "images") can be identified by the presence of Jubilee themes and motifs (sometimes made visible by certain words). Ringe, "Jubilee Proclamation," 118–20. The difficulties with this approach are highlighted in chapter 6 where suggested Jubilee themes are addressed.

there is no need to assess this criterion with each passage from Luke-Acts, since the historical situation of the biblical author and his audience does not change from text to text. In total, there are three of Hays's criteria which do not need to be systematically addressed in relation to each specific suggested allusion: availability, recurrence, and historical plausibility.

In relation to Hays's criterion of availability, it is difficult to know which Old Testament reference to the Jubilee should be prioritized as "the" source text. The passage which is most frequently cited as a reference to the Jubilee is Isaiah 61, which is addressed in detail in chapter 4. In any case, the availability of Luke having access to various source texts is addressed in chapter 1 (see the section "Luke's Use of the Old Testament") and the availability of source texts to Luke's audience is addressed in chapter 3 (see the section "The Implied Audience of Luke-Acts"). Similarly, the criterion of historical plausibility is addressed in chapter 3 (see the section "The Implied Audience of Luke-Acts"). The third criterion (recurrence) is, in one sense, the subject of this entire study, which is a sustained argument that suggested references to the Jubilee throughout the entirety of Luke-Acts can be better explained in other terms. Since this is the case, this criterion is not specifically addressed in any particular section. Finally, the criterion of historical interpretation is briefly addressed in relation to each specific suggested Jubilary allusion. The wider survey of Jubilee interpretation throughout the ages, however, has been included as an appendix.

1

Basileia of God and Jubilee Traditions in the Old Testament

Introduction

One of the central questions of this study pertains to how Jubilee and *basileia* of God traditions should be understood within their Old Testament contexts.[1] There are several reasons why this is particularly important in the case of Luke's work. Firstly, even a cursory reading of Luke-Acts indicates that Luke was familiar with and deeply influenced by Israel's Scriptures; there are frequent Old Testament quotations and allusions throughout his two-part work.[2] Secondly, some of the key texts that have been associated with the Jubilee or the *basileia* of God are citations from, or clear allusions to, the Old Testament.[3] It is therefore of paramount importance for understanding the meaning of these texts that we should examine their Old Testament context/s (especially given

---

1. For the sake of consistency, I use "*basileia* of God" to refer to the Old Testament references to God's kingdom.

2. I use "Luke" (and on occasion "his audience") to refer to the implied author of the Gospel (and the implied audience/s of that text) because my thesis rests on the interrogation of texts rather than authorial intentions or particular views of the Gospel's origin. I will point out in chapter 3 below that traditional views of authorship and provenance are consistent with, and supportive of, the results of my examination of the texts, but that is an aside to the major arguments of this thesis.

3. For example, Luke 4:18–19; 7:21–22, 27–28; 8:10; 17:20–37.

Luke's hermeneutical approach—see further below). Thirdly, while there are no explicit references to the Jubilee in Luke's work, he was unmistakably concerned about the *basileia* of God. Indeed, there are forty-six explicit references to the *basileia* of God throughout Luke-Acts.[4] Luke did not, however, present any detailed explanation as to how the *basileia* is to be understood, which suggests that the idea of God's *basileia* was well known to both Luke and his intended audience. If the Old Testament was indeed a formative influence on Luke's work, understanding how the Old Testament portrays the *basileia* of God may provide some valuable insight into Luke's understanding of the concept. Finally, since there are some who have argued that Luke viewed the Jubilee as an expression of the *basileia*,[5] it is important to ascertain whether a literary relationship exists between the two concepts.

This chapter will therefore examine Luke's use of the Old Testament, before surveying the presence and development of *basileia* of God and Jubilee traditions. On the basis of this survey, the study will then examine whether there is any clear literary or semantic relationship between the *basileia* of God and the Jubilee.

Luke's Use of the Old Testament

The role of Old Testament references within Luke-Acts has received much attention. This is for good reason; in Luke's Gospel alone there are ten quotations from the Pentateuch, seven from the prophets, and seven quotations from the Psalms.[6] Moreover, Kimball has found 525 Old Testament allusions throughout Luke's Gospel.[7] It seems Luke may have had access to a variety of Old Testament texts, including a rendering of the Masoretic Text, the Samaritan Pentateuch, the Targums, Community Testimonia, and a version of the Septuagint. This is particularly evident in citations from books other than Isaiah and the Minor Prophets, where Luke is less consistent in following one textual tradition.[8] It seems his tradition of preference, however, was the Septuagint; there are no occasions in Luke-Acts when citations follow the Masoretic text rather than the Greek text.[9] In relation to Hays's

---

4. See the section on "The *Basilea* of God in Luke" in chapter 3.
5. See, for example, Hertig, "Jubilee Mission," 173–74 and Blosser, "Jubilee," 147.
6. Pao and Schnabel, "Luke," 251.
7. Kimball, *Jesus' Exposition*, 206–12.
8. Bock, *Proclamation*, 16 and Kimball, *Jesus' Exposition*, 15–16.
9. Fitzmyer, "Old Testament," 534.

criterion of availability, therefore, it seems likely that Luke would have had access to source texts which refer to the Jubilee.

There are many who have argued that Luke's purpose in using the Old Testament should be understood in terms of proof from Scripture or prophecy and fulfillment.[10] There are, however, a number of scholars who now dispute the proof from prophecy motif, since it seems that Luke was not only interested in using the Old Testament for apologetic purposes.[11] Fitzmyer has emphasized that Luke presented the narratives of Jesus and the early church as a continuation of biblical history by writing his two-part work in a fashion similar to Old Testament historiography.[12] Brodie sees Hellenistic *imitatio* at play throughout Luke's work and argues that Luke shaped his entire work based on the Elijah-Elisha narratives (1 Kgs 17:1–2; 2 Kgs 18:15), which were foundational to understanding Jesus and his mission.[13] Joel Green and others have focused on intertextuality, arguing that Luke used repetition to produce a text that interplays with other texts to produce a system of references.[14] Hays, on the other hand, has recently argued that Luke employed intertextual narration to highlight seven themes: 1) narrative continuity between the Old Testament and the story of Jesus; 2) the faithfulness of God to his covenant promises; 3) the reality of suffering for Jesus and his followers; 4) God's concern for the poor and helpless; 5) good news for all nations; 6) the countercultural relations between God's elect and the prevailing world structures; and 7) the identity of Jesus as the Lord of all.[15]

While these and other viewpoints present varying (and at times conflicting) perspectives on Luke's use of the Old Testament, there are some

---

10. Conzelmann, *Theology*, 157, 161–62; Bovon, *Luke the Theologian*, 93; and Müller, "Reception," 324.

11. For two excellent surveys of dissenting views, see Bock, *Proclamation*, 27–37 and Litwak, *Echoes*, 8–25.

12. Fitzmyer, "Old Testament," 525. Arnold and Bovon also argue for some type of continuity between Israel and believers in Luke-Acts. Arnold, "Luke's Characterizing Use," 300–302 and Bovon, *Luke the Theologian*, 93.

The idea that Luke has presented his work as a continuation of the biblical narrative is not new, though the relationship between Luke's work and the Old Testament texts has been interpreted a number of different ways. Arnold notes that the debate seems to center on whether Luke is dependent on Israel's Scriptures for exclusively theological purposes, or whether he also wants to emulate their literary style. Moreover, if Luke did intend to imitate their literary style, the question then becomes whether he also sought to imitate the organization and structure of the Old Testament. Arnold, "Luke's Characterizing Use," 301.

13. Brodie, "Luke-Acts as an Imitation and Emulation," 78–85.

14. Green, "Internal Repetition," 283–84.

15. Hays, *Echoes of Scripture in the Gospels*, 277–80.

foundational observations which can be made. It seems clear that Luke sought to emphasize the fulfillment of Old Testament texts (see, in particular, Luke 18:31; 22:37; 24:25–27, 44–47) as part of his larger purpose of communicating the history of the people of God, with Christianity being the fulfillment of God's design.[16] That is, Luke seemingly used the Scriptures for both apologetic and christological purposes in order to demonstrate to both insiders and outsiders that Jesus and the church are the continuation and culmination of salvation-history.[17] Importantly, this is consistent with what one might expect if Luke were, in fact, highlighting the significance of the *basileia* (as opposed to the Jubilee, which would better fit within a prophecy/fulfillment schema). Darrell Bock's study on the subject is particularly helpful. He has demonstrated convincingly that Luke's purpose in using the Old Testament is best described in terms of "proclamation from prophecy and pattern," since "Luke sees the Scripture fulfilled in Jesus in terms of the fulfillment of OT prophecy and in terms of the reintroduction and fulfillment of OT patterns that point to the presence of God's saving work."[18] He and others have noted that Luke often utilized Jewish exegetical techniques and shared the Jewish view of Scripture having a "double context," such that Old Testament passages had historical significance for their original situation, but also contained a picture of God's ultimate purpose/s (which Luke interpreted christologically).[19] There is therefore a two-way relationship between a particular text and an event which Luke viewed as its fulfillment (sometimes called typological exegesis). That is, when Luke "Christianized" a text, he took into account the original Scriptural context before adapting it for his own purposes. The Old Testament texts which

---

16. This is consistent with the theocentric hermeneutic of other New Testament authors who used the Old Testament, as it seems they were increasingly interested in what God was saying to them in their time. Sanders, "The Prophetic Use," 191–94 and Arnold, "Luke's Characterizing Use," 300.

There are, of course, some scholars who disagree with this. Litwak, for example, argues that the 'promise-fulfillment' view does not represent Luke's primary use of Scripture, and instead views Luke's use of Scripture as essentially centering on the continuation of salvation history. He argues that πληρόω can and frequently should be translated in ways other than with regard to fulfillment, and that Luke's use of Scripture can be summarized as 'Framing in Discourse.' Litwak, *Echoes*, 16–17.

17. Juel, *Messianic Exegesis*, 140; Fitzmyer, "Old Testament," 525; Hays, *Echoes of Scripture in the Gospels*, 191, 277; and McCracken, "Interpretation of Scripture," 198.

18. Bock, *Proclamation*, 253.

19. Bock, *Proclamation*, 271–72; McCracken, "Interpretation of Scripture," 200; and Ellis, *Old Testament*, 62–63. Luke's use of introductory formulas for Old Testament citations is also directly paralleled in the Qumran literature, which supports the notion that his use of Scripture may share some similarities with other exegetical traditions. McCracken, "Interpretation of Scripture," 198.

Luke used were often well-known messianic, prophetic, or eschatological texts which provided some details about a coming specific event, and the occurrence of the specific New Testament event then served to clarify the exact content of the Old Testament text.[20]

The *Basileia* of God in the Old Testament

While the *basileia* of God is frequently acknowledged as a central tenet of Jesus' teaching in the New Testament, locating the presence and role of the *basileia* in the Old Testament is far more problematic.[21] One of the main difficulties is the lack of explicit references to the *basileia*. Indeed, the phrase "kingdom of God" (where God is אֱלֹהִים) does not occur at all, and the phrase "kingdom of Yahweh" occurs in various forms only fifteen times.[22] Since this is the case, many scholars have instead concentrated on finding narratives which express the rule of God over his people.[23] This is a frequent Old Testament theme; Yahweh is often referred to as king (over both Israel and the whole earth) and is portrayed having inherent sovereign authority.[24] Indeed, Köhler has argued that the "one fundamental statement in the theology of the Old Testament is this: God is the ruling Lord."[25]

Since God's sovereign rule is not often associated with the abstract notion of a *basileia*, there are some who view the search for *basileia* references as forcing a New Testament theme into Old Testament narratives.[26] However, as Patrick has noted, concepts can be present with or without specific identifying expressions.[27] Thus, a "narrative in which YHWH commands a human to perform some action embodies the idea of divine sovereignty, with or without the expression 'Kingdom of God.'"[28] Other scholars such as Waltke have also argued that the concept of the "kingdom of God" can be

---

20. Bock, *Proclamation*, 273.

21. Selman, "Kingdom," 161.

22. 1 Chr 17:14; 28:5; 29:11; 2 Chr 13:8; Pss 22:9; 103:19; 145:11–13; Dan 2:44; 3:33; 4:31; 6:27; 7:14, 18, 27. See also Patrick, "Kingdom," 72 and Selman, "Kingdom," 162.

23. Bright, *The Kingdom of God*, 18; Patrick, "Kingdom," 69; and Beasley-Murray, *Jesus and the Kingdom of God*, 17.

24. Deut 9:26; 1 Sam 12:12; Pss 24:10; 29:10; Isa 6:5; 33:22; Zeph 3:15; Zech 14:16–17. Yahweh is also ascribed a royal throne in Pss 9:4; 45:6; 47:8; Isa 6:1; 66:1; Ezek 1:26.

25. Köhler, *Old Testament Theology*, 30.

26. See, for example, Selman, "Kingdom," 161–62, which also includes several other criticisms.

27. Patrick, "Kingdom," 69.

28. Patrick, "Kingdom," 69.

seen throughout the entire Old Testament corpus.[29] The following survey will therefore include texts which refer to God's ruling activity even if the word "kingdom" is absent.

The Pentateuch

The sovereignty of God is a key theme throughout the Pentateuch. God is described as reigning forever (Exod 15:18), creating all things (Gen 1; 14:19, 22), owning the whole earth (Exod 19:5), and being sovereign over human kings (Exod 14:8; Num 21:33–34; Deut 2:24, 30; 3:2–3, 21; 7:24; 11:3; 31:4). Yahweh's sovereign transcendence is the fundamental grounds behind the commandment prohibiting idolatry (Exod 20:4; Deut 5:8).[30] It is Yahweh's fulfillment of promises to the patriarchs, however, which forms the central focus of the Pentateuch, particularly in relation to the establishment of Israel as a nation, the formation of the Sinaitic covenant, and the conquest of the land of Canaan.[31] Each of these promises requires and underscores God's sovereign rule. The Sinaitic covenant between Yahweh and Israel has particular significance, since it established Yahweh's *basileia* in terms of the people of Israel (Exod 19:3–8).[32] The Israelites were themselves designated to be Yahweh's "kingdom of priests and a holy nation" (Exod 19:6). While this does not necessarily indicate that the covenant should be considered in royal terms, the formation of the covenant nonetheless established Yahweh's rule over Israel; Israel was obliged to obey God's law as given to them and was subject to his sovereign authority.[33]

---

29. Waltke, *An Old Testament Theology*, 143–47. See also Walther Eichrodt's *Theology of the Old Testament*, in which he argues that "that which binds together indivisibly the two realms of the Old and New Testament—different in externals though they may be—is the irruption of the Kingship of God into this world and its establishment here." Eichrodt, *Theology of the Old Testament*, 26.

30. Chilton, *Pure Kingdom*, 23.

31. Clines, *The Theme of the Pentateuch*, 30 and Wenham, *Exploring the Old Testament*, 145–58.

32. While the Sinaitic covenant established Israel as Yahweh's rule, the idea of Yahweh's kingship was already evident in Genesis. See Lasine, "Everything," 31–57.

33. It is at this point that some scholars such as Bright and Patrick consider the *basileia* of God to have started. This, however, is clearly dependent on how one defines the *basileia* of God, since the Pentateuch affirms God's sovereign rule long before the Sinaitic covenant. Bright, *The Kingdom of God*, 18 and Patrick, "Kingdom," 76.

While some scholars argue that the covenant should be understood in royal terms, there is no explicit mention of Yahweh as king, which one would expect if this were one of the core outcomes of the covenant. Moreover, the scarcity of references to Yahweh as king throughout the Pentateuch make it highly unlikely that Israelite thinking clearly distinguished the covenant as enacting Yahweh's kingship. See Preuss, *Old Testament*

While Yahweh's kingship over the people of Israel is not a pervasive theme throughout the Pentateuch, it is explicitly affirmed on two occasions (Num 23:21; Deut 33:5). It is also clear that Yahweh has authority over Israel's human king (Deut 17:14–15; 28:36). This, in turn, provides an early indication that the Davidic monarchs would themselves be mediators of God's kingly rule.[34]

The Historical Books

In the historical books, the *basileia* of Yahweh is only explicitly mentioned on four occasions, all of which occur in 1 and 2 Chronicles.[35] One of these texts presents Yahweh's reign as encompassing "all that is in the heavens and in the earth" (1 Chr 29:11), however the remaining three references present the kingdom as Israel.[36] Even these three references, however, suggest that something more may be intended beyond a political kingdom, since each presents the kingdom as lasting forever.[37]

While the Chronicler may have had a more spiritual focus than earlier authors who viewed Yahweh's rule in a more earthly sense, his presentation in 1 and 2 Chronicles is nonetheless consistent with the wider sense of God's sovereignty in the historical books.[38] Yahweh is frequently referred to as being sovereign over Israel[39] and as having authority over Israel's king.[40] He is also, however, presented as being sovereign over other nations[41] and their

---

Theology, 154.

Nevertheless, Glock's study into the archaeological evidence suggests that even if Yahweh's kingship was not a dominant theme in Israelite thinking, Israel nonetheless effectively operated as a vassal state under Yahweh's rule. Glock, "Early Israel," 601–3.

34. This is consistent with three of the four earlier references to future Israelite kings (Gen 17:6, 16; 35:11; 36:31) which present the Israelite kingship within the context of God's sovereignty (the exception to this is Gen 36:31).

35. These four passages are 1 Chr 17:14; 28:5; 29:11; 2 Chr 13:8. As has already been mentioned, the phrase "Kingdom of God" does not occur in the Old Testament.

36. While in the case of 1 Chr 28:5 this is explicit, the context intimates that it is also the case in 1 Chr 17:14 and 2 Chr 13:8.

37. 1 Chr 17:14, 28:5–7; 2 Chr 13:5–8.

38. von Rad, "מֶלֶךְ and מַלְכוּת," 565–71.

39. Judg 3:8, 12; 4:2; 1 Sam 12:25; 1 Kgs 11:14–21, 29–39; 2 Kgs 17:7–8; 24:20; 1 Chr 5:26; 9:1; 2 Chr 17:5.

40. 1 Sam 2:10; 12:25; 2 Sam 5:2, 3, 12; 8:11–14; 12:7; 24:18–25; 1 Kgs 14:14; 2 Kgs 15:5; 23:25; 1 Chr 14:2; 28:4; 2 Chr 1:8–12; 9:8.

41. 2 Sam 7:1; 18:28; 2 Kgs 6:8–23; 19:32; 1 Chr 18:6; 2 Chr 20:29–30.

kings,[42] as well as being sovereign over other gods.[43] Other miracles such as the healing of Naaman (2 Kgs 5:1–14) and the raising of the Shunammite's son (2 Kgs 4:18–37) also underscore Yahweh's concern over those outside of Israel and his sovereign power.[44]

The anointing of Saul as Israel's king (1 Sam 8–10) marked an important shift in Yahweh's rule over Israel. His apointment was designed to be a mediatorial role between Yahweh and the Israelites (though in practice this was frequently not the case). The Davidic covenant (2 Sam 7:5–16; 1 Chr 17:4–14) later formalized this mediation, engrafting the dynastic monarchy into the framework of the Sinaitic covenant which regulated Israel's national life.[45] The transferral of Yahweh's kingdom to David and his line (1 Chr 10:14; 2 Chr 13:5), however, again suggests that something more was meant than the political kingdom of Israel. As Selman has noted, "The fact that it is Yahweh who is said to give the kingdom to David and his descendants carries the clear implication that God is here exercising his own kingship. If God has a kingdom to give, then he too must have a kingship of his own, and one that is of a higher order than that which is here entrusted to Saul, David, or Abijah."[46] This kingdom would ultimately be made known through the Davidic dynasty, in spite of the failings of those in the Davidic line.[47] Moreover, the description of the eternal nature of the kingdom (2 Sam 7:13, 16; 1 Chr 17:12, 14) served as an oblique messianic reference; a messiah from the line of David would ultimately inherit Yahweh's kingdom.[48]

---

42. Josh 2:10; 5:1; 6:2; 8:1–2; 10:30, 42; Judg 3:10; 4:23; 2 Chr 36:23; Ezra 1:2; 4:3; 7:6, 27; Neh 2:8.

43. 1 Kgs 18:20–40.

44. Luke's later reference to these two episodes in the Nazareth episode demonstrates that they influenced his understanding of the *basileia* of God.

45. Dumbrell, "The Davidic Covenant," 40. Gary Knoppers's study on the relation between the Davidic and Sinaitic promises is particularly helpful. He concludes that many of the ancient Israelite authors also saw a distinct connection between the two covenants. Knoppers, "David's Relation to Moses," 91–118.

46. Selman, "Kingdom," 166.

47. See, for example, 2 Chr 13:5 where the Chronicler records Abijah claiming the Davidic covenant blessings despite Abijah's disobedience to Yahweh.

48. While Nathan's prophecy is largely concerned about Solomon, the fact that the kingdom will last forever intimates its messianic nature. See Steinmann, "What did David Understand?" 21.

The Psalms and the Wisdom Literature

The sovereign rule of Yahweh is a frequent theme in the Psalms and the wisdom literature.[49] The fear of Yahweh is the key to much of the wisdom literature, especially Proverbs, Ecclesiastes, and Job. This fear is expressed chiefly through obedience to the law of God and can thus be aptly characterized as submission to the reign of Yahweh.[50] It is the Psalms, however, which provide the richest presentation of Yahweh's divine kingship, both within the wisdom literature and the entire Old Testament corpus.[51] Indeed, Mays has argued that the reign of Yahweh can be considered the central organizing theme for all the Psalms.[52] While this may be true, it is the Enthronement Psalms (which proclaim and celebrate Yahweh's kingly reign) and the Royal Psalms (which focus on the kingship of the Davidic rulers) which have a particular focus on Yahweh's reign.

The Enthronement Psalms (Pss 47, 93, and 95–99), are a small group of thematically related Psalms which characteristically contain מָלַךְ אֱלֹהִים (God reigns) or יְהוָה מָלָךְ (Yahweh reigns).[53] While Yahweh's kingship is common in the Psalter as a whole, it serves the purpose in the Enthronement Psalms of offsetting Israel's disappointment with its earthly king by pointing to Yahweh's rule.[54] The rule of Yahweh in the Enthronement Psalms has been characterized in a number of different ways, most notably by Gunkel, who viewed God's rule as being primarily eschatological, and his student Mowinckel, who viewed יְהוָהמָלָךְ chiefly in terms of a cultic festival where Yahweh was enthroned as king (thus the title "Enthronement Psalms").[55]

---

49. See, for example, Job 12:9–25; 21:17–26; 23:8–17; 38:1—42:17; Prov 21:1; Eccl 12:13.

50. Waltke, *An Old Testament Theology*, 160–62.

51. Chilton, *Pure Kingdom*, 31.

52. Mays, *The Lord Reigns*, 12 and Mays, "The Language of the Reign of God," 118.

53. The expression יְהוָה מָלָךְ occurs in Pss 93:1; 96:10; 97:1 and 99:1, and מָלַךְ אֱלֹהִים occurs in Ps 47:8. While the expression does not occur in Pss 95 or 98, the thematic similarities between these two Psalms and the other Enthronement Psalms are very clear. Bullock, *Encountering the Book of Psalms*, 188–89 and Petersen, *Royal God*, 15.

The classification of these Psalms as "Enthronement Psalms" has been challenged on numerous points by many scholars. While they would perhaps be better classified as "Kingship Psalms," they will nonetheless be referred to as Enthronement Psalms for the sake of continuity with other Psalmic studies. Significant works which are critical of the classification of these psalms as "Enthronement Psalms" include Kraus, *Theology of the Psalms*, 84–100; Petersen, *Royal God*, 26–31; and Brettler, *God is King*, 125–58.

54. Bullock, *Encountering the Book of Psalms*, 190.

55. Both Gunkel and Mowickel (and many others since) translated יְהוָהמָלָךְ as "Yahweh has become king." Gunkel and Begrich, *Introduction*, 66–69 and Mowinckel, *The Psalms in Israel's Worship*, 106–92.

While discussion regarding the nature of these Psalms continues, it seems that the central motif of these Psalms is Yahweh's eternal reign, expressed partially in the present and awaiting final fulfillment and vindication in the future. They also express Yahweh's special reign over Israel (Pss 95:7–11; 98:3; 99:2–9), over the other peoples of the world (Pss 47:1–9; 96:1–5; 97:6–7; 99:1–3), and indeed over all of creation itself (Pss 93:1–4; 95:3–5; 98:7–8). Finally, Yahweh's reign is also expressed in terms of his righteousness and justice (Pss 96:10–13; 97:2, 10–12; 99:4) and the coming judgment on Israel and the rest of the world (Pss 95:7–10; 96:10; 98:9; 99:8).[56]

While the Enthronement Psalms focus on Yahweh's kingship, the Royal Psalms are chiefly concerned with the Davidic monarchs. Gunkel's list of eleven Royal Psalms (Pss 2; 18; 20; 21; 45; 72; 89; 101; 110; 132; 144:1–11) is still considered standard, though there are some scholars who see kingship themes in many more Psalms.[57] These Psalms, though different in genre, are nonetheless classified together because of their common focus on the Davidic king. While the king is not mentioned by name or title in all of these psalms, he is undoubtedly the main character; he is presented as a military and diplomatic leader and as the upholder of domestic peace and justice.[58] It is his close relationship with God, however, which is most striking—Israel's king is presented as mediating God's rule over the nation of Israel (see Ps 2:6). He is anointed by God for this task (Pss 2:2; 18:50; 20:6; 45:2; 89:20, 38, 51; 132:10) and enjoys a Father-son relationship with God (Pss 2:7; 89:27; 110:3). God also enables the king's military conquests (Pss 2:8–9; 18:3, 16–19, 37–45; 20:6–7; 21:1–12; 110:1–7; 132:18; 144:1–2) and endows the king with the strength and ability to reign as God calls him to (Pss 18:1–2, 31–36; 45:2; 72:1–2; 89:19). Thus, while the Royal Psalms focus on the Davidic king's reign, they also serve to underscore Yahweh's sovereign reign.

The Royal Psalms are also significant, however, because they provide a powerful source of messianic hope. While the Psalms originally referred to historical Davidic monarchs, the failure of the Davidic line eventually led to the royal figure being viewed as the coming messiah.[59] The nine references to the מָשִׁיחַ ("anointed one") in these Psalms further cemented the notion that the king spoken of was an eschatological figure who would "truly fulfill

---

56. Bullock, *Encountering the Book of Psalms*, 190–94.

57. Gunkel and Begrich, *Introduction*, 99. Eaton disagrees with Gunkel's classification, and instead lists twenty-four characteristics which he believes may indicate a royal background to a psalm. His classification method identified sixty-four psalms as being based in kingship. See Eaton, *Kingship in the Psalms*, 26–49.

58. Gottwald, "Kingship in the Book of Psalms," 438.

59. Grant, "Psalms," 112.

the righteous reign God intended, and he would hold dominion over all the nations of the world as God designed."[60] This messianic hope gradually increased, particularly during the postexilic period (by which time the historical king was a distant memory).[61]

In light of the Psalter's explicit and thematic references to Yahweh's reign, a number of observations can be made. Firstly, while eschatological elements of God's *basileia* frequently appear throughout the Psalter, they are more often concerned with his present reign (that is, God's *basileia* is primarily viewed as a visible reality). Secondly, both Yahweh's dynamic reign and his kingship are presented universally; they encompass the heavens, all of creation, all nations, and all deities. Thirdly, Yahweh's kingship is expressed most clearly and directly in relation to Israel, and this kingship is mediated through the Davidic line. This royal figure would later become a major source of messianic hope. Fourthly, Zion (usually understood in terms of the temple, though sometimes as the city of Jerusalem) was the earthly seat of Yahweh's divine rule.[62] Fifthly, God's reign is presented as righteous and pure, and therefore those people who are concerned about their ethical conduct will enjoy the divine king's blessing.[63] Finally, Yahweh's *basileia* is also implicitly exemplified through the frequent references to coming judgment, since, as Chilton has recognized, "what is wicked in this world must be overcome if God's final power is to permeate his creation."[64] Significantly, many of these observations are also seen in Luke's Gospel. Indeed, as will be discussed in chapter 3, Luke's Gospel seemingly calls humanity to turn their allegiance from human rulers (such as Caeser) and kingdoms to another Lord and kingdom.

The Prophets

While the *basileia* of God is evident to some degree in all of the prophetic writings, it is seen most clearly in Isaiah and Daniel. Isaiah's vision of Yahweh eternally reigning recurs constantly throughout the book.[65] Indeed, Houston argues that the fundamental message of Isaiah is "the kingship of

---

60. Bullock, *Encountering the Book of Psalms*, 182–83.
61. Grant, "Psalms," 112.
62. Roberts, "Enthronement," 685–86 and Selman, "Kingdom," 179.
63. This is seen particularly clearly in Pss 5 and 24. Chilton, *Pure Kingdom*, 38–39.
64. Chilton, *Pure Kingdom*, 36.
65. For the purposes of this study, the book of Isaiah will be treated as a whole, since in its final form it has been passed on in the tradition as a single work, and is assumed to be such in Luke's narrative (Luke 4:17).

God now visible to the eye of faith and to be made visible to all in the new world that is about to dawn."[66] In a similar way to the Psalms, Yahweh is described as sovereign over all the kingdoms of the world (Isa 13–24; 37:16–20; 60:12), as sovereign over other gods (Isa 2:20; 40:12–20; 43:10; 46:1–2), and as exercising a particular rule over Israel, who frequently spurned his kingship (Isa 1–2; 5:1–7; 10:1–2, 20–25; 27:1–6).[67] His reign is presented in broad and sometimes cosmic terms, and is presented in imagery which reflects the festival worship of the Jerusalem temple which celebrated annually the renewal of God's goodness.[68] In line with the focus on Jerusalem are frequent references to the Davidic ruler, who would be established by Yahweh to reign over Israel.[69] There is also a strong focus on Yahweh's righteousness (צְדָקָה), which characterizes both his actions and the community of people whom he delivers.[70]

The text in Daniel, however, presents a somewhat different picture of the *basileia*.[71] It focuses instead on the difference between Yahweh's *basileia* and that of other earthly kingdoms and presents the coming of Yahweh as a time when evil will be subdued and his people will be delivered. The *basileia* of God is presented as being from heaven (2:44), as lasting forever (2:44; 4:3, 34; 6:26; 7:14, 18, 27), and as being primarily a future reign (2:44; 7:14, 18, 27), where the kingdoms of this world are present, temporary, and earthly

---

66. In terms of the future aspects of Yahweh's reign, most of the Isaianic passages are unspecific about their timing; many of them could be viewed as either a time in the near future (presumably during the prophet's life) or a time in the distant future. Regardless of this, the picture of God's *basileia* nonetheless remains as both present and future. This of course mirrors much of what is seen in Luke's writings (see particularly chapter 3—"The *Basileia* and Jubilee in Luke"). That is, there is some continuity between the Isaianic and Lukan presentations of the *basileia* and eschatology.

Houston also argues that Isaiah's vision of the Lord of Hosts enthroned as the king (Isa 6) is the "symbolic center" of the Isaianic text, though the climax of the text is in 52:7–10, where the herald proclaims, "Your God reigns." Houston, "Kingdom," 31–34.

67. God's particular reign over Israel is evident both in the expectations he places on them to obey him and in the way he is described; he is presented as the "Holy One of Israel" twenty-one times and the "God of Israel" thirteen times.

68. Houston, "Kingdom," 31.

69. References to the Davidic ruler include Isa 9:6–7; 11:1–5, 10–11, 16:5; 55:3–4.

70. There is a clear development in how צְדָקָה is used in Isaiah; in chapters 1–39, it is frequently associated with justice (מִשְׁפָּט). In chapters 40–55, however, the focus shifts to God's redemptive/salvific work (see particularly Isa 52:7). The final section of the book (chapters 56–66), however, connects צְדָקָה to salvation/deliverance and justice in a way which also necessitates a human response to his work. That is, God's true victory encapsulates the human exercise of righteousness/justice. Houston, "Kingdom," 34–37 and Ringgren, "Behold," 210–11.

71. See Dan 2:44; 4:3, 17, 25, 32, 34; 6:26; 7:14, 18, 27.

(2:31–44).⁷² Interestingly, as Selman has observed, Daniel never explicitly associates the *basileia* of God with the Davidic monarchy.⁷³ There are, however, clear parallels between the Davidic monarch who represents Yahweh's rule over Israel as seen in Isaiah (above) and the "son of man" (7:13–14) who reigns over Yahweh's kingdom coupled with the giving of the kingdom to the holy people of the Most High (7:18, 27).

Many of the prophets associated the Assyrian and Babylonian conquests with Israel's and Judah's continued disobedience to the Sinaitic covenant, which effectively signaled a rejection of Yahweh's reign.⁷⁴ The promise of a new covenant (see especially Jer 31:31–34; 32:38–41; Ezek 16:60; 34:20–31; 37:22–28), therefore, was not only a promise of restored fellowship between God's people and God, it also heralded a recommencement of God's everlasting reign over his people.⁷⁵ While a thorough exploration into the details of this covenant and its relationship with the previous covenant lie beyond the scope of this study, it is clear that the old and new covenants were both built on the foundation of Yahweh's sovereign rule over his people. Moreover, the descriptions of the covenant indicate that election was no longer "applied automatically to the 'Israel of the flesh'" and was instead framed in terms of a worthy remnant.⁷⁶

Associated with the new covenant is the expectation of a messianic figure from the line of David who would inaugurate an era of salvation. His relationship to the new covenant is pronounced most clearly in Ezekiel 34:23–24 and 37:24–28, where David (described as a "prince," "shepherd," and "king") will reign as Yahweh's servant and representative when the covenant of peace is enacted. The coming of the messiah is described in relation to the future Day of the Lord, the *basileia* of God, and the new age, all of which are concerned with divine visitation for judgment and salvation.⁷⁷

---

72. Though the description of the kingdom as enduring from generation to generation in Dan 4:3 and 4:34 also suggests that it is a present reality.

73. Nor is there any mention of the temple. Selman, "Kingdom," 171.

74. Israel's and Judah's disobedience to Yahweh and the resulting punishment is a frequent theme throughout many of the prophets, including Isaiah (particularly chapters 1–39), Micah, Amos, Hosea, Zephaniah, Jeremiah, and Ezekiel. Prophetic texts which refer to the breaking of the covenant include Jer 11:1–8; 22:8–9; Ezek 16:59; 44:7; Hos 6:7; and 8:1–6.

75. The new covenant is described as an "everlasting covenant" (Isa 24:5; 55:3; 61:8; Jer 32:40; 50:5; Ezek 16:60; 37:26); "a covenant of peace" (Isa 54:10; Ezek 34:25); "a covenant" (Isa 49:8; Hos 2:18); and "My covenant" (Isa 59:21). See Adeyemi, "New Covenant 'Law,'" 314.

76. Gray, *Biblical Doctrine*, 157.

77. The role of the messiah in the coming kingdom is complex and has been the subject of much debate. In particular, discussion has focused on whether the coming

While difficulties in dating and the interpretation of key texts can cloud how messianic thinking might have developed, the hope of the establishment/reestablishment of a Davidic king (who would mediate the rule of Yahweh) echoes clearly throughout many of the prophetic texts.[78]

There are a number of other general observations that can be made about the prophetic teaching on the *basileia* of God. Firstly, there is an increased presentation of God's *basileia* in eschatological terms. While God's reign continues to be presented in a this-worldly manner, there is also a distinct shift to the hope of God establishing his reign in the future.[79] Secondly, in a similar way to some of the Psalms, God's *basileia* is sometimes symbolized by his throne, usually located in Zion.[80] Thirdly, Yahweh's rule and kingship is again presented as being universal. While there is a focus on Israel's wholehearted allegiance to Yahweh, the other nations are frequently presented as turning to Yahweh.[81] Fourthly, it is clear that the *basileia* will be characterized by righteousness, both in terms of the actions of Yahweh and his messiah, and in respect to the people who will be under God's reign.[82] Fifthly, when God ultimately establishes his reign, there will be everlasting peace. This not only includes the absence of war; it also includes peace in the animal kingdom and, most importantly, peace between God and people.[83] Finally, Yahweh's kingship is demonstrated in historical events. This is

---

of Yahweh and the coming of the messiah are effectively two alien concepts. While this debate lies beyond the scope of this study, it is clear that the prophetic teaching presents the messiah as being uniquely related to God and humanity, and that he is to be the instrument of Yahweh's rule.

Beasley-Murray, *Jesus and the Kingdom of God*, 22–23 and Metts, "The Kingdom of God," 60.

78. Collins and Collins, *King and Messiah*, 43–46.

79. Aside from the frequent eschatological references in Isaiah, Ezekiel, and Daniel, one explicit reference to the coming day of the Lord resulting in the *basileia* being the Lord's is Obad 21. See also Patrick, "Kingdom," 76.

80. See, for example, Jer 17:12 and Ezek 43:7. God's throne is also described as being in heaven (Isa 66:1) and with the exiles in Babylon (Ezek 1:26). Selman, "Kingdom," 177.

81. The turning of the nations to Yahweh is sometimes presented as those nations being in submission to Israel (Amos 9:11–12; Mic 4:13; 7:8–17; Isa 49:22–26; 60:4–16), though many texts depict the nations being included in the *basileia* (Isa 25:6–7; 45:21–22; 51:4–5; 52:10–11; 56:3–4; Jer 3:17; Zeph 3:8–9; Zech 8:20–21; 14:9). Beasley-Murray, *Jesus and the Kingdom of God*, 20.

82. The righteousness of Yahweh's actions is seen in Isa 1:25–26; 4:3–4; 32:15–16; Jer 31:31–32; Ezek 36:25–26; 37:23–24. The righteousness of the messiah is seen in Isa 11:3–5 and Jer 23:5–6. Finally, the righteousness of the people of God is seen in passages such as Isa 26:2 and 28:5–6. Beasley-Murray, *Jesus and the Kingdom of God*, 20.

83. Since peace denotes harmony between God and people, it is also used as a synonym for salvation (Isa 12; 21:17–24; 33:17–24; 41:21–22; Jer 31:1–14; Hos 2:14–15;

seen most clearly in the proclamation that "Yahweh reigns" in Isaiah 40–55, which was a declaration that the people were to return from exile to their land.[84] Thus, according to the prophetic writings, the goal of history is "... the revelation and universal acknowledgement of Yahweh's sovereignty, the triumph of righteousness, and the establishment of peace and salvation in the world."[85]

Summary of Findings

While the phrase "*basileia* of God" does not occur in the Old Testament, the concept occurs frequently. God's מַלְכוּת in the Old Testament refers to his kingship (Yahweh is, at times, enthroned or affirmed as king), to the act of his governing/reigning, and to the realm over which he reigns.[86] These various allusions to the *basileia* of God reveal a number of things:

1. The reign of God extends over all creation (including the heavens and all the nations). From the beginning of Genesis onwards, God is portrayed as the Creator of all things and as having sovereign authority over all those in heaven and on earth. There is no person or thing which is presented as being outside his sovereign rule.

2. God's kingship was particularly evident over the nation of Israel (centered particularly on Zion). While God is king over all, he is frequently depicted as having a distinct, personal, and active rule over Israel his people.[87] Indeed, this aspect of God's rule dominates much of the Old Testament's presentation of God's reign. The Sinaitic covenant formalized Yahweh's reign over his people, and the later engrafting of the Davidic promises into this covenant established the monarchs as mediators of Yahweh's rule.

3. Israel's worship was dominated by a liturgical representation of God's dominion over creation from the beginning, his control over present history, and his eschatological kingship.[88] While the reign of Yahweh is usually depicted in the temporal present, there is nonetheless a strong

---

14:4–5; Zeph 3:14–20). Beasley-Murray, *Jesus and the Kingdom of God*, 20.

84. Selman, "Kingdom," 178.

85. Beasley-Murray, *Jesus and the Kingdom of God*, 20.

86. Viviano, *Trinity—Kingdom—Church*, 143.

87. The relationship is so personal that on nine occasions, God is described as the Father of Israel (Deut 32:6; Isa 63:16 [twice]; 64:8; Jer 3:4, 19; 31:9; Mal 1:6; 2:10).

88. Schnackenburg, *God's Rule*, 26–27.

sense that his present omnipotence can be seen in the roots of the past and from the hope of the final fulfillment in the future.[89]

4. The hope of Yahweh's reign is particularly evident in many of the prophetic texts, particularly in the postexilic period.[90] His reign is presented as being synonymous with salvation and is characterized by peace and righteousness.[91]

5. The eschatological hope of God's reign is frequently tied to a final judgment on the nations and on Israel herself. This judgment is itself presented as part of God's redeeming work; the punishment meted out is accompanied by the vindication of God's justice and the deliverance of those who have suffered unfairly.[92]

6. There was a deep-seated expectation of a Davidic messiah who would usher in and mediate the eschatological reign of God.[93] The Davidic line would last forever (2 Sam 7:16; 23:5; Ps 89:35–36) and the Davidic figure would enjoy a sonship relationship with God (2 Sam 7:14; 1 Chr 17:13; 28:6; Pss 2:7; 89:26), extend his rule internationally (Isa 42:1–6; 49:1–7, 22–26; 51:4–6; Amos 9:11–12), and be inextricably bound to Jerusalem (particularly the temple).[94]

---

89. Patrick, "Kingdom," 76 and Schnackenburg, *God's Rule*, 30.

90. This hope was fuelled by disillusionment with the monarchy, Israel's proclivity for rebellion against God's rule, and the exile. This is seen to some degree in Luke's Gospel—the only Gospel to refer explicitly to the "exodus" (ἔξοδον αὐτοῦ) of Jesus (see Luke 9:31).

91. The synonymy of God's reign with salvation is a significant part of Luke's presentation of the *basileia*—see chapter 3, "The *Basileia* and Jubilee in Luke."

92. Dyrness, *Themes*, 235. Indeed, the failure of the monarchy was eventually interpreted as being divine judgment upon the people and its leaders (Isa 40:2).

93. The subject of the messiah in the Old Testament literature is highly controversial. Indeed, as Clements has noted, there are many Old Testament theology books which entirely avoid the subject. More recently, however, scholars such as Mark Boda have observed that the term "messiah" appears to have been used generically for religious functionaries in Israelite society and tradition (particularly those with an enduring role), and therefore exploration into messianism in the Old Testament is not so daring a task as was once believed. In any case, this study is focused on Luke's interpretation of the Old Testament which viewed many texts as messianic. Boda, "Figuring the Future," 45 and Clements, "The Messianic Hope," 4. Importantly, it is clear that Luke portrays Jesus as the Davidic messiah, sent to inaugurate and mediate the reign of God.

94. Hahn, "Kingdom and Church," 300–301. This is also seen in Luke's work—see chapter 3, "The *Basileia* and Jubilee in Luke."

The Jubilee in the Old Testament[95]

The Pentateuch[96]

The Jubilee Provisions in Leviticus 25:8–55

The text in Leviticus 25:8–55 begins with instructions regarding the timing

---

95. Relative to the at times indistinct but widely prevalent *basileia* traditions in the Old Testament, the Jubilee traditions are only found in certain sections of the Pentateuch and the prophetic writings, alongside several possible allusions in the historical books. Since this is the case, there is no discussion here of texts pertaining to the Psalms or the wisdom literature.

One possible exception to this is Psalm 146 (LXX 145), which Ringe believes is a liturgical celebration of divine sovereignty that serves as an image of the Jubilee. She argues that the terms used for the marginalized are similar to those seen in other Jubilee texts (particularly Lev 25, and Isa 58, 61). Ringe, "Jubilee Proclamation," 70–71. While her arguments have some merit, the most one can say is that the Psalm may echo some aspects of the Jubilee release (which is Ringe's conclusion). Importantly, however, it is highly unlikely that Luke would have connected the verse with the aforementioned Jubilee texts on the basis of the references to the marginalized, given that the language used for the marginalized in the Septuagint's translation of the psalm is significantly different from the language used in Lev 25, and Isa 58 and 61. Indeed, the only exceptions to this are πεινάω (Isa 58:7, 10), τυφλός (Isa 61:1), δίκαιος (Isa 61:8), and προσήλυτος (Lev 25:23, 25, 47), none of which are distinctly Jubilean terms.

96. There are a number of similarities between the Jubilee legislation in the Pentateuch and that of other Ancient Near Eastern cultures which have led some scholars to argue that the biblical text must have relied on other earlier works. For example, some scholars have noted the apparent parallels between Israel's Jubilee and some Hittite, Egyptian, and Mesopotamian laws. See Lewy and Lewy, "Origin," 1–152; North, *Sociology*, 46–69; and Bergsma, *Jubilee*, 19–37. Another connection between the biblical text and other ancient texts is the likelihood that the word דְּרוֹר ("emancipation"/"freedom") used in Jubilee texts such as Lev 25:10 and Isa 61:1 was derived from the Akkadian word *durāru* (and the closely related *andurāru*). The word *andurāru* appears in legal documents pertaining to the emancipation of slaves to reunite families and the release of property, which is consistent with the Jubilee ordinances. Lewy, "Biblical Institution," 21–22. Similarly, in the Akkadian period and the Old Babylonian period, many kings issued a royal decree of *mīšarum* ("justice"), whereby certain taxes were canceled, some debt-slaves were released, loans (particularly personal loans) were canceled, and mortgaged property was released. Blosser, "Jubilee," 8–9.

While these parallels with Israel's Jubilee ordinances are clear, the differences between the biblical text and other Ancient Near Eastern texts are also significant. For example, the extant evidence suggests that both *mīšarum* and *andurāru* were proclaimed sporadically, unlike the Jubilee's regular fifty-year cycle. Westbrook, cited in Hartley, views this difference as being so fundamental that *mīšarum* and the Israelite Jubilee must be viewed as being categorically different. See Hartley, *Leviticus*, 434 and Milgrom, *Leviticus 23–27*, 2169. Additionally, Israel's Jubilee affected the entire nation; the Mesopotamian laws only concerned certain pockets of society. These and other differences demonstrate the difficulty in determining the level of influence these Ancient Near Eastern documents had on the Jubilee texts.

and proclamation of the Jubilee. Debate continues regarding the question of whether the Jubilee was proclaimed every fifty or forty-nine years.[97] The proclamation of the Jubilee coincided with the Day of Atonement (Lev 25:9). A trumpet was sounded, liberty was proclaimed, and the year was set aside as holy (25:9–12). There were also several other provisions, which can be summarized as rest for the land (25:11–12, 18–24), the redemption of property (25:14–17, 23–34), and the redemption of slaves (25:39–55).

The provision to let the land lie fallow is analogous to the restrictions for Sabbath years (25:4–7). The Year of Jubilee was to be a time when there were no organized farming practices; the Israelites were to pick and eat what they found and continue to eat from what they had previously stored (25:19–22). This provision would therefore allow the land its rest, remind the Israelites of their pre-conquest nomadic lifestyle, and would provide sustenance for the poor. It would also teach the Israelites to have a renewed sense of trust in Yahweh, both for the provision of food and for protection against marauding bands who could raid the Israelites' food supplies (25:18–22).

The next major provision of the Jubilee was that all property was to be returned to its original owner or his family, in accordance with the Mosaic distribution. During the Jubilee, the Israelites were also to return to their property (25:10, 13). Land itself was not to be permanently bought or sold; it was leased until the next Jubilee. The price for the lease was determined according to the number of years until the next Jubilee (and hence how many crops could be harvested), and the Israelites were instructed to "not take advantage of each other, but fear your God" (25:17). Moreover, the right to recover the land prior to the next Jubilee was reserved by the land's owner or his nearest relative if they had the financial means (25:25–28). These provisions did not, however, apply to dwellings within walled cities or the possessions of the Levites (see 25:29–34 for details).

Guillaume has taken these verses to mean that the Jubilee was the point at which antichretic loans reached their maturity.[98] He argues that landowners who borrowed from creditors rarely moved away from their land (though they might possibly move to their creditor's farm); they instead worked their land which was given as a pledge, and the creditor collected

---

97. See Kawashima, "The Jubilee," 117–20; Bergsma, "Once Again," 121–25; and the excursus in Hartley, *Leviticus*, 434–36. This is of relevance for (and the ambiguity partly undermines) the argument that Luke's distinctive use of "fifty" (Luke 7:41; 9:14; 16:6; Acts 13:20) is a Jubilary allusion. See further below (chapter 6).

98. Guillaume, *Land, Credit and Crisis*, 195. Antichretic loans are those whereby a debtor pledges real property to his/her creditor as security for a debt (and oftentimes the fruits of the property are able to be deducted from the debt and/or the interest).

a portion of the harvest.[99] Therefore, the "return" of the land "was not the consequence of a cancellation of debt, but the result of the synchronization of loans which were granted at most until the date of the next Jubilee."[100] It is difficult, however, to reconcile Guillaume's thesis with a plain reading of the text, which instructs that those who have sold land must return *to their property* (as well as have their property returned to them).[101] Moreover, the precepts referring to the sale and redemption of land correspond to the ensuing legislation which addresses the sale and redemption of houses, which Guillaume's system of loans cannot account for.

The fundamental theological principle underlying the redemption of property was Yahweh's ownership of the land, stated explicitly in 25:23. Both within the Holiness Code and the Pentateuch at large, there are frequent reiterations that it is God who gave Israel the land (Gen 15:7; 17:8; 24:7; Exod 6:4; Lev 20:24; 25:2, 38; Deut 5:16).[102] Thus, while the redemption of property served to prevent *latifundia*, it also continually reminded the Israelites of Yahweh's ultimate ownership.

The provision regarding the redemption of slaves pertained to those Israelites who had sold themselves into slavery as a result of serious debt. The Jubilee legislation ensured that the Israelite slaves would be treated as humanely as possible. Indeed, they were to be treated as hired workers rather than slaves (25:39–42). Israelites who sold themselves into slavery were redeemed at the next Year of Jubilee (25:42 and 54). Aliens (both from within Israel and the surrounding nations), however, were not afforded the same provisions; they were not released during the Jubilee (25:44–46). Furthermore, if an Israelite sold himself as a slave to an alien (or the descendant of an alien) living within Israel, the Israelite slave retained the right to purchase their release or be redeemed by a blood relative at any time, with the price for redemption determined by the number of years left until the next Jubilee (25:47–53).

There are some who have argued that the Jubilee laws provided a new paradigm for Hebrew slavery within Israel. Levinson, for example, argues that the syntax of 25:46 should be translated such that it is only non-Israelites who may be regarded as being slaves for life.[103] He goes on to argue that the writer of the Holiness Code rejected both the institution and the language

---

99. Guillaume, *Land, Credit and Crisis*, 195.
100. Guillaume, *Land, Credit and Crisis*, 195–96.
101. See Lev 25:13, 27, and 28.
102. Wenham, *The Book of Leviticus*, 320.
103. Levinson, "Manumission," 310

of slavery in his redaction of Exodus 21 and Deuteronomy 15.[104] While Levinson's syntactical observations do not necessitate all of his conclusions, it is clear that the language of slavery in Leviticus 25 does give greater dignity to Israelite slaves than the Covenant Code or the Deuteronomic Code affords.

The theological reasoning behind the redemption of Israelite slaves, their humane treatment, and their right of release was that they had been redeemed from servitude in Egypt (25:38, 42, 55) and were Yahweh's servants (25:42, 55). They should therefore never permanently belong to anyone except Yahweh.

While the cancellation of debts is not explicitly mentioned in Leviticus 25, the redemption of property and debt-slaves would effectively result in debt cancellation.[105] It is possible that debt cancellation was not specified in the Jubilee legislation because it followed a Sabbath year during which debts were canceled, or that the Jubilee was viewed as a heightened Sabbath year and therefore debt cancellation was practiced due to the Sabbath year laws.[106] In any case, Josephus later included debt cancellation as a provision of the Jubilee in his *Antiquities*.[107]

Other Pentateuchal Texts

The Jubilee is mentioned in several other texts in the Pentateuch. In Leviticus 27:16–24, further provisions are listed concerning the dedication of property to Yahweh. In Numbers 36:4, there is a reference to the extraordinary case of Zelophehad's daughters, who, despite the provisions of the Jubilee, were in danger of losing their ancestral land if they married outside their tribal clan. As Bergsma has noted, the narrative highlights the significance of the perpetuation of one's name within ancient Israel, which suggests that the Jubilee had eschatological implications in maintaining the bond between family and ancestral land.[108]

Within the Covenant Code, there are three texts (Exod 21:2–11, 22:25–26; 23:10–11) that have similarities to the Jubilee legislation in Leviticus 25.

---

104. Levinson, "Manumission," 305–07.

105. Contra Harbin, "Jubilee and Social Justice," 689–91, 698–99.

106. Sloan, *Favorable Year*, 20–21 and North, *Sociology*, 2.

107. *Josephus*, 4:454–55. Even if one takes debt cancellation to be a Jubilee provision, however, it is clearly not an important theme in Luke's work (see chapter 6). Moreover, as will be discussed in chapter 4, Luke never presented Jesus as freeing people in literal slavery or captivity.

108. Bergsma, *Jubilee*, 124–25.

In Exodus 21:2–11, the seven-year redemption of Hebrew male servants has some resemblance to the redemption of Israelite slaves in the Jubilee legislation. The correlation between Leviticus 25 and Exodus 23:10–11, however, is much clearer; both texts legislate that land will lie fallow each seventh year. There is, however, an apparent difference in motivation. The Exodus text is more concerned with socioeconomic justice, whereas in Leviticus the cultic significance of the Sabbath is stressed.[109] In both Exodus 22:25–26 and Leviticus 25:35–38, though, there is a corresponding humanitarian focus, as both texts prohibit the Israelites from charging interest to the poor.

Deuteronomy 15:1–18 also addresses debts and the redemption of Hebrew slaves at the end of a seven-year period. While it is clear that there are thematic similarities between this passage and the Jubilee legislation, there are also some striking differences. The Deuteronomic text does not mention an agricultural fallow year, it includes provisions for Hebrew slave-women, and there is some question over whether the text legislates the cancellation of debts or only their suspension every seven years.[110]

The Historical Books

There are several texts in the historical books which have underlying motifs reminiscent of the Jubilee legislation. In 1 Kings 21:1–18, the account of Ahab being lawfully unable to confiscate Naboth's vineyard until his death suggests that the Jubilee legislation was being practiced. Indeed, it is the only biblical legal text which protects family property in perpetuity.[111] In Nehemiah 5:1–13, Nehemiah called the people to a major reform, whereby Jewish slaves were redeemed, property was returned, and debts were canceled. While Nehemiah's reforms were not based explicitly on the Jubilee legislation, the thematic parallels with the Jubilee legislation are clear. Similarly, in 2 Chronicles 36:20–23, the Chronicler states that the length of the exile was proportionate to the number of Sabbath years owed to the land (see Lev 26:43–45). Cyrus's ensuing proclamation for the Jews to return to their ancestral land may have then been viewed by the Chronicler as having an underlying Jubilee motif.[112]

---

109. Blosser, "Jubilee," 28.

110. Indeed, Lemche argues that the absence of references to the restoration of land implies that there could not have been a completely new start at the end of the seven-year period. Lemche, "Manumission," 45. For a recent discussion of the relationship between Deut 15 and Lev 25, see Bergsma, *Jubilee*, 125–46.

111. Cogan, *1 Kings*, 486.

112. Johnstone, "Hope of Jubilee," 311.

The Prophets

There are several possible references to the Jubilee in Ezekiel. In 46:1–18, the prophet refers to a year of freedom (46:17) whereby land is to be returned to its patrimonial heirs.[113] In 40:1, the date is recounted as the "twenty-fifth year of our exile," which may allude to the midpoint of a Jubilee cycle.[114] Other possible references include 7:13–14 and 11:15–21; however, neither of these contain any explicit mentions of the Jubilee legislation.

Jeremiah also contains several possible references to the Jubilee legislation. In 34:8–22, Jeremiah addresses Zedekiah's decision to reverse his earlier proclamation of emancipation for slaves. While Zedekiah's proclamation of liberty has some similarities to the Jubilee laws, it is more likely that it reflects an amalgam of Exodus 21, Leviticus 25, and Deuteronomy 15.[115] Jeremiah 32:1–15 records the redemption of Hanamel's field, which appears to parallel the principle of the redemption of land in Leviticus 25. The account does not, however, provide enough historical data to determine whether the Jubilee laws were in play.[116] Finally, it is unlikely that Jeremiah's references to the seventy-year exile (25:1–12; 29:10) were originally intended to be associated with Jubilee years (though later writings may have drawn a connection).[117]

There is no specific mention of the Jubilee in Daniel, although the "seven week" divisions of time in Daniel 9:24–27 were later used in Second Temple literature in connection with Jubilee cycles (see below). Whether this was Daniel's intention is disputed; the passage is notoriously difficult and one cannot say with any certainty that the seventy "sevens" refer to "a sabbatical-cycle schematisation of history."[118]

---

113. It is, however, also possible that the verse is a reference to the Sabbath year. North, *Sociology*, 39–40.

114. Block, *The Book of Ezekiel*, 512; Allen, *Ezekiel 20–48*, 229; Ringe, "Jubilee Proclamation," 34–39.

115. Holladay, *Jeremiah*, 2:238.

116. This is particularly so in light of the exchange of money for the field (Jer 32:7–10), which is not required under the Jubilee laws. See Bergsma, *Jubilee*, 157–60. While there are some commentators (Fried and Freedman) who argue that there is sufficient evidence to conclude that the account is evidence of a Jubilee year, others (such as Robert Carroll) see the lack of historical data as evidence that the account was never intended to be read as a real historical event. Rather, it is a "paradigmatic account of how the future was secured by Jeremiah the prophet." Fried and Freedman, "Was the Jubilee Observed," 2257–70 and Carroll, *Jeremiah*, 621.

117. Bergsma, *Jubilee*, 170–76.

118. Meadowcroft, "Exploring the Dismal Swamp," 447. Indeed, Goldingay (among others) argues that the 490-year period should be viewed as chronography rather than chronology. That is, Daniel's intention was to provide a stylized system of interpretation

The most important prophetic book with regard to references to the Jubilee is Isaiah. From Isaiah 40–66 there are a significant number of references to Israel as a debt-slave, the Lord as the redeemer, and the restoration of land.[119] Moreover, as Baltzer has noted, the Isaianic references to "redemption" cannot be distinguished from "liberation."[120] Thus freedom from debt-slavery (the exile) ultimately results in a new beginning, which has obvious Jubilee significance. Of the myriad of redemption passages in Isaiah 40–66, those which are associated most clearly with the Jubilee legislation are 49:8–13, 58, and 61:1–3. Isaiah 58:6 and 61:1–2a are of particular interest to this study and will be examined in further detail later (see chapter 5).

In Isaiah 49:7–13, there are clear parallels between the return from exile and Leviticus 25; land is restored and reassigned, captives and those in darkness are freed, and there is general prosperity (including provision for the poor). While the Jubilee is not explicitly indicated, the passage corresponds to Isaiah 61:1–3, which has clearer associations with Leviticus 25.

Isaiah 58 is not normally associated with the Jubilee; however, there are some scholars who see clear Jubilee connections.[121] The arguments in favor of an association between Isaiah 58 and the Jubilee are generally centered on the belief that the fast in Isaiah 58 was a reference to the fast on the Day of Atonement (which marked the beginning of a Jubilee year) and on possible literary and thematic parallels between the text of Isaiah 58:1–12 and the legislation in Leviticus 25.[122] It is far from clear, however, whether or

---

to account for historical data. Goldingay, *Daniel*, 257–60.

119. Bergsma notes that the verb גאל ("to redeem") is used twenty-two times within this section of Isaiah. See Bergsma, *Jubilee*, 191–93.

120. Baltzer, "Liberation from Debt Slavery," 477–84.

121. See, for example, Hanks, *Third World*, 98–104; Tanenbaum, "Holy Year 1975," 65; and Brueggemann, *Isaiah 40–66*, 189.

122. Thomas Hanks has provided the most systematic argument for associating Isa 58 with the Jubilee. He argues that: 1) Isaiah 58:1–12 appears in a section framed by teachings referring to the Sabbath in a manner akin to Lev 25; 2) while several fasts were commanded in the postexilic era, the only fast commanded in the law was that on the Day of Atonement. Therefore, the focus on fasting in Isa 58 refers back to the Day of Atonement, which was the first day of the Jubilee; 3) the prophetic proclamation in Isa 58 and the proclamation of a Jubilee year were both announced by the sounding of a trumpet (שׁוֹפָר); 4) Isaiah 58:2 refers to an ordinance of God which has been forsaken, which could be a reminder of the Jubilee laws which were also forsaken; 5) Isaiah 58:5 refers to the day of fasting as רָצוֹן ("acceptable") in the same way that Isa 61:2 refers to the Jubilee year; 6) both Isa 58:6 and the Jubilee ordinances mention the liberation of slaves; 7) Isaiah 58:8 demonstrates a concern for poor Jews, which parallels the Jubilee provisions in Lev 25:35–37; 8) when translated properly, Isa 58:3–4 refers to debts and debtors, which is reminiscent of the cancellation of debts in the Jubilee legislation (Lev 25:10 and 35–55); and 9) Isaiah 58:9 demonstrates that people were rationalizing injustice, just as the Israelites who ignored the Jubilee legislation had done. Hanks, *Third*

not the fast in Isaiah 58 was referring to the Day of Atonement, particularly since there were four other fasts observed in the postexilic period.[123] Moreover, even if it is understood to be a reference to the Day of Atonement, the Jubilee may still not be in focus, since the Day of Atonement and the Jubilee only coincided once every fifty years. Similarly, the suggested parallels between Isaiah 58 and the Jubilee legislation of Leviticus 25 are far from conclusive. Nonetheless, it seems possible that Isa 58 draws on Jubilee themes and images without explicitly referring to them. Since the prophet was undoubtedly familiar with the Levitical legislation, Isaiah 58 may be an ethical reinterpretation of the Jubilee, whereby its "principles and postures could be enacted immediately without the implementation of all the particulars of the traditional law."[124]

The clearest Isaianic allusion to the Jubilee is in chapter 61, particularly verses 1–3.[125] Parallels between this chapter and the themes in Leviticus 25 are apparent in the opening verses; they both refer to justice, the release of captives, the proclamation of a special year, and provision for those in need. Similarly, the word דְּרוֹר ("emancipation"/"freedom") in 61:1 has clear associations with the Jubilee, being only used in texts associated with the "year of release" (Lev 25:10, Jer 34:8, 15, 17; Ezek 46:17).[126]

World, 97–104. While a thorough examination of Hanks's arguments lies beyond the scope of this study, it is apparent that the controlling metaphor in arguments 1) and 3) is the Sabbath in general (marked by trumpets sounded from the temple) rather than the Jubilee in particular, and that this is a wider concern in the prophetic literature, as are the forsaking of God's ordinances (argument 4), the concern for the poor (argument 7), the care for the oppressed (argument 6, which includes all the oppressed, not just slaves; and argument 8, no matter which translation is followed), and the excuses given by the powerful for injustice (argument 9). None of these references provide a *necessary* connection to the Jubilee itself, since they are clearly widespread in the prophetic oracles of Isaiah and beyond. So, too, is the reference to "acceptable" (in Greek or in Hebrew, argument 5) which occurs in Isaiah, Malachi, and Jeremiah (including Isa 61) and in Leviticus, but not in Lev 25. Surely this range of evidence supports the general relationship of Isa 58 to the prophetic literature rather than the particular association with the Jubilee in Lev 25.

123. Watts, *Isaiah 34–66*, 842.

124. Bergsma, *Jubilee*, 198.

125. Collins holds that Lev 25 is not necessarily in view in Isa 61, though the two texts were later brought together at Qumran by the author of 11QMelch. The thematic similarities between the two texts, however, seem to favor the presence of a literary link between the two texts. Collins, "Herald," 228–29.

126. The proclamation of a release here has been seen by some as an attempt to support land claims by those returning from the Babylonian exile. As Brett has noted, however, when one considers the "hierarchical integration of foreigners" in chapters 60–62, it seems more likely that overall reconciliation between the communities is in view. Brett, "Unequal Terms," 252.

While there is general consensus that "the year of the Lord's favor" (61:2a) refers to the new Jubilee age, there is less certainty about "the day of vengeance of our God" (61:2b) since there is no mention of vengeance upon enemies in the Jubilee legislation (nor in Jesus' reading of the text in Luke 4). While different hypotheses have been proposed, the majority view is that the "year" and "day" refer to a concurrent period, since Isaiah elsewhere uses "year" and "day" in parallel (34:8; 49:9; 63:4).[127] Thus, the Jubilee blessings are reserved for Israel and the "day" refers to Yahweh's vengeance on Israel's enemies (see also Isa 34:8; 63:4; Jer 46:10).[128] Since Jubilee imagery is employed here to illustrate the Lord's favor rather than explicate Leviticus 25, there is no difficulty in including vengeance within this passage.

As Sanders has noted, disagreement continues over the meaning of Isaiah 61:1–3 during its first stages of formation. The passage is commonly viewed as a Servant Song, a Midrash on the Servant Songs, or the call of Trito-Isaiah.[129] While all positions can be argued to some extent, a final decision is not necessary, since even if the servant is not in view, the Isaianic herald can be seen to be a picture of the servant figure by drawing on earlier Isaianic associations (Isa 42:1–4; 49:1–11).[130]

As Gregory has noted, the language of Isaiah 61:1–3 also seems to indicate that the author viewed his situation in exilic terms.[131] While there are some who would view this as evidence that the text was written during the Babylonian captivity, others, such as Gregory, have proposed that Isaiah 61:1–3 provides one of the earliest attestations of the exile understood as a theological state, rather than as a historical period.[132] That is, the exile was understood as continuing typologically, since the sins which led to Israel's historical exile had not yet ceased.

The identity of the speaker in Isaiah 61:1–3 has received much attention. Suggestions for the original identity of the speaker include Israel, the high priest, the servant, a Levitical minority, the messiah, the prophet, or a

---

127. Young, *The Book of Isaiah*, 3:460 and Steck, "Der Rachetag," 338. Shalom Paul has also listed occasions whereby "days" and "years" are used synonymously in Ugaritic, Phoenician, Aramaic, Ammonite, and Akkadian inscriptions. See Paul, *Isaiah 40–66*, 540.

128. Paul, *Isaiah 40–66*, 540; Westermann, *Isaiah 40–66*, 367; Whybray, *Isaiah 40–66*, 242; and Young, *The Book of Isaiah*, 3:460.

129. Scholarly opinion is often based on one's view of the literary origin and nature of Isa 56–66. See Bock, *Proclamation*, 108 and Sanders, "From Isaiah 61 to Luke 4," 46–47.

130. Bock, *Proclamation*, 108.

131. Gregory, "The Postexilic Exile," 488.

132. Gregory, "The Postexilic Exile," 488–92. See also McComiskey, "Exile and Restoration," 690.

group of prophets.¹³³ Despite these many suggestions, it seems likely that the figure can be characterized as being both prophetic and royal. His prophetic office seems likely in view of the nature of the eight infinitives in 61:1–3, all of which are consistent with the functions of a prophet. This is consistent with the Targum, which identifies the speaker as an individual prophet, and it parallels Micah 3:8, which also presents a speaker being filled with the Spirit of Yahweh to fulfill prophetic work.¹³⁴ The royalty of the figure is implied by his anointing (61:1). While prophets (1 Kgs 19:16) and priests (Exod 28:41, 29:7; 40:13–15) were also anointed in earlier Old Testament texts, anointing was usually reserved for royalty.¹³⁵ Moreover, the only other Old Testament passages which connect anointing and the impartation of God's Spirit are in connection with David's position as the king of Israel (1 Sam 16:13; 2 Sam 23:1–2). Thus, it seems that the speaker was a unique character, both royal and prophetic, endowed with God's Spirit, anointed by Yahweh, and commissioned to complete a difficult and varied mission. The speaker is also the first figure in Jewish literature directly associated with the proclamation of a new Jubilee age.¹³⁶

The beneficiaries of his ministry were the poor, the marginalized, and those without hope. Thus the socioeconomic aspect of the speaker's work is clear. As Blenkinsopp has noted, however, there are also religious dimensions to the prophet's ministry; "by the time of writing . . . the terms in question (ʿănāvîm, ʿăniyyîm) had acquired a broader and specifically religious connotation without losing their basic meaning of economic deprivation,

---

133. Alexander, *Isaiah*, 397–98; Paul, *Isaiah 40-66*, 538; Wade, *Isaiah*, 386; Westermann, *Isaiah 40-66*, 365–67; Whybray, *Isaiah 40-66*, 240; Young, *The Book of Isaiah*, 458; and Ringe, "Jubilee Proclamation," 54. For a brief summary and evaluation of the different positions, see Blenkinsopp, *Isaiah 56-66*, 220–23.

134. The Tg. Ps.-J opens Isa 61:1 by stating that "the prophet said . . ." (אֲמַר נְבִיָּא). The Targumist evidently viewed the speaker of Isa 61 as a prophet—most probably the prophet Isaiah himself. It is the spirit of prophecy (רוּחַ נְבוּאָה) which rests on the speaker. That is, the speaker is a herald-prophet sent to "proclaim the acceptable year of the Lord and the day of vengeance of our God" (Isa 61:2). While the Tg. Ps.-J is notoriously difficult to date, if it was written by Jonathon ben Uzziel, who was formerly under the tutelage of Rabbi Hillel (as is often argued), then it would have been transcribed sometime during the first century. Thus, it is possible that there was a tradition in the first century which viewed the speaker of Isa 61 as a prophet. This aligns with some of the rabbinic literature, which views Isaiah alone as receiving the Spirit of God (see, for example, Lev. Rab. 10:2). While Luke probably referred to the Septuagint for the Isaianic quotation in Luke 4:18–19, the Targumist's interpretation (or a similar tradition) may nonetheless have had some influence on Luke.

135. See, for example, 1 Sam 9:16; 10:1; 16:3; 2 Sam 2:7; 5:17; 12:7; 19:10; 1 Kgs 1:24; 5:1; 19:15. Bergsma, *Jubilee*, 200 and Westermann, *Isaiah 40-66*, 365.

136. Bergsma, *Jubilee*, 203.

marginalisation, and exploitation."¹³⁷ This coincides with the eschatological view of the Jubilee which pervades the postexilic and Second Temple literature. It was during this period, when the reimplementation of the Jubilee legislation was impossible, that the Law was treated prophetically through a typological hermeneutic.¹³⁸ Jubilee legislation was viewed as having been designed not only for poor Israelites in debt-slavery, but also for the entire nation, who had fallen into debt with God by failing to observe his law.¹³⁹ The speaker in Isaiah 61:1–3 was therefore one who would bring deliverance to the socioeconomically and politically marginalized pockets of society and to the nation of Israel as a whole.

Summary of Findings

There are relatively few passages throughout the Old Testament which explicitly refer to the Jubilee legislation in Leviticus 25, and there are no definite historical occasions where the Jubilee is recorded as being enacted. Implicit references to key Jubilee themes, however, suggest that the Jubilee was not entirely forgotten throughout Israel's history. The redemption of slaves in Nehemiah, Jeremiah, and Isaiah parallels (in part) the ordinances in Leviticus 25:39–55. Similarly, 1 Kings, Nehemiah, Ezekiel, Jeremiah, and Isaiah all record instances of property being redeemed in a way which reflects the provisions in Leviticus 25:14–17 and 25:23–34 (see also Num 36:4). In contrast to the redemption of slaves and property, however, there are no occasions mentioned when the land is given its rest in accordance with the Jubilee provisions.¹⁴⁰

As Bergsma has noted, there appears to be a gradual change in the emphasis of the Jubilee texts.¹⁴¹ The original Pentateuchal references frame

---

137. Blenkinsopp, *Isaiah 56–66*, 224. Blenkinsopp concludes that this religious connotation means that the entire nation could be characterized as "the poor of YHVH," since they had been exploited by imperial forces. Heard agrees that there are religious connotations to the poor; however, he goes further than Blenkinsopp by arguing that the poor were, in fact, those who remained faithful to the Torah (and therefore to God) and chose not to participate in activities that would have led to power and wealth. Thus, the poor in Isa 61 (and indeed generally throughout Isa 56–66) referred to the portion of the nation who chose to follow the Law, which then led to oppression and economic destabilization. While his proposal seems attractive, it is difficult to maintain with any degree of certainty, in part due to the absence of any references to the Law throughout Isa 56–66. Heard, "Luke's Attitude," 48–50.

138. Bergsma, *Jubilee*, 298.

139. Bergsma, *Jubilee*, 299.

140. 2 Chr 36:20–23 refers to the lack of Sabbath rests given to the land.

141. Bergsma, *Jubilee*, 295–304.

the Jubilee provisions in legal terms. While there are eschatological overtones, the Jubilee texts were to be practiced as part of Israel's obedience to the law.[142] In Jeremiah 34:1–8 and Isaiah 58, however, the Jubilee appears to be reinterpreted ethically.[143] That is, the focus of the Jubilee texts moved from literal observance of the legal provisions to a contemporary application of its ethical principles, particularly redemption and justice.[144] Finally, there are some hints of an eschatological emphasis which came to the fore in the postexilic period, demonstrated most clearly by the Spirit-endowed anointed figure of Isaiah 61 who is given the task of proclaiming and inaugurating a new Jubilee age.[145]

The Relationship between the *Basileia* of God and the Jubilee

There are clear difficulties in identifying the presence and/or nature of the relationship between the *basileia* of God and the Jubilee in the Old Testament, partly because of the lack of clear references to the phrase "*basileia* of God." Additionally, none of the various fifteen references to the "*basileia* of Yahweh" are made in connection to the Jubilee, and the Jubilee itself is not very influential throughout the Old Testament. That is to say, there is no explicit association between the *basileia* of God and the Jubilee.

Nevertheless, there are several observations that can be made. The dynamic reign and the kingship of Yahweh can both be seen within the Jubilee legislation. While the legal precepts are themselves a demonstration of Yahweh's reign, they also reiterate that the Israelites belong to Yahweh as his servants (Lev 25:42, 55)—he is the ruling monarch.

While the eschatological hope of Yahweh's *basileia* is present in many of the prophetic texts (particularly those written in the postexilic period), its association with the Jubilee is seen most clearly in Isaiah. In chapters 40–55, the proclamation that "Yahweh reigns" was a declaration to the people that they were to return from the exile to their land.[146] This deliverance from debt-slavery (the exile), return to the land, and the ensuing new beginning has clear Jubilee connotations. Significantly, however, it is the Lord himself who achieves this redemption. That is, the Isaianic text does not call the Israelites to enact Jubilee precepts; rather, the Lord himself achieves

---

142. Sloan, *Favorable Year*, 12–18.
143. Bergsma, *Jubilee*, 297–98.
144. Bergsma, *Jubilee*, 297.
145. Bergsma, *Jubilee*, 298–300.
146. Selman, "Kingdom," 178.

redemption for his people. In accomplishing this redemption, Yahweh not only demonstrates his sovereign rule over the nations, but also his particular concern for and kingship over his people. Thus, it seems Jubilee imagery was employed by the Isaianic author to depict elements of Yahweh's reign.[147]

In the following section of Isaiah (chapters 56–66), Jubilee themes and imagery are used to describe the coming *basileia* of God. This is seen particularly clearly in Isaiah 61, where Jubilee terminology is used to illustrate the nature of God's future *basileia*. That is, the description of the eschatological Jubilee age is used to depict the character of God's future *basileia*. This is underscored by the wider context of the passage, which focuses on the deliverance and final vindication of Zion (Isa 60–62), which is sometimes cited as the location of Yahweh's throne.[148] The eschatological Jubilee is presented as the time when Yahweh's reign over his people would be clear. In a similar way to other prophetic texts, Isaiah 61 presents the coming age chiefly in terms of righteousness and justice. The righteousness of the *basileia* (mentioned explicitly in verses 3, 10, and 11) is portrayed through Jubilee imagery in verses 1–2. Similarly, God's justice is connected to the Jubilee age in verse 2, whereby the proclamation of the year of the Lord's favor is accompanied by the day of vengeance. The description of the *basileia* in Jubilee terms is therefore consistent with the wider picture of the eschatological *basileia*.

It is also significant that Isaiah 56–66 portrays the coming *basileia* as a time of salvation for God's people, whose sins have separated them from God.[149] It is these sins which led to the later theological interpretation of the exile (described in Jubilee terminology in Isaiah 61:1–3). This time of salvation is again reminiscent of the Jubilee, which began with the Day of Atonement and was largely concerned with the redemption of the Israelites.

Since the eschatological Jubilee is a depiction of the future reign of God, it is not surprising that it is ushered in by a figure analogous to the Davidic messiah. In a similar way to the Davidic monarchs, the speaker in Isaiah 61:1–3 is an earthly representative of Yahweh's rule. Additionally, the anointing of the Lord and the royal and prophetic aspects to the figure are all consistent with the messianic expectation in the prophetic texts.[150] Finally,

---

147. This is seen particularly clearly in Isa 49.

148. Selman, "Kingdom," 177. It is also underscored by the mention of the new covenant in Isa 61:8 and the extension of God's reign over other nations in Isa 61:4–6, both of which are related to the reign of God in the Old Testament.

149. See especially chapters 58–59. This is consistent with other portrayals of the *basileia* (particularly in the prophetic texts), which emphasize that when God establishes his reign there will be everlasting peace, including peace between God and people.

150. Boda, "Figuring the Future," 73–74.

the beneficiaries of the speaker's ministry in Isaiah 61:1–3 (both the socio-economically and politically marginalized, as well as the entire nation of Israel who had sinned against God) are consistent with those of the Davidic messiah, who would mediate Yahweh's reign over a society characterized by righteousness and justice.

Conclusion

As mentioned above, the frequency and location of Old Testament citations and allusions in Luke's Gospel indicate how influential the Scriptures were in his thinking. While Luke was concerned about the fulfillment of Israel's Scriptures (particularly christologically), he was also influenced by and concerned with their literary context. In particular, it seems Luke was influenced by the prophetic writings, especially Isaiah. Indeed, there are three explicit references to Isaiah in the Gospel and five in Acts, and there are a number of Isaianic phrases and themes that Luke used at critical places within his narrative to shape his overall work.[151] It is therefore unsurprising that Luke's presentation of the *basileia* of God resonates most closely with its depiction in the prophetic literature. As will be seen in chapter 3, many aspects of the concept of the *basileia* of God in the Old Testament (and especially the prophetic texts) are present in Luke's Gospel. Indeed, Luke was deeply influenced by the eschatological nature of the *basileia* (seen particularly in the postexilic writings), the synonymy of God's reign with salvation, the character of that salvation, the importance of Jerusalem and the temple, and the central role that the Davidic messiah would play in inaugurating God's reign. Significantly, Luke's presentation of Jesus as the Davidic messiah underscores the importance of the reign of God, which would be inaugurated and mediated by the Davidic king.

The prophetic literature's ethical reinterpretation of the Jubilee texts to emphasize redemption and justice is also consistent with what is seen in Luke's narrative. Both of these themes are highly significant throughout Luke-Acts. This does not, however, indicate that Luke was necessarily influenced by Jubilee traditions *per se*; the themes of redemption and justice permeate through many of the prophetic writings which are unconnected with the Jubilee. Indeed, where the prophetic literature employs Jubilee imagery, it is used to elucidate the themes of justice and redemption (rather than

---

151. Koet, "Isaiah in Luke-Acts," 98 and Sanders, "Isaiah in Luke," 20. Isaianic references in Luke-Acts are found in Luke 3:4–6 (Isa 40:3–5); 4:18–19 (Isa 58:6 and 61:1–2); 22:37 (Isa 53:12); Acts 7:49–50 (Isa 66:1–2a); 8:32–33 (Isa 53:7–8); 13:34 (Isa 55:3), 47 (49:6); 28:26–27 (Isa 6:9–11).

justice and redemption elucidating the Jubilee). This parallels the relationship between *basileia* of God and the Jubilee; while there is no explicit literary association between the two traditions, the Isaianic text makes use of some Jubilee terminology and imagery to depict elements of Yahweh's reign. Thus, Luke's quotation of and allusions to Isaiah 61 (which have been identified by some as the most explicit references to the Jubilee) do not necessarily indicate that he was interested in the Jubilee, so much as it indicates his interest in the age of salvation and its inauguration by the Isaianic herald.

2

Basileia of God and Jubilee Traditions in Second Temple Literature

Introduction

While Luke did not explicitly quote any Second Temple documents, he (and his source material) was undoubtedly influenced to some degree by the traditions of his day. Indeed, the fact that Luke considered the *basileia* of God to be such an important concept in his work and yet neglected to define it suggests that the *basileia* was familiar to both him and his audience. This chapter will therefore examine Luke's use of Second Temple literature to assess what traditions may have influenced him (or his source material). After this, the various *basileia* of God and Jubilee traditions in the Second Temple literature will be surveyed to ascertain how the two concepts were alluded to and interpreted. This will then be followed by an exploration into the nature of any relationship between the *basileia* of God and the Jubilee traditions: Is one used to evoke the other? Do they inhabit the same semantic domain? Are there any explicit literary connections? Does the distinctive terminology of each tradition overlap?

Luke's Use of Second Temple Literature

It is quite clear that Luke was significantly influenced by his Hellenistic-Roman context. Talbert goes so far as to say that Luke-Acts has been organized "both as a whole and in its parts" in a similar way to Vergil's *Aeneid*, and that Luke's text has been modeled after such authors as Aristotle, Suetonius, Lucian, and Pliny.[1] There is also little doubt that Luke was influenced by contemporary Jewish traditions. Though there are no explicit quotations from the Second Temple documents in the Gospel, Luke's knowledge of the Old Testament Scriptures suggests that he may have been familiar with other Jewish writings (see below). There are also clear thematic similarities between Luke's narrative and some contemporarily available Jewish works. Moreover, Luke's presentation of Christianity as a continuation of salvation-history and as the fulfillment of Jewish prophecies suggests that he was acquainted with Jewish messianic expectations.

In particular, it seems that Luke (or his source material) may have been aware of some of the Qumran traditions. Indeed, Evans has argued that every major theme and emphasis in Luke's narrative has a close parallel in the Qumran scrolls (especially the "core" scrolls).[2] These parallels include: Luke's distinctive association between spirituality and one's attitude toward money and possessions, his designation of the Christian movement as "the Way," the positive description of the communal sharing of property, and the focus on election (though Luke's interpretation differs significantly from the Qumran writings).[3]

It also seems evident that Luke was familiar with other Jewish literature. Possibly the greatest example of this is the apparent parallels between Luke's Gospel and the 1 Enoch (particularly 1 En. 92–105).[4] The literary and theological similarities between the two documents are striking, particularly with regard to how judgment is described and the association between riches and sudden judgment.[5] Indeed, Aalen has gone so far as to suggest

---

1. Talbert even goes so far as to cite specific texts: Aristotle, *Poet.* 17:5–10; Suetonius, *Vit.* 22–23; Lucian, *Quom. Hist. conscr. sit* 48; and Pliny the Younger, *Ep.* 9:36. Talbert, *Literary Patterns*, 67–68, 141.

2. Evans, "Synoptic Gospels," 75, 95.

3. See Evans, "Synoptic Gospels," 89–95 for a list of Lukan passages and their parallels in the scrolls. Other similarities between the scrolls and Luke-Acts include the description of how one must rebuke a fellow member of the community, a list of beatitudes, disputes concerning the Sabbath, discourse on the Holy Spirit, the designations "Son of God" and "Son of the Most High" as messianic titles, the description of crucifixion as "hanging on a tree," a dying or conquering messiah, and the messianic banquet. See Flint, *The Dead Sea Scrolls*, 187–89.

4. Two more prominent parallels are Luke 12:16–21 and 1 En. 97:8–10, and Luke 16:19–31 and the last chapters of 1 Enoch.
Aalen, "St. Luke's Gospel," 1–13; Nickelsburg, "Revisiting," 547–71; Nickelsburg, "Riches," 521–46; and Kloppenborg, "Response," 572–85.

5. Nickelsburg, "Revisiting," 565–67.

that Luke was either personally acquainted with the translator of 1 Enoch, or that he translated the work himself.[6] While Aalen's conclusions are difficult to substantiate, it does seem that the epistle was widely influential in the first century (there were twenty remains of 1 Enoch scrolls identified at Qumran alone), and it seems likely that the author of Luke-Acts was familiar with it.

In addition to 1 Enoch, R. H. Charles has also demonstrated that Luke included ideas and phrases which mirror sections from Jubilees.[7] Similarly, Charlesworth has argued that the hymns in Luke's Gospel have their origins in various sections of the Pseudepigrapha.[8] Luke's conception of the Davidic messiah also parallels what is seen in many Jewish documents.[9]

Thus, while Luke was most probably a gentile, he nevertheless seemed to be conversant with at least some Jewish traditions. He utilized the vocabulary and literary style of Jewish works, and he (or his source material) was influenced, to some degree, by Second Temple theology. He was evidently comfortable redacting these traditions, however, for his own social context and literary purposes.[10] For the purposes of this study, it is therefore important to establish what influence (if any) the Second Temple *basileia* and Jubilee traditions may have had on his work.

The *Basileia* of God in Late Second Temple Judaism

The Old Testament Apocrypha and Pseudepigrapha

Apocalyptic Works

The apocalyptic material in the Apocrypha and Pseudepigrapha contains thirty-nine references to a "kingdom" in relation to God.[11] Of these references,

---

6. Aalen, "St. Luke's Gospel," 13.

7. According to Charles, similarities between Jubilees and Luke-Acts (and indeed the entire New Testament) are mainly seen with respect to angels and demons. Textual parallels include: Luke 6:49 and Jub. 1:12; Acts 7:15–16 and Jub. 46:9; Acts 7:23 and Jub. 47:10–12; Acts 7:30 and Jub. 48:1; Acts 7:53 and Jub. 1:14, 27; and Acts 9:2 and Jub. 23:20. See Charles, *The Book of Jubilees*, lxxxiii–lxxxv.

Charles's conclusions have been reaffirmed by other more recent works. See Wintermute, "Jubilees," and Charlesworth, *The Old Testament Pseudepigrapha*, 41.

8. Charlesworth, *The Old Testament Pseudepigrapha*, xiv.

9. See, for example, the Pss. Sol. 17:21–32 and the Tg. Ps.-J to Ps 80:16. See also the Dead Sea Scrolls 4QFlor 1:10–13, 4QpIsa 3:11–25, lQSb 5:20–29, and 4QpGen 5:1–6.

10. Kloppenborg, "Response," 579.

11. 1 En. 84:2; 103:1; 2 En. 1a:3; 45:2; 3 En. 6:3; 35:6; 39:2; 44:7–8; 48A:5; Sib. Or. 2.347; 3.46, 767; 12:293; 4 Ezra 2:35; Vis. Ezra 66; Apoc. Sedr. 1:22; 15:5; 2 Bar. 73:1; 3 Bar. 11:2; Apoc. El. 4:27; T. Jos. 19:12; T. Benj. 9:1; T. Isaac 1:7; 2:8; 6:11; 7:2; 8:5–6;

the actual phrase "kingdom of God" only occurs on four occasions,[12] while the phrase "kingdom of heaven" occurs twelve times.[13] The theme of the *basileia* of God is, however, far more prevalent. Indeed, many apocalyptic works contain two central motifs: 1) that the present world order is evil and oppressive, controlled by Satan and his accomplices (be they fallen angels or humans), and 2) that this world order will soon be destroyed by God and a new and perfect order will be established (reminiscent of Eden before the fall).[14] In this sense, one might say that apocalyptic literature is, by its very nature, focused on the establishment of the *basileia* of God. The highly symbolic nature of much of the language, however, coupled with the variation of beliefs between the different apocalyptic authors makes it difficult to articulate a systematic treatment of the doctrine.[15] Nonetheless, it is clear that the apocalypticists viewed the *basileia* of God as very significant.

In a similar way to some Old Testament texts, many of the apocalypticists explicitly referred to God as king.[16] He was also frequently affirmed as being sovereign over creation,[17] earthly rulers,[18] and over other gods.[19] There is no question of God's kingship or his sovereign reign throughout the apocalyptic literature. Indeed, it is God's ultimate sovereignty which undergirds the apocalypticists' conviction that the present order will soon be destroyed when God's *basileia* comes. He is the eternal sovereign ruler,

---

T. Jac. 2:25; 7:11, 19–20, 23, 25, 27; 8:3, 5; T. Mos. 10:1. Admittedly, some of these works (such as Apocalypse of Sedrach) were most likely written after Luke wrote his two works.

12. T. Isaac 1:7; T. Jac. 7:19–20, 23.

13. Vis. Ezra 66; Apoc. Sedr. 1:22; 3 Bar. 11:2; T. Isaac 2:8; 7:2; 8:5–6; T. Jac. 2:25; 7:11, 25, 28; 8:3.

14. Aune, *Apocalypticism, Prophecy and Magic in Early Christianity*, 4. There are, of course, many other suggestions as to how apocalypses can be identified. Koch, for example, lists eight motifs that he argues are present in apocalyptic literature. Koch, *Rediscovery of Apocalyptic*, 28–33.

15. Beasley-Murray, *Jesus and the Kingdom of God*, 46.

16. 1 En. 12:3; 25:3, 5, 7; 27:3; 81:3; 84:2, 5; 2 En. 39:8; 64:4; 3 En. 3:2; 24:15; 25:4; Sib. Or. 1.73; 3.48, 56, 499, 617, 717; 5.499; 8.242; T. Benj. 10:7; T. Ab. 15:15; 16:2; T. Mos. 4:2.

17. 1 En. 1:3; 9:4; 84:2–3; 2 En. 15:1–3; 28:1–5; 66:5; 70:22; 73:4; Sib. Or. Prologue.94–99; 1.192–94; 3.19–23. Apocalyptic literature also, however, characteristically portrays Satan as being the ruler of this world, and his rule is occasionally described as extending to nature (3 En. 23:16). There are also some texts which present Satan as the creator of the world. Andersen, "2 (Slavonic Apocalypse of) Enoch," 141.

18. 1 En. 9:4; 84:2; Sib. Or. 2.220; 3.165–170.

19. 1 En. 9:4; 2 En. 34:1–2; Sib. Or. 3:8–45, 199–201; 5.495–99.

and the final salvation event (that is, the in-breaking of his *basileia*) is the manifestation of his eternal kingship.[20]

As might be expected, the apocalypticists' focus on the in-breaking of God's final *basileia* is frequently accompanied by a strong judgment motif.[21] The depictions of this judgment, however, vary considerably. Paolo Sacchi argues that this is mainly due to developments in Jewish apocalyptic thought.[22] He argues that apocalyptic works from their beginnings to approximately 200 BCE depict good and evil beings as being separated after death while awaiting the great judgment, after which the verdict (which has already been unofficially determined) confirms eternal salvation or eternal condemnation.[23] Works from 200 BCE to 100 BCE focus their attention on sin (over messianism or eschatology) and how the continual increase of sin throughout history (particularly angelic sin) will unavoidably lead to the eschaton, at which point God will eliminate evil.[24] Apocalyptic literature from 100 BCE to 50 CE has a far greater focus on human responsibility for sin, and in some documents a messianic figure comes to the fore as the agent of God's judgment, who will vindicate the righteous elect and condemn those who practice evil.[25] Finally, Sacchi argues that apocalyptic works from 50 CE to 120 CE again have a clear focus on human responsibility for sin (over and against angelic responsibility)—all humans are sinful.[26] A messianic figure is again visible in some works, however it is God himself who performs the last judgment.[27] While Sacchi's observations are clearly dependent on how one defines apocalyptic literature and how that literature is dated, they nonetheless provide helpful insight into the development of Jewish apocalyptic thought, particularly with regard to the growing focus

---

20. Perrin, *The Kingdom of God*, 168 and Fuellenbach, *The Kingdom of God*, 35. References to God's eternal nature include 1 En. 25:7; 75:3; 2 En. 1:8; 3 En. 15B:3; Sib. Or. 1.54, 56, 73, 332; 2.219, 287; 3.56, 600, and 616.

21. The references to judgment in the apocalyptic literature are too numerous to list—it is a constant theme throughout most of the apocalyptic documents. Some more explicit examples of the apocalypticists' focus on judgment include: 1 En. 1–5; 38; 45–48; 50; 53:1—56:4; 65–67; 90; 100–108; 2 En. 7; 18; 36; 39–40; 44; 48–53; 3 En. 32; 48C; Sib. Or. 2.255–83; 4.40–48, 179–92; 6.11; 8.92, 213, 217–250; Apocr. Ezek. 2:1–11; Apoc. Zeph. 2:1–6:17; 4 Ezra 6:35—9:25; Gk. Apoc. Ezra 2:18–5:28; 2 Bar. 20:5—30:5; and Apoc. El. (C) 5:24–29.

22. Sacchi, *Apocalyptic*, 109–10.

23. Sacchi, *Apocalyptic*, 110–11.

24. Sacchi, *Apocalyptic*, 111–13.

25. Sacchi, *Apocalyptic*, 113–22.

26. Sacchi, *Apocalyptic*, 122–25.

27. Sacchi, *Apocalyptic*, 122–23.

on human responsibility for sin and divine judgment, which came to the fore in the late first century.

In some Jewish apocalyptic documents, the establishment of the eternal *basileia* of God was preceded by a temporary messianic kingdom.[28] This kingdom functioned as a transition between the present period and the age to come, and between human monarchy and theocracy.[29] The importance and description of the messiah's role in relation to the *basileia* of God, however, varied greatly between different authors. Indeed, there are only four Jewish apocalyptic works which explicitly mention a messiah (2 Bar. 29; 39–42; 72–74; 4 Ezra 7; 11:37—12:34; 13:3—14:9; 1 En. 48:10; 52:4; 3 En. 45:5).[30] While there are clearly variations in thought between the different apocalypticists, it seems that their focus was not on a coming messiah (and certainly not on the character of the messiah) so much as it was on the establishment of the *basileia* of God, where God himself ruled as the king.[31]

Of all of the apocalyptic works in the Second Temple Literature, it is 1 Enoch which seems to provide the clearest exposition of the *basileia* of God. It is also important for this study because of Luke's apparent awareness of the Enochian text (see above). The first part of the book (chapters 1–36) describes how the present sinful condition of the earth is largely due to angelic wickedness, and how an eschatological judgment is coming for the righteous and the wicked. Significantly, salvation is described as including all nations (as also in Luke-Acts); gentiles will also be converted and included in the eschatological *basileia*.[32] The second part of the book (chapters

---

28. The concept of a temporary messianic kingdom is mentioned explicitly in only three early Jewish apocalypses: 1 En. 91:12–17, 93:1–10; 4 Ezra 7:26–44; 12:31–34; and 2 Bar. 29:3—30:1; 40:1–4; 72:2—74:3. Russell, *Jewish Apocalyptic*, 291–97; Aune et al., "Apocalypticism," 50; and Beasley-Murray, *Jesus and the Kingdom of God*, 47–48.

29. Aune et al., "Apocalypticism," 50.

30. Importantly, the authors of 2 Baruch and 4 Ezra were contemporaries of Luke. It is only 4 Ezra, however, which refers to the messiah in Davidic terms (in a similar way to Luke's Gospel). There are also many other non-apocalyptic Jewish documents that contain references to the messiah, as well as many later Christian apocalyptic works that also highlight a messianic figure. See Charlesworth, *The Old Testament Pseudepigrapha*, xxxii–xxxiii. References to the messiah in the apocalyptic works are, however, frequently disputed. This is partly due to difficulties in determining whether certain literary figures are in fact messianic. While many scholars argue that messianism was essentially dormant from the fifth century through to the late second century BCE, there are some who argue that that messianic hope was strong throughout the Persian period. See Collins, *Scepter*, 50–51 and Horbury, *Jewish Messianism*, 63. For a helpful list of possible messianic figures in different apocalyptic works described in a myriad of different ways, see Perrin, *The Kingdom of God*, 165–66.

31. Rowland, *The Open Heaven*, 176–78 and Aune et al., "Apocalypticism," 50.

32. Ladd, "The Kingdom of God in 1 Enoch," 36.

37–71) presents the *basileia* as coming via the heavenly "Son of Man" (also called the Elect One) who also performs the final judgment (see, in particular, 1 En. 46, 48, 60, 62–63, 69, 71). While scholarship remains divided as to how this figure should be interpreted within its literary context, if Luke was indeed familiar with the Enochian text it seems likely that he would have associated the Son of Man in his Gospel with this figure.[33] The third section of the book (chapters 72–82) is less concerned with the *basileia* of God (except insofar as God is viewed as sovereign over creation), however the fourth and fifth sections return to the judgment motif. Both final sections also affirm God as king, address the final destiny of the righteous and the wicked, and include a righteous figure who achieves justice and who protects his people.[34]

Jubilees[35]

Jubilees only explicitly refers to God's *basileia* on one occasion; however, the theme is addressed in a number of different places.[36] The description of the kingdom has some similarities to what is seen in the apocalyptic material; there is a period of deep trouble before judgment and the inauguration of the *basileia*.[37] The description of the *basileia* is also striking; God's sanctuary would be established in Jerusalem on Mount Zion, where he would reign as king (Jub. 1:27–29). Those who enjoy the blessings of the kingdom are the elect of Israel, whereas gentiles are described as "the sinners" (Jub. 23:24). While gentiles are used by God to judge Israel, they have no part in the

---

33. This section of 1 Enoch has received an extraordinary amount of scholarly attention. Scholars usually identify the "Son of Man" as being a corporate expression, a title, or as being synonymous with "man."

Luke presented Jesus as the Son of Man on twenty-five occasions (not including textual variation in Luke 9:55–56). There are also numerous similarities between the Son of Man in the Similitudes and in Luke's Gospel (though, admittedly, there also some differences).

34. God is affirmed as king in 1 En. 84:2, 5; 91:13. For passages concerning the righteous figure, see particularly 1 En. 90–92.

Importantly, the subject of divine justice is also a key theme in Luke's work. Indeed, words such as ἐκδίκησις (Luke 18:7, 8; 21:22; Acts 7:24) and ἐκδικέω (Luke 18:3, 5) are not seen in the other Gospels.

35. While some scholars categorize *Jubilees* as apocalyptic, there are at least three differences between the document and apocalyptic works: it does not contain bizarre imagery, there is little esoteric appeal, and eschatology is not a major focus. See Wintermute, "Jubilees," 37.

36. The one occasion where "kingdom" is used explicitly in relation to God is Jub. 12:19.

37. Ladd, "Jewish Apocryphal Literature," 168.

people of God and are destined for destruction (Jub. 23:22–24, 30). The elect will experience increasing longevity and will live in peace and joy (Jub. 23:27–29). Meanwhile, all their enemies (including Satan) will be driven out and cursed (Jub. 23:29).

Toward the end of the description of the *basileia*, the author seems to indicate that at the end of the thousand-year period the righteous will physically die but their spirits will live forever and will experience increasing joy (Jub. 23:31). This is quite unusual, given that bodily physical resurrection is a frequent feature of Palestinian Jewish literature.[38] While different explanations have been proposed, it seems most likely that the author is mixing Old Testament terminology with his own expectations of the future.[39]

Other Documents

The *basileia* of God is not mentioned frequently in the other Apocryphal and Pseudepigraphal works. Indeed, the phrase itself only occurs on five other occasions, all of which reflect the hope of entering the eschatological *basileia* (Hist. Rech. 12:9; T. Isaac 1:7; T. Jacob 7:20 [twice], 23). The phrase "kingdom of heaven" is used in much the same way—it is only present in a few texts and reflects the eschatological hope of entering God's presence (T. Isaac 2:8; 7:2; 8:5–6; T. Jacob 2:25; 7:11, 25, 27; 8:3). On the seventeen other occasions where the word "kingdom" is used in relation to God, it is usually eschatological in character and refers to God's unending reign over his people.[40]

God's kingship is mentioned more frequently than God's *basileia*.[41] In a similar way to the apocalyptic material, it seems God's eternal kingship is awaiting manifestation. That is, a time is coming when injustice will end (including foreign rule) and God's eschatological reign will be established

---

38. The preexistence and immortality of one's soul is more often associated with Hellenistic thought, however Greek thinking is conspicuously absent from the majority of the work. It is therefore unlikely that the concept is a reflection of Hellenistic influences. Ladd, "Jewish Apocryphal Literature" 172.

39. Ladd, "Jewish Apocryphal Literature" 172–73.

40. Pss. Sol. 5:18; 17:3; Hel. Syn. Pr. 4:36; 13:10; Odes Sol. 18:3; 22:12; 23:12; T. Jos. 19:12; T. Benj. 9:1; T. Isaac 6:11, 13–14, 18, 22; 8:6; T. Jac. 8:5; T. Mos. 10:1. Admittedly, most of these references are Christian, and some of them (such as the Testament of Isaac) were probably written after Luke penned his Gospel. References which are not necessarily eschatological include Odes Sol. 18:3 and 22:12.

41. Jos. Asen. 16:16; 19:5; 19:9; LAE 29:4; LAB 22:5; Lad. Jac. 2:19; Jan. Jam. 22:a; 3 Macc 2:2, 9, 13; 5:31; 6:2; Pss. Sol. 2:30, 32; 5:19; 17:1, 34, 46; Hel. Syn. Pr. 2:1; 3:1; 12:11; 13:13; T. Ab. 2:6, 11; 7:7; 8:3; 15:15; 16:2; T. Mos. 4:2; 10:3.

for his people (frequently Israel). On occasion, a kingly messianic figure is also mentioned as the mediator of God's rule.[42]

Collins has noted that in some circles of diaspora Judaism, the *basileia* took on a more spiritual or ethical character.[43] In the Wisdom of Solomon, for example, the *basileia* is frequently related to wisdom and righteousness, which is the root of immortality.[44] That is, there is not a strong expectation that the *basileia* of God will break into this world as a physical manifestation of God's sovereignty.[45] Similarly, in 4 Maccabees 2:23, one reads that a man who submits his intellect to the law will reign over a *basileia* that is temperate, just, good, and brave. While this perception of the *basileia* was not the dominant understanding, it was clearly influential in some more Hellenistic contexts.

The Dead Sea Scrolls

There are a number of complicating factors which can make it difficult to draw firm conclusions about the nature of God's *basileia* in the Dead Sea Scrolls. Firstly, due to the fragmentary state of many of the scrolls, it is not always clear whether references to a "kingdom" or "kingship" are associated with God (as opposed to an earthly ruler).[46] Secondly, even where it is clear that divine rulership is intended, the fragmentary context of some of these references can make it difficult to draw any firm conclusions about the nature of God's reign.[47] Thirdly, there is some variation within the scrolls' presentation of God's reign, which suggests that there was some difference in how the *basileia* of God was understood.[48] Fourthly, the doctrine of the *basileia* of God is not a dominant theme in any of the Qumran scrolls.[49]

---

42. Pss. Sol. 17:32; T. Sim. 7:2; T. Levi 18:3; T. Isaac 8:6.

43. Collins, "Kingdom," 87.

44. See especially Wis 15:3. Collins, "Kingdom," 87.

45. Collins, "Kingdom," 87.

46. See, for example, 4Q554 2 III, 20–22. In this passage, it seems that the kingdom being referred to is the kingdom of Israel, but it may also be a reference to the messianic kingdom. See also 4Q286 7 I, 4–5 and 4Q287 5, 8–10.

47. Viviano, "Kingdom of God," 101.

48. As Collins has noted, "The sectarian texts are not without their internal tensions . . . It is reasonable to suppose that there was some change and development in the history of the sect, even though we cannot trace it with any confidence. The sect was not organized on the basis of a creed, and there may well have been variation in what the members believed" (Collins, *Apocalypticism*, 150). See also Davies, "Eschatology at Qumran," 39–42.

49. Lattke, "Jewish Background," 83.

Finally, there is some uncertainty as to how various scrolls should be dated, which impedes discussion about how certain doctrines such as the *basileia* of God might have developed over time.[50]

Despite these difficulties, a number of observations can still be made. Firstly, it seems that the apocalyptic vision of God's reign breaking into human history, which dominated the Apocryphal and Pseudepigraphal works, was also very influential at Qumran. Indeed, some have even labeled the Dead Sea sect as an "apocalyptic community."[51] The apocalyptic thinking at Qumran, however, had some distinctive elements, particularly with regard to the priesthood and the centrality of the Torah.[52] Most important, however, was the idea that the community was already participating in eschatological salvation and that they already belonged to the heavenly Jerusalem.[53] That is, the Qumran community juxtaposed present and future notions of the eschatological *basileia*.[54]

While there is some variation in the Dead Sea Scrolls' presentation of eschatology, all the scrolls agree that God's sovereign rule extends over all creation and beings. This is seen explicitly in the Thanksgiving Hymns:

> See, you are the prince of gods and the king of the glorious ones, lord of every spirit, ruler of every creature. Apart from you nothing happens, and nothing is known without your will. There is no-one besides you, no-one matches your strength, nothing equals your glory, there is no price on your might. (1QHa XVIII, 8–10)[55]

Thus, God was viewed as the great king (though, he was not always given that title).[56] While earthly kings are frequently mentioned, Michael/Melchizedek is named the king of righteousness, and a Davidic ruler or messiah is sometimes described as king.[57] There is never any question, however, that it is God who possesses all authority as the sovereign ruler. As

---

50. Schiffman, "Messianic Figures," 116. This section will focus only on the Dead Sea Scrolls which have not been mentioned earlier (that is, it will not include scrolls such as 1 Enoch or Jubilees).

51. Collins, *Apocalypticism*, 150.

52. Collins, *Apocalypticism*, 153–54.

53. Beasley-Murray, *Jesus and the Kingdom of God*, 49.

54. Beasley-Murray, *Jesus and the Kingdom of God*, 51.

55. Martínez and Tigchelaar, *Dead Sea Scrolls*, 1:187.

56. For references to God's kingship, see particularly the Songs of the Sabbath Sacrifice (4Q400–4Q407 and 11Q17) and the War Scroll.

57. While Melchizedek can be translated "king of righteousness," Michael may also be given that title in the fragmentary text 4Q544 3, 2 (though this is uncertain).

such, the Dead Sea writings align with other apocalyptic texts in presenting God as the eternal sovereign ruler whose *basileia* will be established as a manifestation and vindication of his ultimate kingship.

As mentioned above, God's *basileia* is sometimes mentioned in relation to a coming messianic figure who would mediate Yahweh's reign. In 4Q174, for example, Exodus 15:18 is quoted: "Yahweh shall reign forever and ever."[58] Soon after this, however, the scroll states that Yahweh will establish the throne of the coming Davidic messiah forever.[59] The two statements are not contradictory; the coming Davidic figure was to be established as the mediator of God's reign forever. The same idea is evident in 4Q252, where the Davidic messiah is given "the covenant of kingship of his people for everlasting generations."[60] While the Dead Sea Scrolls present the messiah as a priest, teacher, anointed prophet, Son of God, heavenly Son of Man, the servant, or a combination of these (or they suggest that there are to be two messiahs), the dominant presentation of the messiah is that he would be a Davidic ruler who would restore the kingdom of Israel.[61] Importantly, the texts which emphasize the Davidic figure tend toward restorative messianism, which focus on developments which result in the future peace and prosperity of God's people (as opposed to utopian messianism, which concentrates more on the cataclysmic annihilation of all evil, which then leads to a new perfect and ideal world).[62]

Probably the most important scroll in relation to the *basileia* of God is the War Scroll. Indeed, Lattke argues that "of all the writings from Qumran only the War Scroll really remains as a testimony to or reference to God's royal rule."[63] The scroll details two imminent wars (the War against the Kittim and the War of Divisions) and the final divine intervention whereby God acts on behalf of the sons of light. The scroll describes the final kingdom as belonging to Israel under God's kingship[64] and as being characterized by

58. 4Q174 1 I, 3. Martínez and Tigchelaar, *Dead Sea Scrolls*, 1:353.

59. 4Q174 1 I, 10–11.

60. 4Q252 V, 4. Martínez and Tigchelaar, *Dead Sea Scrolls*, 1:505.

61. Contra Cooper, "Qumran and the Messianic Hope," 77.

References to the Davidic messiah include 4Q174 1 I, 10–11; 4Q252 V, 4; 4Q285 5, 2–4 (depending on whether the prince is translated as the subject or object of the verb "to kill"); and CD-A VII, 19. Moreover, Isa 11:1–5 is cited as a reference to a Davidic messiah in 4Q285, 4QpIsa, and 1QSb. Collins, *Scepter*, 53–78.

The understanding that the hope of a messiah was not a uniform expectation across Judaism is now accepted by the majority of scholars. Charlesworth "From Messianology to Christology," 5.

62. Schiffman, "Messianic Figures," 129.

63. Lattke, "Jewish Background," 83.

64. 1QM XII, 3, 16; XIX, 8. It is difficult to know whether the connection between

justice, peace, and prosperity.⁶⁵ Significantly, there is no mention of a messianic figure (though the angel Michael is mentioned); it is God himself who achieves salvation for his people and who establishes his reign.⁶⁶

The Targums to the Prophets

The Targums to the Prophets, while difficult to date, probably represent some first-century traditions.⁶⁷ Since they present a distinctive perspective on the *basileia* of God, it seems important that they be included in this study.

In the Targum Isaiah, Chilton points out that the "kingdom of God" (or "kingdom of the Lord") is "a distinctive, though comparatively rare, periphrasis for God himself, employed in respect of divine and saving revelation, particularly on Mount Zion."⁶⁸ This is seen, for example, in 24:23b which states, "Because the kingdom of the LORD of hosts will be revealed on Mount Zion" (MT: "Because the LORD of hosts will reign on Mount Zion") and 31:4c which says, "So the kingdom of the LORD of hosts will be revealed to dwell on Mount Zion" (MT: "So the LORD of hosts will descend to fight upon Mount Zion").⁶⁹ On the basis of these two references, Collins argues that the Targumic references to the *basileia* of God emphasize a coming eschatological event, possibly apocalyptic.⁷⁰ This, however, is by no means certain, particularly since at least two other Targumic references to the *basileia* (Isa 40:9d; 52:7) frame the *basileia* as revealed in the present.⁷¹ More important is the association of the *basileia* with Mount Zion (particularly given Luke's distinct emphasis on Jerusalem and the temple) and its description in largely earthly terms.

God's dominion and Israel's dominion was widely accepted throughout the Qumran community, however, given the lack of parallels in other scrolls and the War Scroll's uniqueness amongst all of the Qumran literature.

65. 1QM XVII, 7–8.
66. Lattke, "Jewish Background," 83.
67. Chilton, *Kingdom of God*, 22. For the relevance of the Targums to the New Testament, see Shepherd, "Targums," 45–58.
68. Chilton, *Glory*, 77.
69. Chilton, *Glory*, 77–78.
70. Collins, "Kingdom," 94.
71. Isaiah 40:9d states, "The kingdom of your God is revealed" (MT: "Behold your God") and Isa 52:7 states, "The kingdom of your God is revealed" (MT: "Your God reigns"). Additionally, there is no need to necessarily associate the *basileia* of God with apocalyptic material simply because it is presented as a "revelation." The Aramaic translation is a straightforward reflection of the Hebrew text. Contra Collins, "Kingdom," 94.

The Targums to Zechariah and Obadiah have similar renderings to the Targum Isaiah, however they both present the *basileia* of the Lord as existing over all the peoples of the earth. That is, there is no explicit association with Mount Zion. In Zechariah 14:9a, for example, the Targumist writes, "The kingdom of the LORD will be revealed upon all the dwellers of the earth" (MT: "The Lord will reign upon all the earth").[72] Similarly, Obad 21b reads, "The kingdom of the Lord will be revealed upon all the dwellers of the earth" (MT: "The kingdom will be the Lord's").[73] Chilton sees this universal focus as representing an earlier tradition which was later superseded by the Targum to Isaiah in response to the destruction of the temple (70 CE), after which the restoration of Jerusalem would have been viewed as divine vindication.[74] It is not necessary to see a discrepancy between the different Targums, however, since the biblical Isaiah already viewed God's reign as universal, albeit centered on Zion.[75]

The Targums also display a definite focus on messianism. The targumic renderings of many texts reveal a focus on messianism which coincides to some degree with the Christian interpretations (though there was undoubtedly some level of independence).[76] In particular, there is clear interest in the messiah as a Davidic figure, and he is frequently associated with Jerusalem, though different Targums had varying messianic emphases. The Jeremiah Targum focuses on the messiah as an agent of eschatological hope who would restore Israel's geographical and cultural integrity.[77] The Ezekiel Targum, however, has the expectation of a son of David, appointed by God, who would act as an agent of God's vindication of his people and effect great blessings.[78] The Targum Isaiah emphasizes the messiah's role as a teacher of the Law who seeks the repentance of the house of Israel.[79] Overall, it seems that the messiah would play an integral role in establishing the *basileia* of God. As Koch has noted, "The kingdom of God, the kingdom of the Messiah, and the dominion of Israel (over the nations) belong together for the Targum."[80]

---

72. Chilton, *Glory*, 78.
73. Chilton, *Glory*, 77–78.
74. Chilton, *Glory*, 78–79.
75. Collins, "Kingdom," 94.
76. Shepherd, "Targums," 57.
77. Chilton, *Glory*, 116.
78. Chilton, *Glory*, 116.
79. Chilton, *Glory*, 116. For a summary of the references to the messiah in the Targum Isaiah, see Chilton, *Glory*, 86–96.
80. Cited in Collins, "Kingdom," 95.

The Mishnah[81]

The Mishnah provides some insights into early Jewish views of the *basileia* of God. While the document was redacted and published in its final form from approximately 200 CE onwards, it nonetheless contains rabbinic sayings and laws from pre-Christian times (as attested by parallel traditions in the Qumran scrolls).[82]

The Mishnah refers to the *basileia* in relation to God in the treatises Berakot and Yoma. In Berakot, the *basileia* of heaven is mentioned twice, both times in relation to the Shema (*m. Ber.* 2:2, 5). The recitation of the Shema is equated with taking on oneself the "yoke of the kingdom of heaven" (*m. Ber.* 2:2, 5), which effectively denotes the acknowledgment of Israel's God as the only king and ruler.[83] The treatise Yoma focuses on the ceremonial requirements of the Day of Atonement. On four occasions, the people were required to respond to the high priest's prayer or actions with the statement: "Blessed be the name of the glory of his kingdom for ever and ever" (*m. Yoma* 3:8; 4:1, 2; 6:2).[84] Thus, the glory of God's *basileia* is specifically linked to the atonement of Israel's sin, and it seems that God's *basileia* is equated with the house of Israel. This, of course, is similar to the release from sin seen in Luke's Gospel, which is clearly linked to entrance into the *basileia* of God (see the following chapter).

God is referred to as king on four occasions, three of which describe him as "the King of kings, the Holy One."[85] The fourth reference to God as king is in Tamid 7:4, which cites Psalm 93:1.[86] There are not, however, many passages in the Mishnah which refer to a messianic figure, and as such there is no clear literary relationship between God's reign and a messiah.[87] There

---

81. This study has limited the examination of codified rabbinic works to the Mishnah. Citations have been taken from Danby, *The Mishnah*.

82. Neusner, "Form and Meaning," 28 and Lattke, "Jewish Background," 76–77.

83. Dalman, "Heaven," 298.

84. Three of these occurrences directly follow a high priestly prayer for forgiveness (*m. Yoma* 3:8; 4:2; 6:2), while the other occurs after the selection (through the high priest's casting of lots) of which goat would be slaughtered and which would be sent for Azazel (*m. Yoma* 4:1).

85. *m. Sanh.* 4:5; *m. ʿAbot* 3:1; 4:22.

86. *m. Šabbat* 14:4 also states that "all Israelites are kings' children," and *m. Roš HaŠ.* 4:5 states that the sovereignty verses (which refer to God's kingship) are to be read during the festival.

87. The majority of references to the word "messiah" refer to priests. Evans, "Mishna and Messiah," 266. The two key references to the messiah are *m. Ber.* 1:5 and *m. Soṭah* 9:15. The lack of references to a messianic figure is explained in different ways depending on how one classifies the genre of the Mishnah. For two differing views, see

also appears to be little continuity between the Mishnah and the earlier apocalyptic literature.[88] Nonetheless, there is no question that the authors of the Mishnah viewed God as being the sovereign ruler over everyone and everything.

Philo

The phrase "kingdom of God" appears only once in Philo's works, where Exodus 19:6 is quoted to describe Israel as the βασίλειον καί ἱεράτευμα θεοῦ.[89] In other sections of his work, however, Philo equated wisdom with the kingdom (or kingship), "for we pronounce the wise man to be a king."[90] This is reminiscent of the Stoic idea that the wise person is also a king.[91] For Philo, a kingdom established by God (in contrast to evil human kingdoms) "comes by the gift of God, and the virtuous man who receives it brings no harm to anyone, but the acquisition and enjoyment of good things to all his subjects, to whom he is the herald of peace and order."[92] Thus, Philo's dominant description of God's *basileia* presented it as having spiritual and moral qualities. His understanding was therefore similar to that of other diaspora authors (such as the authors of the Wisdom of Solomon and 4 Maccabees).

Josephus

Josephus does not employ the phrase "kingdom of God," nor does he refer to the *basileia* in reference to Yahweh (kingdoms are usually associated with human rulers). He does, however, occasionally portray human kingdoms as being under God's sovereign rule.[93] More importantly, however, Josephus also mentions a number of messianic movements, centered on a charismatic "king" who sought to "overthrow Herodian and Roman domination and to restore the traditional ideals of a free and egalitarian society."[94] Significantly,

---

Neusner, "Mishnah and Messiah," 267–82 and Evans, "Mishna and Messiah," 274–89.

88. This may be due to the disastrous Jewish revolts against Rome in 66–70 CE and 132–35 CE. Collins, *Apocalypticism*, 164.

89. Philo, *Sobriety* 66.

90. Philo, *Migration* 197. [Colson and Whitaker, LCL]

91. Collins, "Kingdom," 88.

92. Philo, *Abraham* 261. [Colson, LCL]

93. See, for example, Josephus, *Ant.* 10:217, 244–45.

94. For example, Judas, the son of Ezekias, had a "zealous pursuit of royal rank" (Josephus, *Ant.* 17:271–72). Simon, a former servant of Herod, was prepared to "don the diadem" and was proclaimed king by his followers (Josephus, *Ant.* 17:273–74). Finally,

Josephus avoided such phrases as "son of David," "messiah," or "branch"—his language was instead focused on the kingship of the leaders.[95] The movements were, in large part, reactions to the socioeconomic conditions of the period.[96] In this sense, Josephus presents the messianic movements as being focused on the establishment of a Davidic kingdom. He makes no mention, however, of any of these leaders seeking to mediate the rule of Yahweh (indeed, God is conspicuously absent from all of the accounts of the messianic movements).

Summary of Findings

The theme of the *basileia* of God is presented in many varying ways throughout the Second Temple literature. In a similar way to the Old Testament, there are frequent examples of God's kingship, his sovereign act of reigning, and his *basileia* in the sense of the realm over which God rules.

The apocalyptic views of God's *basileia* were particularly influential. The hope of God's eschatological intervention into history to end the present world order to establish his kingdom (that is, realm) as a manifestation and vindication of his ultimate kingship and sovereign reign is a dominant theme in the Apocrypha and Pseudepigrapha, as well as many of the Qumran scrolls. Its influence continued well into the first century when the New Testament was written. Most of the apocalyptic material presents the subjects of God's eschatological *basileia* as Israel, though there are notable exceptions to this (including 1 Enoch). All of the apocalyptic works, however, present God's *basileia* as diametrically opposed to foreign rule. This is also similar to what is seen in Luke's presentation of the *basileia* (see the following chapter), which is not too surprising, given Luke's apparent familiarity with the Qumran traditions, the Epistle of Enoch, and Jubilees.

The Qumran scrolls have a particularly important contribution. They present God's eschatological salvation as presently occurring (they already belong to the heavenly Jerusalem), though awaiting final conclusion. That is, they juxtapose present and future notions of the eschatological *basileia*

Athronges "aspire[d] for kingship" and later put on a diadem and was called "king" by his followers (Josephus, *Ant.* 17:278–81). Horsley and Hanson, *Bandits*, 116.

95. Horsley and Hanson, *Bandits*, 114.

96. They differed from banditry, however, as they were informed by the memory of King David or other anointed figures and therefore had a political consciousness and a corresponding program of action. Horsley, "Movements," 494–95. Luke 13:1 references one such occasion whereby some Galileans were killed by Pilate, however it is difficult to know for certain whether this occasion is represented in Josephus's works (or other ancient writings). See Marshall, *The Gospel of Luke*, 553.

(in a similar way to what is seen in Luke's work—see the following chapter). Developments in the apocalyptic judgment motifs are also significant; the later apocalyptic works (written during the same period as the New Testament) focused on human sin and the culpability of humans for their own sins.[97]

There are also several other understandings of the *basileia* of God. In Philo's work and in some circles of diaspora Judaism, God's *basileia* is presented as having spiritual and moral qualities.[98] In the Targums to the prophets, the "kingdom of God" is used as a periphrasis for God himself, used in relation to the revelation of his saving work (particularly in respect to Mount Zion).[99] The Mishnah refers to the *basileia* in relation to God to denote taking on the rule of the law, and in relation to the atonement of Israel's sin. This second meaning is comparable to the late apocalyptic focus on judgment for one's sin (though other differences between the Mishnah and the apocalyptic works are substantial).

Finally, as has been identified by many scholars, the Second Temple literature does not present a single unified view of the messiah. Indeed, within the Dead Sea Scrolls alone, the messiah is presented as a priest, teacher, anointed prophet, Son of God, heavenly Son of Man, the servant, a combination of these, or they suggest that there are to be two messiahs. Despite these varying views, it seems that the expectation of a Davidic ruler was the predominant perception (in a similar way to what is seen in Luke's work—see below). There are also varying views on the messiah's role in establishing the *basileia* of God. There are many documents which completely omit the role of a messianic figure in establishing God's *basileia*, others which present the messiah as the mediator of God's rule when the *basileia* manifests, and still others which describe a messianic kingdom which would precede the *basileia* of God. Thus, there were a number of varying messianic traditions at the time Luke's Gospel was written.

---

97. This is again similar to what one sees in Luke. See, for example, the parable of Lazarus and the Dives in Luke 16:19–31.

98. Collins, "Kingdom," 86–88. The similarities between this and Luke's presentation of the *basileia* are seen in the following chapter, where it is demonstrated that spiritual release is a core focus of Luke's understanding of the *basileia*.

99. Chilton, *Glory*, 77.

The Jubilee in Late Second Temple Judaism

The Old Testament Apocrypha and Pseudepigrapha

Jubilees

Jubilees primarily presents Jubilee years as having calendrical significance. Jubilee years are forty-nine-year periods (or seven "year-weeks") based on solar years (364 days).[100] The author uses these Jubilee years to demarcate human history from creation through to Moses, a time period which finishes during the fiftieth Jubilee. Jubilee years are used as markers for significant dates and as descriptors for how long a person has lived, rather than referring to years of redemption as detailed in the Leviticus legislation.

One reference which suggests a depth to the Jubilee beyond its calendrical import is in chapter 50: "The land will keep its Sabbaths when they dwell upon it. And they will know the year of Jubilee" (Jub. 50:3).[101] The author then describes a time when Israel will be purified from all sin, the people will dwell in the land, Satan and all other evil will depart, and the land will be purified (Jub. 50:5).[102] Some parallels with the Jubilee precepts are evident; the purification from sin is analogous to the Day of Atonement which marked the beginning of the Jubilee year (Lev 25:9). The reference to dwelling "in confidence in all the land" (Jub. 50:5)[103] suggests that land will no longer be able to be captured or sold; it is permanently redeemed (Lev 25:14-17, 23-34). The eradication of Satan and all other evil may in some way parallel the injustices which the year of Jubilee redressed. Finally, purification of the land suggests that it is to be freed from practices that harm it; it is to enjoy ongoing rest (Lev 25:18-24). Despite these similarities, however, the Jubilee precepts are not explicitly listed. It is therefore difficult to know how much meaning the author attached to Jubilee years beyond their use as a measurement of time.

A year of redemption may also be alluded to in 7:37-38: "And in the seventh year make its release so that you might release it in righteousness and uprightness. And you will be righteous and all your plants will be upright."[104] There are, however, significant difficulties associated with the text; the manuscript evidence suggests that the text should read "fifth year" rather than "seventh year." Charlesworth viewed the passage as probably

---

100. Morgenstern, "Calendar," 34-36.
101. Wintermute, "Jubilees," 2:142.
102. Wintermute, "Jubilees," 2:142.
103. Wintermute, "Jubilees," 2:142.
104. Wintermute, "Jubilees," 2:71.

containing a lacuna, and therefore assumed that the missing portion would introduce the "seventh year."[105] Similarly, Wintermute translated the text as "seventh year" despite the unanimous witness of the Ethiopian manuscripts reading "fifth year."[106]

If indeed a seventh year time of redemption is in view, the text of Deuteronomy 15 bears closer resemblance to the passage than Leviticus 25. There are, however, some thematic similarities to the Jubilee precepts regardless of how the "year" should be translated. The twofold release parallels the themes of redemption that permeate many biblical Jubilee texts. Similarly, the reference to plants being blessed bears some resemblance to Leviticus 25:21, which records how the Lord will bless obedience with an abundance of food. The differences, however, are also significant; there is no explicit mention of the redemption of property or slaves, or the cancellation of debts (both in this text or any other passage within the book). Thus, despite its name, Jubilees makes few if any explicit references to the earlier Jubilee traditions, apart from the idea of seven times seven (plus one).

Testaments of the Twelve Patriarchs

Within the Testaments of the Twelve Patriarchs, it is only the Testament of Levi that references the Jubilee. It is explicitly mentioned in the seventeenth chapter:

> Because you have heard about the seventy weeks, listen also concerning the priesthood. In each Jubilee there shall be a priesthood. In the first Jubilee the first person to be anointed to the priesthood will be great, and he shall speak to God as father; and his priesthood shall be fully satisfactory to the Lord, and in the days of his joy, he shall rise up for the salvation of the world. In the second Jubilee the Anointed One shall be conceived in sorrow of the beloved one, and his priesthood shall be prized and shall be glorified by all.[107]

These three verses are then followed by a brief description of the following five Jubilee periods, all of which are characterized by a particular priest or priesthood. Thus, the author uses Jubilee years to divide Israel's history into seven distinct periods. The Jubilee is therefore understood as

---

105. Wintermute, "Jubilees," 70.
106. Wintermute, "Jubilees," 70.
107. T. Levi 17:1-4. [Citation from Kee, "Testaments," 794.]

a measurement of time rather than a year of redemption, though the testament does not explicitly state how long a Jubilee period is.

In the eighteenth chapter, the focus shifts from the seven Jubilee periods to a time when "the Lord will raise up a new priest to whom all the words of the Lord shall be revealed."[108] This person is portrayed as having both kingly and priestly qualities and is described in part by references to Isaiah 11 and 44.[109] He is one who will cause the angels to rejoice (T. 12 Patr. 18:5), who will be sanctified (18:6), who will have no successor (18:8), who will have sin cease in his priesthood (18:9), and who will allow the saints to eat of the tree of life (18:11). The testament therefore also associates the Jubilee with a coming messianic figure.[110]

Other Thematic Parallels

While the Jubilee is explicitly mentioned in Jubilees and the Testament of Levi, there are other texts that have thematic similarities to the original Jubilee legislation. In particular, Sirach and 1 Maccabees record instances where land is redeemed, money is freely loaned, debts are canceled, and rest is given to the land.

Sirach is largely a collection of moral teachings both for individuals and society at large. In Sirach 22:23, poverty is viewed as a temporary state: "Gain the trust of your neighbor in his poverty, so that you may rejoice with him in his prosperity. Stand by him in time of distress, so that you may share with him in his inheritance." While the Jubilee does not appear to be in focus, the thematic likeness to the redemption of land in the Jubilee legislation is clear. Similarly, Sirach 29:1–2 is a call to lend money in a way which resembles Leviticus 25:35–38: "The merciful lend to their neighbors; by holding out a helping hand they keep the commandments. Lend to your neighbor in his time of need; repay your neighbor when a loan falls due." While there is no explicit direction to charge no interest, the ensuing verses of Sirach 29 command that mercy and compassion be practiced, with verse 20 summarizing the author's intent: "Assist your neighbor to the best of your ability."

---

108. T. 12 Patr. 18:2. [Kee]

109. T. 12 Patr. 18. [Kee]

110. Some of these descriptions, of course, can be likened to what one finds in Luke's work. For example, the angels rejoiced at Jesus' coming (Luke 2:13–14) and salvation was proclaimed (in a similar way to the tree of life being offered)—see the following chapter.

Unlike Sirach, 1 Maccabees is a historical document which details the Jewish struggle for religious and political freedom, mainly during the Macedonian dynasty. Blosser has noted two occasions of debt cancellation which are thematically comparable to the Jubilee provisions.[111] In 1 Macc 10:26-45, Demetrius wrote to the Jews to promise them certain benefits in return for their support against his enemies. In verses 34-35, Demetrius allowed the Jews freedom to continue their cultic practices: "All the festivals and sabbaths and new moons and appointed days, and the three days before a festival and the three after a festival—let them all be days of immunity and release for all the Jews who are in my kingdom. No one shall have authority to exact anything from them." Later, Antiochus VII Sidetes sought Jewish support in chapter 15 by offering release from royal debts: "Now therefore I confirm to you all the tax remissions that the kings before me have granted you, and a release from all the other payments from which they have released you . . . Every debt you owe to the royal treasury and any such future debts shall be canceled for you from henceforth and for all time." As mentioned in the previous chapter, however, debt cancellation was not an explicit requirement of the Jubilee legislation, so it is difficult to place too much weight on these two texts in connection to the Jubilee.

The Dead Sea Scrolls

There are several references to the Jubilee in the Dead Sea Scrolls. As Bergsma has noted, it seems that these texts refer to the Jubilee for historiographical purposes (to determine the chronology of past events), cultic-calendrical purposes (to calculate when certain cultic activities should occur), and eschatological purposes (to predict the arrival of the final age).[112]

The three explicit historiographical references to the Jubilee are in the Genesis Apocryphon (or 1Qap Genar), 4Q372, and 11Q12. The Genesis Apocryphon 6.9-10 uses Jubilee time periods to calculate the length of Noah's life, Fragment 12 of 4Q372 refers to the entrance of Israel into Canaan as being a Jubilee year, and 11Q12 is a quotation from Jub. 4:6-11.[113] Thus, the three texts briefly mention the Jubilee in a manner reminiscent of (or as a citation from) Jubilees, which is not surprising given the significant influence it had on the Qumran community.[114]

---

111. Blosser, "Jubilee," 44.

112. Bergsma, *Jubilee*, 251.

113. Interestingly, the reference in 4Q372 refers to the Jubilee as the "year of the Jubilees."

114. Fourteen copies of Jubilees were found at Qumran, and it clearly influenced at

The explicit cultic-calendrical uses of the Jubilee are limited to two texts: 4Q319 and 4Q320. In 4Q319, the writer employs a mathematical system to explore the relationship between Jubilee periods (forty-nine years), priestly rotations (every sixth year), and sabbatical years (every seventh year).[115] In 4Q320, the Jubilee is mentioned twice in connection with the priestly divisions who served in the sanctuary.[116] Another important text with a cultic-calendrical focus is 1Q22 which summarizes the Scriptural provisions for sabbatical years and years of release, however there are significant portions of the text missing. Interestingly, there is no scroll that summarizes the Scriptural provisions for Jubilee years, though it is possible that a text did once exist and has been lost.[117]

Most of the Qumran literature pertaining to the Jubilee refers to it in terms of its eschatological significance. Fragment 2 of 4Q463 mentions the Jubilee in connection with a rebuke of Belial and other enemies, which may allude to an eschatological event. The text, however, is too fragmentary to determine any precise meaning. Similarly, the brief mention of the Jubilee in 6Q12 seems to be eschatological; however, too much of the text is missing to be sure. Fragments 1 and 2 of 4Q390 also mention Jubilee years as part of a description of Israel's history and the eschatological age. Unfortunately, however, the descriptions are too general to establish what historical events the author is referring to.[118]

11Q13 also refers to the Jubilee in terms of its eschatological fulfillment, however it is significantly more detailed than other eschatological texts. The text is a fragmentary eschatological Midrash which presents Melchizedek as an agent of salvation who will bring deliverance at the time of the tenth Jubilee.[119] The identity and role of Melchizedek has received much scholarly attention; he is exalted above other heavenly beings, an earthly herald of salvation, the high priest, anointed by the Spirit, an eschatological agent of divine judgment, and is described as the equivalent of the Lord.[120] He is to execute God's judgments in accompaniment with God's angels, and in so

---

least seven Dead Sea Scrolls. See VanderKam, *The Book of Jubilees*, 143–46.

115. Wise et al., *The Dead Sea Scrolls*, 305–6.

116. The two references are Frag. 2 col. 1.6 and Frag 4 col. 2.13. Wise et al., *The Dead Sea Scrolls*, 310.

117. Bergsma argues that it is likely that the Jubilee was the original subject of the text in 1Q22 3.8–12. Bergsma, *Jubilee*, 256.

118. See Bergsma, *Jubilee*, 265–76 for a helpful discussion of the texts.

119. 11Q13 2.5–9; Miner, "A Suggested Reading," 144.

120. Delcor, "Melchizedek," 124–25; Ringe, "Jubilee Proclamation," 111–12; Bergsma, *Jubilee*, 286–87; Fitzmyer, "Further Light," 29–31; and Miller, "Function," 468.

doing will inaugurate the time of salvation.[121] This salvation corresponds to an eschatological Jubilee; creditors cancel debts owed to them (line 3); captives (belonging to Melchizedek) are freed (line 4); and liberty is proclaimed (by Melchizedek) (line 6). Significantly, the debt of the captives' iniquities is also canceled, which constitutes a spiritualization of the original institution.

Freedom from the debt of iniquities accords with the Day of Atonement, listed in the text as marking the end of the tenth Jubilee.[122] Why the Jubilee ends with the Day of Atonement rather than begins with it (as in Lev 25:9) is unclear. It may possibly serve as a climactic ending in keeping with other eschatological events in Second Temple literature which have dramatic closing stages.[123]

One of the more intriguing sections of the scroll is lines 18–20. Here, the author links the seventy "sevens" of Daniel 9:24–27 to the coming of the anointed messenger. The author correlates the seventy sevens (490 years) with the tenth Jubilee (also 490 years) to support his interpretation of the timing of the coming anointed one. This has led to a degree of excitement within some pockets of the scholarly community who have calculated the arrival of the anointed one as roughly coinciding with the beginning of Jesus' ministry.[124] This interpretation, of course, is dependent on when one marks the beginning of the seventy sevens, which seems, in some cases, to be a fairly arbitrary exercise.[125]

The scroll is largely an exegetical text, quoting a range of Scriptures (Lev 25; Deut 15; Pss 7; 82; Isa 52; Dan 9). It is clear, however, that Isaiah 61:1–2 also permeates the text and provides the "eschatological context for the pesher of the Jubilee year."[126] The captives (line 4) resemble those in Isaiah 61:1, the "year of the Lord's favor" (Isa 61:2) is stated as "the [year of grace] of Melchizedek," the messenger is anointed in the Spirit (line 18) in a manner analogous to Isaiah 61:1, and the central motifs of salvation and justice correspond to the year of favor and day of vengeance in Isaiah 61:2.[127] The spiritualization of the Jubilee, however, adds a further dimension to the

---

121. De Jonge and Van Der Woude, "11Q Melchizedek and the New Testament," 304–05.

122. 11Q132.7–8.

123. Bergsma, *Jubilee*, 286.

124. Barker, "The Time is Fulfilled," 24–25 and Strobel, "Ausrufung," 40–46. Barker argues that the tenth Jubilee can be dated sometime during 17–19 CE and Strobel argues that it occurred later in approximately 26–27 CE.

125. Goldingay, *Daniel*, 257.

126. Miller, "Function," 469.

127. Miller, "Function," 467–68.

Isaianic passage, as the Qumran text views the eschatological Jubilee as a time of both physical (socioeconomic) and spiritual redemption.

The Mishnah

The Mishnah refers to the Jubilee in *Roš Haššanah*, *Qiddušin*, *Bekorot*, and *ʿArakhin*.[128] In *Roš Haššanah*, the first day of Tishre is listed as the New Year for the reckoning of Jubilee years, to be announced by the sounding of antelopes' horns (*m. Roš Haš.* 1:1, 3:5). The timing of the announcement of Jubilee years seems, therefore, to be earlier than what is prescribed in Leviticus 25:9-10, where Jubilee years are proclaimed on the Day of Atonement (the tenth day of Tishri). *Qiddušin* briefly mentions the Jubilee as a means for slaves to acquire their freedom (*m. Qidd.* 1:2). *Bekorot* 8:10 itemizes what is not redeemed in Jubilee years: "These do not revert [to their first owners] in the year of Jubilee: the Firstborn's portion, what a man inherits from his wife, what he inherits that performs levirate marriage, and what is given as a gift. So R. Meir."

The longest treatment of the Jubilee in the Mishnah, however, occurs in *m. ʿArak.* 7-9. Chapters 7-8 examine various practices related to the redemption of fields, and chapter 9 primarily addresses the redemption of houses in walled cities. While the text refers to some of the precepts in Leviticus 25 and 27,[129] it clarifies certain points and occasionally adds to what was originally written.[130] Clarifications include discussions regarding what would occur if the Jubilee arrived and a field was not redeemed (*m. ʿArak.* 7:4) and what is considered a dwelling house in a walled city (*m. ʿArak.* 9:5-7). Additions include rules regarding when one can redeem a field (*m. ʿArak.* 9:1) and whether one can redeem a field in halves (*m. ʿArak.* 9:2).[131]

---

128. As mentioned earlier, the exploration into the codified rabbinic works has been limited to the Mishnah. While the document was redacted and published in approximately 200 CE, it nonetheless contains rabbinic sayings and laws from the first century (and earlier), and as such provides some valuable insights into early Jewish views of the Jubilee.

129. *m. ʿArak.* 7:5 cites Lev 27:22; *m. ʿArak.* 8:5 cites Lev 25:34; *m. ʿArak.* 8:6 cites Lev 27:21, 28; *m. ʿArak.* 8:7 cites Lev 27:26; *m. ʿArak.* 9:1 cites Lev 25:15; *m. ʿArak.* 9:2 cites Lev 25:27; *m. ʿArak.* 9:3 cites Lev 25:30; *m. ʿArak.* 9:4 cites Lev 25:30; *m. ʿArak.* 9:5 cites Lev 25:29, and *m. ʿArak.* 9:8 cites Lev 25:32-33.

130. This is consistent with the wider text. Indeed, as Neusner has noted, "Arakhin is an effort to amplify and augment the basic rules of Scripture." Neusner, "From Scripture to Mishnah," 277.

131. The Mishnah also details rules concerning the prosbul—a legal fiction which annuls the cancellation of debts in sabbatical years (which Lev 25:8 details as having some connection to the Jubilee). As *Šebiʿt* 10:3 records, Rabbi Hillel noticed that as

Philo

Philo's work addresses the Jubilee on several occasions. In his treatise *On the Special Laws*, Philo briefly provided a brief apology for the importance of rest, before expounding the ordinances relating to the Jubilee in 2.22–25, describing it as "the subject of many special enactments, all of remarkable excellence, apart from those which are common to other seventh years."[132] The majority of the references to the Jubilee in this work focus on the redemption of property. Philo summarized the return of ancestral land (2.22.111–15), the laws regarding the return of rural houses and city houses (2.23.116–17), the provision for non-Jews (2.23.118–19), and the laws regarding Levitical dwellings (2.24.120–21). The subject of Jubilee laws addressing the redemption of slaves and the lending of money to the poor is then discussed.[133]

The above references reveal that Philo was concerned with the cultic and ethical motivations behind the Jubilee precepts.[134] The text therefore seems to be as much an apology for the Levitical laws as an exposition of them, which is unsurprising given Philo's use of Midrash.[135] As North has noted, the Jubilee references appear to be "purely theoretical."[136] However, this is again unsurprising given the nature of the document as an exposition of the Torah. Interestingly, the Jubilee is stated to be a fifty-year event, though Philo offers no explanation as to why this is the case. There is also an emphasis on the redemption of property in a manner disproportionate to the original Levitical laws.

Philo's discussion of the Jubilee in *On the Virtues* is significantly shorter than *On the Special Laws*. After briefly summarizing the regulations regarding Sabbath years (19.97–98), Philo then venerated the Jubilee, describing

---

Sabbath years approached, some Jewish lenders were withholding loans from others for fear of not being paid back (despite Deut 15:7–11 specifically prohibiting such practices). He therefore instituted prosbuls, which effectively provided a means for lenders to determine whether they would cancel debts during Sabbath years or not (*m. Šeb.* 10:3; see also *m. Git.* 4:3).

132. Philo, *Spec. Laws* 2.22.110.

133. Philo, *Spec. Laws* 2.25.122. Additionally, debt cancellation (Deut 15:1–6) is addressed in 2.17.71–72; the lending of money (Deut 15:7–11) is addressed in 2.17.73–78; freedom for slaves (Exod 21:1–11; Deut 15:12–18) is addressed in 2.18.79–85; and letting the land lie fallow for the sake of the poor is addressed in 2.21.105–6.

134. Ringe, "Jubilee Proclamation," 84. For a cultic motivation, see in particular Philo, *Spec. Laws* 2.22.113. For an ethical motivation, see in particular Philo, *Spec. Laws* 2.23.118.

135. Cohen, "Philo and Midrash," 196.

136. North, *Sociology*, 74.

it as having "most sweet and lovely principles."[137] He only specifically mentioned the redemption of property; the other precepts are implied by the denotation of the Jubilee as containing the ordinances of the seventh years[138] and by his summarizing statement: "The particular enactments include a host of others bearing on conduct to fellow-countrymen."[139]

The references to the Jubilee in *On the Virtues* have some similarities to those in *On the Special Laws*: they are focused on the redemption of property, they stem from homiletic hermeneutics, and they seem to be largely theoretical. In *On the Virtues*, however, there is no apparent cultic motivation. Philo instead emphasized provision for the poor. This is in keeping with the rest of the treatise where 123 of the 227 paragraphs focus on kind-heartedness.[140]

The Jubilee is also briefly mentioned in a few other texts. In *On the Decalogue*, the Jubilee is alluded to as part of Philo's discussion about keeping the Sabbath.[141] He emphasized the restitution of the land and apparently believed that the Jubilee was practiced.[142] In *Hypothetica*, the Jubilee is mentioned as part of an argument for the importance of resting from cultivating the land (particularly during Sabbath years).[143] In *Questions and Answers on Genesis*, Philo mentioned the Jubilee in connection with the number fifty as part of his explanation for the measurements of the ark.[144] The Jubilee also is mentioned as part of an explanation regarding Abraham's age, where the number fifty is again cited as having significance.[145]

Philo therefore highlighted a number of aspects of the Jubilee. Its cultic importance was emphasized in book 2 of *On the Special Laws*. The ethical significance was emphasized in both *On the Special Laws* and *On the Virtues*, where Philo accentuated the importance of providing for the needy. And finally, the Jubilee's numerical value was emphasized in *Questions and Answers on Genesis*, where the importance of the number fifty was emphasized by its association with the Jubilee. Consequently, it is clear that Philo viewed the Jubilee as having practical worth (despite the uncertainty

---

137. Philo, *Virtues* 19.99. [Colson, LCL]
138. Philo, *Virtues* 19.100. [Colson, LCL]
139. Philo, *Virtues* 19.101. [Colson, LCL]
140. North, *Sociology*, 77.
141. Philo, *Decalogue* 164.
142. Philo, *Decalogue* 164.
143. Philo, *Hypothetica* 7.15–18.
144. Philo, *QG* 2, 5.

145. Philo, *QG* 2, 3:39. As has already been mentioned, the number fifty is seen a few times in Luke's work. The question of whether is should be linked to the Jubilee is addressed in chapter 6.

over whether or not it was ever enacted). While he applied a homiletic hermeneutic, he nonetheless wrote about the Jubilee in highly pragmatic terms. It is, however, difficult to know how widely his expositions were accepted within the Jewish and primitive Christian communities (and therefore whether they affected Luke's work).[146]

Josephus

The Jubilee is mentioned on two occasions in Josephus's works.[147] On the first occasion, Josephus summarized the Sabbath year laws regarding land lying fallow (Lev 25:1–7) before writing that this was to be done

> at the end of the seventh week of years. This is the period amounting to fifty years in all, of which the fiftieth year is called by the Hebrews *Jôbêl*; at that season debtors are absolved from their debts and slaves are set at liberty, that is to say those who are members of the race and having transgressed some requirement of the law have by it been punished by reduction to a servile condition, without being condemned to death. Now too he restores estates to their original owners after the following fashion. When the *Jôbêl* comes round—the name denotes "liberty"—the vendor and the purchaser of the site meet together and reckon up the products of the site and the outgoings expended upon it. Then if the proceeds are found to exceed the outgoings, the vendor recovers the estate; but if the expenditure preponderates, he must pay a sufficient sum to cover the deficit or forfeit the property if, lastly, the figures for revenue and expenditure are equal, the legislator restores the land to its former possessors.[148]

As North has noted, there are three important differences between the original Jubilee legislation in Leviticus 25 and the above citation. Firstly, Josephus explicitly listed debt cancellation as a Jubilee provision, though it is only implied in the Leviticus text.[149] Secondly, the Leviticus legislation does not include a provision that precludes the redemption of land if the overheads exceed the surplus.[150] Finally, Josephus (or his source) evidently misunderstood the calculation of the value of ancestral land (see Lev 25:14–17)

146. Hilgert, "Central Issues," 17–18.
147. Josephus, *Ant.* 3:281–286; 4:273.
148. Josephus, *Ant.* 3:282–284. [Thackeray, LCL]
149. North, *Sociology*, 84–85.
150. North, *Sociology*, 84.

as being a Jubilee year practice rather than occurring at the time of sale or of repurchase outside Jubilee years.[151]

Since the *Antiquities* were probably written as an apologetic for Judaism, it is little wonder that Josephus stated in no uncertain terms that the Jews of his time kept the entire law (including stipulations regarding the Jubilee): "Certainly there is not a Hebrew who does not, just as if he were still there and ready to punish him for any breach of discipline, obey the laws laid down by Moses, even though in violating them he could escape detection."[152] Whether or not Jubilee years were actually practiced, however, is less clear. Josephus failed to mention any specific instances when Jubilee years were observed.[153] Moreover, the basic mistakes he made in paraphrasing the Jubilee legislation imply that Jubilee years were not being widely practiced and that he was not overly familiar with the Levitical text. Nevertheless, it seems the idea of the Jubilee had not altogether disappeared in the first century.

Summary of Findings

The Second Temple literature indicates that there was an apparent change in the emphases of the Jubilee texts. In the Old Testament Apocrypha and Pseudepigrapha, the Jubilee was primarily used as a chronological division to delineate Israel's history. The Qumran community, however, viewed the Jubilee has having three purposes: historiographical (for delineating history), cultic-calendrical (for ordering cultic activities), and eschatological (for predicting parts of the future age).[154] The later rabbinical writings and the works of Philo and Josephus returned to a focus on the legislative importance of the Jubilee. The contributors to the Jubilee texts in the Mishnah were primarily concerned with the application of the precepts in a manner that ensured fidelity to the law (particularly of Lev 25 and 27). Philo emphasized the cultic and ethical significance of the Jubilee (as well as mentioning its numerical worth) within the context of expositing the law. He evidently viewed the Jubilee as a set of legal precepts to be interpreted literally and applied. Similarly, Josephus recounted the Levitical laws as a set of legal provisions which were to be obeyed if Israel ever regained enough sovereignty to enact them.

---

151. North, *Sociology*, 84.

152. Josephus, *Ant.* 3:317. [Thackeray, LCL]

153. Though he mentioned several instances when Sabbath year laws were observed (Josephus *Ant.* 3:338; 8:234; 9:378; 14:202).

154. Bergsma, *Jubilee*, 251.

Thus, by the time of the first century, there were at least eight traditions or interpretations associated with the Jubilee; it was interpreted 1) ethically, 2) historiographically, 3) eschatologically, 4) numerically, 5) apocalyptically, 6) calendrically, 7) legally, and 8) religiously (that is, in terms of its cultic significance). Thus, as Ringe has noted, the only generalization one can take from Second Temple Judaism is that "it would seem this literature is marked by a fragmentary and piecemeal approach to the traditions."[155] There was no single overriding picture of the Jubilee, and even individual writers such as Philo approached the Jubilee from a myriad of different angles. To some degree, this may be attributed to the range of emphases within the Old Testament texts, though there are clearly some new interpretations (most notably the calendrical focus). This, of course, creates some difficulties for those who wish to argue that Jubilean material forms an important part of Luke's work, since one must first establish what interpretation of the Jubilee is supposedly in view.

The Relationship between the *Basileia* of God and the Jubilee

As with the Old Testament, it is difficult to establish whether any literary relationship exists between the *basileia* of God and the Jubilee in the Second Temple literature. While both concepts occur far more frequently in Second Temple works than they do in the Old Testament, there is only one occasion (in the Dead Sea Scroll 11Q13) when they are explicitly mentioned together.

Nonetheless, some other implicit connections can be made. The mention of the legislative requirements of the Jubilee in the Mishnah and some of Philo's and Josephus's work implicitly exemplify Yahweh's kingship as the lawgiver. Importantly, however, none of these authors mention the Jubilee in order to highlight God's sovereignty. Philo and Josephus were more concerned with providing an apology for Israel's legal ordinances, while the rabbinic authors in the Mishnah concentrated on clarifying and elaborating the original Scriptures. That is, the kingship of God as the divine lawgiver was not the central thrust of their works.

Jubilees provides other implicit connections between the Jubilee and the *basileia* of God. The sole occasion when the *basileia* is mentioned in relation to God occurs during the fortieth Jubilee, though there is no relationship between the two concepts. The kingdom is mentioned as part of Abram's prayer, and the fortieth Jubilee is mentioned ten verses earlier to provide a historiographical setting for the events that followed (Jub. 12:9,

---

155. Ringe, "Jubilee Proclamation," 115.

19). Jubilees also describes an eschatological age, analogous to the apocalyptic vision of God's *basileia*, which would be established during the final Jubilee. This eschatological age has some similarities with the Jubilee precepts; sins would be purified (in a way analogous to the Day of Atonement) and injustice would end. Nevertheless, the word "Jubilee" is only explicitly used to demarcate history. The eschatological description of God's *basileia* occurring during the final Jubilee is not mentioned to highlight the Jubilee itself, so much as it is designed to emphasize that at the end of all things, God's righteous *basileia* will be established and evil will be destroyed. Jubilee years are used purely to delineate history; the fact that God's eschatological *basileia* involves redemption in a comparable way to the Jubilee precepts is not an association which the author shows any interest in.

The same implicit connection is seen in the Testament of Levi, where Jubilee years are used to divide Israel's history into seven distinct periods (T. Levi 17:1–11). At the end of these seven periods, a new figure who is both priestly and kingly shall be raised who will inaugurate a time of salvation analogous to the *basileia* of God. That is, the saints will enjoy life, sin will cease, the angels will rejoice, and the glory of God will be manifested for all to see (T. Levi 18:1–14). This vision of God's *basileia* occurring after the seventh Jubilee is seemingly not, however, designed to highlight a relationship between the two concepts, except insofar as a mathematical/chronological relationship might exist. That is, the only association is that Jubilee years are used to demarcate history, which ultimately culminates in God's *basileia* being established.

The Qumran scrolls provide possibly the clearest association between the *basileia* of God and the Jubilee. While the Qumran community had no scroll which summarized the Jubilee legislation, its three distinct usages in the scrolls underscore the concept's importance to the community. With regard to God's *basileia*, it is the eschatological use of the Jubilee which is most relevant. In particular, it is 11Q13 which associates the Jubilee and the *basileia* of God most clearly. In this scroll, the tenth and final eschatological Jubilee is presented as the time when God will establish his reign on earth through Melchizedek. The vision of the *basileia* accords with many other apocalyptic works—judgment occurs, evil is destroyed, and God's righteous rule is established. The text also cites Isaiah 52:7 which explicitly refers to the reign of God.[156] Importantly, however, the text also describes the reign of God by using imagery that accords with the original Jubilee precepts. That is, God's reign includes the cancellation of debts, the freeing of captives,

---

156. ["How] beautiful upon the mountains are the feet [of] the messen[ger who] announces peace, the mess[enger of good who announces salvati]on, [sa]ying to Zion: your God [reigns."] 11Q13 2.15–16. Martínez and Tigchelaar, *Dead Sea Scrolls*, 1209.

and an eschatological Day of Atonement. Thus, in 11Q13 the Jubilee is used both calendrically and to provide imagery for the eschatological *basileia*.

Thus, aside from 11Q13, the Second Temple literature presents the Jubilee and the *basileia* of God as ethically and theologically separate concepts. The few occasions when the Jubilee and God's *basileia* are implicitly connected through the Jubilee's calendrical use and the apocalyptic expectation of God's rule (as in Jubilees and the Testament of Levi) are not indicative of a substantive relationship in the traditions of Israel.

Conclusion

The *basileia* of God and the Jubilee were markedly more popular in the Second Temple literature than they were in the Old Testament. Both concepts, however, were also interpreted in a variety of different ways. The expression of the *basileia* of God was understood in at least four ways, though the apocalyptic view (or views) was the most dominant. The identity and role (or non-role) of a messianic figure in establishing the *basileia* was also interpreted in various ways. The Jubilee was interpreted in at least eight distinct ways, many of which were unseen in the Old Testament. Thus, the Second Temple literature does not present a single unified understanding of the *basileia* of God or the Jubilee.

The author of Luke-Acts seems to have been familiar with some of this literature. While his writings seem to have been influenced by his Hellenistic-Roman context, they may also have been affected by some Qumran traditions and other Jewish literature. This is unsurprising, given his familiarity with the Old Testament Scriptures. Given the frequency of Jubilee and *basileia* of God traditions, it seems possible that Luke would have been aware of both concepts. This is particularly the case for the *basileia* of God, which is explicitly and frequently mentioned throughout his Gospel.

How references to the Jubilee would have been viewed in the first century is a separate question (and one which cannot be definitively answered). Indeed, the wide variation in how the Jubilee was interpreted makes it impossible to know how a first-century audience may have understood the concept (or if, indeed, they would have been aware of it). With regard to the *basileia* of God, however, it seems likely that Luke would have been aware of the apocalyptic picture of God's *basileia*, given his apparent familiarity with some Qumran traditions, the Epistle of Enoch, and Jubilees. All of these documents (including the majority of the Qumran material) frame the *basileia* in apocalyptic terms. It is also possible that Luke (and/or his source material) was aware of the tradition which viewed God's *basileia* as having spiritual or moral qualities, as evidenced in Philo's work and some other literature from diaspora Judaism. While the provenance and literary *milieu* of Luke's Gospel are notoriously difficult subjects, there are aspects of Luke's presentation of the *basileia* which accord with this spiritual understanding.

In any case, unless the author of Luke was familiar with 11Q13, it is very unlikely that he (or his source material or audience) would have connected the two concepts. While both concepts became increasingly important in Second Temple literature, they remained largely unconnected, as we have seen above. Since this is the case, it seems unlikely that Luke would have used the ethics and theology of the Jubilee as an expression of the *basileia* of God. This challenges the conclusions of other scholars, such as Arias, who argues that Luke specifically presented Jesus as coming "to announce the kingdom of God" and that "he did it in Jubilee language."[157] While it is conceivable that Luke may have associated the two concepts, there is no reason to assume that this is the case based on the Old Testament and Second Temple literature. This assumption will be scrutinized further as we turn our attention to the Lukan text.

---

157. Arias, "Mission and Liberation," 36. See also Sloan, *Favorable Year*, 166 and Ringe, "Jubilee Proclamation," 295.

3

The *Basileia* and Jubilee in Luke
Setting the Scene

Introduction

There are several subjects which need to be examined for the purposes of this study, both because of their own intrinsic importance and because they establish background information vital for the later investigation of Lukan texts. This chapter deals with these subjects. In particular, there is a discussion about the implied audience of Luke's Gospel, and the implications if one argues for the presence of references to the Jubilee. The chapter then examines the word ἄφεσις and the related verb ἀφίημι, both of which have featured heavily in discussions about suggested Jubilee texts in Luke-Acts. Finally, the chapter addresses the *basileia* of God in Luke-Acts, since if one is to determine that proposed Jubilee references are frequently better understood in terms of the *basileia* of God, one must first establish how the *basileia* is presented in Luke's two-part corpus.

The Implied Audience of Luke's Gospel

While there is a division within contemporary literary criticism as to how one should emphasize the author, text, and audience (then and now), there is nonetheless consensus that the interplay between all three plays in integral role in understanding the "meaning" of a text.[1] In the case of Luke's

---

1. Stanley, *Arguing*, 59. As was briefly mentioned in the introduction, although I

Gospel, however, identifying the wider audience is no easy task since, apart from the initial reference to Theophilus (Luke 1:3; Acts 1:1), there is no explicit reference to, or description of, the intended recipients. Where there was once virtual unanimity amongst scholars in identifying Luke's audience as totally or predominately gentile, there are now some scholars who argue that Luke's audience was a mixture of Jews and gentiles, or even that it was predominately Jewish.[2] The difficulty is compounded by speculation over the dating of Luke and its relationship to Acts, which affects the likely ethnic composition of the church community or communities Luke was addressing (which is also unknown). The issue is further complicated by the complex ethnic hybridity of the first-century Roman Empire, where a myriad of people groups and belief systems coexisted in the major urban centers. Nonetheless, there are some observations which can be made.

The identity of Theophilus remains a mystery. There is virtually nothing definite which is known about his character, background, ethnicity, position, and relationship to Luke.[3] This has led some scholars to argue that he may well be a symbolic figure, representative of "any well-disposed 'lover of God.'"[4] This seems unlikely, however, given the common use of Θεόφιλος as a Greek name, the personal description of Theophilus as κράτιστε (1:3),[5] the use of the singular in Luke 1:3-4 (σοι, ἐπιγνῷς, κατηχήθης), suggesting that the recipient was an individual, and the normal literary practice of addressing a letter or prescript to an individual by name.[6]

---

see no reason to doubt the traditional understandings of the authorship of Luke and Acts, they are not the focus of my research or thesis. I simpy note in passing that my conclusions are not inconsistent with the view that the implied author was a second- or third-generation gentile Christian called Luke. Nevertheless, when I use "Luke" I refer primarily to the text and implied author behind that text.

2. Esler and Moscato, for example, both believe that Luke's audience was a mixture of Jews and gentiles, while Anderson argues that it was predominately Jewish. See Esler, *Community and Gospel*, 30-45; Moscato, "Current Theories," 360-61; and Anderson, "Theophilus," 202-5.

3. In relation to Theophilus's ethnicity, most commentators argue that he was a gentile, though there are some who argue that he was Jewish. Importantly, many of those that argue that Theophilus was Jewish do not rule out the wider audience of Luke-Acts as being predominately gentile. Esler, for example, argues that "Theophilus may or may not have been typical of the reading public for whom the work was intended; its real readers may have been different" (Esler, *Community and Gospel*, 24).

4. Shellard, *New Light*, 41.

5. A description which is used by Luke on three other occasions, all in connection with addressing an individual (Acts 24:3; 24:5; 26:25).

6. Strelan, *Luke the Priest*, 107.

Aside from Theophilus, it seems very likely that Luke's work was intended to be circulated amongst a wider audience.[7] This audience was most likely comprised of followers of Jesus (the name "Christian" occurs later in the Acts narrative).[8] There are also a number of factors which suggest that Luke was writing for communities that were predominately gentile. These include:

1. The focus throughout Luke-Acts on God's concern for the gentiles. From Simeon's statement concerning Jesus as the "light for revelation to the gentiles" (Luke 2:32) through to the Pauline statement that "God's salvation has been sent to the gentiles" (Acts 28:28), there is a definite focus on the gentile mission.
2. The use of Greco-Roman literary style (particularly in the preface).
3. The tracing of Jesus' genealogy to Adam (Luke 3:38).
4. The provision of explanations for Jewish traditions and customs.[9]
5. The exclusion of episodes pertaining to Jewish traditions or customs.[10]
6. The substitution of Greek names for Hebrew or Aramaic names. For example, Luke replaces the Jewish ῥαββουνί or ῥαββί with κύριος or ἐπιστάτης (see Mark 9:5; 10:51 versus Luke 9:33; 18:41) and at times, Luke replaces γραμματεύς with νομικός (see Mark 12:28; Matt 23:13 versus Luke 10:25; 11:52).[11]

Luke's apparent concern for gentile Christians does not, however, negate the possibility that he also wrote for the benefit of Jewish Christians and God-fearers. It seems unlikely that Luke would have thought his work would not have been read by Jewish Christians, given the proportion of Jewish Christians in the early church and Luke's presentation of Christianity as a continuation of Judaism. The mention of God-fearers in Acts 13

---

7. Reasons for this include: 1) the ecumenical outlook of Acts, 2) if the author was indeed the companion of Paul, it would seem his identity is not attached to a particular community; and 3) the generality of Luke's purpose/s and prologue. See Barton, "Gospel Audiences," 186–89.

8. Reasons for this include: 1) Luke's assumption that his readers were familiar with the Old Testament; 2) the lack of an explanation for expressions such as "Son of Man" and "kingdom of God"; and 3) Luke's pastoral concerns; he assured Christians that suffering is part of God's plans, and both Jesus and Stephen died honorable martyrs' deaths. Shellard, *New Light*, 51 and Esler, *Community and Gospel*, 25.

9. See, for example, Luke 22:1, 7. Stein, *Luke*, 26.

10. See, in contrast, Matt 5:21–48; 6:1–6, 16–18; 17:24–27; Mark 7:1–23; 10:1–12. Fitzmyer, *Luke (I–IX)*, 26.

11. Fitzmyer, *Luke (I–IX)*, 58.

(especially verses 16 and 26) may also indicate that they were part of the intended readership. Nonetheless, it seems Luke wrote his work primarily for the benefit of gentile believers from a range of religious backgrounds.

Given this plausible scenario, it seems unlikely that Luke's Gospel would simply include unexplained Jubilee imagery to elucidate Jesus' ministry. As mentioned above, when the Gospel text includes distinctly Jewish customs and traditions, it frequently also adds explanatory notes for a gentile readership. There is no such explanatory note for the Jubilee as such. This cannot be excused by suggesting that gentiles were familiar with the Jubilee, since it was a distinctly Jewish institution. Indeed, there is a complete lack of explicit references to the Jubilee in any Greco-Roman literature of the time. If Luke did indeed write his Gospel in order that his readers might "know the certainty of the things they were taught" (1:4), it would have been counterproductive for him to use unexplained and veiled references to an unfamiliar institution.

Nevertheless, it might be argued that Luke's gentile readership would have required instruction in Jesus' messianic fulfillment of Old Testament texts and institutions, such as the Jubilee. This is particularly the case in Luke's Gospel, where fulfillment of the Old Testament Scriptures is emphasized (Luke 18:31; 22:37; 24:25–27, 44–47). This kind of educational aim, however, seems unlikely given that there is no mention of the word "Jubilee," nor is there any explicit reference in Luke to the original Jubilee legislation in Leviticus. Additionally, as Stanley has noted, it is highly unlikely that the early Christian readership would have had access to the full range of Scriptures, and it is also unlikely that they would have been able to study these Scriptures by themselves, given the likely low levels of literacy in the first century.[12] The only references that Luke's audience would definitely have recognized would have been those clearly marked within the text. Indeed, with regard to Old Testament allusions, Stanley has noted that one should not presume that a first-century audience would have recognized and appreciated an unmarked reference to a particular text or theme.[13] This is all the more the case given the likely composition of Luke's audience. Given that Luke's audience would have been unlikely to have access to the proposed source texts—let alone being familiar with Jubilee allusions—it seems

---

12. See Stanley, *Arguing*, 41–46. The subject of literacy rates in the first-century Roman Empire is a complicated. The most well-known work on the topic is William Harris's *Ancient Literacy*, which addresses literacy rates during the classical, Hellenistic, and Roman imperialistic periods. After a thorough investigation into many Ancient Near Eastern sources, he concluded that no more than 10 to 20 percent of the populace would have been able to read and write. Harris, *Ancient Literacy*, 272, 284, 328–30.

13. Stanley, "Pearls Before Swine," 132–33.

clear that Hays's criteria of availability (which addresses the likelihood of the audience having access to the relevant source texts) and historical plausibility (which addresses the likelihood of the intended audience understanding the proposed meaning) do not support the presence of Jubilary allusions in Luke-Acts.

This, of course, is clearly not the case with regard to the subject of the *basileia* of God. There are frequent explicit references to the *basileia* of God throughout Luke's work. While Luke does not give a concrete definition of what he means by this term, the frequency of the expression (and its variations) in all the Gospels indicates that it was a familiar concept to the first-century Christian communities. Thus, the nature of Luke's implied audience supports the contention of this thesis: that suggested references to the Jubilee are better understood in relation to the ethics and theology of the *basileia* of God as manifested in the ministry, teaching, and parables of Jesus.

Ἄφεσις and Ἀφίημι in Luke

One of the reasons why some writers see Jubilee references in Luke-Acts is because of the relatively frequent appearance of ἄφεσις and the related verb ἀφίημι. Ἄφεσις in particular has strong literary links with the Jubilee throughout the Septuagint (see below), which has led some scholars to argue that passages such as Luke 4:18, where Luke uses ἄφεσις twice as part of a quotation from Isaiah, are clear evidence of a reference to the biblical Jubilee.[14] Other passages where Luke uses ἄφεσις and ἀφίημι have added more ammunition to these arguments. As is evident below, however, the semantic development of both words suggests that neither word was explicitly associated with the Jubilee by the time Luke authored his Gospel.

It is clear that throughout the course of the Septuagint, ἄφεσις is frequently related to the Jubilee. Of the forty-nine times that ἄφεσις is used, it is used in connection to the Jubilee at least twenty-three times.[15] It is also used in relation to Sabbath years on at least eight occasions.[16] Indeed, there are only ten occasions when it is clear that ἄφεσις is not used in relation to the

---

14. See, for example, Bruno, "Jesus is our Jubilee," 96; Ringe, "Jubilee Proclamation," 215–20; Koet, *Five Studies*, 31–32; and Sloan, *Favorable Year*, 118–21.

15. Lev 25:10 (twice), 11, 12, 13, 28 (twice), 30, 31, 33, 40, 41, 50, 52, 54; 27:17, 18 (twice), 21, 23, 24; Num 36:4; Isa 61:1. There are also seven other occasions when ἄφεσις is used in a way which may be a reference to the Jubilee, though this is not certain (Isa 58:6; Jer 34:8, 17 (twice), 25; Ezek 46:17; Dan 12:7).

16. Exod 23:11; Deut 15:1, 2 (twice), 3, 9; 31:10; 1 Macc 10:34.

Jubilee or Sabbath years.[17] Within the Septuagint, ἄφεσις is used to translate יוֹבֵל ("ram's horn" or "a year of release" which was inaugurated by the blowing of a ram's horn) in Leviticus 25 and 27; שְׁמִטָּה or שָׁמַט ("remission"/"to release" or "to remit") in Exodus 23:11 and Deuteronomy 15:1 and 31:10; and דְּרוֹר ("emancipation," particularly in relation to slaves) in Leviticus 25:10, Isaiah 61:1, and Jeremiah 34:8.[18] It is only used once as a reference to "forgiveness" (Lev 16:26).[19]

Ἀφίημι, on the other hand, appears 133 times throughout the Septuagint and is never explicitly used in relation to the Jubilee and only once in connection with the Sabbath year (Deut 15:2).[20] The word is used for a range of Hebrew words to denote a) "release"/"surrender" and "leave"/"leave in peace" or b) "remission"/"forgiveness."[21] When used in terms of "remission"/"forgiveness" (over twenty times) the object is sin or guilt (usually ἁμαρτία, though also ἀνομία, ἀσέβεια, and αἰτία) and God is the agent.[22]

In classical Greek literature, ἄφεσις and ἀφίημι referred to a person's release, usually from an office, marriage, obligation, or debt.[23] Both words were used in the context of human relationships—they were not used in a religious sense.[24] By the time of Philo and Josephus, however, ἄφεσις was commonly used to mean "liberty" or "acquittal," particularly in relation to the remission of sins.[25]

In the New Testament, both ἄφεσις and ἀφίημι refer to forgiveness, though ἀφίημι has a range of other meanings as well.[26] Ἄφεσις always refers, at least in part, to the forgiveness of sins and is never given a secular

---

17. Exod 18:2; 2 Sam 22:16; 1 Esd 4:62; Esth 2:18; Jdt 11:14; 1 Macc 13:34; Joel 1:20, 4:18; Lam 3:48; Ezek 47:3.

18. Bultmann, "ἀφίημι, ἄφεσις, παρίημι, πάρεσις," 510. It is also used to mean "amnesty" or "exemption from taxation" in Esth 2:18.

19. Perhaps with the connotation of "sending out." Silva, "ἀφίημι, ἄφεσις," 445.

20. There are also some parallels to years of redemption in 1 Macc 13 and 15 when both Demetrius and Antiochus wrote to Simon; however, these parallels are not explicit.

21. Bultmann, "ἀφίημι, ἄφεσις, παρίημι, πάρεσις," 510.

22. Bultmann, "ἀφίημι, ἄφεσις, παρίημι, πάρεσις," 510 and Silva, "ἀφίημι, ἄφεσις," 444–45.

23. Bultmann, "ἀφίημι, ἄφεσις, παρίημι, πάρεσις," 510 and Silva, "ἀφίημι, ἄφεσις," 444.

24. Silva, "ἀφίημι, ἄφεσις," 444.

25. *TLNT* 1:238–44.

26. These include "to let go," "to leave," "to set aside," "to leave behind," "to let alone," "to leave in peace," "to permit," and "to allow." Silva, "ἀφίημι, ἄφεσις," 447 and Bultmann, "ἀφίημι, ἄφεσις, παρίημι, πάρεσις," 510–11. See also BDAG 156–57.

meaning.²⁷ Moreover, it is almost always God who is the one who forgives.²⁸ The word has a clear and consistent meaning throughout the New Testament and is later strongly connected with Jesus' death on the cross, which is the basis for the forgiveness of sins.²⁹ Similarly, when ἀφίημι is used in reference to forgiveness, the objects of the verb are τὰς ἁμαρτίας (sins), τὰ ἁμαρτήματα (sins), τὰ παραπτώματα (trespasses), αἱ ἀνομίαι, (iniquities), and ἡ ἐπίνοια τῆς καρδίας σου (the intent of your heart).³⁰

This is consistent with Luke's use of the two words. Luke uses ἄφεσις ten times throughout the course of Luke-Acts, and ἀφίημι thirty-four times.³¹ Apart from the Isaianic quotation in Luke 4:18–19, ἄφεσις is always used directly in relation to ἁμαρτία (the "forgiveness of sins"). That is, Luke did not use ἄφεσις in the variety of ways in which it was used in classical Greek literature or the Septuagint. He instead used the word in the same way that the other New Testament authors used it—exclusively in connection to God's forgiveness of human sins. Luke's use of ἀφίημι also reflects the wider New Testament usage. While he sometimes used ἀφίημι in the sense of the forgiveness of sins, Luke also used the word in a variety of other ways.³² Luke, therefore, did not attach the same exclusive meaning to ἀφίημι as he did to ἄφεσις.

That is not to say ἄφεσις does not have a multi-layered meaning. Luke himself conflated physical deliverance from one's enemies and deliverance from Satan with the forgiveness (ἄφεσις) of sins.³³ Moreover, given the association Luke makes between Isaiah 61 (where ἄφεσις appears) and the exorcism of demons (Luke 4:16–37; 7:21–22; Acts 10:38), it seems that the redemption (ἄφεσις) which the Isaianic text refers to was also viewed in relation to freedom from the bondage of evil spirits. Nonetheless, the fundamental and foremost meaning of ἄφεσις throughout the New Testament

---

27. *TLNT* 1:242. See also Tuckett, "Luke 4,16–30," 348 and Rese, *Alttestamentliche Motive*, 145–46.

28. Bultmann, "ἀφίημι, ἄφεσις, παρίημι, πάρεσις," 511.

29. *TLNT* 1:243-44.

30. Bultmann, "ἀφίημι, ἄφεσις, παρίημι, πάρεσις," 511.

31. Ἄφεσις is found in Luke 1:77; 3:3; 4:18 (twice); 24:47; Acts 2:38; 5:31; 10:43; 13:38; and 26:18. Ἀφίημι is found in Luke 4:39; 5:11, 20, 21, 23, 24; 6:42; 7:47 (twice), 48, 49; 8:51; 9:60; 10:30; 11:4 (twice), 42; 12:10 (twice), 39; 13:8, 35; 17:3, 4, 34, 35; 18:16, 28, 29; 19:44; 21:6; 23:34; Acts 8:22; 14:17.

32. See Luke 7:47 for an example of ἀφίημι being used in connection with the forgiveness of sins (ἁμαρτίαι). For some other uses of the word, see Luke 13:8; 19:44; Acts 14:17.

33. Luke 1:77; Acts 26:18.

is centered on the forgiveness of sins.³⁴ Indeed, as O'Brien has noted, "One need not have recourse to the Jubilee Year legislation . . . in order to explain the multivalent meanings of ἄφεσις."³⁵

Since the New Testament authors consistently use ἄφεσις with this distinct focus, Spicq has suggested that "all these NT usages, which are so perfectly homogeneous, presuppose a catechesis—whose scope and evolution are unknown to us—that added the term *aphesis* to the Christian vocabulary with a precise and exclusive theological meaning."³⁶ If this is true, then one would expect that other early Christian writers aside from Luke would also use ἄφεσις in association with the forgiveness of sins, without importing Jubilee ideology. O'Brien's survey of the early Christian material confirms that this is the case—every early church writer employed ἄφεσις exclusively in connection with the forgiveness of sins.³⁷ There are no early Christian authors who associated ἄφεσις with the Jubilee. In the citation of Isaiah 61 in the epistle of Barnabas, for example, the proclamation of ἄφεσις is understood in terms of the forgiveness of sins for those who are in darkness.³⁸ Similarly, in Irenaeus's multiple citations of Isaiah 61, there are no references to the Jubilee at all, nor is there a reference to the Jubilee in any of his extant writings.³⁹ Indeed, as O'Brien has noted, it is not until Origen

---

34. As Wright has noted, however, this forgiveness of sins announced by Jesus should not be primarily viewed in individual terms. Rather, "the most natural meaning of the phrase 'the forgiveness of sins' to a first-century Jew is not in the first instance the remission of *individual* sins, but the putting away of the whole nation's sins." This is particularly relevant given the exilic nature of the Isaianic text (the nation was in an enduring theological exile due to her ongoing sins). Liberation from this exile was signified by the forgiveness of the nation's sins. Thus, the ἄφεσις which Jesus proclaimed was directed at the entire nation, which was captive and oppressed because of her sin. Consequently, it seems that the eschatological use of Isa 61 in Luke-Acts is not so far from the "literal sense" of the Isaianic passage as was once thought. Luke may have included the text (at least in part) to present Jesus as the one who would bring an end to the exile caused by the sins of the nation. He presented Jesus as a proclaimer of spiritual release, centered on the forgiveness of sins. Where Jesus' original listeners may have heard Isa 61 in terms of release from Roman domination, Luke may have intended it in terms of release from theological exile. While this is in no way certain, it does seem plausible, given this quotation's focus on "release" and Luke's general approach to and use of the Old Testament. See Wright, *The New Testament*, 273 and Gregory, "The Postexilic Exile," 496.

35. O'Brien, "Comparison," 440.

36. *TLNT* 1:244.

37. O'Brien, "Comparison," 440–41.

38. O'Brien, "Comparison," 440.

39. Irenaeus refers to Isa 61 in *Against Heresies* 2.22; 3.9.3; 3.17.1; and 4.23.1. O'Brien, "A Comparison," 440.

in the third century that ἄφεσις is associated with the Jubilee.⁴⁰ Even here, however, the word is used in relation to the forgiveness of sins.⁴¹ Origen argued that the reason why the crowds sat in groups of fifty at the feeding of the five thousand was because the number fifty "embraces the remission of sins, in accordance with the mystery of the Jubilee, and of the feast at Pentecost."⁴²

Thus, Spicq's suggestion that ἄφεσις entered the early Christian catechetical material is congruent with the historical and literary evidence, since ἄφεσις was employed by early church authors with an exclusive meaning centered on the forgiveness of sins. There is no reason why one should import the Septuagintal semantic range of ἄφεσις into Luke's work. All early church authors, including Luke, used ἄφεσις without any explicit association with the Jubilee.

Despite this weight of evidence, there are some scholars who still believe that ἄφεσις should be read in relation to the biblical Jubilee. Ringe has presented perhaps the most systematic case as to why "one should not lose sight of OT Jubilee traditions in attempting to understand the meaning of forgiveness in the Synoptic Gospels' interpretation of Jesus and his message."⁴³ Her four arguments for this position are summarized below:

1. The word ἄφεσις occurs in "Jubilee texts" such as Luke 4:18 and Luke 7:18–23.

2. The Greek meaning of ἄφεσις (as a release from legal obligations) influenced the Hebrew notion of forgiveness, which gave it a more ethical or covenantal thrust, in a way reminiscent of the Jubilee traditions.

3. The Synoptic accounts use ἄφεσις and ἀφίημι to refer to the release of debts as well as forgiveness.

4. The Jubilee traditions in Second and Third Isaiah point to release from the old order into God's eschatological reign, which parallels the Synoptic Gospels' understanding of forgiveness being an eschatological event which inaugurates God's reign.⁴⁴

Her arguments can be addressed as follows:

1. Ringe's first argument is clearly circular. It relies on the presumption that Luke 4:18 and 7:18–23 are, in fact, "Jubilee texts." Neither passage,

---

40. O'Brien, "Comparison," 441.
41. Origen, *Comm. Matt.* 6.1 (*ANF* 8:841).
42. Origen, *Comm. Matt.* 6.1 (*ANF* 8:841).
43. Ringe, "Jubilee Proclamation," 219.
44. Ringe, "Jubilee Proclamation," 219–20.

however, has any reference to the Jubilee. There is no mention of the word "Jubilee," no mention of ancestral land, no mention of the number fifty (which was strongly associated with the Jubilee in Second Temple literature), no blowing of the trumpet, and no redemption of houses. Presumably, Ringe means that the texts allude to Isaiah 61, which, in its Old Testament context, does employ Jubilee imagery. As has already been demonstrated, however, it is unlikely that Luke or his readers would have associated Isaiah 61 with the Jubilee. It is more likely that it would have been understood in relation to the *basileia* of God (see the following chapter).

2. As has been stated above, the New Testament authors' use of ἄφεσις is manifestly different from its use in the Septuagint and classical Greek literature. While the semantic development of ἄφεσις is not clear, its use in the New Testament and in early church documents is clearly distinct from its use in the Septuagint in relation to the Jubilee. Even in non-Christian literature such as the works of Philo and Josephus, it is clear that the meaning of ἄφεσις had developed such that it was frequently associated with the remission of sins.[45]

3. The argument that the Synoptic accounts use ἄφεσις and ἀφίημι to refer to the release of debts as well as forgiveness misrepresents the distinct use of each word. Ἄφεσις is *not* used to refer to the release of debts by the Synoptic authors—it is only used in reference to the forgiveness of sins (if one includes Luke 4:18—see chapter 4).[46] While ἀφίημι is used to refer to the release of debts, it has a broad semantic range (it is also used to mean "to let go," "to leave in peace," and "to permit"). Moreover, ἀφίημι does not carry the same Jubilee connotations as ἄφεσις—there is no discernible link between ἀφίημι and the Jubilee anywhere in the Septuagint, or indeed in any Greek literature (including the New Testament).

4. While Ringe's fourth argument has some merit, in actuality it serves to support the contention of this thesis. It is true that the Isaianic texts referred to in Luke-Acts (such as Isa 61) use Jubilee imagery to highlight release from the old order unto God's eschatological reign. It does not, however, follow that this Old Testament Jubilee imagery should be kept in view when one reads Luke's narrative. On the contrary, if Luke alluded to or quoted Isaianic references to release/redemption in order

---

45. *TLNT* 1:238-44.

46. Matt 26:28; Mark 1:4; 3:29; Luke 1:77; 3:3; 24:47.
Indeed, there is a "striking contrast" between the exclusivity of ἄφεσις and the wider semantic range of ἀφίημι. Silva, "ἀφίημι, ἄφεσις," 447.

to parallel or exemplify the Synoptic Gospels' presentation of forgiveness which inaugurates God's reign in his people, it makes more sense to view these texts from Isaiah in relation to the *basileia* of God. This is particularly the case since texts such as Isaiah 61 were elsewhere related to God's *basileia* in the first century (see the previous chapter).

Moreover, as has been demonstrated above, the literary relationship which existed in the Isaianic text between the *basileia* of God and the Jubilee (whereby the Jubilee highlighted aspects of God's reign) diminished significantly throughout the Second Temple period. Indeed, despite the fact that both concepts grew remarkably in their popularity and influence, the only document in the Second Temple literature which posits a relationship between the two concepts is 11Q13, which is unlikely to have exerted any influence over Luke's work (see the following chapter).

Sloan takes a different approach. He concedes that ἄφεσις should be primarily understood in terms of the forgiveness of sin, however he links this forgiveness with the Day of Atonement, which marked the start of Jubilee years.[47] Thus, he argues that notions of forgiveness are "cultically bound up . . . with the day of Jubilee."[48] It seems highly unlikely, however, that Luke would have employed ἄφεσις to signal continuity between the Day of Atonement and Jesus' ministry, given that the word ἄφεσις is largely absent from Pentateuchal accounts of the Day of Atonement.[49] Even if, however, Luke did see continuity between the Day of Atonement and the word ἄφεσις, there is again no need to seek recourse to the Jubilee legislation. The Day of Atonement was a Jewish institution in its own right, celebrated every year (Lev 16:34). Its association with the Jubilee only occurred once every fifty years.

In summary, there is no doubt that ἄφεσις was strongly associated with the Jubilee in the Septuagint. The related verb ἀφίημι, however, was unconnected with the Jubilee, both in the Old Testament texts and in later documents (including the New Testament). The semantic meaning of both words developed, as seen in many classical works, such that by the time of Philo and Josephus, ἄφεσις in particular was commonly used in relation to the remission of sins. Within the New Testament (including Luke-Acts), ἄφεσις has a uniform and exclusive meaning, centered on the forgiveness of sins. This is echoed clearly in other early church literature. Unlike in the

---

47. Sloan, *Favorable Year*, 160.
48. Sloan, *Favorable Year*, 160.
49. Its one occurrence in the Day of Atonement legislation is in Lev 16:26.

Septuagint, ἄφεσις is not associated with the Jubilee. There is therefore no need to resort to Old Testament texts to identify or elucidate the word's meaning, and to do so would result in skewing one's understanding of the word's distinct meaning for Luke and his audience.

The *Basileia* of God in Luke

If it is to be established that the Lukan passages which are frequently associated with the Jubilee are, in fact, better understood in terms of the *basileia* of God, it is important to briefly examine how Luke portrayed this *basileia*. While each of the so-called Lukan "Jubilee passages" and Jubilee themes will be examined in later chapters, it is important first to establish how Luke presented the *basileia* to provide a framework for viewing these passages and themes in relation to the *basileia*.

The *basileia* of God is a major theme throughout Luke's two-part corpus. In Luke's Gospel, the *basileia* is explicitly referred to thirty-nine times (the actual phrase "*basileia* of God" is used thirty-two times)[50] and in Acts the *basileia* is explicitly mentioned seven times (the phrase "*basileia* of God" is used six times).[51] These references, aside from being frequent, are also positioned at key points throughout Luke's corpus to underscore the *basileia*'s importance in the overall Luke-Acts narrative. In fact, Luke routinely used the proclamation of the *basileia* of God as a summary of Jesus' ministry and that of his followers.[52]

Luke's use of *basileia* was fairly consistent. While there are some occasions where Luke presented the βασιλεία τοῦ θεοῦ in the sense of a realm (Luke 13:28–29), and God's sovereign kingship is at times emphasized (Acts 4:26),[53] Luke usually employed *basileia* in the dynamic sense of the word (that is, in the sense of God's reign or rule). God's dynamic reign is a central theological point in Luke's thinking. It is emphasized through Luke's presentation of salvation-history, in which God controls and directs human history in accordance with his plans. Indeed, as Marshall has noted, the

---

50. In Luke's Gospel, the phrase "*basileia* of God" occurs in Luke 4:43; 6:20; 7:28; 8:1, 10; 9:2, 11, 27, 60, 62; 10:9, 11; 11:20; 13:18, 20, 28, 29; 14:15; 16:16; 17:20 (twice), 21; 18:16, 17, 24, 25, 29; 19:11; 21:31; 22:16, 18, and 23:51. It is also explicitly referred to in Luke 1:33; 11:2; 12:31–32; 22:29–30; 23:42.

51. In Acts, the phrase "*basileia* of God" occurs in Acts 1:3; 8:12; 14:22; 19:8; 28:23, 31. It is also explicitly mentioned in Acts 20:25 (and arguably in 1:6).

52. Luke 4:43; 8:1; 9:2; 16:16; Acts 1:3; 28:31. See also O'Toole, "Kingdom," 153.

53. Within Luke-Acts, the language of kingship is more frequently applied to Jesus than God (Luke 1:32–33, 19:11–27; Acts 17:7); however, Luke leaves his readers in no doubt that it is God who has given Jesus the throne (Luke 1:32).

term *"basileia"* is used mainly of the action of God in intervening in human history to establish his rule. Thus, as has been mentioned above, there is some continuity between the Lukan presentation of the *basileia* of God and that of the Old Testament prophetic literature and Second Temple apocalyptic traditions. This is unsurprising given Luke's focus on the fulfillment of Scripture, since for Luke, salvation history consisted of two stages: the period of promise and the period of fulfillment characterized by the coming of the *basileia* (Luke 16:16; Acts 13:32–33).[54]

Sloan argues that Lukan references to the *basileia* should be read in relation to the Jubilee.[55] His argument, in brief, is that references to the kingdom must be read in connection with εὐαγγελίζω, which must always be viewed in light of the Isaianic quotation in Nazareth, and therefore the Old Testament prophetic vision of the Jubilee in Isaiah 61:1–3 forms the background of *basileia* references.[56] His argument is as unsustainable as it is convoluted. While it is true that the Isaianic quotation in the Nazareth episode denotes the character of the *basileia*, it would be a mistake to assume every Lukan reference must be read in that light, particularly since the word *basileia* is not found in the Isaianic text. Moreover, as will be explained in the following chapter, while Luke employed Isaiah 61 for distinct and important literary purposes, none of these included drawing attention to the Jubilee. Finally, as has already been established in the previous two chapters, links between the Jubilee and the *basileia* of God in the Old Testament and the Second Temple literature are extremely tenuous, so to argue that Luke associated the Jubilee with the *basileia* presumes both an innovation and a lack of clarity that is difficult to reconcile.

Luke portrays the *basileia* of God as God's gift and his action (that is, he brings the *basileia*); this is the primary meaning of the genitive τοῦ θεοῦ in Luke-Acts.[57] Significantly, however, the concept of God ruling is relatively infrequent throughout Luke's Gospel. The emphasis is instead placed on the agent of God through whom God's rule is manifested.[58] In a similar way to many of the Old Testament and Second Temple texts, Luke frequently presents this agent of God as the Davidic messiah.[59] In fact, Luke, at times,

---

54. Stein, *Luke*, 46.

55. Sloan, *Favorable Year*, 160.

56. Sloan, *Favorable Year*, 160.

57. O'Toole, "Kingdom," 148. God's giving of the *basileia* is seen in Luke 12:32 and 11:2, and his bringing of the *basileia* is seen in Luke 11:20.

58. Marshall, *The Gospel of Luke*, 129.

59. For a list of the direct and indirect references to Jesus as the Davidic messiah, see Hahn, "Kingdom and Church," 297–99. The relationship of Jesus to the *basileia* of God in Luke-Acts is complex and unique. Ziccardi's study on the subject has identified that

mentions the *basileia* of God and Jesus interchangeably, which suggests that in some ways he saw them as being identical.[60]

There are several other observations about Luke's presentation of the *basileia* of God which are noteworthy. These include:

1. It is both a present inaugurated reality (Luke 7:28) and a future not-yet-realized dimension (Luke 17:22–37; 21:5–38).[61]

2. It can be described in terms of status inversion, whereby the righteous and sinners exchange places, and those who have no wealth, power, or status are honored above those who do.[62]

3. There is a unique relationship between the *basileia* and the Holy Spirit throughout Luke-Acts, particularly in the empowerment of the proclamation of the *basileia*.[63] Stein even argues that the Spirit's presence (particularly in relation to Jesus' baptism in 3:21–22 and the coming of the Spirit at Pentecost in Acts 2:1–2) is the clearest indicator of the realized eschatological dimension of God's *basileia*.[64]

---

while the *basileia* can be considered to be belonging to Jesus, he is also the agent of the realization of the *basileia* and the preacher of the *basileia*. Moreover, his identity as the Davidic messiah and the Son of God is necessarily related to the *basileia*. See Ziccardi, *Relationship*, 261–64, 371–74, 499–503.

60. The interchangeableness of Jesus and the *basileia* of God is seen in Luke 14:26 and 18:29. Additionally, as O'Toole has noted, if Luke 18:29 is sourced from Mark 10:29 (Matt 19:29), then Luke substituted "for the sake of the kingdom of God" for the original "for my sake and for the gospel." Finally, there are numerous times when Luke refers to the whole gospel message in terms of Jesus (Acts 5:42; 8:35; 11:20) and similarly he refers to the whole gospel message in terms of the *basileia* of God (Luke 4:43; 8:1; 16:16). O'Toole, "Kingdom," 150–51.

61. As has already been mentioned, this parallels, to some degree, the Jubilee hope given in 11Q13; however, the differences between this text and Luke's work are so profound that it is unlikely that it exerted any influence over his work (see the following chapter).

Luke's eschatological view on the *basileia* of God has attracted significant attention. Conzelmann's position on Luke's eschatology has been extremely influential amongst Lukan scholars; however, it seems that many have now abandoned his ideas as being overly forced and exegetically unsound. Stagg, for example, has scathingly denounced Conzelmann's views: "How a theory so poorly based exegetically, so forced, so arbitrary, and so dogmatic could so capture so many scholars is a modern marvel!" Cited in Garland, *Luke*, 36.

There is not yet, however, any scholarly consensus about Luke's eschatological position. Indeed, John T. Carroll's study summarizes the varying views on Lukan eschatology under seven distinct headings, all of which continue to be influential. Carroll, *Response*, 1–36.

62. Carroll, *Luke*, 10.

63. Cho, "Spirit and Kingdom," 197.

64. Stein, *Luke*, 47.

4. Jerusalem, and in particular the temple, is exemplified as the place where the good news of the *basileia* of God and demonstrations of salvation are presented to Israel.[65]

5. The preaching of the *basileia* was frequently accompanied by acts of healing, both within Jesus' ministry and that of the apostles in Acts (though in Acts, Luke favors "the word" over "the *basileia* of God").[66]

6. As in the Old Testament, the eschatological hope of God's reign is frequently tied to a final judgment of sin.[67]

7. Jesus is presented as the Davidic king who rules over the earth. Moreover, there is also a shift in focus from the earthly to the heavenly sphere, since Christ's present rule is from heaven (Acts 2:33a) and since citizens of the *basileia* are also in heaven.[68]

Sloan has argued that Luke's presentation of the *basileia* of God as existing both on earth and in heaven must, to some degree, have drawn metaphorical content from the restoration of lands that occurred in the Jubilee years.[69] It is difficult, however, to see any type of relationship between the two concepts. The restoration of lands in the Jubilee legislation pertained to

---

65. As has been mentioned in chapter 1, the Old Testament portrays the temple in Jerusalem as being the seat of God's reign. While there is some controversy as to the meaning Luke placed on Jerusalem, there is little doubt that he viewed it (and the temple) as profoundly important (of 146 New Testament references to Jerusalem, 95 are found in Luke-Acts).

66. The connection between the preaching of the *basileia* of God and acts of healing is seen in many Lukan texts, including Luke 4:40–43; 6:18–20; 8:1–2; 9:2, 6, 11; 10:9; Acts 4:29–30; 8:4–7. There are, however, many occasions when healing does not accompany the preaching of the *basileia*, and the preaching of the *basileia* is not accompanied by healing.

The subject of healing in Luke-Acts is again highly controversial. It seems that Luke viewed at least some sicknesses as evidence of a person being under "the power of the devil" (Acts 10:38), in which case it is easy to see how a person coming under the reign of God would be released from sickness. On other occasions, those who are healed are described as still outside the *basileia* (Luke 10:9), so there is no definite correlation between healing and entering into the reign of God. It would seem Luke viewed healing as an accompanying confirmation of the proclamation of the *basileia* of God, rather than an outworking of a person submitted to the reign of God.

67. The relationship between judgment and the eschatological *basileia* of God is seen most clearly in Luke 13:28: "There will be weeping and gnashing of teeth, when you see Abraham, Isaac and Jacob and all the prophets in the kingdom of God, but you yourselves thrown out." Other examples include: Luke 11:50–51; 12:20, 45–48, 57–59; 13:1–9, 22–30; 16:19–31; 17:26–37; Acts 17:30–33; 24:24–25.

68. Passages which emphasize Jesus' Davidic rule on earth include Luke 1:32–33, 46–55, and 69–75.

69. Sloan, *Favorable Year*, 126.

the return of land purchased from an Israelite by a fellow Israelite. It is categorically different from Luke's presentation of Christ's reign on earth as the Davidic king. The only parallel which seems possible is the apparent ongoing sense of theological exile which continued during the Roman rule, and the hope of release from exile featured in some Old Testament Jubilee texts (such as Isa 49:7–13), which included the redemption of land. Yet there is no evidence that Luke's portrayal of Jesus' reign over earth and heaven should be viewed in this light. Indeed, Luke's focus (in relation to this aspect of the *basileia* of God) was on Christ's present reign over the Davidic kingdom.

Luke also presents the *basileia* of God and salvation as being inextricably linked. In Luke's Gospel, the relationship between the two is seen explicitly in 13:28–29 where entering the *basileia* of God is contrasted with weeping and gnashing of teeth; in 18:18–30 where entering the *basileia* of God is equated with being saved (18:24–25) and with inheriting eternal life (18:29–30); in 21:28–31 where the *basileia* is equated with redemption (which Luke used interchangeably with "salvation"—see Luke 1:68–71); and in 23:42–43 where being in the *basileia* is equated with being in paradise. Similarly, in Acts, Luke associated the *basileia* of God with belief and baptism in 8:12–13, and he connected the *basileia* of God with salvation in 28:23–31 (see especially verses 28–31). Moreover, throughout Luke-Acts, the *basileia* of God is frequently presented in connection with the gospel (in fact, the content of the good news is frequently portrayed as the *basileia* of God), which is presented as the message of salvation.[70] Luke therefore saw no difference between the reign of God in a person's life and the salvation of that person. To be saved is to have entered into the reign/*basileia* of God.

Since this is the case, Luke's soteriology cannot be isolated from his understanding of the *basileia* of God. In the case of Luke's work, this is particularly important because, as Marshall has observed, the "central theme in

---

70. The *basileia* of God and the gospel are explicitly linked in Luke 4:43; 7:22–28; 9:2–6, 16:16; and Acts 8:12. The good news is portrayed as the message of salvation in Luke 2:10–11; 3:16–18; Acts 8:12; 10:34–48; 13:32–48; 17:18–34. Given Luke's holistic view of salvation (see below), the good news is also seen as the message of salvation in Luke 4:18–21; 7:21–22; 8:1–2; 9:6. Significantly, while the good news is predominately presented as the *basileia* of God (particularly in Luke's Gospel), in Acts it is also described as the good news that Jesus is the Messiah (Acts 5:42), the good news of the *basileia* of God and the name of Jesus Christ (Acts 8:12), the good news about Jesus (Acts 8:35), the good news of peace through Jesus Christ, who is Lord of all (Acts 10:36), the good news about the Lord Jesus (Acts 11:20), the good news of the fulfillment of Scripture (Acts 13:32), the good news of how one can turn from worthless things to the living God (Acts 14:15), the good news about Jesus and the resurrection (Acts 17:18), and the good news of God's grace (Acts 20:24). All of these descriptions can therefore be viewed as equivalent, to some degree, with Luke's conception of the *basileia* of God.

Luke's writings is that Jesus offers salvation to men."[71] That is, salvation in Luke focuses on the person and ministry of Jesus rather than a scheme of history (as in Conzelmann's writings).[72] This salvation concerns the totality of human life and relationships (see, for example, Luke 5:23); Luke never makes a clear distinction between the physical, spiritual, and social aspects of salvation.[73]

Nevertheless, it is clear that Luke is particularly interested in the spiritual deliverance that occurred when a person was saved. Of Luke's thirty uses of σῴζω ("to save"), eighteen emphasize spiritual liberation.[74] Indeed, as Green has noted, Luke's use of σῴζω stands in sharp contrast to Matthew's and Mark's use of the word, since Luke is "much more apt to use the verb in its transcendent, spiritual sense."[75] Similarly, Luke's use of the nouns for salvation (σωτήριον and σωτηρία) are frequently linked with spiritual deliverance (see particularly Luke 1:77).[76] Luke also employs the noun μετάνοια ("repentance") eleven times (half of all the word's uses in the New Testament), and he uses the verb μετανοέω ("to repent") fourteen times.[77] On some occasions, the link with the *basileia* of God is quite explicit. Indeed, in Luke 9:23-27 and 17:20-35, the reign of God is consonant with people losing their lives (that is, repenting) in order to gain eternal life.[78] Repentance is

71. Marshall, *Luke: Historian and Theologian*, 116.
72. Leifeld, "Luke," 811.
73. Powell, "Salvation in Luke-Acts," 8 and Carey, *God's Salvation*, 37-38.
74. Luke 7:50; 8:12, 36; 9:24 (twice); 13:23; 18:26; 19:10; Acts 2:21, 40, 47; 4:9, 12; 11:14; 15:1, 11; 16:30, 31. Σῴζω is used to refer to physical deliverance in Luke 6:9; 8:48, 50; 17:19; 18:42; 23:35 (twice), 37, 39; Acts 4:9; 14:9; 27:20, 31.
75. Green, "'The Message of Salvation,'" 28.
76. Luke uses the word "salvation" on six occasions in his Gospel: 1:69, 71, 77; 2:30; 3:6; and 19:9. Luke 1:77 relates salvation to the forgiveness of sins. In Luke 3:6, God's salvation is preached by John in the context of preaching baptism and the forgiveness of sins (3:3). Similarly, Zacchaeus's salvation (19:9) is based on his repentance. In Acts, Luke again used the word "salvation" on seven occasions (Acts 4:12; 7:25; 13:26, 47; 16:17; 27:34; 28:28). On five of these occasions (4:12; 13:26, 47; 16:17; 28:28), the word is used in connection with the message of salvation, which, in 13:46-48, is shown to be the message that gives eternal life. That is, in Acts the word is explicitly linked to spiritual redemption five times.
77. Luke uses μετάνοια in Luke 3:3, 8; 5:32; 15:7; 24:47; Acts 5:31; 11:18; 13:24; 19:4; 20:21; 26:20. He uses μετανοέω in Luke 10:13; 11:32; 13:3, 5; 15:7, 10; 16:30; 17:3, 4; Acts 2:38; 3:19; 8:22; 17:30; 26:20.
78. Otto Betz argues that while the relationship between repentance and the *basileia* of God is explicit in Mark (Mark 6:12), Luke's work instead emphasizes a connection between the *basileia* of God and realized eschatology. See Betz, *Jesus, der Messias Israels*, 258. The distinction, however, is both untrue and unnecessary. As has already been mentioned, the link between repentance and the *basileia* of God is quite explicit in Luke's material. Indeed, the dynamic meaning of the *basileia* of God (the reign of God)

frequently linked with the forgiveness of sins, such that "when Luke speaks of forgiveness he presumes repentance, and vice-versa."[79] Moreover, as Bock has noted, Luke frequently presents the benefits of salvation in spiritual terms: there is forgiveness of sins, eternal life, the Holy Spirit, peace, grace, and justification (in a nontechnical sense).[80] Thus, while there are many dimensions to salvation in Luke-Acts, it is clear that the Lukan Jesus had a distinct focus on people being released from spiritual bondage.

The Lukan connection between the *basileia* of God and spiritual release also includes release from the power of evil spirits. Indeed, as Evans has convincingly demonstrated, Jesus' exorcism ministry was inextricably linked to his proclamation of the *basileia* of God, since the exorcisms served to demonstrate the reality of God's reign.[81] Much of the Second Temple literature presented the eventual triumph of God's *basileia* as leading to the destruction of Satan's *basileia*.[82] Thus, "for Jesus and his following, the exorcisms offered dramatic proof of the defeat and retreat of Satan's kingdom in the face of the advancing rule of God."[83] In Luke's Gospel, Jesus' proclamation at Nazareth (which, chapter 5 will demonstrate, served as a proclamation of the *basileia* of God) was followed by the driving out of an evil spirit at Capernaum (Luke 4:31–37), as if to demonstrate the spiritual release which was just proclaimed. Luke 4 then concludes with a summary of Jesus' ministry, described in terms of exorcisms and the preaching of the *basileia* of God (Luke 4:41–43). Later in Luke's Gospel, the association between the preaching and presence of the *basileia* of God and deliverance from evil spirits is seen in 7:21–28, 8:1–2, 9:1–2, and 11:20, which is, perhaps, the most explicit: "If I drive out demons by the finger of God, then the kingdom of God has come to you." Similarly, in Acts 8:4–7, the preaching of the word (the character of which is the *basileia* of God) is accompanied by exorcisms, and in Acts 26:18, Saul's commission is described in terms of turning gentiles from the power of Satan to God.

---

is itself expressed by repentance. That is, repentance is presented as the changing of a person's perspective to come under the reign of God. This is then expressed in the totality of a person's life. See Méndez-Moratalla, *Paradigm*, 87. Additionally, the subject of Luke's eschatology is highly controversial. To argue that Luke sought to draw an explicit connection between realized eschatology and the *basileia* of God is very difficult to maintain in light of the many passages referring to God's future reign.

79. Vinson, *Luke*, 14.
80. Bock, *Theology*, 268–72.
81. Evans, "Inaugurating," 49.
82. Evans, "Inaugurating," 63.
83. Evans, "Inaugurating," 75.

It is easy to see how this Lukan focus on spiritual release could be mistakenly viewed as primarily a reference to the Jubilee, since release was a major thematic emphasis of the Jubilee throughout the Old Testament. To view the theme of release as being necessarily related to the Jubilee, however, would be a mistake. Even within the Old Testament corpus, the themes of spiritual release and justice were explicitly associated with the reign of God. In fact, as was shown in chapter 1, where the Old Testament prophetic literature (which Luke was aware of) employed Jubilee imagery in connection with spiritual release, the Jubilee was only referenced to elucidate the theme of spiritual release (rather than the theme of spiritual release being employed to elucidate the Jubilee). In Luke-Acts, there is no need to turn to the Jubilee in connection with the theme of spiritual release, particularly since there is no mention of the Jubilee anywhere in the text. The theme is instead employed to denote (in part) what occurs when one comes under the reign of God.

Luke also paints a consistent picture as to who the recipients of the *basileia* of God are. In one sense, Luke portrays the *basileia* of God as being universally open that all might enter (including gentiles and women).[84] As some scholars have noted, however, despite the universality of the *basileia*, there is a definite practical bias toward the disadvantaged and marginalized.[85] While this is seen in the Isaianic text in Jesus' programmatic statement of mission in Luke 4:18–19 (see the following two chapters), it is also denoted periodically throughout Luke-Acts (most explicitly in Luke 6:20—"Blessed

---

84. The universality of the *basileia* is seen explicity in the Isaianic quotation in Luke 3:6 ("All mankind will see God's salvation") and the quotation from Genesis in Acts 3:25 ("Through your offspring all peoples on earth will be blessed"). There are many women who occupy important roles in Luke-Acts. These include: Elizabeth, the Virgin Mary, the prophetess Anna, the widow at Nain, the nameless sinner in the house of Simon, Mary Magdalene, Joanna, Susanna, the woman subject to bleeding, Martha and Mary, the widow with the two mites, the "daughters of Jerusalem," and the women at the tomb. Plummer, *St. Luke*, xliii. For a recent detailed treatment of this subject, see Forbes and Harrower, *Raised from Obscurity*, 36–218.

Luke's position on Jews and gentiles has attracted much attention. While there is no doubt Luke viewed gentiles favorably, his presentation of the Jews has been strongly criticized. Some, such as Sanders, have even characterized Luke's work as hateful and anti-Semitic. See Sanders, *Jews*, 310–11. Most, however, argue that Luke's presentation of Christianity is grounded in Judaism and Scripture, and that the Christian movement is presented as a continuation of its Jewish heritage. See, for example, Carroll, *Luke*, 11–12; O'Toole, "Kingdom," 152–53; Carey, *God's Salvation*, 39–40; Marshall, *New Testament Theology*, 149–50; Weatherly, "The Jews in Luke-Acts," 107–17; and Brawley, *Luke-Acts and the Jews*, 155–59.

85. Carey, *God's Salvation*, 39; Green, *Theology*, 76–101; Hoesl, "The Kingdom," 57–68; and Tannehill, "What Kind of King?" 20.

are you who are poor, for yours is the kingdom of heaven").[86] Importantly, however, it seems that it is the humble attitude of the disadvantaged and marginalized that is a requirement for entry into the *basileia* of God, rather than their position in life.[87]

This bias toward the marginalized and disadvantaged is frequently described in terms of status reversal. Carroll summarizes it well:

> The reign of God as imagined and enacted by Jesus challenges conventional notions and practices, especially relating to social status. His ministry effects radical status inversion that is both horizontal (sinners and righteous exchange places) and vertical (persons possessing and those lacking wealth, status, and power trade places). Or rather, Jesus invites any and all to a table where the only status and position that matter are those conferred by a gracious, just God.[88]

Green goes so far as to say that status-inversion (or, one might say, entering into the reign of God) is itself presented as salvation in Luke-Acts.[89] While this may be an oversimplification, it is nonetheless clear that the status of those in the *basileia* of God is characterized as completely opposite to what would have been culturally normative.[90]

Karl Allen Kuhn has recently published an alternative view to Luke's presentation of the *basileia* of God.[91] In contrast with many scholars, Kuhn argues that the Lukan view of the *basileia* is not politically or socially benign.[92] On the contrary; he argues that the "gospel proclaimed by Luke is one that calls upon all humanity to turn their allegiance from Caesar and the kingdom of Rome to another realm and another as Lord . . . He considered the reign of God to be not a benign reality but a deeply subversive and disturbing force that was already undermining the foundations of Rome

---

86. Luke 1:46–55; 4:18–19; 6:20–26; 9:46–48; 14:15–24; 16:19–31; 18:15–30; 22:24–27; 23:42–43; Acts 4:32–37; 10:34.

87. Examples of this include the humble tax-collector's prayer (Luke 18:13–14), the children who came to Jesus (Luke 18:16–17), the thief on the cross (Luke 23:40–43), Joseph of Arimathea (Luke 23:51), and Cornelius (Acts 10:4–5, 22, 25).

88. Carroll, *Luke*, 10.

89. Green, *Theology*, 94.

90. This will be explored further in the section on "Reversal of Fortunes" in chapter 6.

91. Kuhn, *The Kingdom*. Kuhn, of course, is not the first scholar to hold this view. Others include Ahn, *The Reign of God*, 89–90 and Cassidy, *Jesus, Politics, and Society*, 77–86.

92. Kuhn, *The Kingdom*, xvii.

and all earthly claims to power."[93] According to Kuhn, Luke wanted to show Theophilus that the advent of the *basileia* was highly disruptive of the elite-controlled forms of Israelite tradition and Roman social order.[94] Luke was not necessarily calling for open insurrection, but he was challenging his readers to change their allegiance to a new king.[95] While Kuhn, at times, overemphasizes Luke's political agenda, his overall thesis is convincing; there is no dichotomy between religion and politics in Luke's world or his narrative. Therefore, for Luke, to come under the reign of God is to give total allegiance to God as king. This is consistent with the apocalyptic material (some of which seemingly influenced Luke), all of which presents God's *basileia* as diametrically opposed to foreign rule (see the previous chapter).

Thus, in sum, the *basileia* of God in Luke-Acts has some continuity with the Old Testament and the apocalyptic literature; however, there are also some clear differences, the most important being the Lukan focus on God's dynamic reign over a person's life. Additionally, Luke connected the reign of God with salvation to such a degree that being saved is presented as being the equivalent of entering into God's *basileia*. Moreover, while Lukan salvation (or entering into the *basileia*) is holistic, there is a definite emphasis on spiritual redemption. It is this redemption which has, at times, been mistakenly interpreted as a reference to the year of Jubilee. In Luke-Acts as in the majority of the Old Testament and the Second-Temple literature, however, no explicit link exists between the *basileia* of God and the Jubilee.

Conclusion

As in many previous studies, this chapter has demonstrated that Luke presented the *basileia* of God as being focused on God's dynamic reign—universal (though biased toward those who are disadvantaged or marginalized), holistic (though focused on spiritual redemption), eschatological, and as directly impacting political allegiances. Since this is the case, it is easy to see how some of these *basileia* emphases might be mistakenly construed as being linked to the Jubilee (especially notions of accommodating the disadvantaged and redemption). As will become increasingly clear in the following exegetical analyses of selected Luke-Acts texts, however, there is no reason to resort to the Jubilee traditions to explain their presence or meaning.

93. Kuhn, *The Kingdom*, xvii.
94. Kuhn, *The Kingdom*, 270.
95. Kuhn, *The Kingdom*, 228.

Additionally, the nature of the implied audience of Luke suggests, at the least, that we should question the assumption that there are Jubilee references in Luke's Gospel. Indeed, it seems unlikely that the implied audience would have had access to the proposed Jubilee source texts, let alone be familiar with Jubilee allusions.[96]

Finally, concerning ἄφεσις and ἀφίημι, Luke evidently used these words in a way consistent with all other New Testament usages, none of which are related explicitly to the Jubilee.[97] Indeed, it seems ἄφεσις entered the vocabulary of New Testament authors with a precise and exclusive meaning, centered on the forgiveness of sins. It is therefore of little wonder that the word is found in texts connected to salvation (Luke 1:77; 3:3; 4:18; 24:47; Acts 2:38; 5:31; 10:43; 13:38; 26:18), which Luke considered to be equivalent to participating in the reign of God. As a prelude to the detailed examination of selected texts in Luke to test these conclusions, I now turn to an analysis of the key background text (Isa 61) for those who argue for the programmatic nature of the Jubilee in Luke's Gospel.

---

96. This has significant implications when one considers Hays's criterion of historical plausibility.

97. As mentioned above, ἀφίημι was not used in connection with the Jubilee in the Old Testament either, and there is no literary evidence to demonstrate that it ever developed Jubilee connotations.

4

The *Basileia* Proclaimed, Explained, and Fulfilled

Isaiah 61 and Luke

Introduction

Passages in Luke-Acts which cite or allude to Isaiah 61 are of central importance in determining the presence or absence of Lukan references to the Jubilee.[1] Indeed, as Ringe has stated, "The principal points of contact between OT Jubilee traditions and the NT are the quotations and paraphrases of Isa 61:1–2 (and related oracles)."[2] Since the Isaianic text refers to the Jubilee (see chapter 1), it is frequently assumed that Luke was similarly drawing on Jubilee motifs or imagery. Sloan goes so far as to state that the reason why Luke used Isaiah 61 was precisely because of its relationship with the Jubilee.[3] It is therefore important to ascertain how early traditions (which may have influenced Luke and its implied audience) interpreted and/or applied Isaiah 61. This is one of the purposes of this chapter. The chapter will also survey how Isaiah 61 was used throughout Luke (and Acts). This will include an exploration into the likelihood of the text being shaped by the Jubilee and/or God's *basileia*.

---

1. The texts which are most often associated with Isa 61 are Luke 4:16–30; 6:20–26; 7:18–35; and Acts 10:34–43.
2. Ringe, "Jubilee Proclamation," 290.
3. Sloan, *Favorable Year*, 115.

Early Isaiah 61 Traditions

The Rabbinic Literature

There are several rabbinic references to Isaiah 61:1-2 worth mentioning.[4] The Mekhilta to Exodus mentions Isaiah 61 alongside some other texts in order to demonstrate the humility of Moses.[5] Similarly, ʿAbodah Zarah states that meekness is the greatest of the virtues and uses Isaiah 61:1 as evidence, since the speaker brings good news to those who are meek (לְבַשֵּׂר עֲנָוִים).[6] Isaiah 61:1 is also quoted in the Midrash to Leviticus to support the argument that prophets received their gift of prophecy from the Holy One. The same verse is also cited in the Midrash to Lamentations, where the Holy Spirit is mentioned in relation to the redemption of the end time.[7] And finally, in the Targum of Pseudo Jonathan on Numbers 25:12, Isaiah 61:1 is associated with Malachi 3:1 in reference to the eschatological mission of Elijah who would announce the coming of the messiah.[8]

One study which surveys all references to Isaiah 61 in early Jewish sources is Larrimore Crockett's doctoral dissertation.[9] In addition to the humility highlighted in the Mekhilta to Exodus mentioned above, he also linked Daniel 7:14-18 with Isaiah 57:15 and 61:1 such that those who "inherit the land" (Isa 57:13b; 61:7) are those who will "receive the kingdom" (Dan 7:18), and the "poor" and "contrite in spirit" (Isa 57:15; 61:1) are the "saints of the Most High God (Dan 7:18), which he then associated with the first Matthean beatitude ("Blessed are the poor in spirit, for theirs is the kingdom of heaven").[10] Crockett also explored the use of Isaiah 61 in the Leviticus Rabbah Midrash, where the prophet is told that his mission to the children of Israel will mean rejection and degradation, before Isaiah 61:1 is cited to highlight the Spirit of God on Isaiah and his anointing for God's mission (as mentioned above).[11] Crockett's overall summary of the Jewish

---

4. Sanders notes that Isa 61:1 is cited nine times through Ibn Bakudah, though many of these are passing references with no real interest in the Isaianic text. See Sanders, "Isaiah 61," 53.

5. Mek. Exod 20:21.

6. ʿAbod. Zar. 20b.

7. Mid. Lam 3:49-50 (73a). Elias notes similarities between this text and the Yalkut Makiri. Elias, "Beginning," 135.

8. Elias, "Beginning," 135.

9. Crockett, "Old Testament," 248-76.

10. Matt 5:3. Crockett, "Old Testament," 269-71. Luke's version of this beatitude (6:20) can be similarly linked to the Isaianic text.

11. See Lev Rab 10:2. Crockett, "Old Testament," 273-75.

Midrashic treatment of Isaiah 61 is compelling: he sees the Isaianic speaker as one who "sees ahead to the last days in the specific sense of knowing that his mission to Israel will mean humiliation and rejection."[12]

Overall, it seems that the rabbinic literature increasingly presented Isaiah 61 as having eschatological importance.[13] That is, the original Isaianic release from the diaspora was increasingly viewed as being relevant to the Roman context. It is also clear that the speaker was viewed as a prophet (particularly in the Targum Isaiah) who would serve Israel and whose mission would end in rejection. There is not, however, any clear evidence in the rabbinic literature that the speaker in Isaiah 61 was interpreted messianically, though this is unsurprising given the general lack of messianic references in the Mishnah (there are only two)[14] and the lack of a systematic approach to the topic[15]—nor is there any evidence that the Jubilee was specifically associated with the text.

The parallels with the rabbinic traditions and Luke's use of Isaiah 61 are clear. The eschatological use of Isaiah 61 is evident in Luke-Acts, particularly in Luke 4:18–21 where Jesus reads from Isaiah 61:1–2 and then states that the text has been "fulfilled." Jesus' role as a prophet is also evident (Luke 4:24; 7:16; 24:19; Acts 3:22; 7:37), as is his rejection during the passion narrative (see particularly Luke 9:22; 17:25; 20:17). The episode at Nazareth (Luke 4:16–30) where Jesus reads from Isaiah 61 acts this out in miniature—after reading from the text, Jesus refers to himself as a prophet (4:24) and is rejected by the synagogue crowd (4:28–30). Part of the reason for his rejection was no doubt because Jesus' ministry included gentiles (4:25–27), in direct contradiction to the rabbinic traditions which focused on the Isaianic speaker's ministry to Israel (see the following chapter). In contrast to the rabbinic material, it is clear that Luke also viewed the text as having messianic significance. Indeed, the passage is used on three occasions to identify Jesus as the promised messiah (Luke 4:16–30; 7:18–35; Acts 10:34–43).

The Dead Sea Scrolls

In contrast to the rabbinic literature which focused on Midrashic exegesis, the community at Qumran frequently employed pesher exegesis. That is, they interpreted and applied Scriptures as being fulfilled or about to be

---

12. Crockett, "Old Testament," 276.
13. Sanders, "Isaiah 61," 54.
14. Evans, "Mishna and Messiah," 275.
15. Neusner, "Messianic Themes," 366.

fulfilled in their present context. It is this pesher exegesis, practiced by the Qumran community, which is of great significance for interpreting the New Testament (particularly Luke's work), since a recurring motif in the use of the Old Testament in the New is that past prophecies are now being fulfilled (sometimes again) through Jesus' person and ministry.[16] A clear example of this is Jesus' application of Isaiah 61:1-2 to himself in Luke 4:21: "Today this Scripture has been fulfilled in your hearing."

Both the Rule of the Community (1QS) and the War Scroll (1QM) refer to the "day of vengeance" (Isa 61:2b). In the Rule of the Community, the writer makes clear that the Instructor at Qumran will be one who will seek and delight in God's will and who will welcome the coming vengeance.[17] Sanders notes that this text is an example of the dual aspect of the "year of the Lord" as understood at Qumran. It was to be a time of bliss for all who were part of the true Israel and damnation for those who were "men of the pit."[18] In the War Scroll, the day of vengeance is again briefly mentioned as a way of describing the coming eschatological battle between the sons of light and the sons of darkness.[19] Thus both texts refer to the day of vengeance eschatologically—it is a time when those who oppose God will be conquered and those who follow him will enjoy peace under his reign. Given that the day of vengeance is noticeably absent from every Lukan allusion to Isaiah 61, however, it seems unlikely that the Rule of the Community and the War Scroll were of primary importance in Luke's understanding of Isaiah 61. This is particularly the case given that both scrolls do not mention Isaiah 61:1-2a (the verses which are Luke's focus). That is not to say that Luke was purposefully avoiding the subject of vengeance, as there are several occasions where Jesus is presented as proclaiming the coming judgment (Luke 18:7; 19:43-44; 21:22). None of these occurrences, however, are linked to Isaiah 61.

The association between the Thanksgiving Hymns (1QHa) and Isaiah 61:1-3 has long been recognized.[20] In 1QHa 18:14-15 there are multiple parallels to the Isaianic text: the speaker states that he is a messenger of goodness; that he will proclaim mercy to the meek and the contrite; and that he will announce a message of joy for those who mourn. It is, however, unclear as to who the speaker is, so it is difficult to determine the degree to

---

16. Elias, "Beginning," 141.
17. 1QS 9:21-23; 10:19-21.
18. 1QS 9:22; 10:20; Sanders, "Isaiah 61," 55.
19. 1QM 7:5.
20. Elias, "Beginning," 142.

which Luke's portrayal of Jesus is analogous to the speaker in the Qumran scroll.[21]

As has already been mentioned in chapter 2, 11Q13 also features Isaiah 61:1–2. In this scroll, the writer presents Melchizedek as an agent of redemption and judgment who will bring deliverance at the time of the tenth Jubilee. A pesher hermeneutic of Isaiah 61:1–2 is employed to describe Melchizedek as a messenger who will proclaim the eschatological freedom of the people of God. His identity and qualifications are described in the language of Isaiah 61:1—he is a herald of good tidings who is anointed by the spirit for his work.[22] Though the text of Isaiah 61:1–2 is not explicitly quoted, it is "woven into the fabric of the commentary material."[23] 11Q13 refers to captives (line 4), a proclamation of liberty (line 6), a year of grace (line 9), the vengeance of God (line 13), the anointing by the Spirit of a messenger (line 18), and the pronouncement of comfort for the afflicted (line 20), all of which are paralleled in the Isaianic text. The author also cites Leviticus 25:13, Psalms 7:8–9 and 82:1–2, Deuteronomy 15:2, and Isaiah 52:7 in relation to different sections of Isaiah 61:1–2 in order to demonstrate that the author's argument is supported by all of the Scriptures.

There are many scholars who argue that 11Q13 is of great importance in relation to the interpretation of Luke's work.[24] Indeed, it is precisely because of the suggested relationship between 11Q13 and Luke's use of Isaiah 61 in 4:18–19 (which is a programmatic text for Luke's Gospel) that the Jubilee has been highlighted as a key Lukan motif.[25] There are, however, several reasons why one should be cautious in associating the scroll with Luke-Acts.

Firstly, the Qumran scroll has as one of its emphases the anointed servant's role in carrying out the vengeance of God.[26] As has been mentioned above, however, Luke never employed Isaiah 61 in a context where vengeance or judgment are present (though he did address the subject of judgment on several occasions). (Indeed, the "day of vengeance" text is very

---

21. Collins states that the speaker may "plausibly be identified as the Teacher of Righteousness"; however, ultimately this is uncertain. Collins, "Herald," 231.

22. 11Q13 2.6, 18. See also Miller, "Function," 468–69.

23. Miller, "Function," 469.

24. Bruno, "Jesus is our Jubilee," 95; Kimball, *Jesus' Exposition*, 103; Ford, *My Enemy is My Guest*, 56–59; Garland, *Luke*, 200; Marshall, *The Gospel of Luke*, 182; Betz, *Jesus, der Messias Israels*, 260–62; Pilgrim, *Good News to the Poor*, 71; and De Jonge and Van Der Woude, "11Q Melchizedek," 309–10.

25. See, for example, Bruno, who only includes 11QMelch in his references to pertinent Second Temple literature. Bruno, "Jesus is our Jubilee," 94–95.

26. For explicit mentions of vengeance, see 11Q13 2.13 and 3.7.

obviously left unread by Jesus in Luke's account and is thus *not* part of what is fulfilled "this day." Secondly, in the Lukan text, there is also no mention of Melchizedek, Belial, or the Jubilee, all of which feature heavily in 11Q13. Thirdly, the fragmentary state of the scroll should not be overlooked. There are few firm conclusions which one can make about how the scroll should be understood, which makes it very difficult to determine if and how it might have influenced authors such as Luke.[27] Fourthly, the nature of 11Q13 identifies it as a scroll exclusively for the Qumran cult, which highlights both the difference between it and Luke's text (which emphasizes universal salvation) and the unlikelihood that Luke would have had access to the text. Fifthly, 11Q13 emphasizes that salvation is for the "sons of God" (2.14), who are "the small group of faithful Jews for whom the author writes his Midrash."[28] Those who were not part of the community were to be judged and then punished as objects of God's vengeance. On two of the occasions when Luke-Acts refers to Isaiah 61, the beneficiaries of the ministry of the Isaianic speaker (Jesus) are explicitly identified as Jews and gentiles (Luke 4:16–30; Acts 10:34–43). It could, no doubt, be argued that this difference was intentional. That is, Luke's audience might have been familiar with a tradition similar to 11Q13, and therefore the inclusion of gentiles as beneficiaries of the Isaiah 61 prophecy could have been a powerful polemical tool. As has been noted above, however, the rabbinic traditions also viewed the beneficiaries of the Isaianic speaker's ministry as being limited to Israel, so there is no need to recourse to 11Q13 to validate this possibility. In sum, the differences in how Isaiah 61 is used in 11Q13 and Luke-Acts make it highly unlikely that Luke was dependent in any way on this Qumran scroll.

4Q521 (the Messianic Apocalypse) also provides insight into the Qumran community's understanding of Isaiah 61:1–2. While there are again significant portions of the text missing, it seems that the scroll describes events that were expected to occur in the eschatological messianic era.[29] Unlike 11Q13, however, there is no mention of (or allusion to) the Jubilee. When the text was first published, parallels between it and Luke 7:22 (and Matt 11:5) were quickly identified.[30] Since Luke 7:22 and Matt 11:5 are often viewed as being sourced from Q 7.22, it has been thought that the author/s of Q were aware of the Qumran scroll.[31] While this is possible,

---

27. Kratz also argues that there is room for improvement in the hermeneutical methodologies applied to the Dead Sea Scrolls. Kratz, "Das Alte Testament," 198–213.

28. De Jonge and Van Der Woude, "11Q Melchizedek," 312.

29. Wise et al., *The Dead Sea Scrolls*, 421.

30. The first scholars to note the parallel were M. D. Wise and J. D. Tabor. See Evans, "Jesus," 96.

31. See, for example, Evans, "Jesus," 96.

there are also remarkable similarities between the scroll and the quotation of Isaiah 61 in Luke 4:18–19, as can be seen below:

Isa 35	Isa 61	4Q521	Luke 4:18–19	Luke 7:22
	The spirit of the Lord God is upon me,		"The Spirit of the Lord is upon me	
	because the Lord has anointed me;	The heavens and earth will listen to his anointed one.	because he has anointed me	
	he has sent me to bring good news to the oppressed,	He will proclaim good news to the poor,	to preach good news to the poor.	The good news is preached to the poor,
	to heal the brokenhearted,	he will heal the badly wounded,		
	to proclaim liberty to the captives	freeing prisoners,	He has sent me to proclaim release to the captives	
The eyes of the blind will be opened.	and release to the prisoners (Septuagint = "the blind"),	giving sight to the blind,	and recovery of sight to the blind,	the blind receive sight,
				those who have leprosy are cured,
The ears of the deaf will be unstopped.				the deaf hear,
The lame will leap like a deer.				the lame walk,
		straightening out the twisted.		
			to let the oppressed go free,	
		He will make the dead live.		the dead are raised.

Isa 35	Isa 61	4Q521	Luke 4:18-19	Luke 7:22
	to proclaim the year of the Lord's favor.		to proclaim the year of the Lord's favor."	

Table 1: A Comparison between the text of 4Q521 and texts in Isaiah and Luke

Of all the Dead Sea Scrolls which refer to Isaiah 61, it is this scroll which seems to be most consistent with what is seen in Luke's work. Aside from the textual similarities, there are also similarities in how the text is interpreted. Neither Luke-Acts nor 4Q521 limit the beneficiaries of the Isaianic prophecy to Israel. 4Q521 states that those who will be ministered to are "the pious" (2 II, 5 and 2 II, 7), while in Acts 10:35 Luke defined the beneficiaries as those "from every nation who fear [God] and do what is right." 4Q521 attributes the redemptive Isaianic ministry to the Lord himself (though it could equally well be understood as the work of a herald or prophet who attributes all work to God).[32] The Lukan presentation of Jesus as the Isaianic figure who achieves redemption corresponds to this. As Collins has noted, 4Q521 establishes a messianic *Gestalt* which describes the activities of a coming prophetic messiah.[33] The interpretation of the text by Jesus clearly accords with this messianic expectation.

It also seems possible that Luke may have had access to a tradition with similar messianic expectations to 4Q521.[34] Unlike 11Q13, there is "nothing in 4Q521 that points to a sectarian origin, and the motif of resurrection rather suggests that the text did not originate in the same community as the sectarian scrolls."[35] That is, it is possible that a tradition similar to the scroll's tradition was widely accessible and that the original Gospel writers and readers may have had access to it.[36] This is particularly likely for Luke, who may have been influenced by Qumran documents more than the other Synoptic authors.[37]

If Luke was indeed influenced by a similar tradition to 4Q521 in his understanding of Isaiah 61, there are far-reaching consequences for this study. Firstly, it establishes a clear link between Isaiah 61 and the *basileia* of

---

32. Collins, "Works," 101-2 and Collins, "Herald," 234-35. See also Neirynck, "Q 6,20b-21," 51-58.
33. Collins, *Scepter*, 131-35.
34. Brooke, *Dead Sea Scrolls*, 14 and Strathearn, "4Q521," 396-97.
35. Collins, "Herald," 238.
36. Wise et al., *The Dead Sea Scrolls*, 420.
37. Brooke, *Dead Sea Scrolls*, 158-65.

God, since 4Q521 states that the beneficiaries of the Isaianic prophecy will be included in God's *basileia*: "For he will honor the pious upon the throne of an eternal kingdom, freeing prisoners, giving sight to the blind . . ."[38] It also removes the perceived need to link the text with the Jubilee traditions. The Qumran scroll not only excludes references to the word "Jubilee," it also omits Isa 61:2a ("to proclaim the year of the Lord's favor"), which is the most explicit Isaianic reference to the Jubilee.

Other Sources

In considering what traditions may have influenced Luke, one must also consider Luke's own immediate sources, which were "handed down to us by those who from the first were eyewitnesses and servants of the word" (Luke 1:2). Q is particularly pertinent to this section since reconstructions of the Q material include Luke 6:20-21 and 7:18-23, both of which are passages that contain allusions to Isaiah 61.[39] According to Tuckett, Isaiah 61:1-2 was a particularly important text within the Q corpus.[40] Indeed, he argues that the entire teaching of Jesus seems to be placed "under the over-arching rubric of the affirmation and re-presentation of the promises made in Isa. 61:1-2."[41] For Q, Jesus was the eschatological prophet of Isaiah 61:1-2 who brought good news to the poor and affirmed and reaffirmed to them that the *basileia* of God would be theirs.[42] Luke's use of Q and his references to Isaiah 61 at key places in his narrative would suggest he was influenced by this view.

There is also general consensus that Luke followed the Septuagint in a form similar to what is available today.[43] With regard to Isaiah 61, Luke's dependence on the Greek text is seen most clearly in Luke 4:18-19 where the

---

38. 4Q521 2 II, 7-8.

39. Mack, *The Lost Gospel*, 260; Neirynck, "Q 6,20b-21," 27-64; Tuckett, "Isaiah in Q," 53-57; and Hoffman, "Vom Freudenboten," 87-106. Schürmann has argued that these two texts reflect a later insertion into Q, at which time the Nazareth discourse (Luke 4:16-30) was also inserted. Schürmann, *Das Lukasevangelium*, 234.

40. Tuckett, "Isaiah in Q," 57.

41. Tuckett, "Isaiah in Q," 57.

42. Tuckett, "Isaiah in Q," 57.

43. That is not to say that he quoted the LXX verbatim, as there are times when he clearly departs from the LXX either intentionally or possibly inadvertently. These redactions can, at times, give some indication of Luke's doctrinal positions and literary purposes. Scholars who see the LXX as Luke's source text include: Bock, *Proclamation*, 16; Bovon, *Luke the Theologian*, 111; Kimball, *Jesus' Exposition*, 16; Mallen, *Isaiah in Luke-Acts*, 73; and Goulder, *Luke*, 1:203-4.

text is almost identical to the Septuagint (see chapter 5). It is possible that he may have relied on an early Christian compilation of Old Testament texts which included references to Old Testament passages (including Isaiah 61) which were considered to be testimonies to Christianity (the Testimonia), though this is by no means certain.[44]

Summary of Findings

When one considers the above survey, a number of observations can be made. Firstly, in a similar way to Luke's narrative, many of the early Isaiah 61 traditions interpreted the prophecy eschatologically. It is the Dead Sea Scrolls with their frequent pesher exegesis, however, which correspond most closely to Luke's approach to Old Testament texts (including Isaiah). The Tg. Isa., some of the rabbinic literature, some of the Dead Sea Scrolls, and Q expect the eschatological Isaianic agent of redemption to be a prophet. This resounds with Jesus' self-description as a prophet ("no prophet is accepted in his hometown") after the Isaiah 61 synagogue reading in Luke 4. While the eschatological Isaianic prophet's messiahship is not clear in the Old Testament text/s or the rabbinic literature, 4Q521 and Q both view the speaker in Isaiah 61:1-2 to be Israel's messiah. With regard to the beneficiaries of the prophet's ministry, there is a correlation between the rabbinic Mekhilta to Exodus and Q, both of which emphasize the poor over other possible beneficiaries from the Isaianic text. Interestingly, there is no evidence of any Second Temple tradition where the beneficiaries are explicitly mentioned as those outside of Israel. On the contrary, many of the rabbinic texts and

---

44. The original proponent of this theory, James Rendel Harris, argued that Isa 61:1-2 was included in the testimony book because it is a christological text which highlights the personhood of Jesus. After Harris, C. H. Dodd substantially reworked Harris's thesis, arguing instead that the *testimonia* was a system of Old Testament interpretation and an oral tradition that provides the framework for New Testament theology. Dodd argued that although "it is only in Luke 4:18-19 that Isaiah 61:1-2 is expressly quoted, it seems to be treated as a source of testimonia in the kerygmatic passage of Acts 10, which almost certainly rests upon an earlier tradition, and in the 'Q' stratum of Matthew and Luke, which, whether or not it had the character of a documentary source, also represents an early independent tradition." See Dodd, *According to the Scriptures*, 53 and 126. Hodgson has since argued that the Isaianic text quoted in Luke 4:18-19 may have had its origin in the testimony tradition, which, he argues, means that the concepts of the apostolic office and the gospel are ultimately derived from the *testimonia*. Hodgson, "The Testimony Hypothesis," 375. The *testimonia* hypothesis has received a mixed reaction; there are some scholars who deny its claims and others who firmly accept the hypothesis. In any case, it is difficult to posit the degree to which Luke may have used the *testimonia* (if it existed) and whether it impacted his hermeneutical methodology.

Dead Sea Scrolls explicitly cite Israel as being the recipients of the prophet's ministry, which may help to explain the reaction of the synagogue crowd in Luke 4:28-29 and that of the Jewish leaders in Luke 7:34.

Furthermore, contrary to what has frequently been presumed, it seems highly unlikely that Luke was dependant on 11Q13. This has far-reaching consequences, since of all the Second Temple literature, it is only this document which explicitly links Isaiah 61:1-2 with the biblical Jubilee (see chapter 2). Since Luke was almost certainly influenced by traditions other than 11Q13, there is no necessary need to link his references to Isaiah 61 with the Jubilee. Similarly, there is no need to presume that he viewed the biblical Jubilee as having an intrinsic link to God's *basileia*, or that he used it to illustrate or emphasize aspects of the *basileia*. Indeed, none of the traditions which are likely to have influenced Luke make this connection.

It does, however, seem likely that Luke associated Isaiah 61 with the *basileia* of God. As Crockett has noted, some of the rabbinic references to Isaiah 61 can be read in connection to Daniel 7:14-18, which explicitly refers to God's *basileia*. In reconstructions of Q (which was probably one of Luke's sources), Isaiah 61:1-2 is again linked with the *basileia*. Most important, however, is the Dead Sea Scroll 4Q521, which draws attention to the beneficiaries of the Isaianic speaker's ministry as those who will partake in the *basileia* of God. As has been outlined above, there are remarkable similarities between how that Qumran text and Luke's narrative employ the Isaiah 61 prophecy. It seems possible that Luke was influenced by this scroll (or a similar tradition), particularly when one considers the similarities between Luke's treatment of Old Testament prophecies and the Qumran pesher exegesis. It therefore seems reasonable to conclude that, since the Isaiah 61 traditions available to Luke would have connected the Isaianic prophecy with God's *basileia*, he also would have made this connection. As has been stated earlier (see chapter 1), this is also consistent with the Isaianic text itself, which frequently highlights the reign of God.

Significantly, the above observations are supported by other early church writings. There is no clear association made between Isaiah 61 and the Jubilee in any early church documents.[45] Rather, Isaiah 61:1-2 was

---

45. See, for example, the *Epistle of Barnabas*, where the author argues (particularly from chapter 4 onwards) that God has fulfilled his covenantal promises to the patriarchs through the message and ministry of Jesus, and that Christians are free from the Mosaic regulations. The author refers to many Old Testament texts to support his case, and in chapter 14 he cites Isaiah 61:1-2a as part of his case. There is no reference or allusion to the Jubilee. Instead, the author uses the text to argue that Jesus, "having suffered on our behalf, hath given it [the new testament of the Lord] to us, that we should be the people of inheritance." *Epistle of Barnabas* 14 (*ANF* 1:146, 147).

Similarly, in Irenaeus's *Haer.*, Isa 61 is cited on four occasions, none of which refer to

largely employed in early church texts to elucidate and defend Jesus' *basileia* ministry. It seems unlikely that Luke's literary purposes would have been ignored or misconstrued by the time of these later Christian authors, particularly given the programmatic importance of the allusions to Isaiah 61 in the Luke-Acts corpus. It is far more likely that Luke, like other early Christian authors, did not explicitly associate Isaiah 61 with the Jubilee. Rather, the evidence in these first-century traditions and the exegetical evidence in the Luke-Acts corpus (see below) support the notion that Luke connected the text with Jesus' proclamation of the *basileia* of God.

Luke's Use of Isaiah 61

References to Isaiah play a particularly important role in the unfolding of Luke's narrative and the Luke-Acts corpus. Indeed, the number, accuracy and locations of Isaianic quotations, from the infancy narratives through to the final scene in Acts, all suggest that the Lukan tradition deliberately focuses its attention on Isaiah to clarify certain theological themes and to support its literary purposes.[46] Within the Isaianic corpus, chapter 61 is one of Luke's favorite texts. In particular, Luke focuses on Isaiah 61:1-2a. While the text is only quoted once (Luke 4:18-19), it is explicitly referenced on several other occasions.[47] More importantly, the locations and manner in which Luke employs Isaiah 61 underscore its significance within Luke-Acts. The use of the Isaiah 61 quotation in Luke 4:18-19, for example, has long been recognized as a programmatic description of Jesus' mission and ministry.[48] Similarly, in Luke 7:21-22, the text is used to summarize Jesus'

---

the Jubilee. See Irenaeus, *Against Heresies* 2.22 (*ANF* 1:1005-06); 3.9.3 (*ANF* 1:1078); 3.17.1 (*ANF* 1:1121); and 4.23.1 (*ANF* 1:1230). In fact, as O'Brien has noted, even when Irenaeus discussed themes such as the "inheritance of corruption" and the "new covenant of liberty" which could easily have lent themselves to Jubilean interpretation, he made no mention of the Jubilee legislation. Irenaeus, *Against Heresies* 3.12.14 (*ANF* 1:1102-03) and O'Brien, "Comparison," 440.

While a detailed investigation into all of the early church literature which cites Isa 61 is beyond the scope of this study, it is evident that Isa 61 was not associated with the Jubilee year. Indeed, as appendix 2 demonstrates, no early church references to the Jubilee mentioned or alluded to Isa 61.

46. Mallen, *Isaiah in Luke-Acts*, 198.

47. The clearest allusions are Luke 6:17-20; 7:18-35; and Acts 10:34-43. There are, however, many other occasions where an association with Isa 61 is evident. These are discussed below.

48. Scholars who have recognized Luke 4:16-30 as a programmatic text include: Marshall, *The Gospel of Luke*, 177-78; Craddock, *Luke*, 61; Metzger, *Consumption and Wealth*, 25; Green, *Theology*, 76; Hill, "Rejection," 170; Tannehill, "The Mission of Jesus," 51; Green, *Luke*, 207; Ellis, *The Gospel of Luke*, 95-96; Garland, *Luke*, 189; Sabourin, *St*

ministry in response to doubts from John. In Acts 10:38, Isaiah 61 is referenced as part of Peter's speech about Jesus to Cornelius and his relatives and friends—the point in Luke's narrative where attention is turned to the gentile mission. It is beyond reasonable doubt that Luke specifically chose and highlighted Isaiah 61 as a central Old Testament text which exemplified Jesus' identity and ministry. The following section will therefore address how Luke interpreted and employed the various sections of Isaiah 61:1–2a.

Isaiah 61:1–2a[49]

πνεῦμα κυρίου ἐπ' ἐμέ οὗ εἵνεκεν ἔχρισέν με	The Spirit of the Lord is upon me because he has anointed me
εὐαγγελίσασθαι πτωχοῖς ἀπέσταλκέν με	he has sent me to bring good news to the poor,
ἰάσασθαι τοὺς συντετριμμένους τῇ καρδίᾳ	to heal the brokenhearted,
κηρύξαι αἰχμαλώτοις ἄφεσιν	to proclaim release to the captives
καὶ τυφλοῖς ἀνάβλεψιν	and recovery of sight to the blind
καλέσαι ἐνιαυτὸν κυρίου δεκτὸν	to proclaim the acceptable year of the Lord

Table 2: Text and Translation of Isa 61:1–2a

Luke, 135; Blosser, "Jubilee," 147; Tiede, Luke, 101; Wilson, Gentiles, 40; Falcetta, The Call of Nazareth, 12; Spencer, Rhetorical Texture, 6; Tiede, Prophecy & History, 19; Rice, "Thematic Use," 54–55; Abogunrin, "Declaration at Nazareth," 227; Anderson, "Horizons," 260; Kimball, "Jesus' Exposition," 180; Busse, Das Nazareth-Manifest Jesu, 77–81; Talbert, Reading Luke, 57; Lieu, The Gospel of Luke, 31; Johnson, Luke, 81; Carroll, Luke, 116; Byrne, Hospitality, 45; Bock, Theology, 136; Rowe, Early Narrative Christology, 78–80; Kodell, "Luke's Gospel in a Nutshell," 18; Caird, The Gospel of Luke, 86; Tannehill, Narrative Unity, 62; Bruno, "Jesus is our Jubilee," 84; Brawley, Luke-Acts and the Jews, 12; Rodgers, "Luke 4:16–30," 81; Schweizer, Good News, 84; Mallen, Isaiah in Luke-Acts, 299; Koet, Five Studies, 24; Evans, Saint Luke, 267; Stein, Luke, 152; Nolland, Luke, 195; Hartsock, Sight and Blindness in Luke-Acts, 174; Elias, "Beginning," 1–3; Sanders, Jews, 165; Busse, Die Wunder des Propheten Jesus, 58; Völkel, "'Reiches Gottes' bei Lukas," 63–65; Evans, "Function," 76; Vinson, Luke, 116; Willoughby, "Concept of Jubilee", 42; and Schreck, "Nazareth Pericope," 399.

49. As has already been mentioned, Luke uses the Septuagint when referring to Isaiah. While Luke amended Isa 61:1–2a slightly in the quotation in Luke 4:18–19 (see the next chapter), this section will address the Septuagintal version of text.

Πνεῦμα κυρίου ἐπ' ἐμέ οὗ εἵνεκεν ἔχρισέν με

On several occasions, Luke presented Jesus as fulfilling the role of the Isaianic speaker (Luke 4:18–21; 7:21–22; Acts 10:37–38). He is referred to as being anointed by God on three occasions (Luke 4:18; Acts 4:27; 10:38), and the activity of the Spirit in his life is seen throughout Luke's work (Luke 1:15, 35; 3:22; 4:1 (twice), 14, 18; 10:21; Acts 1:2; 10:38). Importantly, Luke often denotes the Holy Spirit's chief work as enabling the proclamation of the *basileia* of God.[50] As in Isaiah 61, therefore, the Spirit of the Lord resting on Jesus is what enables and testifies to his ministry, which in Luke-Acts centers on the proclamation of God's *basileia*.

While there is no doubt that Jesus was presented as the Isaianic speaker, there is no clear consensus as to how the Lukan tradition may have viewed this figure. There are at least six proposals for the speaker's identity:

1. The eschatological prophet
2. The messiah
3. A priestly messiah
4. A combination of the eschatological prophet and the messiah
5. A combination of the eschatological prophet and the Isaianic servant
6. A combination of the eschatological prophet, the messiah, and the servant[51]

While there continues to be scholarly disagreement over which figure/s is in view, it seems likely that Luke viewed Jesus in prophetic terms, given the close textual connection between two of the main references to Isaiah 61 and Jesus' identity as a prophet.[52] Additionally, Luke may have been influenced by documents such as Tg. Isa., which emphasize the Isaianic speaker as being a prophet. It is also likely that Luke viewed the Isaianic speaker as the messiah, given Luke's likely access to the scroll 4Q521 which associates Isaiah 61 with an eschatological messiah.[53] Similarly, Luke may have con-

---

50. Cho, "Spirit and Kingdom," 173–97.

51. There are no doubt other views which have also been proposed. This summary has been limited to six views and is based on Charles Kimball's survey. See Kimball, *Jesus' Exposition*, 111–12.

52. The Isaianic quotation in Luke 4:18–19 is closely followed by references to prophets to whom Jesus is compared (Luke 4:24–27), and the reference to Isa 61 in Luke 7:21–22 is closely preceded by Jesus being identified as "a great prophet" (Luke 7:16). This is consistent with Luke's wider presentation of Jesus, which also identifies him as a prophet (see, for example, Luke 13:33 and 24:19).

53. Additionally, the juxtaposition of Isa 58:6 with Isa 61:1–2 in Luke 4:18–19 also

nected the anointing of the Isaianic figure (Isa 61:1) with a messiah, given the linguistic relationship between χρίω ("to anoint") and χριστός ("anointed one"/"messiah").[54] Finally, it is also possible that Luke had the servant figure in mind, since, as has been mentioned above, if Isaiah 61 is not a Servant Song, the Isaianic herald can still be pictured as the servant figure by drawing on earlier Isaianic associations (Isa 42:1–4; 49:1–11).[55] There is less evidence, however, to support the view that Jesus was intentionally depicted as the servant (and less again that Luke used Isaiah 61 to depict Jesus as the servant). Thus, it would seem Luke viewed the speaker of Isaiah 61 as being both prophetic and messianic, which is consistent with his portrayal of Jesus throughout the two-part corpus of Luke-Acts.

Εὐαγγελίσασθαι πτωχοῖς ἀπέσταλκέν με

In addition to presenting Jesus as the Isaianic speaker, Luke also describes Jesus' ministry using the language of Isaiah 61:1–2. The first act of the Isaianic speaker—being sent to proclaim good news to the poor (εὐαγγελίσασθαι πτωχοῖς ἀπέσταλκέν με)—is of central concern throughout Luke-Acts. Luke uses εὐαγγελίζω and πτωχοῖς much more than any other New Testament author.[56] Εὐαγγελίζω is used in a variety of ways: in connection with John's ministry (Luke 1:19; 3:18), Jesus' birth (Luke 2:10), the word (Acts 8:4; 15:35), repentance (Acts 14:15), Jesus' fulfillment of Old Testament prophecies (Acts 8:35; 13:32), and as a general reference to salvation through Jesus (Acts 5:42; 10:36; 11:20; 17:18). It is also, however, frequently used in connection with the *basileia* of God (Luke 4:43; 7:22–28; 8:1; 9:2–6; 16:16; Acts

---

supports the view that Jesus was to be viewed as a messianic liberation figure who would bring justice to the nation.

54. While Luke includes χρίω as part of the Isa 61 quotation in Luke 4:18 and the allusion to Isa 61 in Acts 10:38, it is difficult to determine whether he associated the word with the messiah. While he did juxtapose χριστοῦ ("messiah"/"anointed one") and ἔχρισας ("you anointed") in Acts 4:26–27, the natural sense of the anointing in the Isaianic text in Luke 4:18 is prophetic. Moreover, other uses of χρίω in the New Testament make clear that it does not necessarily have messianic connotations. Χρίω is used five times in the New Testament: Luke 4:18; Acts 4:27; 10:38; 2 Cor 1:21; and Heb 1:9. While four of these occasions are in reference to Jesus, in 2 Cor 1:21 the word is used to communicate the anointing of all Christians. Thus, while it seems likely that Luke viewed the Isaianic speaker as a messianic figure, the use of χρίω does not in itself prove this.

55. Bock, *Proclamation*, 108 and Koet, "Isaiah in Luke-Acts," 84.

56. Of the fifty-four uses of εὐαγγελίζω in the New Testament, it occurs twenty-five times in Luke-Acts (Luke 1:19; 2:10; 3:18; 4:18, 43; 7:22; 8:1; 9:6; 16:16; 20:1; Acts 5:42; 8:4, 12, 25, 35, 40; 10:36; 11:20; 13:32; 14:7, 15, 21; 15:35; 16:10; 17:18). Luke employed πτωχός ten times, all of which occur in the Gospel (Luke 4:18; 6:20; 7:22; 14:13, 21; 16:20, 22; 18:22; 19:8; 21:3).

8:12). Indeed, the nature of Luke's use of εὐαγγελίζω and its frequent links with the *basileia* of God has led Friedrich to conclude that "the task of Jesus was to proclaim the βασιλεία τοῦ θεοῦ."[57]

Luke uses πτωχός consistently throughout his Gospel to refer to those who are economically poor.[58] His references to the poor in passages which cite or allude to Isaiah 61, therefore, must be taken in that light. Aside from this primary meaning, however, it seems possible that he also understood πτωχός as including those who are spiritually poor.[59] It seems likely that

---

57. Friedrich, "εὐαγγελίζομαι," 707–21. Contra Sabourin, *St Luke*, 136, who argues that the *basileia* is not the epitome of the good news—Luke is more concerned with proclamation/evangelization. This is an unnecessary distinction; Luke frequently presents the message being proclaimed/evangelized *as being* the *basileia* of God (see the references in the text).

58. While there are two occasions where the context does not make it immediately obvious that Luke was using πτωχός to refer to those who are economically poor (Luke 4:18 and 6:20), the word's clear and consistent use throughout the remainder of Luke's Gospel make it clear that the word is best understood this way. Importantly, the two unclear uses of πτωχός are both part of texts which reference Isa 61:1. Luke 7:22, however, which is also a reference to Isa 61:1, makes it clear that πτωχός is employed to denote those who are economically poor.

59. Aside from the reasons given in the body of the text, there are several additional reasons why Luke may have viewed the poor as including those who are spiritually impoverished:

1. As Bailey has noted, there were some traditions in the first century which identified the poor as religious believers. Two examples include the Hymns of the Poor (4Q434), where the Qumran community equates being poor with piety, and the practice of some early Jewish Christians calling themselves the Ebionites (poor). Bailey, *Jesus through Middle Eastern Eyes*, 158–59.

2. Bock has shown that the use of ταπεινός ("humble") in Luke 1:52 is parallel to the poor in Luke's Gospel, which therefore demonstrates that a covenant relationship forms part of the backdrop to πτωχός. He also argues that in Luke 6:23, the poor are likened to the Old Testament prophets (that is, those who accepted and testified to the message of God) and the rich are likened to false prophets. Bock, *Luke*, 408.

3. In the Septuagint, πτωχός occurs nearly one hundred times and translates six Hebrew terms, the most common term being עָנִי, which has both socioeconomic and religious connotations. The עָנִי refers to those who are powerless and dependent, and who are therefore vulnerable to exploitation. Thus, even with regard to the socioeconomic connotation, the emphasis is on relationship (that is, one's dependent relationship to those in power) rather than whether or not one has material possessions *per se*. The humble posture of the עָנִי can therefore lend itself to exemplify those who depend on God and are devoid of any pretention (Pss 14:6; 22:24; 25:16; 34:6; 40:17; 69:29; 82:3; 86:1; 88:15). As Guelich has noted, "The poor in Judaism, referred to those in desperate need (socioeconomic element) whose helplessness drove them to a dependent relationship with God (religious element) for the supplying of their needs and vindication." See Guelich, *The Sermon on the Mount*, 68–69.

the captives, blind, and oppressed in the following lines are also to be understood metaphorically (at least in part), given that Jesus never liberated actual captives or those who were militarily oppressed.[60] In fact, as Green has noted, the captives, blind, and oppressed serve to clarify who the poor are. Indeed, seven of Luke's uses of πτωχός come as part of a list of adjectives which elucidate the wider meaning of the poor (Luke 4:18; 6:20; 7:22; 14:13, 21; 16:20, 22).[61] Moreover, as has been mentioned earlier, the Old Testament's presentation of the poor in Isa 61:1 includes religious connotations (without losing the basic meaning of economic deprivation).[62] Finally, when one considers that Luke presented the good news as the message of the *basileia* of God, it is clear that Luke did not view Jesus as isolating the message from those who had more money.[63] Nevertheless, it is clear that Luke primarily viewed the πτωχός as those who are genuinely poor.[64]

Interestingly, however, while the Lukan Jesus' teaching frequently focuses on the blessedness of being poor and the difficulties which accompany material wealth (see, for example, 12:13-21 and 16:19-31), there are no occasions where Luke explicitly states that Jesus actually verbally preached good news to the poor. Even when Jesus ministered to the poor in some other way, there is no explicit indication that the good news was verbally preached to those people at that time.[65] Nonetheless, Luke not only presented this as one of Jesus' ministry emphases, he also believed that Jesus accomplished it (see Luke 7:22). It therefore seems likely that Luke considered

---

60. One possible exception to this is the account of the Gerasene demoniac (Luke 8:26-39), which has recently been interpreted post-colonially. According to this reading, the "pigs" represent the Roman military, and the demoniac represents the conquered, colonized people. Jesus' ministry to the demoniac is therefore an example of Jesus bringing peace to those who are politically oppressed. See Arnold and McConnell, "Hijacked Humanity," 591-606. Even if one accepts this reading of the text, however, there nonetheless remains a definite difference between physical freedom from a military oppression and internal/emotional/spiritual release.

61. Green, "Good News," 68.

62. Heard, "Luke's Attitude," 50.

63. See, for example, Jesus' interaction with the tax collectors in Luke 5:27-32; 7:29-34; 15:1; and 19:1-10.

64. This may be because those who are literally poor often recognize their needs in the greatest way (in all facets of life) and are therefore the most likely to respond to Jesus' message. Bock, *Luke*, 408 and Green, "Good News," 62-4.

65. Even on the other occasions when Jesus healed people who weren't specifically identified as being poor, Luke does not clearly record the good news having being preached to those who were healed (Luke 4:38-40; 5:12-25; 6:6-10, 18-19; 7:1-10, 21-22; 8:43-46; 13:10-13; 14:1-4; 17:11-14; 18:35-43). There is, however, the possibility that "preaching" may have been considered unnecessary, if the poor had already responded in faith.

much of Jesus' audience to be the poor, even though he did not clearly designate them as such.

This is consistent with Luke's wider portrait of the recipients of the *basileia* of God. As mentioned in the previous chapter, Luke portrayed the *basileia* as being universally open, though practically biased toward the disadvantaged and marginalized. Given Luke's wider presentation of the *basileia* of God, it is little wonder that he chose Isaiah 61 to exemplify Jesus' proclamation of that *basileia*.

The sending (ἀποστέλλω) of the Isaianic speaker to preach good news to the poor also demonstrates Luke's association of Isaiah 61 with the *basileia* of God. After the Isaianic quotation in Luke 4:18-19, which twice mentions the Isaianic speaker being sent, the next (and only other) explicit occasion where Jesus is described as being sent in Luke's Gospel is in Luke 4:43, a text which emphasizes Jesus being sent to preach the good news of the *basileia* of God to other towns (καὶ ταῖς ἑτέραις πόλεσιν εὐαγγελίσασθαί με δεῖ τὴν βασιλείαν τοῦ θεοῦ, ὅτι ἐπὶ τοῦτο ἀπεστάλην). Similarly, Luke twice records Jesus sending out his disciples to proclaim the *basileia* of God (Luke 9:2 and 10:1-16). While there are lots of occasions where ἀποστέλλω is used in contexts other than the proclamation of the *basileia* of God, it is nonetheless clear that those who do proclaim the *basileia* have been sent, and this sense of being sent finds its Scriptural grounding in Isaiah 61:1.

ἰάσασθαι τοὺς συντετριμμένους τῇ καρδίᾳ

The healing of the brokenhearted is never explicitly mentioned in Luke-Acts, though the theme is evident through Luke's work. The Isaianic quotation in Luke 4:18-19 omits this line and inserts Isaiah 58:6 instead (see the next chapter). While Luke does employ ἰάομαι on fifteen occasions, it is usually associated with physical healing and is never used in connection with the healing of the brokenhearted, though of course the two may frequently overlap (Luke 5:17; 6:18, 19; 7:7; 8:47; 9:2, 11, 42; 14:4; 17:15; 22:51; Acts 9:34; 10:38; 28:8, 37). In Luke 9:39-42, however, Jesus heals (ἰάομαι) a possessed man who is described as being crushed (συντρίβω) by the demon. If this text is associated with Isaiah 61:1, it would suggest that the brokenhearted include those who were under the power of the devil. While this association is far from clear, it seems possible when one considers Acts 10:38—a text which clearly alludes to Isaiah 61—where Jesus is described as healing (ἰώμενος) those under the power of the devil. Moreover, as is demonstrated below, it is clear that the subsequent lines of the Isaianic text refer, at least in part, to the freeing of people from spiritual oppression.

Nevertheless, it is difficult to be certain that Luke viewed Jesus as fulfilling this Isaianic prophecy through his ministry of exorcism.

κηρύξαι αἰχμαλώτοις ἄφεσιν

While Luke only mentioned the freeing of captives (αἰχμαλώτοις) once (in the Isaianic quotation in Luke 4:18–19), it seems likely he viewed Jesus' ministry as accomplishing this through people being released from sin and demonic oppression. That is, Jesus' ministry accomplished spiritual release for people. There are a number of reasons for this:

1. The use of ἄφεσις, which Luke always used in contexts of spiritual release/forgiveness (see the previous chapter).

2. The freeing of captives (αἰχμαλώτοις) is only mentioned in the Nazareth pericope, which is immediately followed by the driving out of an evil spirit in Capernaum (Luke 4:31–37), thus illustrating (in part) Jesus' fulfillment of the Isaianic text.

3. Given that Luke's solitary use of αἰχμάλωτος is in a passage which is programmatic for Luke-Acts, one would expect to see Jesus' fulfillment of this text throughout the course of Luke's Gospel.[66]

4. Luke never presented Jesus as freeing people in actual physical captivity. In Luke 3, John the Baptist is left imprisoned, where he remained until his death (Luke 3:20). In fact, in Luke's Gospel, there is only Barabbas's actual release from captivity. Moreover, in Acts 16 and 27, prisoners are miraculously given the opportunity to escape, though they chose to remain incarcerated.[67] Indeed, as Dowling has noted, Luke was seemingly disinterested in addressing actual physical captivity.[68] His focus was instead on those in spiritual bondage.

---

66. Regarding Jesus' exorcism ministry, aside from the account of the man with the demon in Capernaum mentioned above, Luke also includes four other examples of Jesus exorcising a demon/demons out of people (Luke 8:26–39; 9:37–43; 11:14–16; 13:10–17). Four of Luke's statements summarizing Jesus' ministry also refer to his exorcism ministry (Luke 4:41; 6:18; 8:1–2; 13:32). For Luke, Jesus' ministry to those possessed by evil spirits was clearly of great significance. Similarly, Jesus' ministry of forgiveness was of central concern. See, for example, Luke 1:77; 5:17–24; 7:48–49; 23:34; and 24:47, as well as the section on Ἄφεσις and Ἀφίημι in Luke-Acts in the previous chapter.

67. Tuckett, "Luke 4,16–30," 348.

68. Dowling, "Slaves," 140.

Sloan has argued that Luke considered the word αἰχμάλωτος as having Jubilary import.[69] He believes that the word probably refers to those who have debilitating debts due to social and/or economic conditions.[70] He also argues that even if the αἰχμάλωτοι are understood to be prisoners of war (which is the literal meaning of the word), it still has relevance to the Jubilee since it evokes imagery of a nation of exiles (prisoners of war) returning to their homeland, paralleling Jubilee land restoration.[71] Both of these positions, however, ignore the Lukan literary purposes and context. Luke never presents Jesus as someone who frees people from social or economic debts, nor does he ever encourage or even mention land reclamation. When one considers the word's solitary appearance in the programmatic text in Luke 4, Sloan's argument seems even more untenable.

Once again, the word is better understood in relation to the *basileia* of God than the Jubilee. For Luke, forgiveness and repentance are connected so often that when one is mentioned, Luke presumes the other.[72] This is significant, since repentance is another way of expressing the dynamic reign of God in one's life (see the previous chapter). For Luke, to be forgiven is to enter the *basileia* of God. Similarly, as demonstrated above, Jesus' exorcism ministry and the reality of the presence of the *basileia* are closely linked, since the exorcisms themselves demonstrate the reign of God.[73] Finally, the Isaianic proclamation (κηρύσσω) of release to the captives is also important, since Luke frequently linked κηρύσσω with the *basileia* of God (Luke 4:43–44; 8:1; 9:2; Acts 20:25; 28:31). Thus, for Luke, the proclamation of freedom for the captives (that is, spiritual release from sin and Satan) was a clear expression of the reality of the presence of the *basileia* of God.

καὶ τυφλοῖς ἀνάβλεψιν

Throughout Luke-Acts, blindness and one's need for sight is used both literally and figuratively. Luke refers to those who are physically blind on several occasions (Luke 7:21; 14:13, 21; 18:35–43) and includes two specific instances of physical recovery of sight (Luke 18:35–43; Acts 9:9–19).[74]

69. Sloan, *Favorable Year*, 38.
70. Sloan, *Favorable Year*, 38.
71. Sloan, *Favorable Year*, 38–39.
72. Vinson, *Luke*, 14.
73. Evans, "Inaugurating," 49.
74. The account of Paul's sight being restored is actually recorded three times: Acts 9:1–19; 22:6–13; and 26:13–18. Interestingly, this final account does not mention Paul's physical healing, though Paul does mention the "opening of eyes" in a figurative way

The figurative use of blindness is employed in a parable (Luke 6:39) to denote a person experiencing salvation (Luke 1:79; 3:6; Acts 26:17–18) and to express a person understanding (or not understanding) God's plan of salvation being achieved through Jesus (Luke 24:31; Acts 28:27).[75] Indeed, as Green has noted, the recovery of sight is often "presented as a metaphor for receiving revelation and experiencing salvation and inclusion in God's family."[76] Since this is the case, one might also say that gaining figurative sight is equivalent to entering into the reign of God, since Luke equates salvation with God's *basileia* (see the previous chapter).

Jesus' ministry to the blind is mentioned in two passages which clearly refer to Isaiah 61: Luke 4:18 and 7:21–22. Only Luke 4:18, however, uses ἀνάβλεψις to describe the recovery of sight which the blind receive. In Luke 7:21–22, the blind are those who are physically blind—Jesus has healed their physical need for sight. In Luke 4:18, however, it seems likely that it is both the physically blind and the spiritually blind who are in view, since all the other lines of the Isaianic quotation have figurative significance. Additionally, given the programmatic nature of Luke 4:18–19, it seems unlikely that Luke would have understood Jesus' ministry as a physical healer of sight as being a focal point of his ministry, given that there is only one specific occasion which recounts Jesus physically healing a person of blindness (Luke 18:35–43).[77] Finally, 4Q521 (which may represent a tradition which may have been known to Luke) also uses "the recovery of sight" from Isaiah 61:1 figuratively.[78] Thus, the explicit Isaianic references to recovery of sight for the blind and the wider Lukan text point to Jesus' ministry as healing both physical and spiritual blindness, the latter of which can be equated with entering into the *basileia* of God.[79]

καλέσαι ἐνιαυτὸν κυρίου δεκτόν

The final line of the Isaianic text which Luke picks up on underscores the present period as the time of God's grace and favor. It is the time of salvation,

---

in relation to the gentiles turning from the power of Satan to God. Elymas the magician was also blinded in Acts 13:4–12 and was also presumably healed based on 13:11, though his healing is not recorded.

75. Garland, *Luke*, 199.
76. Green, *Theology*, 79.
77. Hartsock, *Sight and Blindness in Luke-Acts*, 173–79.
78. Kvalbein, "Metaphoric Language," 96–97.
79. Interestingly, in the Ancient Near East, the accession of a new king was commonly accompanied by the healing of the blind, deaf, and lame. Ringgren, "Behold," 210.

when the message of the *basileia* of God is preached and the reality of the presence of the *basileia* of God is seen.

Luke includes the Isaianic description of the present period as a "year" (ἐνιαυτόν) on one occasion as part of the quotation from Isaiah 61 (Luke 4:19); however, in a similar vein as the rest of the Isaianic text, he clearly viewed it figuratively—it is an indefinite period of salvation.[80] Sloan has argued that the word should be read as a parallel to ἐνιαυτὸς ἀφέσεως ("year of release") in Leviticus 25:10.[81] There is nothing in the Lukan text, however, to suggest that this is how Luke intended the word be understood. The most one can say is that the use of ἐνιαυτόν is demonstrative of the original Isaianic author's intention to use Jubilee imagery (though even this is unclear).

The description of this period of salvation as acceptable (δεκτός) is important. The word only appears five times in the New Testament, three of those occasions being in Luke-Acts. All three of these Lukan occurences are in passages which feature Isaiah 61—Luke 4:19; 4:24; and Acts 10:35. The word is used to denote that all people (including gentiles) are now acceptable for entry into the *basileia* of God. This is consistent with the Lukan contexts in which the word is used, as it is used in two sermons about the acceptance of gentiles into the God's *basileia*. Indeed, as Byrne has noted, the "whole idea of 'acceptance/non-acceptance' is pivotal to Luke's understanding of who may enter the *basileia* of God. The 'acceptable year of the Lord' is the season of God's 'hospitality' to the human race, which it is Jesus' mission to proclaim and enact."[82]

Sloan has managed to see a connection between δεκτός and the Jubilee. He forces a convoluted literary link by arguing that the verbal form of the Hebrew noun (רָצוֹן) which δεκτός often translates sometimes has connotations of debts being paid.[83] This association, however, is highly questionable, particularly since neither the noun (רָצוֹן) nor the verb (רָצָה) appear in the Jubilee legislation of Leviticus 25. The word is better understood as conveying that all people are now able to be accepted into God's *basileia*.

---

80. This is in distinction to his two other uses of ἐνιαυτός (Acts 11:26; 18:11), both of which refer to a literal year.

81. Sloan, *Favorable Year*, 33–34.

82. Byrne, *Hospitality*, 50.

83. Sloan, *Favorable Year*, 34–35. This is only one of a myriad of meanings for the verb. BDB 953 and Gerleman, "רצה," 1259–61.

Summary of findings

While Isaiah 61 is only clearly referred to on four occasions, it serves a number of key purposes in Luke's narrative. Firstly, it clarifies Jesus' identity as the eschatological prophet and messiah. Luke uses Jesus' references to Isaiah 61 in Luke 4:16–30 and 7:18–23 to simultaneously proclaim the *basileia* of God and Jesus' role in relation to it. Secondly, Isaiah 61 is used to describe and summarize Jesus' ministry. This ministry is presented in terms of the proclamation of the *basileia* of God, addressing people's physical needs and providing spiritual release from sin and Satan. Thirdly, Isaiah 61 is used to clarify that all people (including gentiles) would be beneficiaries of Jesus' ministry. While the Isaianic text includes a focus on the poor and marginalized and the spiritually oppressed, it culminates in a proclamation of acceptance for all people. Fourthly, the text from Isaiah is used to announce the dawning of the new age of God's grace and favor (that is, the time of salvation). This is parallel to proclaiming the presence of the *basileia* of God. Fifthly, the text is used to illustrate that Jesus' identity and ministry fulfills Scripture.[84]

Luke makes no mention of the text in Isaiah 61 after verse 2a.[85] It is important to note, however, that Luke's treatment of Isaiah (and indeed the entire Old Testament) frequently took into account the wider context of the passage.[86] In the case of Isaiah 61, the immediate context has in view the beneficiaries of the Isaianic speaker's ministry being called generations of righteousness (κληθήσονται γενεαὶ δικαιοσύνης), while the wider context emphasizes the role of the Anointed One in restoring Zion, the seat and center of God's reign. Both the immediate and wider contexts, therefore, correspond to the proclamation of the reign of God.

Moreover, as has already been noted, the language of Isaiah 61:1–3 also seems to indicate that the Isaianic author viewed his situation in exilic terms.[87] If, therefore, Luke also viewed Isaiah 61 in exilic terms, the eschatological use of Isaiah 61 in Luke-Acts is not so far from the "literal sense" of the Isaianic passage as was once thought.[88] Luke may have included the ac-

---

84. This is seen explicitly in Luke 4:21.

85. Importantly, if Luke did in fact seek to emphasize Jubilee terminology or imagery, it would have made more sense at least to include the following line, given that the Hebrew word for "vengeance" (נָקָם) was translated ἀνταπόδοσις ("reward"/"repayment"/"recompense") in the Septuagint. The correspondence between the notion of repayment and the Jubilee legislation are obvious.

86. Koet, "Isaiah in Luke-Acts," 79.

87. Gregory, "The Postexilic Exile," 488.

88. The question of the ongoing exile of Israel is, of course, a highly controversial

count (at least in part) to present Jesus as the one who would bring an end to the exile caused by the sins of the nation. He presented Jesus as a proclaimer of spiritual release, which centered on the forgiveness of sins. While this is in no way certain, it does seem possible given Luke's approach to and use of the Old Testament and the Isaianic text's focus on release.

Conclusion

In many ways, the use of Isaiah 61 throughout the two-part Lukan narrative is consistent with how it is used in other early traditions, particularly those from Qumran. The pesher exegesis, seen frequently in the Dead Sea Scrolls, mirrors Luke's focus on the fulfillment of Scripture, which is mentioned in relation to Isaiah 61 in Luke 4:21. In a similar way to other traditions, Luke also identifies the Isaianic speaker (Jesus) as the eschatological prophet and messiah.

Luke, however, presents the beneficiaries of Jesus' ministry somewhat differently than other Isaiah 61 traditions. While he emphasizes the beneficiaries of the Isaianic speaker's ministry as the poor and underprivileged in a similar way to the Mekhilta to Exodus, Luke also presents the beneficiaries as including those outside of Israel. This is not seen in other early Isaiah 61 traditions. Moreover, throughout Luke's corpus, the descriptions of the beneficiaries are seen to include those who are spiritually needy (though some of the beneficiaries are also described in physical terms). While this is consistent with how ἄφεσις was employed in the first century (see above), in Luke's text the spiritualized sense of the beneficiaries is widened in a way that is not seen in other early Isaianic material.

It is also clear that Luke connected this passage with the *basileia* of God. Within the Luke-Acts corpus, Jesus' proclamation of the *basileia* is elucidated in terms of the Isaiah 61 text. That is, the Isaianic passage is used to present the presence and character of the *basileia*. This connection between the *basileia* and Isaiah 61 is not unique to Luke; there are a number of early works which juxtapose the Isaianic text with the notion of God's reign. Of these, it seems possible that Luke was influenced by a similar tradition to 4Q521 given the similarity in thought between the scroll's use of Isaiah 61 and Luke's text.

Since Luke usually denotes the *basileia* in the dynamic sense of God's reign, it makes sense that Luke would use the passage to present the beneficiaries of the Isaianic speaker's ministry (in part) as those who are spiritually

---

subject, and critical analysis lies beyond the scope of this study. Gregory, "The Postexilic Exile," 496.

needy, those in bondage to sin and Satan, those seeking salvation, and those awaiting acceptance by God during the coming era of salvation. These descriptions fit with Luke's wider focus on forgiveness and repentance, which demonstrate the presence of the dynamic reign of God in a person's life.

It therefore seems that Luke employed Isaiah 61 to highlight several key points: 1) to emphasize that the Holy Spirit was on Jesus; 2) to present Jesus as the eschatological prophet and messiah; 3) to communicate the nature of Jesus' mission (including the nature of those whom he was ministering to), giving particular emphasis to forgiveness/spiritual release; and 4) to communicate that Jesus inaugurated the new age (that is, the *basileia* of God). While other early church authors used the Isaianic text for different literary purposes, they accord with Luke in using Isaiah 61:1–2 as a means to elucidate Jesus' ministry.

Finally, there is no substantive evidence that Luke associated Isaiah 61 with the Jubilee. This is unsurprising, given that the vast majority of other early traditions also ignored this literary link. The only tradition which explicitly links the Isaianic text with the Jubilee is 11Q13, which is unlikely to have exerted any influence outside of Qumran and which almost certainly had no bearing on Luke's work. Additionally, there is no evidence that Luke used the Isaianic text to connect the Jubilee with the *basileia* of God, or that the Jubilee was used to elucidate certain aspects of God's *basileia*.[89] In short, Isaiah 61 is not associated with the Jubilee in any Second Temple works which may have influenced Luke, nor is it associated with the Jubilee within the Luke-Acts corpus. Since this is the case, with regard to Hays's criterion of availability (which addresses whether the author had access to the proposed source text), even if Luke did have direct access to Isaiah 61 (which is the source text most connected with the Jubilee in Luke-Acts) there is no reason to assume that it was associated with the Jubilee.

---

89. As has been mentioned above, the only Second Temple work to associate the Jubilee with the *basileia* of God is 11Q13, which, in all likelihood, had no influence on Luke's work.

5

The Event at Nazareth

Luke 4:14–30

Introduction

The event at Nazareth (Luke 4:14–30) is frequently cited as the clearest reference to the Jubilee in the New Testament.[1] Consequently, in this chapter we will examine it in significantly more detail than other passages. While the verses addressed in this chapter are traditionally separated into two sections (4:14–15 and 4:16–30), they have both been included in this chapter since 4:14–15 presents a summary of Jesus' Galilean ministry and 4:16–30 provides a specific example of that ministry (that is, Luke 4:14–15 provides the historical and literary context for what follows). While the quotation of Isaiah 61 (Luke 4:18–19) has already been addressed to a large extent in the previous chapter, this chapter will include additional remarks relevant to the Lukan text. Finally, the chapter will also include an examination into the presence of proposed Jubilary allusions on the basis of Hays's criteria.

---

1. See, for example, Bruno, "Jesus is our Jubilee," 95.

Text and Translation of Luke 4:14–30

14 Καὶ ὑπέστρεψεν ὁ Ἰησοῦς ἐν τῇ δυνάμει τοῦ πνεύματος εἰς τὴν Γαλιλαίαν. καὶ φήμη ἐξῆλθεν καθ' ὅλης τῆς περιχώρου περὶ αὐτοῦ.

14 And Jesus returned in the power of the Spirit into Galilee, and a report about him spread throughout the entire region.

15 καὶ αὐτὸς ἐδίδασκεν ἐν ταῖς συναγωγαῖς αὐτῶν δοξαζόμενος ὑπὸ πάντων.

15 And he was teaching in their synagogues being praised by everyone.

16 Καὶ ἦλθεν εἰς Ναζαρά, οὗ ἦν τεθραμμένος, καὶ εἰσῆλθεν κατὰ τὸ εἰωθὸς αὐτῷ ἐν τῇ ἡμέρᾳ τῶν σαββάτων εἰς τὴν συναγωγὴν καὶ ἀνέστη ἀναγνῶναι.

16 And when he came into Nazareth, where he had been brought up, he went into the synagogue on the Sabbath day, according to his custom, and he stood up to read.

17 καὶ ἐπεδόθη αὐτῷ βιβλίον τοῦ προφήτου Ἠσαΐου καὶ ἀναπτύξας τὸ βιβλίον εὗρεν τὸν τόπον οὗ ἦν γεγραμμένον·

17 And the scroll of the prophet Isaiah was given to him, and he unrolled the scroll and found the place where it was written:

18 Πνεῦμα κυρίου ἐπ' ἐμὲ οὗ εἵνεκεν ἔχρισέν με.

18 "The Spirit of the Lord is upon me for he has anointed me.

Εὐαγγελίσασθαι πτωχοῖς ἀπέσταλκέν με, κηρύξαι αἰχμαλώτοις ἄφεσιν καὶ τυφλοῖς ἀνάβλεψιν, ἀποστεῖλαι τεθραυσμένους ἐν ἀφέσει,

He has sent me to preach good news to the poor, to proclaim release to the captives and recovery of sight to the blind, to let the oppressed go free,

19 κηρύξαι ἐνιαυτὸν κυρίου δεκτόν.

19 to proclaim an acceptable year of the Lord."

20 καὶ πτύξας τὸ βιβλίον ἀποδοὺς τῷ ὑπηρέτῃ ἐκάθισεν· καὶ πάντων οἱ ὀφθαλμοὶ ἐν τῇ συναγωγῇ ἦσαν ἀτενίζοντες αὐτῷ.

20 And after rolling up the scroll, he gave it back to the attendant, and sat down; and the eyes of all in the synagogue were fixed on him.

21 ἤρξατο δὲ λέγειν πρὸς αὐτοὺς ὅτι σήμερον πεπλήρωται ἡ γραφὴ αὕτη ἐν τοῖς ὠσὶν ὑμῶν.

21 Then he began to say to them, "Today this scripture has been fulfilled in your hearing."

22 Καὶ πάντες ἐμαρτύρουν αὐτῷ καὶ ἐθαύμαζον ἐπὶ τοῖς λόγοις τῆς χάριτος τοῖς ἐκπορευομένοις ἐκ τοῦ στόματος αὐτοῦ καὶ ἔλεγον· οὐχὶ υἱός ἐστιν Ἰωσὴφ οὗτος;

22 And all witnessed to/against him, but were astonished at the words of grace that came from his mouth, and they said, "Is this not Joseph's son?"

23 καὶ εἶπεν πρὸς αὐτούς· πάντως ἐρεῖτέ μοι τὴν παραβολὴν ταύτην· ἰατρέ, θεράπευσον σεαυτόν· ὅσα ἠκούσαμεν γενόμενα εἰς τὴν Καφαρναοὺμ ποίησον καὶ ὧδε ἐν τῇ πατρίδι σου.	23 And he said to them, "Surely you will quote to me this proverb, 'Physician, heal yourself! What things we heard happening in Capernaum, do also here in your hometown.'"
24 εἶπεν δέ· ἀμὴν λέγω ὑμῖν ὅτι οὐδεὶς προφήτης δεκτός ἐστιν ἐν τῇ πατρίδι αὐτοῦ.	24 And he said, "Truly I say to you, no prophet is acceptable in the prophet's hometown.
25 ἐπ' ἀληθείας δὲ λέγω ὑμῖν, πολλαὶ χῆραι ἦσαν ἐν ταῖς ἡμέραις Ἠλίου ἐν τῷ Ἰσραήλ, ὅτε ἐκλείσθη ὁ οὐρανὸς ἐπὶ ἔτη τρία καὶ μῆνας ἕξ, ὡς ἐγένετο λιμὸς μέγας ἐπὶ πᾶσαν τὴν γῆν,	25 But truly I say to you, in the time of Elijah there were many widows in Israel, when the sky was shut for three years and six months, when there was a great famine over all the land;
26 καὶ πρὸς οὐδεμίαν αὐτῶν ἐπέμφθη Ἠλίας εἰ μὴ εἰς Σάρεπτα τῆς Σιδωνίας πρὸς γυναῖκα χήραν.	26 and to none of them was Elijah sent except to a widow in Zarephath in Sidon.
27 καὶ πολλοὶ λεπροὶ ἦσαν ἐν τῷ Ἰσραὴλ ἐπὶ Ἐλισαίου τοῦ προφήτου, καὶ οὐδεὶς αὐτῶν ἐκαθαρίσθη εἰ μὴ Ναιμὰν ὁ Σύρος.	27 And there were many lepers in Israel in the time of Elisha the prophet, and none of them were cleansed except Naaman the Syrian."
28 καὶ ἐπλήσθησαν πάντες θυμοῦ ἐν τῇ συναγωγῇ ἀκούοντες ταῦτα	28 And, hearing these things, all in the synagogue were filled with anger.
29 καὶ ἀναστάντες ἐξέβαλον αὐτὸν ἔξω τῆς πόλεως καὶ ἤγαγον αὐτὸν ἕως ὀφρύος τοῦ ὄρους ἐφ' οὗ ἡ πόλις ᾠκοδόμητο αὐτῶν ὥστε κατακρημνίσαι αὐτόν·	29 And rising up, they drove him outside the city, and led him to the brow of the hill on which their city was built, so that they might cast him down the cliff.
30 αὐτὸς δὲ διελθὼν διὰ μέσου αὐτῶν ἐπορεύετο.	30 But he passed through the midst of them and went.

Table 3: *Text and Translation of Luke 4:14–30*

Comments on Luke 4:14–15

Identifying the source/s for Luke 4:14–15 has attracted some attention. While there are some who would argue that the passage parallels (to some degree) Mark 6:1–6 and Matt 13:53–58, the more likely parallel in Mark's account is 1:14–15 (and other sections of Mark 1).[2] There are clear simi-

---

2. Tannehill, for example, argues that Luke 4:14–15 partially parallels Mark 6:1–6 and Matt 13:53–58, but adds that the accounts in Mark and Matthew occur later in Jesus' ministry and the occasion seems different. Tannehill, *Luke*, 91. See also Klein,

larities between the two accounts, the most obvious being the geographical reference to Galilee (Mark 1:14; Luke 4:14), the focus on teaching, Jesus' teaching in synagogues (Mark 1:21–22; Luke 4:15), and news of Jesus being spread throughout the entire region (Mark 1:28; Luke 4:14). The differences, however, are also significant: Luke omits John's arrest (though admittedly it is already mentioned in 3:19–20); omits a reference to repentance; substitutes ὑπέστρεψεν for ἦλθεν; includes ἐν τῇ δυνάμει τοῦ πνεύματος; and phrases the "spread of the news of Jesus throughout the entire region" (4:14) almost entirely differently from Mark's wording in 1:28.

These differences have led to different conclusions. Many scholars argue that the textual differences are due to Luke's redaction, and that there is insufficient evidence to discount Mark 1:14–15, 28, and 45 as his primary source material.[3] This seems particularly plausible when one considers that the Lukan passage contains five terms frequently seen throughout Luke's wider corpus.[4] Others, however, have argued that Luke relied on another tradition (either Q or L) which paralleled Mark's account.[5] This also seems possible when one considers the distinct textual differences and likelihood that the narratives prior to and following these two verses were dependent on a tradition other than Mark. Thus, the question of Luke's source/s for Luke 4:14–15 remains difficult to resolve. Regardless of his source material, however, it seems likely that the passage describes the same occasion as Mark 1:14–15.

If this is the case, it can be argued that Mark 1:15 has triggered the account of Jesus' teaching ministry in Luke 4:15. That is, Jesus' teaching ministry in Luke 4:15 also centered on a proclamation of the *basileia* of God and the need to repent and believe the good news. The absence of the phrase βασιλεία τοῦ θεοῦ in Luke may be due to differing source material, though it may also represent a difference in Luke's literary purposes. Conzelmann, for example, has argued that while Mark emphasized the nearness of the *basileia* and the need for repentance, Luke was more interested in presenting Jesus' teaching as the message of the *basileia* itself.[6] That is, Jesus'

Das Lukasevangelium, 184–85. Those who argue for a Mark 1:14–15 as Luke's source include Elias, "Beginning," 60, 86; Sabourin, *St Luke*, 133; Garland, *Luke*, 194; and Nolland, *Luke*, 1:185.

3. See, for example, Elias, "Beginning," 64 and Schmidt, *Der Rahmen*, 36–38.

4. The five terms are: ὑποστρέφω, δύναμις, καθ' ὅλης, περίχωρος, and πάντες. Bock, *Luke*, 390.

5. For example, Schürmann (who argues in favor of Q) and Grundmann (who argues that Luke may have used L material). See Schürmann, *Traditionsgeschichtliche Untersuchungen*, 69–80 and Grundmann, *Lukas*, 118.

6. Conzelmann, *Theology*, 114.

teaching ministry was not primarily focused on the coming of the *basileia*; it concentrated instead on the nature of the *basileia* (described in 4:18–21), which presupposes the call to repentance.[7] Conzelmann's view is consistent with the wider Luke-Acts corpus; Luke never explicitly links repentance with a proclamation of the *basileia* of God, despite the frequency of both terms.[8] Thus, it seems plausible that Luke viewed the following account (4:16–30) as a statement of the content of the *basileia*'s program.[9]

Luke also indicates that Jesus' teaching ministry was empowered by the Spirit. He established early in his work that those who have the Spirit are to be viewed positively,[10] and in 4:14, Luke continues the focus on the Spirit's work. The emphasis is on Jesus' teaching and that the Spirit empowered Jesus' proclamation such that news spread throughout the region. Given that Luke frequently associates teaching and the Holy Spirit in the sense of the proclamation of the *basileia* of God, his mention of the Spirit in these verses supports the notion that the content of Jesus' teaching was God's reign.[11]

---

7. Conzelmann, *Theology*, 114. See also Elias, "Beginning," 87.

8. Luke employs μετανοέω more than any other New Testament author (a total of fourteen times across Luke-Acts) and uses the phrase "*basileia* of God" forty times. The two terms, however, are never presented together, except arguably in Luke 10:1–16 (repentance is mentioned in verse 13 and the *basileia* of God is mentioned in verse 9). Interestingly, however, Luke here presents Jesus as instructing the seventy-two to preach that "the *basileia* of God has come near to you" (10:9) rather than to preach the content of the *basileia*. Thus, once again the association is between repentance and the nearness of God's *basileia*, as in Mark, rather than its content.

9. In consideration of the following account (4:16–30), it is also possible that Luke may have viewed Jesus' general teaching methodology as being based on the reading and explication of the Jewish Scriptures. It also seems possible that Jesus' explication of the Scriptures emphasized his own fulfillment of the Old Testament, since this is what occurs in 4:21 and it is consistent with his later interpretation of the Old Testament (see 24:26–27, 44–45). It is therefore plausible that Jesus' teaching ministry in Luke 4:14–15 was centered on a proclamation of the *basileia* of God, which was taught through the reading and exposition of Old Testament texts.

10. John the Baptist in 1:15; Elizabeth in 1:41; Zechariah in 1:67; Mary in 1:35; Simeon in 2:25 and 27; and Jesus in 3:22 and 4:1. Spencer, *Rhetorical Texture*, 64.

11. Cho, "Spirit and Kingdom," 197.

Comments on Luke 4:16–30

Introductory Remarks

Sources and Parallel Texts

Luke 4:16–30 is usually recognized as a parallel occasion to Mark 6:1–6 and Matt 13:53–58.[12] There are clear similarities between the accounts:

1. Entry into the synagogue on the Sabbath (Matt 13:54; Mark 6:2; Luke 4:16)
2. Amazement at Jesus' teaching (Matt 13:54; Mark 6:2; Luke 4:22)
3. Astonishment at Jesus' family heritage (Matt 13:55–6; Mark 6:3; Luke 4:22)
4. Offense taken at Jesus' teaching (Matt 13:57; Mark 6:3; Luke 4:28)
5. Jesus citing a prophet's lack of honor in his hometown (Matt 13:57; Mark 6:4; Luke 2:24)

These similarities make it likely that Matthew, Mark, and Luke all refer to the same occasion.[13]

The differences, however, are also significant. In Luke's account, there is no mention of Jesus' disciples being with him (Mark 6:1), of the crowd's amazement at Jesus' "deeds of power" (Mark 6:2), of the sick being healed (Mark 6:5), or of Jesus' amazement at the crowd's unbelief (Mark 6:6).[14] In Mark's account, there is no mention of a specific sermon or the Isaianic text (Luke 4:17–20) or Jesus' address regarding Elijah and Elisha (Luke 4:24–27), nor is there any mention of the crowd wanting to kill him (Luke 4:29–30). Moreover, the differences in chronology and theological emphases are also significant.

These differences have been explained in a variety of ways. Many have argued that Luke freely rewrote and rearranged Mark 6:1–6 for his own theological purposes.[15] This, however, seems out of character for Luke, who

---

12. Sabourin, *St Luke*, 135; Geldenhuys, *The Gospel of Luke*, 167; Ringe, *Luke*, 67; and Bock, *Luke*, 394. While there is a minority who argue that the two accounts may represent different occasions, there are numerous literary and historical issues associated with this view. See, for example, Leifeld, "Luke," 866.

13. Anderson, "Horizons," 262.

14. Luke also uses Ναζαρά in place of his usual Ναζαρέθ. Mark never uses Ναζαρά (Matthew uses it once in 4:13), which suggests reliance on a source other than Mark.

15. See, for example, Catchpoole, "The Anointed One," 232–36; Nolland, *Luke*, 1:191; and Hill, "Rejection," 162.

often displayed clear historical acumen and limited his editorial work to the transitional sections at the beginning and ending of pericopes.[16] Others have argued for the Lukan redaction of Mark 6:1–6 in combination with another tradition.[17] Still others argue that Luke used entirely non-Markan sources for this episode (though he was aware of Mark's account).[18] Both of these views seem possible; however, the distinct differences between Mark's account and the Lukan text suggest that Luke depended on another source or sources. It also explains how the two accounts can parallel each other without having much verbal overlap.[19] Thus, it seems that if Mark's account did influence Luke's work, it was not his primary source material.

Attempts have been made to separate Luke 4:16–30 into several separate blocks according to different possible sources.[20] It has also been suggested that the passage represents a conflation of at least two distinct events.[21] Since it is clear, however, that the author of Luke intended that Luke 4:16–30 be read as a single event, this study will treat the text as a unified literary unit that fills out the briefer accounts of Jesus returning to his hometown in Mark and Matthew.[22]

The Placement of the Passage

As has already been mentioned, there is almost unanimous scholarly agreement that the Nazareth event is programmatic for Luke's narrative. Indeed, Tannehill has argued that Luke "chose to make this quotation the title under which the whole ministry of Jesus is placed."[23] This is partly due to the text's literary placement in Luke's narrative. In Matthew and Mark, the event occurs much later during Jesus' ministry; however, Luke has brought it forward to mark the beginning of Jesus' ministry in Galilee (which continues until Luke 9:50).[24] Some scholars have postulated that Luke included the event

16. Marshall, *Luke: Historian and Theologian*, 53–76 and Turner, *Power from on High*, 217–18.

17. Schürmann, *Das Lukasevangelium*, 227–28, 241–42 and Fitzmyer, *Luke (I–IX)*, 527.

18. Marshall, *The Gospel of Luke*, 179 and Turner, *Power from on High*, 217.

19. Bock, *Luke*, 397.

20. See, for example, Elias, "Beginning," 59–60.

21. See Luce, *The Gospel According to St. Luke*, 121.

22. There are also form-critical reasons as to why the account should be treated as a single unit. See Bovon, *Lukas*, 1:214–15.

23. Tannehill, "The Mission of Jesus," 72.

24. Matt 13:53–58; Mark 6:1–6. Trocmé argues that Luke's chronology is preferable to the other synoptic authors since it "was logical and congruent with the Old

at the beginning of his narrative in order to follow Q's order and content.[25] Even if this is the case, however, verse 23 and Luke's access to the Markan material suggest that he was aware that the Nazareth event occurred later in Jesus' ministry (sometime after his ministry in 4:31–44).[26] Thus, it seems likely that Luke placed the account early in his narrative for his own literary and theological purposes.

The early placement of the Nazareth event in Luke's Gospel is consistent with Luke's wider approach to his narrative's structure. That is, it seems that Luke's work is frequently "dictated not by strict chronology but by emphases, themes, literary balance, and design."[27] Since this is the case, George Rice has postulated that the pericopes directly following the Nazareth account have been thematically arranged by Luke as his interpretation of the Isaianic quotation (4:18–19).[28] He views the emphasis in the Isaiah passage as being the statement from Isaiah 61:2 ("to proclaim an acceptable year of the Lord"), which he believes is a proclamation of release.[29] This release comes in three ways: 1) release from Satan's power (4:31–44); 2) release from the power of sin (5:1–32); and 3) release from cultic traditions (5:33–6:11).[30]

While Rice's hypothesis is attractive, it has some significant weaknesses. The above analysis of Luke's use of Isaiah 61 (as well as the following comments on Luke 4:18–19) demonstrate that it is highly unlikely that Luke viewed the Isaianic text's release as "release from cultic traditions." Indeed, Luke seemed to view the Isaianic release primarily in terms of release for those imprisoned by sin and Satan. The categorization of 5:1–32 as being primarily about release from sin is also not an accurate reflection of the text—the first sixteen verses of chapter 4 address the calling of Jesus' disciples and the cleansing of a leper. Nonetheless, it does seem possible that Luke viewed the account of demonic release (4:31–37) directly following the Nazareth episode as a demonstration of the Isaianic release. Similarly, many early church commentators on Luke's Gospel frequently interpreted

---

Testament pattern for the Spirit-filled Jesus to begin his ministry in his hometown." This is insufficient grounds to reject Matthew and Mark's chronology. It seems more likely that Luke moved the account forward for his own literary and theological purposes. See Trocmé, *Nonviolent Revolution*, 14.

25. Ringe, "Jubilee Proclamation," 159. See also Tuckett, "Luke 4,16–30," 348–54.

26. It is also possible, however, that verse 23 refers back to Jesus' teaching ministry in 4:14–15.

27. Kistemaker, "Structure," 39.

28. Rice, "Thematic Use," 55.

29. Rice, "Thematic Use," 55.

30. Rice, "Thematic Use," 55; Rice, "Luke 5:33–6:11," 127; and Rice, "Luke 4:31–44," 23.

the text this way.³¹ In fact, there are many commentators who view Luke 4:14–44 as one literary unit.³² Ziccardi, for example, argues that 4:16–30 and 4:31–41 are two complementary halves, sandwiched between an opening and closing frame.³³ No matter how one groups the text, however, it is clear that Luke ordered his narrative purposefully, and so it is no accident that the exorcism account occurred directly after Jesus' proclamation of spiritual release.

The Composition of the Isaianic Quotation

When one compares the text of Luke 4:18–19 with the Septuagint, it is difficult to discount Luke's reliance (or his source's reliance) on the Greek version:³⁴

---

31. See, for example, Cyril of Alexandria, *St. Luke*, 60–61 and Origen, *Homilies on Luke*, 32.

32. See, for example, Busse, *Das Nazareth-Manifest Jesu*, 47–54; Ziccardi, *Relationship*, 318–21; Bock, *Luke*, 389; Green, *Luke*, 203–04; Plummer, *St. Luke*, 116; and Carroll, *Luke*, 106–07.

33. Ziccardi, *Relationship*, 321. Similarly, Green argues that 4:15–16 and 4:42–44 form an inclusio around 4:16–41, which recounts Jesus' proclamation of good news in Jewish synagogues. Green, *Luke*, 203. Even this larger section, however, falls within Luke's wider introduction to Luke-Acts. As Fearghus Ó Fearghail has demonstrated, it seems likely that Luke 1:1–4:44 constitutes Luke's introduction to his two-part work. See Ó Fearghail, *Introduction to Luke-Acts*, 9–38.

34. As has already been mentioned, Luke generally used the Septuagint when referring to Isaiah. It seems unlikely that Luke would have consulted a Targum in this quotation, given the distinct textual differences. For example, the Targum reads, "The spirit of prophecy from before the Lord Elohim is upon me," which clearly departs from the Greek (and Hebrew) text. While the Syriac version Sys supports the Lukan reading, it is far more likely that the Syriac reading is a redaction of the original text rather than a dominical reading. See Bock, *Proclamation*, 107–8.

Luke 4:18-19	LXX Isaiah 61:1-2a and 58:6
πνεῦμα κυρίου ἐπ' ἐμὲ οὗ εἵνεκεν ἔχρισέν με εὐαγγελίσασθαι πτωχοῖς, ἀπέσταλκέν με[35]	πνεῦμα κυρίου ἐπ' ἐμέ οὗ εἵνεκεν ἔχρισέν με εὐαγγελίσασθαι πτωχοῖς ἀπέσταλκέν με
κηρύξαι αἰχμαλώτοις ἄφεσιν	ἰάσασθαι τοὺς συντετριμμένους τῇ καρδίᾳ κηρύξαι αἰχμαλώτοις ἄφεσιν
καὶ τυφλοῖς ἀνάβλεψιν	καὶ τυφλοῖς ἀνάβλεψιν
<u>ἀποστεῖλαι</u> τεθραυσμένους ἐν ἀφέσει	<u>ἀπόστελλε</u> τεθραυσμένους ἐν ἀφέσει (58:6)
<u>κηρύξαι</u> ἐνιαυτὸν κυρίου δεκτόν	<u>καλέσαι</u> ἐνιαυτὸν κυρίου δεκτόν

Table 4: A Comparison between Luke 4:18-19 and Isaiah 61:1-2a and 58:6 in the Septuagint

There are four differences between Luke's version and the Septuagint. Luke omits ἰάσασθαι τοὺς συντετριμμένους τῇ καρδίᾳ ("to heal the brokenhearted"), two verbs are changed (ἀπόστελλε is changed to ἀποστεῖλαι, and καλέσαι is changed to κηρύξαι), and the penultimate line (from Isa 58:6) is inserted.

The change from καλέσαι to κηρύξαι bears little weight on the meaning of the text. It is possible that Luke used κηρύξαι due to his general preference for the verb.[36] In any case, he kept the grammatical form of the verb as aorist infinitive active. Kimball sees a reliance on the Hebrew text here, since in verse 18 לקרא is also rendered κηρύξαι.[37] While this is possible, Luke's

---

35. The punctuation of ἔχρισέν με εὐαγγελίσασθαι πτωχοῖς, ἀπέσταλκέν με is unclear. There is some uncertainty as to whether εὐαγγελίσασθαι ("to preach the good news") should be taken with the preceding ἔχρισέν με ("he anointed me") or with the ensuing ἀπέσταλκέν με ("he has sent me"). Many commentators argue for the former position (that is, Jesus was anointed to preach the good news to the poor). See, for example, UBS5; Bock, *Luke*, 402; Garland, *Luke*, 198; and Stein, *Luke*, 153.

There are some commentators, however, who argue for the latter punctuation, since it accords more with the Masoretic Text and the Septuagint. See Marshall, *The Gospel of Luke*, 183; Fitzmyer, *Luke (I-IX)*, 532; and Nolland, *Luke*, 1:190. I have adopted the latter punctuation here, however I have also related the four infinitives (εὐαγγελίσασθαι, κηρύξαι, ἀποστεῖλαι, and κηρύξαι) to ἀπέσταλκέν με. This is consistent with Luke's interpretation of the quotation in Luke 4:43 and Acts 10:38.

36. Luke uses a form of κηρύσσω in Luke 3:3; 4:18, 19, 44; 8:1, 39; 9:2; 12:3; 24:47; Acts 8:5; 9:20; 10:37, 42; 15:21; 19:13; 20:25; 28:31.

37. Kimball, "Jesus' Exposition," 183-84. See also France, *Jesus and the Old*

reliance on the Septuagint over and against the Hebrew in other sections of the citation makes this unlikely.³⁸ In any case, there is little if any semantic difference between καλέσαι and κηρύξαι.

Sloan has argued that the use of κηρύξαι in the Isaianic quotation in Luke 4:19 should be associated with the proclamation of a Jubilee year seen in Leviticus 25:10.³⁹ His argument, however, has serious flaws, the chief of them being that κηρύξαι (or any form of κηρύσσω) does not appear in any of the Levitical Jubilee legislation. Additionally, while the change in the Lukan quotation from the Septuagint makes little difference to the meaning of the text, it is important to note that if Luke had wanted to draw a literary link with the Levitical text, he would have employed διαβοάω. The presence of κηρύξαι actually draws attention to the *basileia* of God, which is frequently the subject of proclamation in Luke-Acts.

The change to ἀποστεῖλαι from ἀπόστελλε also makes little difference to the overall meaning of the text. Both verbs are derived from ἀποστέλλω; however, Luke used the aorist infinitive in place of the present imperative. He may have done this in keeping with the rest of the Isaianic quotation which includes three other aorist infinitives (εὐαγγελίσασθαι, κηρύξαι, and κηρύξαι).

It is unclear as to why Luke omitted ἰάσασθαι τοὺς συντετριμμένους τῇ καρδίᾳ, particularly in view of the healing motif of verse 23 ("Physician, heal yourself!") and verse 27 (Naaman cleansed of leprosy). While there are a few manuscripts which support the inclusion of the text, it is almost certain that these are scribal supplements which were designed to parallel the Septuagint.⁴⁰ Marshall and Garland both speculate that Luke may have omitted the text because he was reluctant to use ἰάομαι in contexts other than physical healing.⁴¹ This cannot be the case, however, since in Acts 28:27, Luke uses ἰάομαι in a context which is clearly spiritual. Blosser argues that Luke absentmindedly forgot the line, though this seems unlikely, given Luke's careful handling of other texts.⁴² Interestingly, in Acts 10:38, Luke again

---

Testament, 243.

38. For example, the Septuagint (and Luke) omits renderings of יהוה twice, and translates ולאסורים פקח־קוח (literally, "and complete opening to the prisoners") as καὶ τυφλοῖς ἀνάβλεψιν ("and recovery of sight to the blind").

39. Sloan, *Favorable Year*, 35–36.

40. Metzger, *Textual Commentary*, 114. Contra Reicke, "Jesus in Nazareth," 47.

41. Marshall, *The Gospel of Luke*, 182 and Garland, *Luke*, 196.

42. Blosser, "Jubilee," 86. As Chilton has noted, this is unlikely for several reasons: 1) the ἐν in the inserted line from Isa 58:6 is unusual in Luke; 2) verse 17 shows that Luke had a particular passage in mind; and 3) it is unlikely Luke would have omitted the healing phrase in light of the text in verses 23–27 which is concerned with healing.

alludes to Isaiah 61, though in that passage he uses ἰάομαι to describe part of Jesus' ministry. In the case of Luke 4:18, it seems that Luke was either quoting his source material, or he left out the line for his own literary purposes. If the latter, then it may be because Luke wanted to highlight the line from Isaiah 58:6 (ἀποστεῖλαι τεθραυσμένους ἐν ἀφέσει) over and against the original line. Perhaps Luke felt at liberty to change the contents of the citation, though not the structure. Or perhaps Luke was deliberately not mentioning Jesus' healing ministry at this point in his narrative, since Jesus had not yet physically healed anyone. Whatever the case, it is clear that a sense of "healing the brokenhearted" pervades Jesus' ministry in Luke's Gospel, so Luke was certainly not averse to the concept.

The question of why Isaiah 58:6 was inserted into the text is intriguing. There are at least six major views on the topic:[43]

1. Luke cited the text from memory and inserted Isaiah 58:6 by accident.[44]
2. There is no apparent reason for its insertion.[45]
3. Luke related the inserted line to exorcism, and therefore substituted it for the healing line, since Luke sometimes approximated healing with deliverance from evil spirits.[46]
4. It reflects the association of texts in the Dead Sea Scroll 4Q521.[47]
5. It was inserted to refer the audience to Isaiah 58, and thereby increase the focus on the Jubilee nature of Jesus' ministry.[48]
6. It demonstrates the linking of two related texts by a common word/words.[49]

The first view is at odds with Luke's usual careful handling of texts.[50] The second view is worth considering, though it seems that there are plausible explanations for the text's inclusion (examined below). The third view

---

See Chilton, "Announcement in *Nazara*," 163–64.

43. Other perspectives (for example, the text is an early Christian testimony text or it has been inserted to create chiastic parallelism) have not been included since they are either no longer supported or are held by a very small minority of scholars.

44. Plummer, *St. Luke*, 122; Blosser, "Jubilee," 86; and Ringe, "Jubilee Proclamation," 128–29.

45. Marshall, *The Gospel of Luke*, 184.

46. Evans, *Saint Luke*, 271.

47. Flint, *The Dead Sea Scrolls*, 191.

48. Hanks, *Third World*, 99, 103.

49. See Kimball, *Jesus' Exposition*, 106–08.

50. Bock, *Proclamation*, 106.

seems difficult to justify, given that every other use of ἄφεσις by Luke is in relation to the forgiveness of sins (Luke 1:77; 3:3; 24:47; Acts 2:38; 5:31; 10:43; 13:38; 26:18).[51] There is simply a lack of evidence for this position, as there is no reason to suggest that Luke departed from his usual literary practices in this text. The fourth view seems possible, given that Luke may have had access to a tradition similar to 4Q521, though this is far from certain. Peter Flint argues for the association by translating line 8 of 4Q521 (Frags. 2 col. II) as "lifting up those who are opp[ressed]," which parallels Isaiah 58:6.[52] It is unclear, however, as to whether this translation best reflects the language used.[53] Moreover, if Luke did have a tradition similar to 4Q521 in mind, it seems more likely that he would include a citation from Isaiah 35, as it features more heavily than Isaiah 58. The fifth view presupposes that Isaiah 58 does indeed increase the focus on the Jubilee, which seems unlikely, given the vagueness of the Jubilee imagery in that chapter. Indeed, as has already been mentioned in chapter 1, sharing from Isaiah 58 and 61 would more likely point people to the *basileia* of God than to Jubilee imagery.

The view which seems most likely in the end is that there is a literary connection between the two texts, and Isaiah 58:6 has been inserted to highlight that association. The text may demonstrate the use of *gezerah shawah*, whereby two texts are linked by means of a common catchword.[54] Even if *gezerah shawah* was not the approach employed in this text, however, it was nonetheless common practice for early Christian scriptural interpretation to import a second text to illuminate the meaning of the first.[55]

There are several ways that the two texts can be associated. As Bock has noted, a semantic link is possible since שלח ("to let go") is common to both Isaiah 58:6 and 61:1.[56] Bock has also noted that the two texts may be linked by δεκτός or רצון, which is common to Isaiah 61:2 and 58:5.[57] While both of these textual links are possible, it seems more likely that the texts were linked via the use of ἄφεσις (the word is common to both Isa 58:6 and

---

51. See the section "Ἄφεσις and Ἀφίημι in Luke-Acts" in chapter 3.

52. Flint, *The Dead Sea Scrolls*, 190.

53. Indeed, Martínez and Tigchelaar translate the line as "straightening out the twis[ted]," and Wise et al. translate it as "raising up those who are bo[wed down]." Martínez and Tigchelaar, *Dead Sea Scrolls*, 1045 and Wise et al., *The Dead Sea Scrolls*, 421.

54. Kimball, *Jesus' Exposition*, 107 and Koet, *Five Studies*, 29.

55. Byrne, *Hospitality*, 49 and Koet, *Five Studies*, 30.

56. Bock, *Proclamation*, 106. He also notes that רצון appears in both Isa 58:5 and Isa 61:2 in reference to a time acceptable to the Lord.

57. Bock, *Proclamation*, 106.

61:1), particularly given Luke's use of the Septuagint and awareness of the first-century Jewish exegetical milieu.[58]

It is unclear as to whether Jesus, the Lukan sources, or Luke inserted the text. There are several scholars who argue that Jesus had the prophetic authority to conflate the two texts.[59] The text may also, however, represent Lukan redaction; Luke may have combined the two texts for his own literary purposes as outlined in the prologue.[60] As has already been discussed, it is likely that Luke used another source (or sources) in penning the Nazareth discourse. The Isaianic quotation might be a direct quote from Luke's source material, or Luke may have combined two or more historical occasions in his work. This is particularly feasible when one considers the verses that precede the Nazareth episode, which draw attention to Jesus' teaching ministry throughout Galilee. Indeed, it could be that Luke combined two of Jesus' sermonic texts because of the distinct theological similarities between the two passages.

Bovon has a rather unique view and has instead argued that the two texts are connected because Isaiah 57:15—58:14 and 61:1–11 were both associated with Yom Kippur.[61] That is, Isaiah 57:15—58:14 should be associated with Yom Kippur because of the themes of fasting and contrition, and Isaiah 61:1–11 refers to Jubilee years, which began on Yom Kippur.[62] There are, however, several reasons why it is unlikely that Luke had this association in mind. Firstly, there is no mention or hint of Yom Kippur in Luke 4:16–30, which would be expected if Luke included Isaiah 58:6 specifically because of this association. Secondly, it is difficult to see why Luke would want fasting and contrition to be central elements of Jesus' programmatic statement on mission, particularly in place of the line pertaining to healing from Isaiah 61:1 which has been left out of the citation. Finally, if Luke were intending to communicate Yom Kippur imagery, one must question the place of the ensuing Elijah/Elisha sermon, which pertains to gentile inclusion in the *basileia* of God rather than the atonement of the sins of Jews (or gentiles).[63]

---

58. Kimball, *Jesus' Exposition*, 106.

59. Kimball, *Jesus' Exposition*, 107; Willoughby, "Concept of Jubilee," 48; Bailey, *Jesus through Middle Eastern Eyes*, 155–56; and Lee, *Luke's Stories of Jesus*, 255.

60. Composite quotations are not uncommon in the New Testament. See, for example, Acts 3:22–23; Rom 3:10–18; and 2 Cor 6:16.

61. Bovon, *Lukas*, 211–212.

62. Bovon, *Lukas*, 211–212.

63. It is also significant that sacrificial atonement is not emphasized in Luke's theology or passion narrative (particularly in comparison with Matthew's Gospel).

The conclusion of the Isaianic quotation mid-sentence emphasizes the current period as being one of liberation and favor.[64] Indeed, as Stein has identified, the phrase "an acceptable year of the Lord" is synonymous with "the good news of the kingdom of God" (Luke 4:43).[65] Thus, the omission of Isaiah 61:2b was theologically driven; it was designed to underscore that Jesus' ministry was one of grace and not judgment.[66] That is not to say that Luke does not present Jesus as shying away from justice, since Jesus at times proclaims the coming judgment (Luke 18:7; 19:43–44; 21:22). This judgement, however, is reserved for an indefinite time in the future.

Luke 4:16–17

The record of Jesus' entry into the synagogue on the Sabbath day is the oldest available account of a synagogue service.[67] There is still some uncertainty over what was included in these services, though it seems likely that Luke has not included all the service elements.[68] He (or his source/s) probably excluded them because they were superfluous to his literary and theological purposes.[69]

---

64. Scholars who hold this view include Willoughby, "Concept of Jubilee," 45; Evans, *Saint Luke*, 271; Fitzmyer, *Luke (I–IX)*, 533; Stein, *Luke*, 157; Carroll, *Luke*, 112; and Kimball, "Jesus' Exposition," 194.

65. Stein, *Luke*, 157.

66. This point is of some importance for the purposes of this thesis, since it could be argued that the quotation ended with a reference to the "acceptable year of the Lord" in order to emphasize the Jubilee year. Ringe is the only commentator identified over the course of this study who has recognized the possibility that Luke might have finished the Isaianic quotation when he did to emphasize the Jubilee, though she writes that it "is impossible to know whether Luke stopped there in order to avoid those words [Isaiah 61:2b] or if he wanted to emphasize the 'year of the Lord's favor' as the final words cited." Ringe, *Luke*, 68.

67. Morris, *St. Luke*, 105. There are a few scholars who dismiss Luke's account of the synagogue service as being historically unreliable. Michael Cook, for example, argues that readings from the Prophets during synagogue services did not occur until at least six decades after Jesus' time. There are, however, a number of presuppositions which have clearly influenced Cook's conclusions, including his position on Luke's purpose/s in writing, the dating of Luke's Gospel, Luke's reliability as a historian, and his general unease at relying on Luke alone as a precedent for the historicity of prophetic readings in synagogue services. Cook, "Jesus at Nazareth's Synagogue," 133–35.

68. Interestingly, McKay argues that a synagogue service only consisted of the reading and discussion of the Scriptures, and therefore Luke 4:16–30 records all the major elements of the service. McKay does not, however, account for why the Jews called their communal buildings προσευξαι—a strange term if they never used them for prayer. McKay, *Sabbath and Synagogue*, 250–51.

69. Chilton, *God in Strength*, 136.

Bacchiocchi argues that Luke's mention of Jesus' entry into the synagogue on the Sabbath is significant, since Jesus' ensuing Jubilee message (4:18–19) has strong sabbatical overtones.[70] Bacchiocchi believes Jesus' messianic mission fulfilled the Sabbath/Jubilee promises of liberation, since the proclamation was fulfilled on a Sabbath day (see σήμερον in 4:21).[71] There are, however, several reasons why this is unlikely. First and foremost, as has already been explained, it is unlikely that the Isaianic quotation would have been understood in Jubilean terms. Secondly, even if Isaiah 61 were chosen as a narrative strategy to present Jesus' mission in Jubilee language, it does not follow that Jubilean language would have had strong sabbatical overtones for Luke.[72] Indeed, the Sabbath day is not mentioned in Isaiah 61, nor is the Sabbath mentioned in connection with Isaiah 61 elsewhere in Luke's Gospel.[73] Thirdly, even if Luke did indeed seek to connect messianic Jubilee language with the concept of an eschatological Sabbath, there is little evidence that he then took the further step of presenting the week-day Sabbath as the memorial of Jesus' work.[74] Finally, Luke gives no hint that the Isaianic text was chosen because it was a Sabbath day (this is clearly not the intent of σήμερον in verse 21).[75] Indeed, it seems Luke's mention of the Sabbath is somewhat incidental to the scene that follows.

The fact that Jesus "was given" (ἐπεδόθη) the Isaianic scroll does not necessarily indicate whether he had any choice in the matter.[76] It is possible

70. Bacchiocchi, *From Sabbath to Sunday*, 19–21.

71. Bacchiocchi, *From Sabbath to Sunday*, 20–21.

72. As argued by Turner, "Sabbath," 102.

73. Nor is the Sabbath mentioned in the two Qumran peshers which most heavily feature Isa 61 (11Q13 and 4Q521). See Turner, "Sabbath," 102.

74. Turner, "Sabbath," 102.

75. Turner, "Sabbath," 103.

76. Nevertheless, there are a number of perspectives which different scholars have offered. There are some who argue that it is unlikely that Jesus chose either the scroll or the passage. See Schweizer, *Good News*, 88. There are others who argue that εὗρεν indicates that Jesus found the passage himself. See Bock, *Luke*, 404; Fitzmyer, *Luke (I–IX)*, 532; Danker, *Luke*, 106; Keck, *Luke*, 105; and Blosser, "Jubilee," 83. Some who argue for this position also believe that Jesus' reasoning for selecting the text involved (among other things) the proclamation of a Jubilee year. Proponents of this view include Trocmé, *Nonviolent Revolution*, 28–41; Kimball, *Jesus' Exposition*, 102–3; and Arias, "Mission and Liberation," 37. It has also been argued that the Holy Spirit was sovereignly guiding Jesus to find the text, since finding a specific passage would have been a difficult task. See Garland, *Luke*, 196. Luke's text does not, however, make it explicitly clear as to how the passage was chosen, since εὗρεν does not negate the possibility that Jesus merely found a text which had been already selected. If Luke had wanted to emphasize Jesus' choosing of the text, it is more likely that he would have employed ἐκλέγομαι (Luke 6:13; 9:35; 10:42). It seems Luke was not interested in specifying who

that the text was chosen by the attendant (ὁ ὑπηρέτης) mentioned in verse 20; however, it is also possible that Jesus organized to teach from Isaiah before the service started. It has also been argued that Jesus' reading came as part of a fixed triennial lectionary,[77] or that the use of the aorist passive may be Luke's way of designating that the text was ordained by God himself.[78] Whatever the case, Luke's text does not detail why the Isaiah scroll was given to Jesus.[79]

Luke 4:18–19[80]

The first line of the Isaianic quotation emphasizes the Spirit's role in Jesus' ministry and his anointing, which, as has already been mentioned, emphasizes the prophetic and messianic elements of Jesus' ministry. Prior to this quotation, Luke included several references to the Spirit's activity in Jesus' life: Mary was told that the Holy Spirit would come upon her for Jesus' conception (1:35); the Spirit descended on Jesus after his baptism (3:22); Jesus was full of the Holy Spirit and was led by the Spirit into the wilderness (4:1); and Jesus returned to Galilee in the power of the Spirit (4:14). Luke also made clear that Jesus is not to be considered subordinate to the Spirit. Rather, Jesus was a possessor of the Spirit (not an object taken over by the Spirit's power).[81] While the use of the preposition ἐπί with the accusative ἐμέ could denote the Spirit to be either a compelling force or an indwelling presence, the previous references to the Spirit connote Jesus as the subject

---

chose the text.

77. See, for example, Guilding, *The Fourth Gospel*, 109–10. While Luke does not record a reading from the Torah, it is possible that during the first century a fixed reading for the Law had already been established. Crockett's study into the subject has demonstrated, however, there is no clear evidence that there was a fixed lectionary for the prophetic readings at this early stage. Crockett, "Old Testament," 222–47. Heinemann's somewhat pointed observations are correct: there was "no single, generally accepted Sabbath-lectionary in use in the first-century, and . . . all assertions regarding the reading of any particular weekly portion at fixed times of the year are entirely unfounded speculation" (Heinemann, "Triennial," 41).

78. Elias, "Beginning," 101.

79. In another sense, however, the remainder of Luke indicates to us why Isa 61 was chosen—whether by Jesus, the sources, or Luke—because it is a programmatic summary of the ministry of Jesus in Luke.

80. There are already many exegetical comments relating to Isa 61:1–2 in the previous chapter. This section will therefore only address those issues which are specifically pertinent to Luke 4:18–19.

81. Elias, "Beginning," 166–67 and Blosser, "Jubilee," 87.

of the Spirit's activity rather than an object of the Spirit's inspiration.[82] Thus, Luke portrays the Spirit as testifying to and enabling Jesus' ministry.[83] This is consistent with the wider Luke-Acts corpus, where Luke frequently denotes the Spirit as enabling the proclamation of the *basileia* of God.[84]

As mentioned in the previous chapter, the poor (πτωχοῖς) are almost certainly those who are genuinely economically poor, with a secondary meaning being those who are spiritually needy (and who therefore recognize their need for God's help). When one considers Jesus' words at the end of the chapter—"καὶ ταῖς ἑτέραις πόλεσιν εὐαγγελίσασθαί με δεῖ τὴν βασιλείαν τοῦ θεοῦ, ὅτι ἐπὶ τοῦτο ἀπεστάλην" (4:43)—this meaning seems even more likely. Verse 43 is also significant, as it gives context to the double use of ἀποστέλλω in verse 18.

The centrality of the forgiveness of sins in the interpretation of ἄφεσις has been rejected by some scholars. Turner, for example, has presented several reasons as to why forgiveness is not in view in Luke 4:18–19. He argues:

1. The normal meaning of ἄφεσις in Greek (including the Septuagint) was "release," usually in relation to a debt or oppressive conditions.[85] Thus, Luke's audience would not have read it in connection with the forgiveness of sins.

---

82. Elias, "Beginning," 166. This is particularly the case when one considers the difference between Luke's account of Jesus being led by the Spirit (ἤγετο) into the wilderness and Mark's account of Jesus being driven by the Spirit (ἐκβάλλει) into the desert.

83. Contra Garland, *Luke*, 198, who argues that the Spirit should be viewed as a compelling force. Of the synoptic authors, it is Luke who has the greatest interest in the Spirit—he mentions the Spirit on twenty occasions throughout his Gospel, and nine of these occurrences explicate Jesus' own relationship to the Spirit (Luke 1:35; 3:22; 4:1, 2, 14, 18; 10:21; 11:13; 24:49). After the Nazareth episode, however, there is little mention of the Spirit in connection to Jesus. In Luke 10:21, Jesus is presented as rejoicing in the Holy Spirit, and he teaches about the Holy Spirit in Luke 11:13; 12:10–12; and in 24:29. As Fitzmyer has noted, none of the Lukan Jesus' miracles are explicitly related to the Spirit, and similarly the Spirit is not depicted as being operative in Luke's passion narrative or resurrection narrative. Fitzmyer, "Role of the Spirit," 173–74.

The absence of the Spirit in much of the rest of Luke's narrative does not, however, indicate that Luke considered Jesus' relationship to the Holy Spirit as being unimportant. Rather, as Brawley has noted, because Luke "strongly establishes the identity of Jesus as one anointed with the Spirit at the beginning of Jesus' ministry, he is able to assume it through the rest of his gospel with little need for additional resources." See Brawley, *Luke-Acts and the Jews*, 19 and Chilton, "Announcement in *Nazara*," 151. The significance of the Spirit in the Nazareth episode should not, therefore, be understated: it established that all of the Lukan Jesus' ministry was to be viewed as being inseparably linked to the Spirit.

84. Cho, "Spirit and Kingdom," 173–97.

85. Turner, *Power from on High*, 222–23.

2. If Luke had wanted to present ἄφεσις as meaning the forgiveness of sins in Luke 4:18–19, he would have presented it alongside ἁμαρτία (sin) as he did in every other instance in Luke-Acts.[86]

3. Since the Isaianic quotation connects ἄφεσις with αἰχμαλώτοι (captives) and τεθραυσμένοι (the oppressed), the word should be interpreted as "liberation" or "freedom."[87]

4. If Luke had wanted to communicate the forgiveness of sins, he could have done so "by turning to more suitable verses of Isaiah".[88]

Each of these arguments has serious flaws:

1. While it is true that the normal meaning of ἄφεσις in the Septuagint centered on "release," the consistent use of the word throughout the New Testament and the early Christian literature clearly demonstrates that it underwent definite semantic development. Moreover, even in non-Christian literature such as the works of Philo and Josephus, it is clear that the meaning of ἄφεσις had developed such that by the time of Luke's two-part composition, it was frequently associated with the remission of sins.[89]

2. Turner's second argument presupposes that Luke felt literary liberty to freely add or subtract words like ἁμαρτιῶν to quotations from the Septuagint. On the contrary, Luke usually treated Old Testament texts carefully.[90] More importantly, however, Turner has failed to realize that it is precisely because ἄφεσις is linked to ἁμαρτία in every other instance in Luke-Acts that it should be read in relation to the forgiveness of sins in Luke 4:18–19. That is, the uniform use of ἄφεσις in all other Lukan passages serves to clarify how it should be read in Luke 4.

3. It is extremely unlikely that Luke equated ἄφεσις with a literal "freedom" or "liberation," since nowhere in Luke-Acts is Jesus presented as literally freeing prisoners or the oppressed. Instead, Luke used both αἰχμαλώτοι and τεθραυσμένοι symbolically to represent those who are spiritually captive or oppressed (see the previous chapter).

4. Turner's final argument presupposes that Luke's sole purpose in including the Isaianic quotation was to present Jesus' ministry of

---

86. Turner, *Power from on High*, 223. See also Busse, *Die Wunder des Propheten Jesus*, 60.

87. Turner, *Power from on High*, 223.

88. Turner, *Power from on High*, 224.

89. *TLNT* 1:238–44.

90. Bock, *Proclamation*, 106.

forgiveness. As has already been mentioned, however, Luke used Isaiah 61 (including this quotation) for a number of purposes (see the previous chapter).

Bart Koet has presented a different perspective.[91] He agrees that ἄφεσις must be viewed in relation to the remission of sins; however, he also maintains that the word is inextricably linked to Jubilee/Sabbath year traditions.[92] He therefore seeks to connect forgiveness and the Jubilee by arguing that the presence of ἄφεσις in Luke 4:18 denotes a call to repentance for those who have ill-gotten wealth so that they might experience forgiveness.[93] This interpretation, however, largely misses the point of ἄφεσις in the passage. The double use of ἄφεσις is designed to emphasize Jesus' ministry of spiritual release, demonstrated throughout the remainder of Luke's Gospel.[94] That is, the point of the text is to denote Jesus' identity and his ministry, not to call Luke's audience to respond in some particular way. While it is possible that Luke's audience may have understood the double use of ἄφεσις as an implicit call to forgiveness ("come and be beneficiaries of Jesus' ministry of forgiveness"), it seems highly unlikely that the word would have necessarily been understood to be a call only for the wealthy to repent of their riches. That is not to say that Luke was unconcerned with calling the rich to repent of the love of wealth; there are many occasions in Luke's Gospel where this is clearly the case (see, for example, 12:13–21; 16:19–31; and 18:18–25). The use of ἄφεσις in Luke 4:18, however, seems to be a more general call for transformation.

While it has already been noted that the reference to the blind in Luke 4:18 is most likely a reference to the spiritually and physically blind, it is

91. Koet, *Five Studies*, 33–35.
92. Koet, *Five Studies*, 33–34.
93. Koet, *Five Studies*, 34–35.

94. The forgiveness of sins is mentioned twice prior to the Nazareth pericope (1:77; 3:3), both times in connection with John's ministry. After the Nazareth episode, there are numerous references to Jesus' ministry of forgiveness. In Luke 5:17–26, Jesus' ministry focused on the forgiveness of the paralytic's sins. Indeed, the healing of the paralytic served to prove Jesus' authority to be able to forgive sins. Luke 5:27–32 emphasizes Jesus' focus on spiritual liberation; he did not come to "call the righteous, but sinners to repentance" (5:32). A main focus of Luke 7:36–50 is the forgiveness of the sinful woman who anointed Jesus' feet. Similarly, in Luke 15 the three "lost" parables are all concerned with how there is rejoicing in heaven over sinners who repent. After the passion narrative (Luke 22–24), Luke emphasized that Jesus' death and resurrection occurred so that "repentance and forgiveness of sins will be preached in his name to all nations" (24:47). While there are many more references to Jesus' ministry of forgiveness (see, for example, Luke 5:8; 11:4; 12:10; 18:13–14), it is clear that the Isaianic quotation's focus on spiritual liberation was played out in the rest of Luke's Gospel.

also noteworthy that the Nazareth crowd themselves appear to serve as an example of spiritual blindness. Though they thought they knew who Jesus was ("Is this not Joseph's son?"), they were apparently unaware of Jesus' true identity as the eschatological prophet and messiah.[95] Thus, it seems that the spiritually blind are typified immediately after the Isaianic quotation by Jesus' audience.

The release for the oppressed (ἀποστεῖλαι τεθραυσμένους ἐν ἀφέσει) is a reference to those who endure spiritual torment. That is, Jesus' ministry liberates people from the power of Satan (see the following account in 4:31–37) and provides forgiveness (ἄφεσις) for those who recognize the oppressive and devastating nature of their sins. It seems unlikely that Luke viewed the oppression as primarily political (that is, as a promise that the Jewish people would be freed from Roman domination), since his work largely avoids passages that could be interpreted as being directly politically subversive.[96] Luke therefore communicated that Jesus was not only announcing forgiveness and freedom like John the Baptist had in 1:77 and 3:3; he was also the agent who would achieve this spiritual liberation (Isa 58).[97] Thus, Jesus' proclamation of the Isaianic text serves simultaneously to proclaim the *basileia* of God and Jesus' role in relation to it, which is consistent with how Luke presented the *basileia* of God throughout Luke 1–4.[98]

There are some scholars who argue that "the oppressed" in Isaiah 58:6 are those who have economic difficulties, and they should therefore be identified this way in Luke 4:18.[99] Even if one emphasizes the context of Isaiah 58, however, it is clear that the central issue in the Isaianic passage was that the people had forsaken "the judgments of their God" (Isa 58:2). That is, the poor socioeconomic and political conditions described in Isaiah 58 were the result of the people's religious sins. Thus, both Isaiah 58 and Luke 4 emphasize that people are spiritually needy, which Luke addresses by explicating Jesus' ministry as one of forgiveness and spiritual redemption.

Verse 19 has been translated by some commentators as "to proclaim the year of the Lord's favor" in order to emphasize that the Jubilee is in view.[100] This, however, does not accord with Luke's other uses of δεκτός. In Luke 4:24 and Acts 10:35, it is clear that the word is best understood as "acceptable," so

---

95. Hartsock, *Sight and Blindness in Luke-Acts*, 177.

96. Tuckett, "Luke 4,16–30," 348. Though, as mentioned above, accounts such as the Gerasene demoniac (Luke 8:26–39) could be read politically.

97. Schweizer, *Good News*, 446 and Kimball, "Jesus' Exposition," 193.

98. Ziccardi, *Relationship*, 261–64; 352; 371–74; 499–501.

99. See, for example, Sloan, *Favorable Year*, 39.

100. See, for example, Johnson, *Luke*, 79.

the word is best translated that way in Luke 4:19 as well. This is particularly the case since it seems that Luke is making a Midrashic point by employing the same word again in the ensuing sermon (Luke 4:24).[101]

Luke 4:20–30

After Jesus' reading from Isaiah, Luke records him as declaring the text's fulfillment (4:21).[102] It is likely that this is a summary of Jesus' message, given that the text says that Jesus began (ἤρξατο) to speak and given the crowd's reaction to Jesus' words of grace (τοῖς λόγοις τῆς χάριτος).[103] His use of σήμερον ("today") at the beginning of the sentence is emphatic, as it highlights that the era of salvation is present. Luke clearly did not view it as being a literal twenty-four hour period, since some aspects of the quotation (such as the restoring sight to the blind) do not occur until much later in his narrative. Instead, as Leifeld has noted, Luke consistently uses σήμερον to emphasize "the presence of the kingdom and of the time of salvation."[104]

---

101. Kimball, *Jesus' Exposition*, 110–11.

102. The text therefore highlights the fulfillment of Scripture through Jesus' life and ministry. Prior to the Nazareth episode there are several occasions where Scripture is cited and fulfilled. In the Gospel's prologue, Luke describes Jesus' ministry in terms of "the events that have been fulfilled among us" (τῶν πεπληροφορημένων ἐν ἡμῖν πραγμάτων). He then describes Jesus' and John's births in terms of the fulfillment of God's plan (1:35, 38, 57; 2:6, 21–22). The songs of Mary (1:46–56) and Zechariah (1:67–79) also contain allusions to Old Testament texts and images, as does Simeon's prayer (2:29–32). Luke then makes a point of describing Jesus' early childhood in terms of obedience to the Law (2:21–24, 41–42), after which John the Baptist describes Jesus in relation to Isa 40:3–5 (3:4–6) and Jesus resists the devil by citing Scripture (4:3–12).

It is not until the Nazareth episode that the fulfillment of Scripture mentioned in the prologue comes explicitly into view. Indeed, as Elias has noted, the "overarching theological schema in which the Nazareth pericope plays a crucial part is that of promise and fulfillment" (Elias, "Beginning," 283).

Jesus' ministry is described in terms of the fulfillment of Isa 61 (4:18–21) and is clarified and reinforced by the ensuing Elijah/Elisha narrative, which depicts Jesus as the typological fulfillment of the two prophets (4:25–27). While Luke also presents John as an Elijianic figure, he continues to depict Jesus in Elijianic terms throughout his Gospel. Thus, Luke uses the Nazareth pericope to demonstrate that Jesus' entire life and ministry is to be understood within the framework of Scripture fulfillment. That is, the text sets the tone for the rest of Luke's Gospel, in which he continues to clarify and remind his audience that Jesus has fulfilled the Old Testament (9:31; 21:22, 24; 22:16, 37; 24:25–27, 44–47).

103. Plummer, *St. Luke*, 123; Marshall, *The Gospel of Luke*, 185; and Bock, *Luke*, 412.

104. Leifeld, "Luke," 868.

Similarly, the use of πεπλήρωται ("has been fulfilled") in the perfect tense serves to indicate the continuing state of fulfillment. As the previous chapter explained, Luke uses the Isaianic passage to present Jesus as the Spirit-empowered eschatological prophet and messiah, to proclaim the nature of Jesus' mission (giving particular emphasis to spiritual forgiveness/release), and to communicate the inauguration of the new age (that is, the *basileia* of God). Jesus' pronouncement that the text "has been fulfilled" therefore highlights the enduring importance of his own identity and ministry. The phraseology is similar to Mark 1:15, which stresses the imminence of the *basileia*. Luke's account, however, stresses "the nature of the time in the nearness of the person."[105] This is consistent with the wider Lukan narrative, where the first four chapters of the Gospel present God's *basileia* as being uniquely and necessarily related to Jesus, predicated on his identity as the Davidic messiah.[106]

Related to Jesus' fulfillment of Scripture is the inauguration of the new eschatological era.[107] As has been explained above, Jesus' proclamation of the new age of salvation was effectively a declaration of the *basileia*; Luke presents Jesus' fulfillment of Isaiah 61 as a declaration of the inauguration of the reign of God.[108] This is also seen in Luke's two other references to Isaiah 61 in his Gospel.[109] Jesus' declaration that the Isaianic text "has been fulfilled" also corresponds to Luke's later descriptions of the *basileia* of God as a present inaugurated reality (Luke 7:28) with a future not-yet-realized dimension. That is, the use of the perfect tense (πεπλήρωται) denotes the *basileia* (Isa 61) as a present reality. Similarly, Luke's use of σήμερον (4:21) also supports the "already"/"not yet" nature of the *basileia*.[110] Thus, the

---

105. Bock, *Luke*, 413.

106. Ziccardi, *Relationship*, 499–501.

107. Jesus' statement to the synagogue crowd that σήμερον πεπλήρωται ἡ γραφὴ αὕτη ἐν τοῖς ὠσὶν ὑμῶν was a declaration that the Scriptures were fulfilled and the last days had begun.

108. While the phrase "*basileia* of God" is not explicitly used within the Nazareth pericope, Luke later summarized Jesus' message as "the good news of the *basileia* of God" (4:43). The quotations from Isa 61:1 and 58:6 are used to illustrate the characteristics of the reign of God (good news, freedom, justice, and release), and the "acceptable year" (Isa 61:2a) is synonymous with the *basileia* of God. Additionally, if Luke has connected Isa 61 with 4Q521 (as is argued in the previous chapter), then it seems likely that he would have associated the Isaianic text with the scroll's *basileia* terminology.

109. In Luke 7:22, Jesus refers to Isa 61 to elucidate his ministry to John's disciples, connecting it to the *basileia* of God in verse 28. In Luke 6:20, there is an even clearer association between God's *basileia* and the Isaianic text—it is the poor who receive the reign of God. Thus, the Nazareth pericope sets the scene for later references to Isa 61, all of which juxtapose the text with the *basileia* of God.

110. The verses following the Nazareth pericope present Jesus as enacting his

Nazareth episode is the first place in Luke's Gospel where the *basileia* is presented as a present and future reality; this serves as a blueprint for the remainder of Luke's Gospel where the *basileia* increasingly comes into view.

Barker argues that Jesus' fulfillment of the Isaianic quotation signals his inauguration of the final Jubilee year.[111] She argues that various Old Testament texts and documents such as 11Q13 demonstrate that fervor and expectations for the tenth (and final) Jubilee formed the context for Jesus' ministry.[112] Therefore, there is "no other interpretation which can be put on the claim to have fulfilled *that day* (Luke 4:21) [except for] the Jubilee prophecy in Isa 61 which was central to the Melchizedek expectations of the time."[113] Barker's conclusions, however, overstep the literary evidence. As has already been mentioned, the argument that a tenth Jubilee year occurred at the time of Jesus' ministry depends entirely on when one marks the beginning of the seventy sevens (Dan 9:24–27), a point on which there is no scholarly consensus.[114] Moreover, as has already been argued, it is also very unlikely that 11Q13 had any influence outside the Qumran community, let alone on Luke's work. Indeed, there is no evidence that Jesus ministered in a context where there was "Jubilee fervour and expectations," and there is similarly no evidence that Luke viewed Jesus' ministry that way. The fulfillment of the Old Testament text is better understood as a statement that the eschatological prophet's ministry, described in Isaiah 61, has begun—a ministry which centers on a proclamation of the inauguration of the *basileia* of God.

The reaction of those in the synagogue to Jesus' declaration of fulfillment in verse 22 has attracted a significant amount of attention, particularly because of the semantic range of verbs which Luke employs. There continues to be debate over whether ἐμαρτύρουν αὐτῷ should be interpreted as a dative of advantage or disadvantage, or whether it signifies impartial witness.[115] Similarly, the use of ἐθαύμαζον could indicate that the people were

---

Isaianic ministry the very day on which it was proclaimed (4:31–41). The programmatic nature of the passage and Jesus' future ministry also demonstrate, however, that the σήμερον was an ongoing period—the new eschatological age.

111. Barker, "The Time is Fulfilled," 26–27.

112. Barker, "The Time is Fulfilled," 24–25.

113. Barker, "The Time is Fulfilled," 26–27.

114. As has been already mentioned in chapter 2, there are very few scholars who posit that the "seventy sevens" of Dan 9:24–27 are to be taken as a literal reference to 490 years. Even amongst those who do believe that the years are literal, however, there is no agreement as to when the 490 began and concluded.

115. Jeremias, *Promise*, 44; Marshall, *The Gospel of Luke*, 185–86; Prior, *Jesus the Liberator*, 93–95; and Nolland, *Luke*, 1:198.

marveling in admiration, or it could mean that the people were astonished and critical of Jesus' message.[116] Finally, Jesus' τοῖς λόγοις τῆς χάριτος could be taken to mean "words of grace," "winsome words" (descriptive genitives), or even "words about God's grace" (objective genitive).[117]

Many commentators view the verbs as signifying the Nazareans' positive response to Jesus.[118] Such a view leads to difficulties, however, when one considers Jesus' abrupt response to the people in the following verses.[119] It is also inconsistent with the people's remarks about Jesus being Joseph's son, which Mark's parallel account shows to be undoubtedly negative.[120] While more could be said, there are clear difficulties associated with Luke's presentation of the Nazareans as admirers of Jesus in 4:22 and his depiction of them as a murderous rage-filled mob six verses later.

A number of alternate interpretations have been offered, the most well-known being Jeremias's theory. He developed Bornhäuser's and Violet's prior linguistic reconstructions to argue that the synagogue crowd was decidedly angry because Jesus finished the Isaianic quotation prior to the mention of the "day of vengeance of our God" (Isa 61:2b).[121] Thus, Jeremias

---

116. The issue becomes even more complicated, since even within Luke's Gospel, θαυμάζω is used positively (7:9; 8:25; 9:43) and negatively (11:38; 20:26). Green, *Luke*, 214 and Ó Fearghail, "Rejection," 67.

117. Those that interpret the phrase as "words of grace" include Marshall, *The Gospel of Luke*, 186; Nolland, *Luke*, 1:198; Ó Fearghail, "Rejection," 68; and Hertig, "Jubilee Mission," 169–70. Those that interpret the phrase as "winsome words" include Eltester, "Israel," 138. Those that interpret the phrase as "words about grace" include Violet, "Zum rechten Verständnis," 263–68; Jeremias, *Promise*, 44–45; and Tannehill, "The Mission of Jesus," 72.

118. See, for example, Vinson, *Luke*, 122; Green, *Luke*, 214; Bock, *Luke*, 414; Stein, *Luke*, 157; Byrne, *Hospitality*, 51; Keck, *Luke*, 107; and Carroll, *Luke*, 113.

119. Tannehill, for example, notes that Jesus is "remarkably ungracious" in his response to the Nazareans. Similarly, Vinson admits that the positive reading of the people's reaction suggests that Jesus is deliberately provoking them to anger. See Tannehill, *Narrative Unity*, 69 and Vinson, *Luke*, 123.

120. Mark 6:3: οὐχ οὗτός ἐστιν ὁ τέκτων, ὁ υἱὸς τῆς Μαρίας. Green argues that the Nazareans' question about Jesus' parentage is essentially selfish; they are musing to themselves that they will be beneficiaries of the Lord's favor since they saw Jesus as "one of us." Green, *Luke*, 214–15. While this is possible, there is a clear lack of literary evidence in support of it. The tone of the question "Is not this Joseph's son?" is clearly akin to "Is not this the carpenter?" (Mark 6:3). That is, the people in the synagogue were surprised that Jesus, whom they knew the parents and background of, would deliver such a message.

121. Jeremias, *Promise*, 44–46. Bailey agrees with Jeremias; however, he also believes that Jesus' omission of the second stanza (Isa 61:2c–3) and especially the third stanza (Isa 61:4–7) would have contributed to the crowd's anger. See Bailey, *Jesus through Middle Eastern Eyes*, 150–55.

would argue that the hostility in 4:28–29 was already present (to some degree) in 4:22.¹²² Jeremias's theory has attracted some support (most notably Walter Grundmann's); however, it has also been criticized on many fronts, particularly with regard to the supposed Semitic background and interpretation of πάντες ἐμαρτύρουν αὐτῷ and the focus on the omission of Isaiah 61:2b.¹²³ Nonetheless, Jeremias's contribution has gone some way in resolving the literary difficulties associated with translating 4:22 within its wider context.

Other scholars, however, have provided more convincing contributions as to how the verse should be interpreted.¹²⁴ Nolland has demonstrated that Luke's initial use of μαρτυρέω is was probably designed to show "his readers . . . that even people so inimical to the claims of Jesus that they seek his death, nevertheless, cannot but be impressed by the words of this imposing figure."¹²⁵ That is, despite the ensuing rejection, the amazed response of the people is in itself a testimony to Jesus.¹²⁶ Luke's use of θαυμάζω, however, betrays that the people's astonishment was coupled with criticism and rejection.¹²⁷ This becomes particularly clear in view of the ensuing negative question regarding Jesus' parentage in 4:22c.¹²⁸ The synagogue crowd was questioning how Jesus' remarkable teaching and claims could come from one who was the son of a lowly craftsman.¹²⁹ As Rohrbaugh has noted, this type of question had definite social implications; aspersions cast on one's lineage (particularly in relation to one's father) were extremely insulting.¹³⁰

The insult becomes even clearer, however, in light of the description of Jesus' message as τοῖς λόγοις τῆς χάριτος (words of grace), a phrase which suggests that Luke may have viewed the crowd as having identified Jesus' words as a message of salvation to all (not just Jews), a point then reiterated and reinforced through the Elijah/Elisha references in verses 24–27.¹³¹

---

122. Jeremias, *Promise*, 44–45.

123. Grundmann, *Lukas*, 119–22. For a list of the various criticisms leveled against Jeremias's theory, see Hill, "Rejection," 164–65; Anderson, "Horizons," 267–69; Ó Fearghail, "Rejection," 61–63; and Nolland, "Impressed Unbelievers," 220.

124. Nolland, "Impressed Unbelievers," 219–29 and Ó Fearghail, "Rejection," 60–72.

125. Nolland, "Impressed Unbelievers," 229.

126. Nolland, "Impressed Unbelievers," 226–29.

127. Ó Fearghail, "Rejection," 70. This understanding therefore views the καὶ enjoining the πάντες ἐμαρτύρουν αὐτῷ and the ἐθαύμαζον ἐπὶ τοῖς λόγοις τῆς χάριτος epexegetically.

128. Ó Fearghail, "Rejection," 70.

129. Rohrbaugh, "Legitimate Sonship," 194.

130. Rohrbaugh, "Legitimate Sonship," 194.

131. Luke's use of χάρις in Acts 14:3; 20:24; and 20:32 demonstrates that he

Ó Fearghail has noted that this understanding of Jesus' message demonstrates that Jesus' claim in Luke 4:21 indicated that he was not only the bearer of the good news of salvation, but the bearer of salvation itself.[132] Since this is the case, it is easy to see why the crowd's description of Jesus was so grossly inadequate. The crowd's hostility arose because the message of salvation (the Isaianic quotation) came from the mouth of Jesus (τοῖς ἐκπορευομένοις ἐκ τοῦ στόματος αὐτοῦ), whom they only knew as the son of Joseph. They were offended because Jesus declared that he was the Spirit-empowered, anointed prophet of Isaiah 61. Thus, it seems Luke intended that verse 22 present the synagogue audience as expressing hostility toward Jesus, which climaxed in verses 28–29.[133]

In verse 23, Luke presents Jesus as responding frankly to the people's hostility by means of a proverb: ἰατρέ, θεράπευσον σεαυτόν. It is unclear, however, whether σεαυτόν refers to the people in Nazareth or to Jesus himself. That is, it is possible to interpret the proverb and the following statement as a request for Jesus to bring the same blessings to his hometown as he brought to Capernaum, or as a retort that Jesus should prove his verbal claims (as the eschatological prophet who would fulfill the Isaianic text) by miraculous signs.[134] Unfortunately, the proverb's use in other classical

---

sometimes associated the word with salvation. The context of this passage suggests that this is one of those occasions; the content of the Isaianic quotation has clear salvific connotations. This interpretation is supported by other Septuagintal texts and Luke 4:43, which summarizes Jesus' message in the Nazareth episode as a proclamation of the *basileia* of God which must also be preached elsewhere. Ó Fearghail, "Rejection," 68–70.

The view that the phrase τοῖς λόγοις τῆς χάριτος corresponds to Acts 14:3; 20:24; and 20:32 is not unique to Ó Fearghail; there are many commentators who have recognized the parallel (see Hertig, "Jubilee Mission," 169; Prior, *Jesus the Liberator*, 97; Garland, *Luke*, 202; and Danker, *Luke*, 108). Interestingly, some of these commentators also argue that the Isaianic quotation (which "the words of grace" refer to) was largely concerned with the Jubilee. The three parallel Acts passages, however, have no Jubilee connotations whatsoever. (The mention of inheritance in Acts 20:32 has no connection with the Jubilee. The point of Paul's message is that God is able to give an inheritance through the gospel, not that one already has a patriarchal inheritance which can be redeemed or that the people are the inheritance of God.)

132. Ó Fearghail, "Rejection," 70.

133. This is supported by Jesus' description of his Isa 61 ministry in Luke 7:22, after which he stated, "And blessed is the one who is not offended by me" (7:23). Luke's audience would immediately have been reminded of the offense that occurred in 4:22.

134. Those that argue that σεαυτόν refers to either Nazareth or to Israel include Noorda, "'Cure,'" 464–65; Ringe, *Biblical Jubilee*, 41; Garland, *Luke*, 203–4; Keck, *Luke*, 107; and Tannehill, *Luke*, 93.

Those that argue that σεαυτόν refers to Jesus include Bock, *Luke*, 416; Nolland, *Luke*, 1:199; John Nolland, "Classical and Rabbinic Parallels," 207–9; Plummer, *St. Luke*, 126; and Marshall, *The Gospel of Luke*, 187.

and rabbinic literature is also ambiguous.¹³⁵ Given the people's response to Jesus in verse 22, the natural reading of the proverb (whereby σεαυτόν refers to ἰατρέ), the clear personal rejection of Jesus in verse 24, and the frequent requests for signs throughout Jesus' ministry (Luke 4:3; 11:16; 22:64; 23:8, 35–37), it seems more likely that the sense of verse 23 is a retort that Jesus should back up his claims.¹³⁶ That is, the force of verse 23 is, "Who do you think you are to offer us what you do not have yourself? Do here what we have heard you did in Capernaum and prove that you are who you say you are."¹³⁷

Verse 24 then records Jesus giving an even clearer rebuke to the synagogue congregation: οὐδεὶς προφήτης δεκτός ἐστιν ἐν τῇ πατρίδι αὐτοῦ. The wording of the statement is different from its parallels in Matthew, Mark, and John, though it seems the sense is the same (see Matt 13:57; Mark 6:4; and John 4:44). Jesus responds to the crowd's critical attitude reflected in verse 22 and states that it is to be expected since no prophets are welcome in their hometowns. The use of δεκτός, however, adds an extra element; it refers Luke's audience back to the acceptable (δεκτόν) year of the Lord in verse 19, thus making a connection between "sharing in the time of salvation which Jesus announces and the acceptance of Jesus himself."¹³⁸ Significantly, the only other time Luke employs δεκτός is in Acts 10:35, a passage which refers back to the event at Nazareth.¹³⁹ The verse therefore reiterates Jesus' identity as the eschatological prophet and both responds to and anticipates his rejection.¹⁴⁰

Bovon has argued that the mention of Jesus' hometown (πατρίς) in verses 23 and 24 is reminiscent of the Jubilee legislation in Leviticus 25:10, where the Israelites were commanded to return to their own clan (ἕκαστος εἰς τὴν πατρίδα αὐτοῦ ἀπελεύσεσθε).¹⁴¹ This, he believes, is evidence that Jesus' preaching in Nazareth was a pronouncement of the year of Jubilee.¹⁴² His argument is tenuous at best. If it were true, then one might also say that

---

135. See, for example, the surveys of the classical literature by Noorda and Nolland, who both arrive at different conclusions. Noorda, "'Cure,'" 459–67 and Nolland, "Parallels," 193–209.

136. Nolland, *Luke*, 199 and Bock, *Luke*, 416.

137. Nolland, *Luke*, 199 and Bock, *Luke*, 416.

138. Tannehill, "The Mission of Jesus," 57–58.

139. Tannehill, "The Mission of Jesus," 57–58.

140. It is also possible that the introduction of the statement using ἀμὴν λέγω ὑμῖν adds weight to Jesus' self-identification as the eschatological prophet, though this is less certain. Johnson, *Luke*, 80 and Marshall, *The Gospel of Luke*, 187–88.

141. Bovon, *Lukas*, 214–15.

142. Bovon, *Lukas*, 214–15.

Matthew, Mark, and John's use of πατρίς in reference to Jesus' hometown (Matt 13:57; Mark 6:4; John 4:44) was meant to allude to the Jubilee (though no commentator has taken this position). More importantly, it seems odd that Bovon would choose certain sections of the Jubilee legislation in Leviticus 25 as being applicable to Jesus' ministry while ignoring other sections. If one is to assume that Luke viewed Jesus' return to Nazareth as a type of obedience to Leviticus 25, then one would also expect that Jesus' obedience would extend to other sections of the Jubilee legislation, such as only consuming what is taken directly from the fields (Lev 25:12). This, however, is clearly inconsistent with Luke's portrayal of Jesus.[143]

Blosser also sees a reference to the Jubilee year in verses 23–24, though for entirely different reasons. He argues that someone in the crowd must have asked Jesus for proof of the Jubilee age (as mirrored in verse 23), which he says must have been proclaimed moments earlier.[144] Blosser believes that this challenge stemmed from a selective memory of what the Jubilee actually meant; it ignored obedience and instead focused on blessings from God.[145] Luke, therefore, presented Jesus as refusing the command (verse 24) and instead began to redefine the new Jubilee age in terms of obedience to God's will (which comes before the divine blessings).[146] It is difficult to affirm much of what Blosser argues, given his many assumptions. It is possible that there was a more primitive tradition that ascribed the proverb in verse 23 ("Physician, heal yourself") to a person in the crowd, which Luke then changed to come from the lips of Jesus. Even if this is the case, however, there is nonetheless no evidence that the proverb should be taken to mean that Jesus was asked for proof of the new Jubilee age. Indeed, there is no explicit mention of the Jubilee at all, nor is there any mention of how obedience to God's will leads to the attainment of divine blessings.

Verses 25–27 then expand on the prophetic identity of Jesus as mentioned in the previous verses. John Collins has argued that Luke may have been influenced by the Qumran scroll 4Q521, which presents the herald of

---

143. While it is true that on one occasion Jesus did eat what was taken directly from the fields (Luke 6:1), on all other occasions there is no indication that Jesus ate directly from a field. Luke's focus, it would seem, was more on who Jesus was with rather than what he ate. He draws attention to Jesus eating with tax collectors and sinners (Luke 5:29–33; 15:2), Pharisees (Luke 9:36–37; 11:37; 14:1), his disciples (Acts 1:4), and the general populace (Luke 9:10–17). In Luke 24:42, Jesus is said to have eaten a piece of broiled fish, which would have almost certainly been salted, given the fish that was sold in Jerusalem. That is, eating the fish did not comply with the Jubilee legislation (and presumably neither would many of Jesus' other meals).

144. Blosser, "Jubilee," 110, 114.
145. Blosser, "Jubilee," 110, 114.
146. Blosser, "Jubilee," 110, 114.

Isaiah 61 as an eschatological Elijianic figure.[147] Poirier agrees with Collins that the figure in 4Q521 is Elijah, and therefore argues that Luke 4:16–30 should be understood as presenting Jesus as this Elijianic figure.[148] It is unclear, however, whether Luke intended that Jesus be viewed as the Elijianic figure, particularly given that John the Baptist was explicitly referred to as a *type* of Elijah in Luke 7:27.[149] Indeed, Collins views Luke 7:24–28 as a means of refuting the idea that Jesus was *Elijah redivivus*, an idea which might have arisen in view of the description of Jesus' ministry in Luke 7:22.[150] It seems more likely that Luke intended that Jesus be understood as a prophet who was comparable to Elijah and Elisha, particularly concerning his rejection by his own countrymen.[151]

Luke seemingly used the verses for at least five reasons:

1. They relate Jesus' ministry to the ministries of Elijah and Elisha; Jesus is presented as a prophet akin to the prophets of old.[152]

2. They provide two examples of other prophets who were also unwelcome amongst their people (verse 24).[153] It is therefore not unusual that Jesus is rejected by the congregation in Nazareth (4:22, 28–29).

3. They demonstrate that the gentiles are also going to be beneficiaries of Jesus' ministry.[154] The verses therefore redefine the Jewish election traditions to demonstrate that God's messianic blessings are available to those of every ethnicity.[155] Later in Jesus' ministry, the raising of a widow's son in Nain (Luke 7:11–17) would recall Elijah's raising of a widow's son in Zarephath (1 Kgs 17:8–24), and his healing of the

---

147. Collins, "Works," 102–4. For a more detailed assessment of 4Q521, see the previous chapter.

148. Poirier, "Elijianic Figure," 353–59.

149. The question of how Jesus and John the Baptist relate to Elijah and Elisha is admittedly complex and difficult. For a helpful assessment of the relationship, see Fitzmyer, *Luke (I–IX)*, 213–25.

150. Collins, "Works," 107. See also Miller, "Elijah, John, and Jesus," 611–22.

151. Brawley, *Luke-Acts and the Jews*, 10–11.

152. Fitzmyer, *Luke (I–IX)*, 537 and Plummer, *Luke*, 127.

153. Elijah was rejected by the leaders of Israel in 1 Kgs 18–22 and 2 Kgs 1. Elisha was threatened by the king of Israel in 2 Kgs 6:26–32.

154. The verses do not present Jesus as turning his back on Israel (both Elijah and Elisha ministered primarily within the boundaries of Israel), nor do they present his ministry as being programmatically oriented toward the gentiles. They instead reveal that all people can be part of the *basileia* of God. Green, *Luke*, 217–18; Abogunrin, "Declaration at Nazareth," 225–27; Matthey, "Luke 4:16–30," 6; Tannehill, *Luke*, 94; Prior, *Jesus the Liberator*, 142; and Carroll, *Luke*, 115–16.

155. Evans, "Function," 73–75 and Prior, *Jesus the Liberator*, 147.

centurion's servant (Luke 7:1-10) would parallel Naaman's healing through Elisha's ministry (2 Kgs 5:1-19).[156]

4. They give concrete examples of whom Jesus includes amongst the poor (Isa 61:1): a widow and a leper.[157]

5. They foreshadow the coming gentile mission in Acts.[158] Significantly, the point in Acts where the mission to the gentiles begins to spread is in Acts 10:36-38, a text which refers back to the event at Nazareth.

The *basileia* of God is therefore of central concern in the passage. The use of the text to redefine election effectively delineates who is able to enter

---

156. Siker, "Gentiles," 87-89; Evans, "Function," 74; and Garland, *Luke*, 205. Significantly, both of these accounts in Luke happen shortly before Jesus referred to Isa 61 (7:22). It is possible that Luke was again intending to associate Elijah, Elisha, and Isa 61.

It has also been suggested that verses 25-27 also demonstrate a healing motif, particularly in light of Jesus' later healing ministry. This, however, seems unlikely given that the line pertaining to healing in Isa 61:1 was omitted from Luke 4:18. See Tannehill, *Luke*, 94.

157. Hertig, "Jubilee Mission," 170.

158. Siker, "Gentiles," 74; Fitzmyer, *Luke (I-IX)*, 537; Carroll, *Luke*, 115-16; Tannehill, *Narrative Unity*, 71; and Elias, "Beginning," 259. Since there was disagreement in the early church as to whether the gospel extended to gentiles, it has been suggested that verses 25-27 were added by Luke to support the gentile mission. It is not necessary, however, to postulate this possible Lukan agenda since, as has been demonstrated above, the verses follow logically from 4:23-24 as part of Jesus' response to the crowd's initial criticisms. See Ringe, *Biblical Jubilee*, 41. Contra Tannehill, "The Mission of Jesus," 59-61 and Hill, "Rejection," 177.

Crockett is critical of the view that Luke 4:25-27 is designed to foreshadow the gentile mission, instead arguing that the chief importance of the text lies in supporting early Christian relations between Jews and gentiles. He argues that the verses represent Jesus' programmatic announcement that the Old Testament stories of Elijah and Elisha are prophecies which are to be fulfilled. Crockett sees an anticipatory pre-resurrection fulfillment of the Elijah/Elisha narratives in Luke 7 by comparing the raising of the widow's son at Nain (Luke 7:11-17) with the Elijah-widow narrative, and by comparing the healing of the centurion's slave (Luke 7:1-10) with the Elisha-Naaman account. He then argues for a post-resurrection fulfillment by paralleling the Elijah/Elisha stories with various aspects of the account of Peter and Cornelius in Acts 10-11. Thus, for Crockett, these passages should be seen as a prolepsis of "Jewish-gentile *reconciliation*, the *cleansing* of the gentiles which makes it possible for Jews and gentiles to live and eat together in the new age." With regard to Luke 4:25-27, however, Crockett does not explain how the issue of Jewish-gentile relations is an important motif within the Nazareth pericope. Moreover, his view that the accounts in Luke 7 and Acts 10-11 should be understood chiefly in relation to Luke 4:25-27 are unconvincing, particularly in light of some of his questionable literary associations. For example, Crockett argues that the famine mentioned in Luke 4:25 parallels the famine mentioned in Acts 11:28-29. While this association is itself questionable, it is even more doubtful that Luke's main aim in mentioning the severity of the famine was to highlight the fact that Elijah and a gentile ate together. Crockett, "Luke 4:25-27," 178-83.

into and participate in the *basileia* of God.¹⁵⁹ The passage demonstrates that the good news of the *basileia* of God is for the marginalized and the outcasts, including even gentiles.¹⁶⁰ The foreshadowing of the gentile mission in Acts is the foreshadowing of the preaching of the good news of the *basileia* to those who were previously outsiders.¹⁶¹ This is consistent with Luke's use of Elijah and Elisha narratives elsewhere; he employed Elijah/Elisha references to outline the "requirements for membership and participation in the Kingdom of God."¹⁶²

There are some scholars who see verses 25–27 as an extension of the Jubilee year blessings, proclaimed in verses 18–19, to the gentiles.¹⁶³ Lowery,

159. This would have been particularly troubling for Luke's audience (and the original synagogue audience) if they were familiar with the rabbinic traditions that employed Isa 61, all of which emphasized Israel as the recipients of the eschatological prophet's ministry.

There are some commentators who want to draw analogies between Nazareth and Israel, and Capernaum and the gentiles, and who therefore argue that the rejection of Jesus' message by the crowd in Nazareth and Jesus' subsequent journey to Capernaum indicates the Jews' rejection of salvation and the ensuing sending of the gospel to gentiles (see, for example, Sanders, *Jews*, 168). This clearly oversteps the narrative of the Nazareth episode and is inconsistent with the remainder of Luke's Gospel. As Brawley has noted, there is no reason why Nazareth should be viewed as a cipher for Israel and Capernaum as a symbol for gentiles, particularly since nowhere in Luke's Gospel does Jesus carry out a gentile mission. See Brawley, *Luke-Acts and the Jews*, 10–11.

Similarly, this understanding of "the Jews" also freezes into one image what Luke-Acts differentiates and it presumes the separation of Christianity from Judaism (whereas, even by the end of Acts, Christianity is still presented as a Jewish sect). Brawley, "The God of Promises," 279.

160. Tiede, *Luke*, 109 and Talbert, *Reading Luke*, 60.

161. It is frequently argued that Luke 4:25–27 demonstrates a causal link between rejection by Israel and ministry to the gentiles (that is, because Elijah and Elisha were rejected by their own, they consequently ministered to gentiles). It is therefore argued that Luke 4:25–27 shows that the reason why the gentiles are to be beneficiaries of Jesus' ministry is due to his rejection by Israel. See, for example, Nolland, *Luke*, 1:200; Abogunrin, "Declaration at Nazareth," 237; and Willoughby, "Concept of Jubilee," 50. This, however, clearly oversteps the literary evidence; nowhere in these verses did Luke suggest that Jesus' ministry to the gentiles would come as a result of his rejection by his hometown. Indeed, Elijah's ministry to the widow came *before* he was explicitly rejected by Ahab, since the account of Elijah and the widow of Zarephath occurs in 1 Kgs 17:8–24, before he was rejected by King Ahab in 1 Kgs 18, and Elisha's healing of Naaman occurred *before* his life was threatened by the king of Israel (the account of Elisha and Naaman occurs in 2 Kgs 5:1–19, and it is not until 2 Kgs 6:26–32 that Elisha is threatened by the king of Israel). Rather, as Tannehill has noted, "It is not so much that Jesus goes elsewhere because he is rejected as that he is rejected because he announces that it is God's will and his mission to go elsewhere." See Tannehill, "The Mission of Jesus," 62.

162. Evans, "Function," 82.

163. See Lowery, *Sabbath and Jubilee*, 138–39; Sloan, *Favorable Year*, 87–88; and

for example, views the verses as a "Jubilee reversal," whereby those outside of the Jewish community can also partake in the privileges of a Jubilee year.[164] Similarly, Sloan argues that the verses indicate that "Luke's understanding of the Jubilee year seems to extend beyond the boundaries of the Mosaic law, which tended to preserve the blessings of that year for Jews alone."[165] This reading of verses 25–27, however, is difficult to sustain. While it is true that the verses signify that the gentiles would also benefit from Jesus' ministry, there is no indication that Luke intended to communicate that the gentiles would be partakers in Jubilee year blessings. If he were trying to relate the verses to the Jubilee, it is unlikely that he would have used the examples of Elijah and Elisha, since neither example has any connection with the Jubilee. Indeed, the lack of a connection between these verses and the Jubilee may be the reason why some of those who argue that Luke presented Jesus as declaring a Jubilee year in Luke 4:16–22 are seemingly altogether disinterested in Luke 4:23–30, despite the fact that Luke clearly saw the two passages as a single literary unit.[166]

Verses 28–29 then record the people's response to Jesus' Elijah/Elisha discourse; they sought to push him off a cliff (which the Mishnah prescribes as the first step for the ritual of stoning in *m. Sanh.* 6:4).[167] Ringe has noted that the people may have believed that Jesus was a false prophet, in which case his death would have been warranted by the Torah (Deut 13:1–5) and by precedent (Jer 11:21–23).[168] This seems possible, given that the crowd was already offended at Jesus' self-identification as the Spirit-empowered, anointed prophet of Isaiah 61. In any case, Luke presented the Elijah/Elisha discourse as incensing the crowd even further; they were filled with wrath (ἐπλήσθησαν πάντες θυμοῦ) when they heard that the message of the *basileia* of God was also for those of different cultural, racial, and geographical origins. Luke may also have included the text to foreshadow Jesus' later rejection in Jerusalem (Luke 22–23).[169] Indeed, Elias argues that the final three

---

Blosser, "Jubilee," 114–15.

164. Lowery's focus on reversals, however, is not in keeping with the original Jubilee legislation, which was more concerned with rest, redemption, and restoration. Lowery, *Sabbath and Jubilee*, 138–39. Problems associated with relating the theme of "reversal of fortunes" to the Jubilee are explored in the following chapter.

165. Sloan, *Favorable Year*, 88.

166. Two examples of works which ignore Luke 4:22–30 are Kinsler and Kinsler, *The Biblical Jubilee* and Yoder, *Politics*.

167. Poirier, "Elijianic Figure," 361.

168. Ringe, *Biblical Jubilee*, 41–42. See also Elias, "Climax," 90.

169. This is particularly the case when one considers the message of salvation which lay at the core of the Isaianic quotation (see chapter 3); Jesus was rejected when he

verses of the Nazareth episode correspond to the four parts of the passion narrative: 1) 4:28 represents the mounting hostility toward Jesus; 2) 4:29a signifies Jesus' expulsion from Jerusalem; 3) 4:29b represents his death on the cross; and 4) 4:30 represents Jesus' resurrection and ongoing mission.[170]

Finally, in verse 30, Luke records that Jesus passed through the midst of the angry crowd and went away. The verse is vague; Luke does not clearly explain how Jesus was able to escape the crowd. Longenecker has surveyed four prominent possibilities which have been proposed, before arriving at the conclusion that the best explanation for Jesus' escape is divine intervention.[171] Nolland agrees, arguing that ἐπορεύετο ("he went on his way") should perhaps be taken as a reference to the divine pattern laid out for Jesus' life, which found its goal in Jerusalem (see the use of πορεύομαι in Luke 4:42; 7:6, 11; 9:51, 52, 53, 56, 57; 13:33; 17:11; 22:22).[172] While this seems the most likely explanation, Luke does not explicitly state that a miraculous escape is in view.

Conclusion

Luke 4:14–30 serves a variety of functions within Luke's narrative. It presents a concrete example of Jesus' teaching ministry mentioned in 4:14–15 and provides a clear example of what Jesus' synagogue ministry (4:15, 31–37, 44; 6:6; 13:10–17) consisted of.[173] It also contains the first narrated episode of Jesus' public ministry in Luke's Gospel.[174] In addition to these literary functions, however, the passage also provides programmatic insights into Luke's presentation of Jesus and his ministry. These can be summarized under eight headings:

1. Jesus' relationship to the Holy Spirit

---

preached the good news of spiritual release, and he was rejected when he achieved the means of spiritual release through his death on the cross. Stein, *Luke*, 160–61; Byrne, *Hospitality*, 52; Sabourin, *St Luke*, 139; Bovon, *Lukas*, 216; Nolland, *Luke*, 1:200–202; Elias, "Climax," 87–90; Garland, *Luke*, 190; Ringe, *Luke*, 71; Carroll, *Luke*, 108–9; Mallen, *Isaiah in Luke-Acts*, 73; Willoughby, "Concept of Jubilee," 42; and Keck, *Luke*, 104.

170. Elias, "Climax," 87. See also Bailey, *Jesus through Middle Eastern Eyes*, 169.

171. These four possibilities are: 1) Jesus was extraordinarily athletic and avoided capture; 2) Jesus used mind-bending trickery on the crowd; 3) there were some sympathizers in the crowd who aided him; and 4) Luke made up the ending and therefore left out concrete details. Longenecker, *Hearing the Silence*, 24–37, 42–51.

172. Nolland, *Luke*, 202. See also Bock, *Luke*, 420 and Reicke, "Jesus in Nazareth," 539.

173. Green, *Luke*, 207.

174. Green, *Luke*, 207.

2. Jesus' identity as the eschatological prophet and messiah
3. Jesus' fulfillment of Scripture
4. Jesus' inauguration of the new age
5. Jesus' ministry of spiritual release
6. Jesus' ministry to the poor and marginalized
7. Jesus' message is for all people
8. Jesus' future rejection

The main focus of the Nazareth pericope, however, is the nature of Jesus' ministry. As has been demonstrated above, the Nazareth episode indicates that this ministry would center on spiritual release. The double reference to ἄφεσις in the Isaianic quotation emphasizes Jesus' ministry of forgiveness. It also seems that Luke understood ἄφεσις as including release from demonic spirits. Moreover, it seems that Luke understood the beneficiaries of Jesus' ministry primarily in spiritual terms. The freedom for the captives and release for the oppressed (Luke 4:18) refer to liberation from spiritual imprisonment. Similarly, the references to the poor and the blind are figurative as well as literal.

As the above chapter demonstrates, there are no clear literary references to the Jubilee. The reference which most scholars cite as being the most clear is the Isaianic quotation, which, as the previous chapter demonstrated, was probably not viewed in connection with the Jubilee by Luke (or his audience). While there are a number of words in the passage which have been connected with the Jubilee by a few scholars, these connections seem to be extremely tenuous and quite unlikely.

The chapter does, however, clearly refer to the *basileia* of God, albeit indirectly. Luke 4:15 is most likely a reference to Jesus' *basileia* ministry, elucidated in Mark 1:15. The use of certain words such as κηρύξαι and σήμερον emphasize the *basileia*, and concluding the Isaianic text with "an acceptable year of the Lord" highlights the reign of God ushered in through Jesus' ministry. The Spirit (mentioned in 4:14, 18) is frequently used by Luke in connection with the proclamation of the *basileia* of God and should be read in that light. Similarly, the Elijah/Elisha motifs (and the Isaianic quotation), while not explicitly referring to the *basileia*, nonetheless serve to clarify who is able to enter into and participate in the *basileia* of God. Thus, Jesus' proclamation of the Isaianic text serves to simultaneously proclaim the *basileia* of God and Jesus' role in relation to it, which is consistent with how Luke presented the *basileia* of God throughout Luke 1–4.[175]

175. Despite the myriad implicit references to the *basileia* in Luke's opening

There are at least three of Hays's criteria which are addressed in this chapter.[176] In relation to Hays's criterion of volume, there are a number of words and patterns in Luke 4:14–30 which have been cited as an intertextual link to the Old Testament Jubilee. Most notably, these include the use of κηρύξαι in Luke 4:19, the supposed linking of Isaiah 58 with Isaiah 61 on the basis of Yom Kippur, the double use of ἄφεσις, the use of δεκτός, and the mentioning of Jesus' hometown (πατρίς) in verses 23 and 24. Each of these supposed links to the Jubilee are very unlikely. Indeed, it seems there are no terms or syntactical patterns which clearly support the presence of Jubilary allusions in the text.

When one considers the criterion of thematic coherence, it seems even more unlikely that there are Jubilary allusions in the Nazareth pericope. Indeed, the eight purposes of the passage listed above are all manifestly unrelated to the Jubilee provisions of rest for the land, the redemption of property, and the redemption of slaves. Indeed, it would be very difficult to posit any relationship between the Old Testament Jubilee and the themes presented in Luke 4:14–30 and the surrounding text.

Finally, with regard to the criterion of satisfaction, arguing in favor of a Jubilary allusion makes little sense in the immediate literary context, and no sense in the surrounding discourse. The main basis on which the text is linked to the Jubilee is the Isaianic quotation, which, as demonstrated in chapter 4, is unlikely to have been viewed by Luke in connection with the Jubilee. The specific purposes for which Isaiah 61 was employed (and for which the Nazareth pericope was included) do not relate to the biblical Jubilee.

---

chapters, the actual phrase "the *basileia* of God" is not employed until Luke 4:43, after which it is used frequently (see chapter 3). Ziccardi argues that this is because Luke designed the first four chapters to catch up to Mark 1:14–15 (which corresponds to 4:14–44). He argues that the first four chapters of Luke undeniably address the *basileia*, albeit indirectly; they present God's *basileia* as being uniquely and necessarily related to Jesus, predicated on his identity as the Davidic messiah and the Son of God. Moreover, in Luke 3–4, references to the *basileia* are usually achieved by citations of or allusions to *basileia*-related texts from the Old Testament (as in the case of Luke 4:18–19). See Ziccardi, *Relationship*, 261–64; 371–74, 499–501. As Blomberg has noted, this accords with the general synoptic sequence of Jesus' self-disclosure. Blomberg, "Response," 33. Thus, while the exact phrase "*basileia* of God" does not appear in Luke 4:14–30, it is nonetheless a central theme.

176. In relation to the criterion of history of interpretation, appendix 1 demonstrates that there is a long history of the Nazareth pericope (and in particular the Isaianic quotation) being associated with the Jubilee. It is only recently (that is, in the late twentieth century), however, that Luke himself was suggested to have intentionally presented Jubilary allusions in the Nazareth pericope.

6

Beyond Nazareth

Other Themes and Passages in Luke
with Suggested Jubilary Connections

Introduction

While Luke 4:16–30 is the passage which is most often linked with the Jubilee, there are a number of scholars who have suggested various other allusions in Luke-Acts.[1] Indeed, scholars such as Donald Blosser believe that allusions to the Jubilee are so prolific in Luke's work that one cannot understand the ministry of the Lukan Jesus without recognizing the Jubilee theme.[2] This chapter will therefore address the remaining suggested Jubilary allusions throughout Luke-Acts to determine their validity.[3]

---

1. I include the five texts in the Acts of the Apostles for the sake of completeness and as a basis for comparison within the traditional Lukan corpus.

2. Blosser, "Jubilee," 143. See also Willoughby, "Concept of Jubilee", 50–51.

3. The proposed allusions addressed in this chapter include all those mentioned in appendix 1, though many have been grouped together thematically (see the first four sections of this chapter). The examination of each theme or text is achieved with the use of Hays's criteria, and in particular the criteria of volume, thematic coherence, and satisfaction. These criteria are not, however, necessarily explicitly mentioned throughout the treatment of each text.

Reversal of Fortunes

There are many who have recognized the theme of reversal of fortunes in Luke-Acts.[4] God is portrayed as being deeply concerned for those considered to be lowly, marginalized, and outcast, usually characterized by the poor, tax collectors, sinners, Samaritans, gentiles, and women.[5] They are raised up and accepted by God, becoming part of his restored people. Conversely, the rich, powerful, self-righteous, and those esteemed within society are cast down and lowered, and ultimately cut off from the people of God.[6] As York has written,

> God humbles those who exalt themselves and exalts those who humble themselves; he makes last those who are first and first those who are last; he saves those who lose themselves for Jesus' sake and those who seek to save themselves will be lost; he fills the hungry but sends the rich away empty; he causes those weeping to laugh and those laughing to mourn and weep.[7]

The connection between the reversal of fortunes and the *basileia* of God has also been well recognized; the reversal of fortunes is frequently presented as a depiction of the values of the *basileia*.[8] That is, to be under the reign of God is to embrace the reversal of fortunes as described throughout Luke-Acts. For those in Luke's audience familiar with the apocalyptic literature, the reversals would have indicated that the *basileia* had arrived.[9]

It is this theme of reversal of fortunes which some scholars have linked to the Old Testament Jubilee. Blosser, for example, argues that "the reversal of roles is a critical element of the Jubilee."[10] Similarly, Hertig believes that the Jubilee can be summarized as "a reversal of rich and poor, a redistribution of resources, and a flattening of pyramids."[11] Sloan makes the most far-reaching claim by not only arguing that the Old Testament Jubilee

---

4. See, for example, Stein, *Luke*, 49–50; Johnson, *Luke*, 22; York, *Last Shall Be First*, 9–184; Knight, *Luke's Gospel*, 153, 172; and Esler, *Community and Gospel*, 188.

5. Stein, *Luke*, 49–50.

6. Johnson, *Luke*, 22.

7. York, *Last Shall Be First*, 93. York also argues that Luke was more interested in the reversal of accepted categories of shame and honor than in addressing the socioeconomic structures of his day. York, *Last Shall Be First*, 182–84.

8. Knight, *Luke's Gospel*, 172 and Garland, *Luke*, 290. See also the section addressing the *basileia* of God in Luke-Acts in chapter 3.

9. York, *Last Shall Be First*, 183.

10. Blosser, "Jubilee," 141. See also Schürmann, *Das Lukasevangelium*, 76 and Kinsler and Kinsler, *The Biblical Jubilee*, 106–7.

11. Hertig, "Jubilee Mission," 171.

precepts (if they were ever practiced) would have resulted in "a thoroughgoing reversal of all material forms of oppression," but by also arguing that the background to the reversal of fortunes in Luke's Gospel is provided by the Jubilee, which stands "as the controlling metaphorical antecedent."[12] Thus, Sloan argues that the theme of fortune reversal in Luke's Gospel adds weight to the argument that the Gospel is infused throughout with Jubilary imagery.[13]

There are, however, several problems with associating the Jubilee with the theme of reversal:

1. Describing the Jubilee in terms of status reversal (or fortune reversal) is a mischaracterization. If a slave was set free by his master during a Jubilee year, the slave-owner would not become a slave. That is, their roles (or fortunes) would not have been reversed. The Jubilee is better described in terms of status restoration (or the restoration of fortunes).

2. The reversal of fortunes in Luke (such as the poor being blessed, the humble being exalted, and sinners being called to righteousness) is categorically and manifestly different from the Jubilee legislation, whereby land, property, and people were returned (or restored) to their original state.

3. Even if the argument can be made that the Jubilee precepts from Leviticus 25 do exemplify status reversal, there is still no reason to assume that Luke necessarily was considering them when the Gospel tradition was formed. This is particularly the case in view of the next point.

4. There are many examples throughout the Old Testament which exemplify status reversal (or restoration), including the Exodus and the narratives of Esther, Joseph, David, and Daniel. Similarly, the themes of honoring the humble and God's concern for the poor are both seen frequently throughout the prophetic literature. Indeed, the theme of reversal of fortune has a long and far-reaching presence within the Old Testament. There is not, therefore, any need to assume that descriptions of reversal of fortunes in Luke-Acts must be read in connection with the Jubilee legislation, and indeed, there is no evidence that the Lukan theme of reversal of fortunes necessarily needs to be read as having any particular Old Testament background since it is so widely depicted.

---

12. Sloan, *Favorable Year*, 125, 161.
13. Sloan, *Favorable Year*, 125.

Despite the above arguments, the suggested link between the reversal of fortunes and the Jubilee has caused some scholars to argue that certain Lukan passages which incorporate the reversal of fortunes should be read as having Jubilary undertones. These include Mary's Magnificat (Luke 1:14–55), the Beatitudes and Woes (Luke 6:20–26), the parable of the rich fool (Luke 12:13–21), the parable of the great banquet (Luke 14:7–24), and the parable of the rich man and Lazarus (Luke 16:19–31).[14]

In relation to Hays's criterion of volume, there are no words or syntactical patterns which would support any of these texts containing an allusion to the Jubilee, nor can the Jubilee legislation be considered particularly distinctive or prominent overall (which Hays views as an important feature of this criterion).[15] The main textual reason why some scholars have linked these texts to the Jubilee is because of the presence of the word πτωχός (used in four of the five texts).[16] The association, however, is made on the basis of Isaiah 61 (which Luke probably did not associate with the Jubilee) rather than any of the Old Testament Jubilee texts where the word πτωχός does not appear.[17]

Hertig argues that the use of ταπείνωσις in Luke 1:48 should be read as paralleling πτωχός, which is used in the Isaianic quotation in Luke 4:18–19, which, he argues, has Jubilee allusions.[18] The tenuousness of his argument is manifestly apparent. One must assume that Luke definitely viewed ταπείνωσιν as paralleling πτωχός, and then assume that he would

---

14. The Beatitudes and Woes (Luke 6:20–26) have also been linked to the Jubilee on the basis of the Isa 61 background to some of the Beatitudes. This text will therefore be treated again in the section below which addresses texts alluding to Isa 61.

15. Hays, *The Conversion of the Imagination*, 34–37. There are some words which are used in some of these texts which also appear in the Jubilee legislation in Lev 25; however, there is no reason that to assume that they should be associated. In Mary's Magnificat, for example, the words δούλη, γενεά, and πατέρας are all employed, all of which also occur in the Jubilee legislation in Lev 25. They are all so common within the Old Testament (δούλη occurs 38 times, γενεά occurs 184 times, and πατέρας occurs 1109 times), that it would be difficult to argue that Luke definitely connected them with the Jubilee legislation. Significantly, there were no studies found during the course of this research which argue that any of these words signal a Jubilary allusion.

Further, in Luke 6:20–26, the words ἀφορίζω and ἡμέρα are employed in a similar way to the Jubilee legislation in Leviticus, though once again they are used so frequently throughout the Old Testament that there is no reason to assume that Luke associated them exclusively with the Jubilee.

16. The term πτωχός was examined in some detail in chapter 4. It was established that it has no distinct Jubilary connotations.

17. See chapter 4. Scholars who draw a connection between these texts and the Jubilee based on Luke's use of πτωχός include Blosser, "Jubilee," 134, 139–41 and Ringe, "Jubilee Proclamation," 180–88, 211–13.

18. Hertig, "Jubilee Mission," 174.

view all uses of πτωχός in connection to Luke 4:18-19 (even though Mary's Magnificat occurs before the Nazareth pericope), and then assume that he interpreted the Isaianic text in connection to the Jubilee (which, as has already been demonstrated, he probably did not).

Concerning thematic coherence, suggested allusions to the Jubilee in Luke 1:41-55; 6:20-26; 12:13-21; 14:7-24; and 16:19-31 do not serve to illuminate the wider point of any of these texts. While there are many scholars who see the theme of reversal of fortunes highlighted in each of these texts, it is a fallacy to characterize the Jubilee this way (as demonstrated above).[19] In fact, conflating the Lukan theme of reversal of fortunes with the Jubilee can actually serve to cloud the meaning of a text, since Jubilee ideas and imagery are effectively forced upon it. Blosser highlights this point well. He argues that Luke 14:11 ("For everyone who exalts himself will be humbled, and he who humbles himself will be exalted") is "a clear Jubilee principle, for as the land is restored, debts are forgiven and slaves are set free, the lowly are indeed raised up and the high are brought down until they share a place of ... equality."[20] While it is possible that if the Jubilee was practiced there may have been more social equality than if it wasn't practiced (though even this would largely depend on the state of society before a Jubilee year), that is hardly the point of Luke 14:11. Indeed, the Lukan text sees the two positions of humility and exaltation *reversed* rather than equalized. Moreover, importing the ideas of land restoration, debt cancellation, and the release of slaves again serves to complicate the text rather than illuminate it.

Finally, the application of the criteria of history of interpretation and satisfaction again does not support the presence of Jubilary allusions. As appendix 1 demonstrates, there are no ancient commentators and only a few modern scholars (since Trocmé) who argue in favor of Jubilary allusions in Luke 1:41-55; 6:20-26; 12:13-21; 14:7-24; and 16:19-31. This is for good reason; the proposed allusion makes no sense in its immediate context, nor does it serve to illuminate the surrounding discourse.

Texts that Allude to Isaiah 61

As has already been mentioned, texts in Luke-Acts which cite or allude to Isaiah 61 are of central importance in determining the presence or absence

---

19. Those who see the theme of reversal of fortunes in at least some of these texts include Leifeld, "Luke," 836, 891; Garland, *Luke*, 95-99, 266, 592-94, 671-75; Morris, *St. Luke*, 93, 272; Green, *Luke*, 267, 542; Marshall, *The Gospel of Luke*, 632; Johnson, *Luke*, 22, 42; Nolland, *Luke*, 1:72-76, 283; and Edwards, *Luke*, 473.

20. Blosser, "Jubilee," 138.

of Lukan references to the Jubilee, since it is these passages which are frequently viewed as the principal points of contact between the Old Testament Jubilee and the New Testament.[21] As demonstrated in chapter 4, however, there is no evidence that Luke associated Isaiah 61 with the Jubilee, nor are there any Second Temple works that are likely to have influenced Luke which draw an association between the Isaianic text and the Jubilee. While there seems to be an allusion to the Jubilee in the Isaianic text (see chapter 1), Luke employed Isaiah 61 to highlight several key points, all of which center on the elucidation of Jesus' ministry (see chapter 4). This elucidation includes a focus on the *basileia* of God since the Isaianic passage is used to present the presence and character of the *basileia*.

Nevertheless, there are four Lukan texts which are frequently identified as alluding to Isaiah 61 and have therefore also been identified by some scholars as allusions to the Old Testament Jubilee.[22] While one of these texts (Luke 4:16-30) has already been examined in detail in chapter 4, the other three (Luke 6:20-26; 7:18-35; Acts 10:34-43) have not yet been examined in relation to Hays's criteria for determining Old Testament allusions and are addressed below.

In relation to the criterion of volume, Luke 6:20-26; 7:18-35; and Acts 10:34-43 have very few words or syntactical patterns which can be linked to the Old Testament Jubilee. Indeed, the basis on which some scholars see a relationship between the Lukan texts and the Jubilee is simply that Luke was alluding to Isaiah 61, which is thought to be a Jubilee text.[23] If one looks outside Isaiah 61:1-2, there are only two words employed in the three Lukan

---

21. Sloan, *Favorable Year*, 115 and Ringe, "Jubilee Proclamation," 290.

22. Sloan, *Favorable Year*, 123-38; Ringe, "Jubilee Proclamation," 165-76, 180-88, 267-86; Blosser, "Jubilee," 134-36; Kinsler and Kinsler, *The Biblical Jubilee*, 105-6; Edwards, *Luke*, 221-22; Hertig, "Jubilee Mission," 173-74; Tiede, *Luke*, 155; and Trocmé, *Nonviolent Revolution*, 37. The subject of the degree to which Luke quotes Isa 61 or merely alludes to it in each of these texts is a topic addressed by Ringe, though it lies outside the scope of this study.

23. Sloan, *Favorable Year*, 123-38 and Ringe, "Jubilee Proclamation," 165-76, 180-88, 267-86. One exception to this is Blosser, who argues that the six ministry functions which Jesus lists in Luke 7:22 (τυφλοὶ ἀναβλέπουσιν, χωλοὶ περιπατοῦσιν, λεπροὶ καθαρίζονται καὶ κωφοὶ ἀκούουσιν, νεκροὶ ἐγείρονται, πτωχοὶ εὐαγγελίζονται) have their background in Isa 29:18; 35:5; 42:7; and 61:1, and he identifies all of these texts as "Jubilee texts." While it is possible to argue that the background to each of Jesus' ministry functions are found in the various Isaianic texts which Blosser has identified, it is very difficult to posit that all of them have a Jubilary background. Indeed, even Ringe (who sees a Jubilary background to Luke 7:18-35) argues that of all the Isaianic texts which form the background to Luke 7:18-23, it is "only Isa 61:1-2 [which] contains specific Jubilee language in the MT." See Blosser, "Jubilee," 135-36 and Ringe, "Jubilee Proclamation," 166.

texts which could be argued to have a textual relationship with the Jubilee legislation: ἄφεσις and ἀποστέλλω.²⁴ The word ἄφεσις occurs once in Acts 10:43 in reference to the forgiveness of sins. As has already been demonstrated in chapter 3, the word had a clear and distinct meaning throughout all of Luke's work (and indeed, the entire body of New Testament and other early church material), centered on the forgiveness of sins, and as such there is no reason to assume that Luke viewed the word in connection with the Jubilee. The second word, ἀποστέλλω, occurs once in Leviticus 25:21 (in the Jubilee legislation), once in Isaiah 61:1, and is also found in Luke 7:20; 7:27; and Acts 10:36. The frequency of the word throughout the Old and New Testaments, however, makes it very difficult to argue that there is a textual parallel.²⁵

The criterion of thematic coherence also does not support Jubilary allusions in any of the texts in question. Indeed, it is difficult to see how the provisions associated with the biblical Jubilee (which centered on rest for the land and the redemption of property and slaves) could be made to cohere with the blessings and woes (Luke 6:20–26), Jesus' response to John the Baptist's disciples and his explanation of John's ministry (Luke 7:18–35), or to the account of Peter at Cornelius's house (Acts 10:23b–48).²⁶

While the vast majority of Lukan scholars would seemingly concur with this (evidenced in part by the vast majority of studies and commentaries not mentioning the Jubilee in relation to any of these verses), there are nonetheless some who would disagree. Trocmé, for instance, states, "Only in light of the Jubilee can the meaning and scope of [the Lukan Beatitudes]

---

24. Aside from these two words, there are only four words which occur in the Lukan texts in question which point back to the Isaianic text: κηρύσσω (which occurs once in Isa 61:1 and once in both Acts 10:37 and 42); τυφλός (which occurs once in Isa 61:1 and once in both Luke 7:21 and 22); πτωχός (which occurs once in Isa 61:1 and once in both Luke 6:20 and 7:22); and πενθέω (which occurs once in Isa 61:2 and once in Luke 6:25, though its occurrence in Isaiah occurs after the conclusion of the Isaianic quotation in Luke 4). These words were examined in detail in chapter 4 and it was seen that none of them has any Jubilary significance.

25. Indeed, ἀποστέλλω occurs 521 times in the Septuagint and occurs 50 times in Luke-Acts. Additionally, the varied usage of the word demonstrates that Luke was not attaching a specific Jubilary meaning to it even within the Lukan texts in question. In Luke 7:20, it is used in reference to John the Baptist sending his disciples to Jesus; in Luke 7:27 it is used in reference to John being sent before Jesus; and in Acts 10:36 it is used to refer to the word (that is, the good news of Jesus which is sent by God to the people of Israel.

26. With regard to Luke 7:18–35, it is clear that John being in prison is categorically different from the redemption of slaves described in the Jubilee legislation in Leviticus. The allusion to the freeing of captives in Isa 61 should be recognized as a sufficient and more suitable background text.

fully reveal themselves."[27] He argues that the blessedness described in the Beatitudes is reserved for those "who have voluntarily thrown off their possessions to fulfill the Jubilee," after arguing that the Lukan Jesus calls his followers to implement a literal Jubilee year.[28] His argument demonstrates both a misunderstanding of the meaning of the "poor" in Luke's Gospel (see chapter 4) and a misconstrual of why the blessedness of the Beatitudes is bestowed: the emphasis falls more on the assurance that God sees the plight of the poor, hungry, mourners, and persecuted and will intervene on their behalf, rather than on ethical exhortation ("be poor, be hungry, weep, and be persecuted").[29]

In a similar way to the suggested Jubilee texts which feature the theme of reversal of fortunes, the criterion of historical interpretation demonstrates that Luke 6:20-26; 7:18-35; and Acts 10:34-43 have all only recently been connected with the Jubilee (see appendix 1). None of the three texts were associated with the biblical Jubilee before the publication of Trocmé's work in 1961, and even since then there are very few scholars who see a Jubilary allusion.

Finally, the criterion of satisfaction is again unmet for these three texts. As has already been stated, the reason why Luke 6:20-26; 7:18-35; and Acts 10:34-43 have been connected to the Jubilee is on the basis of the allusions to Isaiah 61, which is assumed to be a Jubilee text.[30] As has already been demonstrated in chapter 4, however, it is extremely unlikely that Luke viewed the Isaianic text in relation to the Jubilee; the text was employed for several specific purposes, none of which are connected to the biblical Jubilee.

Debt Cancellation

The subject of debt cancellation can be seen in a number of Lukan texts, particularly Luke 7:36-50; 11:2-4; and 16:1-9. In the first of these (Luke 7:36-50), Jesus employed the idea of debts to represent the notion of sin, with the cancellation of debts thereby representing the forgiveness of sins.

27. Trocmé, *Nonviolent Revolution*, 37.

28. Trocmé, *Nonviolent Revolution*, 37.

29. Garland, *Luke*, 276. A fuller critique of Trocmé's study lies beyond the scope of this study. Suffice to say, however, it seems very unlikely that a key part of the ministry of the historical Jesus would have been a call for the implementation of a Jubilee year, given that there is no evidence of this year ever occurring and there is no mention of the term "Jubilee" in any of the Four Gospels.

30. As shown above, Luke 6:20-26 has also erroneously been linked to the Jubilee on the basis of the theme of reversal of fortunes.

Similarly, in Luke's version of the Lord's Prayer (Luke 11:2–4), the conflation of the ideas of sins and debts is unmistakeable: "Forgive us our sins, for we ourselves also forgive everyone who is indebted to us" (ἄφες ἡμῖν τὰς ἁμαρτίας ἡμῶν, καὶ γὰρ αὐτοὶ ἀφίομεν παντὶ ὀφείλοντι ἡμῖν). This was not an uncommon metaphor; the Jews frequently employed the concept of debt to represent sin.[31] Luke also, however, used the notion of debts for other purposes. While Luke 16:1–9 (the parable of the unjust steward) is one of the most notoriously difficult passages to interpret in all of Luke-Acts, there is little doubt that the notion of debts was not intended to be a metaphor for sins.[32]

Thus, debt cancellation is seemingly not a major theme in Luke's Gospel, nor is it presented as a principle to be practiced literally.[33] Indeed, debt cancellation was instead used to aid in the communication of a wider point. Significantly, it seems the point of at least two of the texts was to highlight aspects of the *basileia* of God. In Luke 7:36–50, Jesus' forgiving of the woman's sin points Luke's audience back to the Nazareth episode, where his ministry of spiritual liberation is made clear (see chapter 5). Similarly, in Luke 11:2–4, the prayer highlights forgiveness from God, and the forgiveness offered by those praying to those who sinned against them. As has already been mentioned, Luke's emphasis on forgiveness is inextricably linked to the reign of God, since it is a person's forgiveness which signals entry into God's *basileia* (see chapter 3). Finally, while a specific conclusion about the point of the parable of the unjust steward lies beyond the scope of this study, it does seem likely that Jesus was relating the parable to the *basileia*, given his closing statement about eternal dwellings (αἰωνίους σκηνάς) and the ensuing teaching regarding service to God rather than finances (Luke 16:10–15). Thus, the instances where images of debt cancellation are employed seem to be understood best in relation to various aspects of the *basileia*.

There are some, however, who see Lukan references to debt cancellation as evidence of reliance upon Jubilee traditions. Yoder, for example, argues that the Jubilee provision of the remission of debts stands in the center of Jesus' teaching and theology.[34] He argues that the Lord's Prayer (Luke

---

31. Stein, *Luke*, 326 and Marshall, *The Gospel of Luke*, 310. This is also seen in Luke 13:1–4, where ἁμαρτωλός (sinner) is used synonymously with ὀφειλέτης (debtor).

32. Goodrich, "Voluntary Debt Remission," 547–48. On pages 548–53, Goodrich also includes a helpful survey of the varying interpretations of the text.

33. Contra Green, who argues that "in Jesus' ministry debts are canceled. His mission is to release persons from evil in all of its guises, including the evil of the never-ending cycle of gifts leading to obligations." See Green, *Luke*, 321 and Reimer, "The Forgiveness of Debts," 162.

34. Yoder, *Politics*, 61.

11:2–4) is a "Jubilary prayer," and that the debt cancellation in the parables of the unmerciful servant (Luke 7:36–50) and the unjust steward (Luke 16:1–9) are two proofs that Jesus really did call for the implementation of a literal Jubilee year.³⁵ While there are few who would agree with Yoder's interpretation, there are nonetheless some others who see debt cancellation in Luke's Gospel as indicative of Jubilee imagery or principles.³⁶ As can be seen through the application of Hays's criteria, however, there is no clear reason that one should see allusions to the Jubilee in any Lukan reference to debt cancellation.

In relation to the criterion of volume, there are two main words which have caused some scholars to see Jubilary allusions. The first is χαρίζομαι, employed twice in Luke 7:42–43 to denote the "canceling" or "remitting" of a debt. Sanders sees this word as being synonymous with ἀφίημι, which he argues has clear Jubilee connotations, and thus one should see the debt cancellation in this light.³⁷ His argument is difficult to maintain. As has already been shown in chapter 3, there is no discernible link between the Jubilee and ἀφίημι (as distinct from ἄφεσις) anywhere in the Septuagint (or indeed in any Greek literature including the New Testament). Even if there were, however, Sanders fails to address adequately why χαρίζομαι should necessarily be read synonymously with ἀφίημι. This is particularly important given the semantic range of both words.³⁸ Additionally, χαρίζομαι is also used by Luke on five other occasions (Luke 7:21; Acts 3:14; 25:11, 16; 27:24), none

---

35. Yoder, *Politics*, 62–69.

36. These include Ringe, *Luke*, 220–30, 243–58; Blosser, "Jubilee," 136–37, 139–40; Sanders, "Sins," 84–92; Pilgrim, *Good News to the Poor*, 137; and Sloan, *Favorable Year*, 139–45. Though it is not strictly pertinent to this study, it is interesting to note that N. T. Wright argues that though the historical Jesus most likely did not institute a literal Jubilee year, it seems he was keen to see his followers adopt the Jubilee principle of debt cancellation. He writes:

> Although Jesus did not envisage that he would persuade Israel as a whole to keep the Jubilee year, *he expected his followers to live by the Jubilee principle among themselves.* He expected, and taught, that they should forgive one another not only "sins" but also debts. This may help to explain the remarkable practice within the early church whereby resources were pooled, in a fashion not unlike the Essene community of goods.

Wright, *Jesus and the Victory of God*, 295.

37. Sanders, "Sins," 87.

38. As has already been mentioned in chapter 3, ἀφίημι is sometimes used to refer to the release of debts; however, it is also used to mean "to let go," "to leave in peace," and "to permit." Χαρίζομαι, on the other hand, can sometimes refer to cancelling (in the contexts of debts); however, it can also mean "to give or grant freely as a favor," "to remit or forgive," and "to show oneself to be gracious."

of which are related to debt cancellation, which again cautions against the assumption that Luke connected the word with the Jubilee.

The other word which has been singled out as having Jubilary content is ὀφείλω, used by Luke in the Lord's Prayer (11:2-4) to denote those who have sinned against others/become indebted ("Forgive us our sins, for we ourselves also forgive everyone who is indebted [ὀφείλοντι] to us"). Sloan argues that Luke has chosen this word over the Matthean ὀφειλέτης because it is also used in the debt cancellation legislation in Deuteronomy 15, which Sloan argues cannot be read apart from the Jubilee legislation in Leviticus 25.[39] There are several problems with Sloan's argument:

1. Luke used ὀφείλω on several other occasions, two of which are unconnected with financial debts (Luke 17:10; Acts 17:29).[40] Luke did not, therefore, treat the word as having an exclusive meaning only related to debt cancellation, and therefore may not have viewed the word in connection to Deuteronomy 15.

2. Even if Luke did associate the word with the Deuteronomic legislation, there is no need to assume that he viewed that legislation in connection with the Jubilee. Indeed, as has already been discussed in chapter 1, the Deuteronomic text is significantly different from the Jubilee text in Leviticus 25. While there are some thematic similarities, the text in Deuteronomy 15 includes specific provisions for Hebrew slave-women, occurs every seven years, does not mention an agricultural fallow year, and there is some question over whether the text legislates the cancellation of debts or merely their suspension every seven years.

3. It is also unlikely that Luke chose ὀφείλω over the Matthean ὀφειλέτης specifically to draw attention to the Deuteronomic legislation. Far more likely is Fitzmyer's suggestion: Luke changed the wording of the sentence from the Matthean text to make the petition more intelligible to his gentile Christian readers.[41]

---

39. Sloan, *Favorable Year*, 139-45.

40. The three other occasions when Luke employed ὀφείλω pertain to the other passages being discussed in this section: Luke 7:41; and 16:5, 7.

41. See Fitzmyer, *Luke (X-XXIV)*, 897 and Nolland, *Luke*, 2:617. While Fitzmyer is speaking particularly of the change from ὀφειλήματα (Matt 6:12) to ἁμαρτίας (Luke 11:4), it was this change in wording which probably prompted the change from ὀφειλέτης to ὀφείλω, since Luke would have been free from the parallelism in the Matthean text (ὀφειλήματα and ὀφειλέτης). He would therefore have felt at liberty to employ his preferred ὀφείλω (which occurs six times in Luke-Acts as opposed to ὀφειλέτης, which occurs only once in Luke 13:4).

In sum, neither χαρίζομαι nor ὀφείλω have any connection with the Jubilee legislation anywhere in the Septuagint, and there is no reason to suggest that Luke viewed the words in this light either. Indeed, there are no words or syntactical patterns in Luke 7:36–50; 11:2–4; or 16:1–9 which would give any reason for one to assume reliance on Jubilee traditions.

Similarly, the criterion of thematic coherence also cautions against assuming an awareness or reliance upon the Old Testament Jubilee. While it is the theme of debt cancellation which has prompted some scholars to see the three Lukan texts as containing Jubilee motifs, it must be remembered that nowhere in the Jubilee legislation is there an explicit call to cancel debts.[42] Even if one associates debt cancellation with the Jubilee, however, it must be noted that the instances of debt cancellation in the three Lukan texts look markedly different from what Jubilee remittance would have entailed. Jubilee debt cancellation would have occurred every fifty years and would have resulted from the prescribed restoration of status and property. Debt cancellation in Luke's work is used as part of Jesus' wider teaching about the relationship between love and the forgiveness of sins (Luke 7:36–50) to highlight that sins are akin to debts which require forgiveness/cancellation (Luke 11:2–4) and as a sub-point within Jesus' wider narrative about the prudence (φρόνιμος) of the steward (Luke 16:1–9). The debt cancellation that would have occurred as a result of a Jubilee year was categorically different from that seen in Luke's Gospel.

Finally, the criteria of history of interpretation and satisfaction also do not support the presence of a Jubilary allusion. With regard to the history of interpretation, there are only a few modern scholars who argue in favor of Jubilary allusions in the three Lukan texts in question (see appendix 1). The criterion of satisfaction is similarly unfulfilled by the suggested allusion. The gulf of difference between the debt cancellation that would have occurred as a result of a Jubilee year and the allusions to debt cancellation as presented in Luke's work is so great that it makes little sense to connect them.

Redistribution of Property

Another area in which Luke is said to have employed Jubilee traditions is in the various passages which contain references to what is sometimes termed the "redistribution of capital." This redistribution was a major emphasis in the Jubilee legislation, whereby property was returned (or redistributed) to its original owners (or their families) in accordance with the Mosaic

---

42. Though, as was explained in chapter 1, the redemption of property and debt-slaves would have effectively resulted in debt cancellation.

distribution (Lev 25:14-17, 23-34). It is argued that the similarities between the Jubilee redistribution and some Lukan texts are indicative of authorial dependence on an intentional allusion.

In particular, there are six texts which some scholars have suggested as having Jubilary allusions in this regard: Luke 12:22-34; 18:18-23; 19:1-10; 21:1-4; Acts 2:42-47; and 4:32-37.[43] The first three of these texts address the giving of finances to the poor. In Luke 12:22-34, Jesus taught his disciples not to worry about earthly treasures, and that they were to instead pursue treasures in heaven. As part of this teaching, he commanded them to sell their possessions and give to the poor (πωλήσατε τὰ ὑπάρχοντα ὑμῶν καὶ δότε ἐλεημοσύνην). Similarly, in Jesus' response to the rich ruler (Luke 18:18-30), the ruler was directed to sell everything he had and to give it all to the poor (πάντα ὅσα ἔχεις πώλησον καὶ διάδος πτωχοῖς) and he would have treasure in heaven (verse 22). Finally, after Zacchaeus met with Jesus he gave half of his possessions to the poor and paid back four times those whom he had cheated (see Luke 19:1-10). It is argued that this giving of one's finances/possessions to the poor is a "Jubilee ordinance,"[44] and that the promise of heavenly treasures if one forfeits earthly wealth mirrors the promise in the Jubilee legislation that God would sovereignly watch over those who are faithful.[45]

There are, however, significant differences between the redistribution entailed in the Jubilee legislation and that indicated in the three Lukan texts. For example, the redistribution which occurred in a Jubilee year was designed to ensure that each family had their property returned to them. Whilst something like this this might have occurred in the case of the Zacchaeus story, in the other two texts Jesus directed his listeners to sell all they had and give to the poor. In other words, Jesus' direction was to give

---

43. Works which argue in favor of Jubilee allusions in these verses include:
    1. Trocmé, *Nonviolent Revolution*, 33-37 (Luke 12:22-34; 18:18-23; 19:1-10; 21:1-4)
    2. Yoder, *Politics*, 69-71 (Luke 12:22-34; 18:18-23; 19:1-10; 21:1-4)
    3. Blosser, "Jubilee," 137 and 141-42 (Luke 12:22-34; 18:18-23; 19:1-10)
    4. Lightfoot, *Whole Works*, 8:75-76 (Acts 2:42-47)
    5. Henry, *Commentary*, 6:747 (4:32-37)
    6. Kinsler and Kinsler, *The Biblical Jubilee*, 141-43.
    7. Reimer, "The Forgiveness of Debts," 165-67.
    8. Richard, "Now is the Time," 54.

Others, such as Ringe, also see Jubilary allusions in some of these verses, though not because of the redistribution of capital. These other suggested allusions are addressed elsewhere in this chapter.

44. Yoder, *Politics*, 70.

45. Blosser, "Jubilee," 141.

graciously to the poor, rather than return to them what was theirs. Additionally, even in the case of Zacchaeus returning property to the poor, it is clear that it was not the strict and literal returning of people's property that was of interest to Jesus, but rather the generous heart behind the giving. If a strict Jubilary return of property was in view, the Lukan Jesus would no doubt have instructed Zacchaeus not to pay back four times the amount, but only what was owed.[46] Finally, it is important to note that where the Lukan Jesus called his disciples effectively to become poor (by the selling and giving away of their possessions), the Jubilee legislation was designed to alleviate poverty in Israel. That is, Jesus' call to embrace poverty in one's own life is entirely different from the Jubilee provisions, which sought to alleviate national poverty. The most one can say is that both the Jubilee legislation and the three Lukan narratives are concerned with the needs of the poor and call for reliance on the sovereignty of God, which is hardly enough grounds to argue for a specific intertextual link.

The account of the widow's offering (Luke 21:1–4) is also said to contain a Jubilary allusion, since it is argued that the widow giving all she had to live on parallels the Jubilee year redistribution of capital that occurred every fifty years.[47] As has already been noted, however, the Jubilee was not a call for people to give away all of their worldly goods or finances. Rather, in relation to property, it was a time when one's family assets would be returned. There is simply no evidence that the widow was following a Jubilee program, nor is there any reason to see an allusion to the Jubilee traditions.

The final two texts, Acts 2:42–47 and 4:32–37, refer to the early church's practice of selling property, houses, and possessions and distributing the proceeds among the community of believers.[48] Two of those who argue that this "community of goods" can be connected to the Jubilee argue that the year Jesus died was, in fact, a literal Jubilee year.[49] According to Lightfoot, the believers chose to sell their possessions rather than have them returned to them as the Jubilee year privileged them.[50] Henry instead argued that since it was a Jubilee year, the lands and possessions would raise a good price when sold (since they would not be returned for a full Jubilee cycle), and so selling the lands would raise the maximum amount of money for

---

46. Contra Reimer, "The Forgiveness of Debts," 165–67.

47. Trocmé, *Nonviolent Revolution*, 35 and Yoder, *Politics*, 70.

48. In Acts 4:35, Luke adds that the proceeds were first laid at the apostles' feet before being distributed.

49. Lightfoot, *Whole Works*, 8:75–76 and Henry, *Commentary*, 6:747. For Lightfoot's full explanation as to why he believed that the year Jesus died was a Jubilee year, see Lightfoot, *Whole Works*, 5:135–36.

50. Lightfoot, *Whole Works*, 8:76.

the Christian community.⁵¹ Thus the distribution of goods in the two Acts passages was not intended to be an implementation of the Jubilee provision of redistribution in Henry's understanding, so much as seizing the opportunity that provision afforded when it was practiced to maximize income to the early believers.⁵²

There are, however, several problems associated with this interpretation. Firstly, as has already been discussed in both the previous chapter and chapter 1, there are different views as to when the Jubilee year would have occurred, mainly since there are different views on when the seventy sevens (490 years) of Daniel 9:24–27 began. Secondly, even many of those who see an allusion to the Jubilee in Jesus' reading of Isaiah 61 in Nazareth argue that he could not have been declaring a literal Jubilee year since so much of his interpretation of the Isaianic text was symbolic.⁵³ Thirdly, Lightfoot's and Henry's conclusions are based on the assumption that the Jubilee year was being widely practiced at the time of the early church; however, as has already been discussed, there is no evidence that the Jubilee provisions were ever followed. In fact, to the contrary, by the time of the first century, Jubilee years were interpreted very differently from the original provisions outlined in Leviticus 25 (see chapter 2). Fourthly, even if there was a Jubilee year practiced at the time of the early church, Henry seems to assume (without citing any evidence) that the new community of Christian believers felt willing to continue to participate in it.⁵⁴ In sum, there is simply no evidence that the occasions referred to in Acts 2:42–47 and 4:32–37 occurred as a result of a Jubilee year being practiced.

Several other scholars also argue that Acts 2:42–47 and 4:32–37 point to a Jubilary allusion, though for different reasons.⁵⁵ They argue that the two passages promote "Sabbath economics—Jubilee spirituality," which they see as a means to overcome poverty, redistribute possessions, and free people

---

51. Henry, *Commentary*, 6:747.

52. There are also a number of scholars who argue that Luke borrowed his phraseology in Acts 4:34 from Deut 15:1–11 (particularly verses 4 and 11), which emphasizes that God's blessing is attached to there being no poor in the community. Even if this linguistic connection exists, however, the previous section demonstrated that there is no connection between the Jubilee legislation and the provisions in Deut 15. Those who see an intertextual connection between Acts 4:34 and Deut 15 include Fitzmyer, *Acts*, 314; Bock, *Acts*, 214–25; Schnabel, *Acts*, 271; and Keener, *Acts*, 1177–78.

53. See particularly Rodgers, "Luke 4:16–30," 80.

54. There is no evidence that this ever occurred. See appendix 2 for the various interpretations of the Jubilee in the early church (none of which call for the literal implementation of a Jubilee year).

55. Kinsler and Kinsler, *The Biblical Jubilee*, 141–43 and Richard, "Now is the Time," 54.

from debts and slavery.[56] Kinsler and Kinsler believe that this Sabbath-Jubilee vision is clear throughout Luke's Gospel, and these two Acts passages demonstrate that Luke then carried the vision into the book of Acts.[57] In particular, they believe that the two Acts texts outline a sharing (or redistribution) amongst the believers, which was reminiscent of the ideology behind some of the original Jubilee provisions.[58]

Many of these arguments have already been addressed.[59] It is important to reiterate, however, that relating the sharing amongst the community of believers in the two Acts passages with the Jubilee provisions in Leviticus 25 is a clear mischaracterization. The redistribution of property in Leviticus 25 was a returning of that property to its original owners (or their families), which stands in stark contrast to what occurred in Acts 2 and 4. In fact, in some ways one might say that the Jubilee provisions were the exact opposite of what occurred in the two Acts texts; in the Leviticus legislation, property was returned and reclaimed by individual family units, whereas in the early Christian community, family property was voluntarily given to the wider collective.

While none of the six texts addressed in this section should be connected with the Jubilee, at least three of them unmistakably refer to the *basileia* of God. In Luke 12:22–34 and 18:18–23, the giving of finances to the poor is clearly linked to being given/entering the *basileia*, since those who treasure earthly finances will ultimately be excluded from God's *basileia* (see in particular Luke 12:31–32; 18:24, 29). Though there is no mention of the *basileia* in the account of Zacchaeus (Luke 19:1–10), the statement Σήμερον σωτηρία τῷ οἴκῳ τούτῳ ἐγένετο should also be understood in relation to the *basileia*, since Luke's soteriology is never isolated from his understanding and portrayal of the *basileia* of God (see chapter 3).

The application of Hays's criteria supports the notion that none of these texts should be associated with the Jubilee. In relation to the criterion of volume, there are no words or linguistic patterns in any of the texts in Luke-Acts which correlate to the Jubilee legislation in Leviticus 25. From the perspective of thematic coherence, the imposition of the Jubilee on the texts either obscures the meaning of the texts (Luke 12:22–34; 18:18–23; 19:1–10; 21:1–4) or provides superfluous (and erroneous) background

56. Kinsler and Kinsler, *The Biblical Jubilee*, 142.
57. Kinsler and Kinsler, *The Biblical Jubilee*, 142.
58. Kinsler and Kinsler, *The Biblical Jubilee*, 142.
59. As has already been mentioned above, debt cancellation is not a major theme in Luke's Gospel, nor is it presented as a principle to be practiced literally. Additionally, as was discussed in chapter 4, Luke never presented Jesus as freeing people in literal slavery or captivity.

information (Acts 2:42–47; 4:32–37). The history of interpretation of each of the texts demonstrates that there are very few scholars who would agree that there are Jubilary allusions in any of the texts in question (see appendix 1).[60] Finally, as has already been demonstrated, the final criterion of satisfaction is also unmet, since in both the immediate and wider contexts, supposed allusions to the Jubilee only serve to obscure the meaning of each of the texts.

Other Suggested References to the Jubilee

Luke 1:68

Verse 68 of Zechariah's song highlights the redemption (λύτρωσις) which the God of Israel would perform for his people. Green sees in this word an echo of the Jubilee, since λύτρωσις was used in both the Jubilee legislation of Leviticus 25 and Isaiah 63:4 (ἡμέρα γὰρ ἀνταποδόσεως ἐπῆλθεν αὐτοῖς καὶ ἐνιαυτὸς λυτρώσεως πάρεστιν).[61] Additionally, the theme of redemption is also common to both the Jubilee and this section of Zechariah's song.[62]

There are several reasons why this association should be considered unlikely. Firstly, Luke's understanding of λύτρωσις in Luke 1:68 is seen clearly in Luke 2:38 (the word's only other usage in Luke-Acts), where Anna looks forward to the redemption of Jerusalem (λύτρωσιν Ἰερουσαλήμ). In that passage the word is used to highlight God's salvific actions on behalf of his people, which is consistent with how the word was used in other Old Testament texts (Pss 110:9; 129:7).[63] When understood in this light, the difference between the way the word is used in Luke and its usage in the Jubilee texts in Leviticus 25 (where the word refers to the redemption of a person's dwelling house in a walled city and the redemption of foreign-owned slaves) is obvious. In fact, given that salvation in Luke-Acts is inextricably linked with the *basileia* of God, the redemption mentioned in Luke 1:68 can again be better explained in relation to the *basileia* (albeit indirectly). Secondly, while it is possible that there is a thematic link between Isaiah 63:4 and Isaiah 61:1–3 (given the double references to the "day of vengeance" and the "acceptable year of the Lord"/"My year of redemption"), it has already

---

60. Indeed, it is only since Trocmé that allusions to the Jubilee have been seen in Luke 12:22–34; 18:18–23; 19:1–10; and 21:1–4 (and these only by a handful of scholars), and it was only in the seventeenth century that two scholars argued in favor of Jubilee allusions in Acts 2:42–47 and 4:32–37.

61. Green, *Luke*, 116–17.

62. Green, *Luke*, 116–17.

63. Bock, *Luke*, 253.

been established that it is unlikely that Luke would have read Isaiah 61 in relation to the Jubilee (see chapter 4). Thirdly, while it is true that the theme of redemption is common to both the Jubilee and Zechariah's song, the Old Testament background to the concept of redemption in Zechariah's song is better understood as being the Exodus.[64]

In relation to Hays's criteria, this supposed allusion is unconvincing. Aside from the above arguments, the history of interpretation is also uncompelling; apart from Green there are no other scholars identified over the course of this study, writing at any point in history, who argue in favor of a Jubilee echo in Luke 1:68 (see appendix 1).

Luke 2:3-4

Another text which is said to have a Jubilee allusion is Luke 2:3-4 because of the similarities between the phrase ἕκαστος εἰς τὴν πατρίδα αὐτοῦ in Leviticus 25:10 and the phrase ἕκαστος εἰς τὴν ἑαυτοῦ πόλιν in Luke 2:3.[65] The allusion is said to be even clearer given Luke's use of πατριά in the next verse.[66]

The connection, however, is unconvincing. With regard to the similarities in phrasing, the same wording can be seen in many other Old Testament texts.[67] There is therefore no need to recourse to the Jubilee to explain its presence in Luke. Moreover, in relation to Luke's use of πατριά, it is important to note that the Jubilee legislation actually employs the word πατρίδα (from πατρίς), which, though related to πατριά, is nonetheless distinct from it.[68] If Luke was alluding to the Jubilee legislation, he could have easily used πατρίς (which he employed twice in Luke 4) without losing the sense of the text. Indeed, as Pao and Schnabel have noted, "The historical practice of returning to one's hometown in the Roman imperial period is sufficient in explaining the appearance of [πατρίδα] in this context."[69]

Given the tenuous nature of the supposed allusion, it is little wonder that it is largely unattested in Lukan studies (see appendix 1). The differences

---

64. Marshall, *The Gospel of Luke*, 90-91.
65. Kilpatrick, "Luke 2,4-5," 264-65 and Leifeld and Pao, "Luke," 76.
66. Kilpatrick, "Luke 2,4-5," 264-65.
67. For other phrases with the "ἕκαστος εἰς τὴν" structure, see Deut 3:20; Josh 1:15; 1 Sam 8:22; 1 Kgs 22:36; 2 Chr 31:1; Jer 27:16; and 28:9 (and John 7:53 in the New Testament). For other similar wording, see Josh 24:28, 33; 1 Sam 10:25; 2 Sam 6:19; 1 Kgs 8:66; 12:24; 22:17; 1 Chr 16:43; 2 Chr 11:4; 18:16; 25:22; and Hag 1:9 (and John 16:32 in the New Testament).
68. Indeed, where πατριά emphasizes one's lineage/family, πατρίς is more concerned with the ancestral land of a particular person/family. See BDAG 788-789.
69. Pao and Schnabel, "Luke," 266.

between the Jubilean return to one's property and family every fifty years and the Roman census mentioned in Luke 2:3-4 are manifold; the suggestion of a Jubilary allusion only serves to obscure the meaning of the Lukan text.

Luke 3:1

Luke's reference to the fifteenth year of the reign of Tiberius Caesar (Luke 3:1) has been used by some scholars to make calculations about when both John and Jesus ministered.[70] The verse (along with other texts) was also used by August Strobel to conclude that according to Jewish chronology, the year was a Jubilee year, which he calculated to be 26-27 CE.[71] According to Strobel, since the year Jesus began his ministry was an actual Jubilee year, this supports the argument that Jesus' Nazareth address (Luke 4:16-30) was a proclamation of Jubilee release.[72]

There are, however, a number of problems with Strobel's hypothesis:

1. There is no firm consensus as to how the fifteenth year of the reign of Tiberius Caesar should be dated. While many of the older commentators dated the year as 25/26 CE or 26/27 CE, the majority of modern Lukan scholars now believe that Tiberius's reign began on August 19, 14 CE, which means the year is more likely to have been 28/29 CE.[73] In any case, it is difficult to date the fifteenth year of Tiberius with any degree of certainty.

2. There is also no firm consensus as to when there would have been a Jubilee year. Though Strobel has calculated that it occurred in 26/27 CE, Barker believes that it began during 17-19 CE, while Lightfoot calculated that the year of Jubilee occurred in the year of Jesus' death, which he believed was 33 CE.[74] As has been mentioned in chapter 2, the dating of the Jubilee year depends in large part on how one dates the "seventy sevens" of Daniel 9:24-27, and there remains no consensus as to how that text should be interpreted or dated.

---

70. For a survey of some of the different calculations, see Messner, "'Fifteenth Year,'" 202-5.
71. See Strobel, "Plädoyer," 466-69 and Strobel, "Ausrufung," 40-46.
72. Strobel, "Plädoyer," 466-69.
73. See Bock, *Luke*, 281-84; Messner, "'Fifteenth Year,'" 210-11; Nolland, *Luke*, 1:139; and Marshall, *The Gospel of Luke*, 133.
74. Lightfoot, *Whole Works*, 8:75-76; Barker, "The Time is Fulfilled," 24-25; and Strobel, "Ausrufung," 40-46.

3. There is no other evidence that an actual Jubilee year was occurring—let alone being observed—at the time of Luke 3:1 (or at any time in Luke-Acts). There was no blowing of the *shofar*, no exhortation for people to return to their patrimonies, no use of the word "Jubilee," no release of slaves, nor any other distinct reference anywhere in Luke-Acts to the Jubilee material of Leviticus 25.[75]

4. It is inconsistent to argue that Jesus deliberately chose a literal year of Jubilee as the occasion when he read from Isaiah 61, given that even in the text's original Old Testament context, the passage refers to the Jubilee symbolically and eschatologically, if at all (and not literally).[76]

As one might expect, there are very few scholars who argue in favor of this allusion. As mentioned above, most see Strobel's dating methods as unreliable. When assessed in relation to Hays's criterion of *History of Interpretation*, therefore, the suggested allusion is seen to be even more unsatisfactory.

Luke 5:17–26

Ringe argues that the account of Jesus healing and forgiving a paralyzed man in Luke 5:17–26 is a demonstration of the Jubilee "release" from both sins and disease.[77] She argues that "in a way, all the healing stories in the gospel might . . . be seen as manifestation of the message of liberation that is part of the Jubilee [since] in those stories the inclusive picture of release from powers inimical to the eschatological sovereignty of God is evident."[78] Ringe bases her conclusions on her understanding of the Lukan theme of release/forgiveness, which is informed by her interpretation of ἄφεσις and ἀφίημι, which she argues cannot be understood without reference to the Old Testament Jubilee.[79]

There is much in Ringe's argument that can be affirmed. The theme of forgiveness is, on occasion, conflated with the idea of healing (as is seen in this passage), and the release/forgiveness of sins is indeed inextricably linked to the reign of God (see chapter 3). As has been shown in chapter

---

75. O'Brien, "Comparison," 438–39.

76. This, of course, is a moot point, given that by the time of the New Testament, Isa 61 was probably not read in relation to the Jubilee (see chapter 4). See also Rodgers, "Luke 4:16–30," 80.

77. Ringe, "Jubilee Proclamation," 230.

78. Ringe, "Jubilee Proclamation," 230–31.

79. Ringe, "Jubilee Proclamation," 219–20.

3, however, neither ἀφίημι nor ἄφεσις were connected with the Jubilee by the time of the New Testament (and in fact, ἀφίημι was not even associated with the Jubilee in the Old Testament). The semantic meaning of ἄφεσις developed such that by the time of the New Testament, it had a uniform and exclusive meaning centered on the forgiveness of sins, entirely unrelated to the Old Testament Jubilee. Additionally, it seems tenuous at best to posit that the accounts of healing in the Synoptic Gospels can be linked to the Jubilee, given that the Jubilee legislation in Leviticus 25 was entirely unconnected to healing or disease.

Aside from Ringe, no other scholars were identified over the course of this study who see a link between Luke 5:17-26 and the Jubilee. Similarly, it seems there are no other scholars who argue that all the accounts of healing, in some way, point to a Jubilee release. While admittedly the absence of scholarly support does not necessarily negate the proposed allusion, when considered in conjunction with the other flaws in Ringe's argument her position seems even more untenable.

Luke 6:27-38

Another passage which is said to contain Jubilary allusions is Luke 6:27-38, and in particular verses 34-36 (which address the free lending of finances). It is argued that the lending of money without expecting repayment corresponds to the Jubilee legislation which prohibits the lending of money with interest.[80] This argument has been developed by other scholars, who have seen in Luke 6:34-36 a dependence on Deuteronomy 15:7-11, which they argue parallels the Jubilee legislation in Leviticus 25:35-38.[81]

It is unclear, however, what is meant by the repayment mentioned in verse 34 (that is, the object of λαβεῖν is uncertain). The three options which are usually cited are: 1) it refers to the recovery of the principal that was loaned; 2) it refers to the full repayment of the principal and interest; or 3) it refers to the opportunity of a reciprocal loan being offered in the future.[82] While there is support for all three positions, most modern scholars prefer the third interpretation, particularly in light of the reciprocity of the previous two verses.[83] There are few scholars who advocate for the first or second

---

80. Trocmé, *Nonviolent Revolution*, 31; Yoder, *Politics*, 66; and Pilgrim, *Good News to the Poor*, 137-38.

81. Sloan, *Favorable Year*, 133 and Blosser, "Jubilee," 134-35.

82. See Stein, *Luke*, 209; Nolland, *Luke*, 299; Marshall, *The Gospel of Luke*, 263; Bock, *Luke*, 600-601; and Bovon, *Lukas*, 317-18.

83. Stein, *Luke*, 209; Nolland, *Luke*, 299; Marshall, *The Gospel of Luke*, 263; and

positions, since, as Marshall has noted, people do not lend solely for the purpose of being paid back (which the ἵνα clause necessitates in the first two views).[84] The significance of this is highlighted when one considers the Jubilee legislation in Leviticus 25:35-38, which pertains to the taking of interest from loans given to fellow Israelites. The Jubilee legislation is only relevant to the Lukan text if one concludes that the second position is the one which is to be accepted. Additionally, even if one posits that the meaning of the text is that lenders are to lend without the expectation of the principal and interest being repaid, there are a number of other Old Testament texts which prohibit or denounce the lending of money with interest, including Exodus 22:25; Deuteronomy 23:20; Ezekiel 18:8, 13, 17; and 22:12. If one accepts the minority view that the principal and interest no longer need to be repaid and one also argues that there must be dependence on an earlier Old Testament tradition, there is still no reason to prioritize the legislation in Leviticus 25 over the other texts listed above.

Finally, if one posits that there is an intertextual relationship between Deuteronomy 15 and the Lukan text (which is possible given the use of the relatively rare word δανείζω in both texts), there is no reason to assume an intertextual link with the Jubilee legislation of Leviticus 25. As shown above ("Debt Cancellation"), the differences between Deuteronomy 15 and Leviticus 25 suggest that they are two entirely separate traditions.

As with all the suggested allusions to the Jubilee in this chapter, there is very little scholarly support for an allusion in Luke 6:27-38. This allusion was first proposed by Trocmé, and while there have been several scholars who have agreed with his position, it remains quite unpopular.

Luke 6:1-11 and 14:1-6

Another argument which has been proposed in favor of Jubilary allusions is that since there was a strong relationship between the Jubilee and the Sabbath in the Old Testament, references to the Sabbath in Luke-Acts can also be taken as having some type of connection to the Jubilee. Some writers refer to the prevalence of the Lukan Sabbath-Jubilee texts and traditions,[85] while others see Luke's apparent interest in the Sabbath and assume interest in the Jubilee as well.[86] Green argues that Jesus' proclamation of an eschatological

---

Bock, *Luke*, 600-601.

84. Marshall, *The Gospel of Luke*, 263.

85. Kinsler and Kinsler, *The Biblical Jubilee*, 103-7 and Sloan, *Favorable Year*, 145-46.

86. Leifeld, "Luke," 888.

Jubilee in Luke 4:16–30 is the interpretive key for the Sabbath texts in Luke 6:1–11 and 14:1–6, since Jesus' Jubilee declaration effectively made Sabbath days (as well as all other days) the time of divine benefaction for the needy.[87] As has already been mentioned in chapter 5, Bacchiocchi goes so far as to say that Jesus chose a Sabbath day to make his Jubilee proclamation in order to make the day a memorial of his redemptive activity.[88]

There is little doubt that the Sabbath is prevalent throughout Luke-Acts. Luke refers to the Sabbath far more than any other New Testament tradition (thirty times throughout his two-part corpus).[89] It is also clear that a textual relationship exists between Sabbath years and the Jubilee years within the Deuteronomic context; the beginning of Leviticus 25 addresses Sabbath years, and Jubilee years were to be measured by the counting of seven Sabbath years (Lev 25:8). There is not, however, any reason to posit a relationship between Jubilee years and Sabbath *days*. This is significant, given that on every occasion Luke used σάββατον, it was always in connection to a Sabbath day. There is no reason to assume that Luke (or his audience) would have heard a reference to Sabbath days and immediately have thought of Sabbath years, much less Jubilee years. Additionally, those who argue in favor of the existence of Sabbath-Jubilee texts in Luke-Acts invariably base many of their arguments on there being a Jubilee proclamation in Luke 4, which has already been demonstrated to be unlikely. In short, there are no specific words or syntactical patterns within any of the Sabbath passages in Luke-Acts which allude to the Jubilee, nor is there any reason to suppose that Luke or his audience would have connected references to Sabbath days with Jubilee years. It is therefore little wonder that there is very little scholarly support for this proposed allusion (see appendix 1).

Luke 9:1–6

Another suggested reference to the Jubilee in Luke's work is Jesus' sending out his twelve disciples in Luke 9:1–6. Donald Blosser argues that the text should be seen in connection to Luke 7:22–23 (which he also sees as a Jubilee text) because of the corresponding references to healing and preaching.[90]

---

87. Green, *Luke*, 252–53, 548.

88. Bacchiocchi, *From Sabbath to Sunday*, 21. Bacchiocchi's claims were addressed in chapter 4.

89. The word σάββατον is used eleven times in Matthew and Mark, thirteen times in John, and twice in Paul's epistles. In contrast, σάββατον occurs twenty times in Luke's Gospel and ten times in Acts.

90. Blosser, "Jubilee," 136. Significantly, there are no other scholars who view this text as a Jubilary allusion (see appendix 1).

Blosser also believes that the use of εὐαγγελιζόμενοι (Luke 9:6) strengthens the connection to 7:22, as well as linking the text to 4:18 and ultimately to Isaiah 61:1–2.[91] He believes that Luke portrayed Jesus as transferring "the Jubilee message and its corresponding activities to his disciples . . . Thus [the] Jubilee moves beyond being simply a proclamation made by Jesus . . . to become the continuing theme of the Gospel which is to be proclaimed throughout all the years."[92]

Blosser's arguments rest on a number of false assumptions, including the linking of εὐαγγελίζω with a Jubilary proclamation, the characterization of Jesus' preaching in Luke 7:22–23 and Luke 4:18–19 as a Jubilee message, and the corresponding characterization of the disciples' message as a Jubilee proclamation. As previously discussed, all of these presuppositions are significantly flawed. Additionally, while it is true that one can link the text with Luke 7:22 and Luke 4:18 on the basis of the motifs of healing and preaching, it seems strange that Blosser would ignore other texts which link the two themes (Luke 4:40–43; 5:15; 6:18; 10:9). More importantly, there is no indication in Luke 9:1–6 that the message of the disciples was to be a Jubilary proclamation (nor indeed is there any indication that the Jubilee was the subject of the preaching in Luke 4:18–19 or 7:22–23). To the contrary, Luke clearly articulated the message which the disciples were to proclaim—they were κηρύσσειν τὴν βασιλείαν τοῦ θεου (Luke 9:2). This is underscored by the use of εὐαγγελίζω in verse 6, which was frequently used by Luke in connection with the proclamation of the βασιλεία τοῦ θεοῦ (see chapter 4). Finally, it seems inconceivable that Luke would view the message of the Jubilee as the key theme of Jesus' and the disciples' preaching, given the complete lack of references to both the word "Jubilee" and its core provisions.

Luke 9:14 and Acts 2:1–4

As noted in appendix 2, there are two references made by Origen to the Jubilee in passages from Luke-Acts, both of which are based on the significance of the number fifty. The first of these, Luke 9:14, comes as part of the narrative of Jesus feeding the five thousand (Luke 9:10–17), whereby the crowd were instructed to sit in groups of fifty (πεντήκοντα). The second (Acts 2:1–4) again draws attention to the numerical significance of the day of Pentecost (πεντηκοστῆς), which occurred fifty days after the Passover. O'Brien has argued that Origen may also have made a connection between the day of Pentecost and the Jubilee, given that ἄφεσις is also used in both

91. Blosser, "Jubilee," 136.
92. Blosser, "Jubilee," 136.

texts.⁹³ More recently, Richard and Kinsler and Kinsler have also highlighted what they believe is the parallelism between Pentecost occurring fifty days after the Passover and the Jubilee occurring every fifty years.⁹⁴

In relation to Origen's interpretation of the two texts, it is unsurprising that significance was attached to the number fifty, given the allegorical approach to interpreting Scripture in the early church and the numerical significance attached to the Jubilee in many of the Second Temple writings (see chapter 2). Significantly, Origen did not advocate that Luke deliberately alluded to the Jubilee, since in fact his reference to Jesus' feeding the five thousand came as part of his commentary on Matthew's Gospel.⁹⁵

Kinsler and Kinsler's argument that there is a parallelism between the occurrence of the Jubilee every fifty years and Pentecost occurring fifty days after the Passover is tenuous at best. The difference between the fifty years and fifty days should not be ignored. The parallelism seems even more unlikely, however, given that according to Leviticus 25:10 a Jubilee proclamation of liberty was to be made in the fiftieth year; however, according to Kinsler and Kinsler, Jesus had already proclaimed the Jubilee message several years before Acts 2 occurred (in Luke 4).⁹⁶ Finally, the likelihood of a Lukan parallelism is diminished even further, given that Luke chose to use the substantive feminine πεντηκοστή rather than πεντηκοστός (which is used in Lev 25).

Acts 6:9

The final proposed reference to the Jubilee is in Acts 6:9, where the Synagogue of the Freedmen is mentioned (τῆς συναγωγῆς τῆς λεγομένης Λιβερτίνων). Lightfoot believed that some of the freedmen in the synagogue may have achieved their freedom because of a Jubilee year.⁹⁷ There is no

---

93. O'Brien, "Comparison," 441.

94. Richard, "Now is the Time," 53–54 and Kinsler and Kinsler, *The Biblical Jubilee*, 141. Interestingly, Acts 2:1–4 is the only proposed allusion supported by both an early church author and two modern scholars. Nevertheless, there remains a lack of historical support for either Luke 9:14 or Acts 2:1–4 as referring to the Jubilee (appendix 1).

95. Origen, *Comm. Matt.* 11.3 (*ANF* 9:433). Additionally, the narrative of the feeding of the five thousand is also represented in Mark 8:1–10 and Matt 15:32–39. It is therefore difficult to argue that Luke included the account because of the Jubilary significance of the number fifty, unless one wishes to argue that Matthew and Mark also had the same aim in mind.

96. Kinsler and Kinsler, *The Biblical Jubilee*, 103–6.

97. Lightfoot, *Whole Works*, 8:414. There were no other scholars identified over the course of this study who saw this verse as a reference to the Jubilee.

evidence for his claims, however, particularly given that there is no evidence that Jubilee years were ever actually practiced. It is far more likely that the text is a general reference for diaspora Jews who were former slaves (or the children of former slaves).[98]

Conclusion

While there are many scholars who argue that a Jubilary allusion exists in Luke 4:16–30, there are far fewer who see allusions outside that text. This in itself is remarkable, given the programmatic importance of the Nazareth pericope. Additionally, the few scholars who do argue in favor of other Jubilary allusions in Luke-Acts have almost all written their works after Trocmé's seminal book *Jesus and the Nonviolent Revolution*. There is not, therefore, widespread support either currently or throughout history for any of the above proposed allusions (see appendix 1). This lack of support is unsurprising, however, when one considers the tenuousness of the arguments in favor of their presence. Indeed, none of the texts seem to meet Hays's criteria for determining the validity of Old Testament allusions.

Significantly, however, there are many of the above passages which can be linked to the *basileia* of God. The theme of reversal of fortunes has clear links with God's reign, as does Isaiah 61 (see chapter 4). In addition, two of the texts which address debt cancellation (Luke 7:36–50; 11:2–4), three of the texts which highlight the redistribution of property (Luke 12:22–34; 18:18–23; 19:1–10), and three of the other suggested allusions to the Jubilee (Luke 1:68; 5:17–26; 9:1–6) are also explicitly associated with the *basileia* of God. That is to say, many of the proposed Lukan allusions to the Jubilee addressed in this chapter are better understood as references to the *basileia* of God.

---

98. Thompson, "Diaspora Jewish Freedmen," 166–67.

Conclusion

Since the publication of André Trocmé's *Jesus and the Nonviolent Revolution*, there has been renewed interest into possible references to the Jubilee in the New Testament, and particularly in Luke-Acts. Much has been written, especially in response to Trocmé, with the focus often being how one should interpret the suggested Jubilee texts. In recent years, however, some scholars have recognized the derivative nature of much of what has been written and have called into question the likelihood of whether or not the author of Luke-Acts was himself at all concerned about the Jubilee.[1] It has been the burden of this study to investigate that question.

To achieve this, the Jubilee and *basileia* of God traditions in both the Old Testament and Second Temple literature were examined to establish how they may have been understood in the Lukan traditions and their intended audience. Following this, there was an examination into several key subjects (how the words ἄφεσις and ἀφίημι should be interpreted in Luke-Acts, and how Luke understood and depicted the *basileia* of God), all of which impact how one might identify and assess the proposed Jubilee allusions. The focus then turned to Isaiah 61 traditions that may have influenced Luke, and how the Isaianic text was used throughout the Luke's work. This was especially important, given that some scholars believe that the principal points of contact between the Jubilee and the New Testament are those passages which cite or allude to Isaiah 61.[2] Finally, there was an examination into every suggested Jubilee allusion in Luke-Acts, with particular attention given to the account in Luke 4:14–30.

As a result of this study, there are a several key conclusions which have been made:

---

1. Stein, *Luke*, 157 and Tannehill, *Narrative Unity*, 68.
2. See, for example, Ringe, "Jubilee Proclamation," 290.

1. Every suggested allusion in Luke-Acts can be satisfactorily explained without reference to the Jubilee.

This first conclusion stands in stark contrast to the findings of some other scholars who have not only argued in favor of a number of Jubilee allusions, but have also argued that the author of Luke-Acts saw the theme of the Jubilee as a central motif.[3] Sloan, for example, believes that "the image of Jubilee is very important for Luke in the construction of his Gospel."[4] The findings of this study, however, suggest that even if Luke was at all acquainted with the Jewish Jubilee institution, there is uncertainty as to how the implied Lukan audience would have interpreted it, given that there were at least eight differing Jubilee interpretations in the Second Temple literature. Further, if the author/s of Luke was a gentile (as many still argue), there is no certainty that he was even aware of the Jubilee, particularly given that it had never been implemented throughout Israel's history and there was no Greco-Roman equivalent.

Additionally, the absence of references to many of the distinct Jubilee year practices is surely significant. There is no blowing of the trumpet, no exhortation for people to return to their ancestral land, and no literal release of slaves, nor is there any mention of the word "Jubilee," and debt cancellation (which itself is not a clear Jubilee year provision) is only mentioned sparingly and never exhortatively. Given that Luke frequently provides explanatory notes for a gentile readership about Jewish customs and traditions, it seems highly unlikely that he was seeking to communicate some type of Jubilee release, much less present it as a key theme. Moreover, the findings of this study indicate that arguing in favor of the various suggested Jubilee allusions can, at times, serve to obscure the meaning of the Lukan text.

There are, however, some who argue that even though Luke may not have known about the Jubilee, there are nonetheless a number of Jubilee images which are present throughout his two-part work.[5] This line of argument largely depends on how one defines and differentiates the terms "images" and "allusions," and how one then chooses to assess the presence (and possible meaning) of an image or allusion. For this study, since both allusions and images were grouped together and were assessed according to Richard Hays's well-known criteria, it was important that suggested Jubilary allusions were historically plausible.

---

3. See, for example, Blosser, "Jubilee," 147–53 and Sloan, *Favorable Year*, 174–75.
4. Sloan, *Favorable Year*, 174.
5. Ringe, "Jubilee Proclamation," 293.

That is, one of the criteria to determine the presence of an allusion to the Jubilee was whether the biblical author could have intended the proposed meaning, and whether his intended audience could have understood it. This difference in approach is possibly part of the reason why this study has arrived at different conclusions from some other studies.[6]

Finally, it is also of significance that the early church did not consider the Jubilee theme to be an explanation or explication of the message of Jesus. Indeed, the survey of references to the Jubilee in the wider early church literature in appendix 2 reveals that there were no distinctively Christian interpretations of the Jubilee until the writings of Hippolytus of Rome and Origen of Alexandria in the early third century. Significantly, they did not view the Jubilee as a summary of Jesus' ministry either. Indeed, appendix 1 demonstrates that it was not until the late Middle Ages that passages such as the Nazareth pericope were read in relation to the Jubilee (possibly in response to the first Christian Jubilee year declared in 1300 CE by Pope Boniface VIII).

2. In the first century, Isaiah 61 was rarely linked to the Jubilee.

As mentioned above, the significance of this finding is highlighted when one considers that quotations and allusions to Isaiah 61 are sometimes considered to be the clearest Lukan references to the Jubilee. Indeed, it has been common in recent times for commentators to see the anointed speaker in Isaiah 61 proclaiming a new Jubilee age and assume that Luke had this image in mind when he penned the Nazareth pericope. This interpretation gains even more traction when one considers Luke's propensity to take into account the original Scriptural context when applying (and detailing the fulfillment of) an Old Testament text. Problems arise, however, when one fails to take into consideration how a text may have been understood by the New Testament authors themselves. That is, there can be an implicit assumption that New Testament authors such as Luke read Old Testament texts in a similar way to how those texts are read today. In the case of Isaiah 61, it is clear that in the first century the text was almost never interpreted in connection with the Jubilee.

Indeed, there is only one Dead Sea Scroll (11Q13) which posits a link between Isaiah 61 and the Jubilee. The scroll has been considered by many as incredibly important in determining how Luke (and the

---

6. Most notably Sharon Ringe's dissertation, which did not address questions of intentionality. Ringe, "Jubilee Proclamation," 293.

historical Jesus) would have understood the text of Isaiah 61.[7] Indeed, for some scholars, it is precisely because of this scroll that a reference to the Jubilee is seen in the Isaianic quotation in Luke 4:18–19.[8] As was determined in chapter 4, however, it seems unlikely that the scroll had any bearing on Luke's work whatsoever. It is more likely that Luke's interpretation of Isaiah 61 was guided by a tradition similar to the scroll 4Q521 (since the way this scroll treats the Isaianic text is very similar to what is seen in Luke-Acts—see chapter 4), though even this is far from certain.

The significance of this is far-reaching. It reveals that by the time of the first century, Isaiah 61 traditions were not necessarily linked with the Jubilee. On the contrary, in the entire body of Second Temple and early church documents which address Isaiah 61, it is only 11Q13 which refers to the Jubilee. That is, the only Second Temple tradition which connects Isaiah 61 with the Jubilee is a fragmentary text which seemingly had no bearing on the traditions of Luke-Acts. There is therefore little reason to assume that either Luke or his audience viewed the Isaianic text in connection with the Jubilee.

When one removes the felt need to read Isaiah 61:1–2 in relation to the Jubilee, the text's meaning becomes far more consistent with what is seen in the remainder of Luke-Acts. This of course is to be expected, given that the Isaianic text stands at the heart of Luke's programmatic description of Jesus' ministry in Luke 4:16–30. Luke's use of words such as ἄφεσις do not need to be read as carrying any Jubilary undertones of release from slavery, financial debts, or marginalization for either Luke or his audience. The word is instead able to be understood as having the same meaning as seen throughout the entire remainder of Luke-Acts, and indeed all early Christian literature: spiritual release, particularly in relation to the forgiveness of sins (which also signaled entry into the *basileia* of God).

3. In the first century, the Jubilee was rarely linked to the *basileia* of God.

Those that argue that Luke sought to present Jesus as proclaiming a Jubilee release often frame this proclamation as part of Jesus' wider

---

7. Bruno, "Jesus is our Jubilee," 95; Kimball, *Jesus' Exposition*, 103; Ford, *My Enemy is My Guest*, 56–59; Garland, *Luke*, 200; Marshall, *The Gospel of Luke*, 182; Betz, *Jesus, der Messias Israels*, 260–62; Pilgrim, *Good News to the Poor*, 71; and De Jonge and Van Der Woude, "11Q Melchizedek," 309–10.

8. See, for example, Bruno, who only includes 11QMelch in his references to pertinent Second Temple literature. Bruno, "Jesus is our Jubilee," 94–95.

teaching on the *basileia* of God.⁹ That is, the suggested Jubilee proclamation (especially with regard to the Nazareth pericope) is frequently viewed as a declaration of the eschatological reign of God. Mortimer Arias, for example, has written that Luke specifically depicted Jesus as coming "to announce the kingdom of God and he did it in Jubilee language."¹⁰ As was demonstrated in chapters 1 and 2, however, there is little reason to assume that Luke would have connected the Jubilee with the concept of the *basileia* of God, either on the basis of the Old Testament texts or the Second Temple literature. Indeed, given the diversity of interpretations of the Jubilee in those Jewish sources that mention it and the wide-ranging meaning of the *basileia* of God, even if Luke was aware of both concepts, one cannot be sure how he would have interpreted either, much less assume that he would have viewed the Jubilee as a picture of God's eschatological reign. This is particularly the case given that interpretations of the Jubilee were relatively infrequent.

In fact, of all the references to the *basileia* of God and the Jubilee in the Second Temple literature, it is once again only the Qumran scroll 11Q13 which explicitly links the motifs of the *basileia* of God with the Jubilee. Given that the scroll probably exerted no influence over Luke's work, there is no reason to posit that the motif of the *basileia* of God in Luke was informed or elucidated by Jubilee allusions.

4. Many of the suggested allusions to the Jubilee are better explained as references to the *basileia* of God.

Many suggested allusions to the Jubilee in Luke-Acts are better seen as revealing and explicating various aspects of the *basileia* of God. Possibly the clearest examples of this are seen in Luke 6:20–26; 7:18–35; 11:2–4; 9:1–6; 12:22–34; 14:7–24; and 18:18–30, all of which explicitly refer to the *basileia*. Similarly, themes such as the reversal of fortunes (which have sometimes been linked to the Jubilee) have long been recognized in connection with the *basileia* of God.

It also seems likely that Luke connected Isaiah 61 (which is the source text of many proposed Jubilee allusions) with God's *basileia*. As shown in chapter 4, the text was used by Luke for a number of purposes, including to describe the nature of the *basileia* of God (Luke 4:16–30; 7:18–23) and Jesus' role in relation to it (which pertained particularly to his ministry of spiritual release). It was also used to

---

9. See, for example, Sloan, *Favorable Year*, 166; Ringe, "Jubilee Proclamation," 295; Hertig, "Jubilee Mission," 176; and Garland, *Luke*, 208–9.

10. Arias, "Mission and Liberation," 36.

clarify those that were to be beneficiaries of Jesus' ministry (especially the poor, marginalized, and spiritually oppressed) and to announce the dawning of the new age of God's grace and favor (which is equivalent to proclaiming the presence of the *basileia* of God). This connection between Isaiah 61 and God's *basileia* is also seen in a number of Second Temple documents. Importantly, the scroll 4Q521 also relates the Isaianic text to the *basileia*.

Areas for Future Study

While the above study has led to a number of significant conclusions, it has also highlighted a number of other areas which could be the subject of future study. Firstly, this study was limited in its scope to Luke-Acts. There are, however, some who would argue in favor of Jubilary allusions in other New Testament books (especially the two other Synoptic Gospels). The findings of this study cast doubt on the validity of other possible Jubilee allusions in the New Testament (particularly when one takes into consideration the survey of Jubilee interpretation in the early church—see appendix 2); however, this needs to be explored more thoroughly.

A related area of study would be to explore the likelihood of the historical Jesus proclaiming a Jubilee release (which, as appendix 1 shows, is the contention of a number of scholars), and what that may have entailed. Much of what has been written, however, has been based on readings of Luke-Acts (and in particular the Nazareth pericope) which this study has shown to be, at times, presumptuous and, in some cases, fallacious. While there is no doubt much in this study which could be aptly applied to a study of the historical Jesus and his possible views on the Jubilee, there may be some points of major difference, especially when one considers the ethnic and cultural differences between a first-century Jew like Jesus and the probable gentile author of Luke.

More fundamentally, this study calls for some widely-held interpretations to be reexamined. The Nazareth episode, for example, can set the tone for how one views the entirety of Jesus' ministry in Luke-Acts. Those that have viewed the passage as Jesus' proclamation of a Jubilee release have, on occasion, read the remainder of Luke's Gospel through that lens and have imported Jubilee thinking into texts where it is not present.[11]

---

11. See in appendix 1 the list of those who see an allusion to the Jubilee in the Nazareth episode and who have gone on to find other Jubilee references throughout Luke-Acts.

Finally, this study calls for a major reassessment of how one understands the practical implications of the Jubilee in the twenty-first century. As mentioned in the introduction and in appendix 1, there are numerous and wide-ranging views as to how the Jubilee should be practiced today, many of which are based on texts in Luke-Acts. My intention has not been to question the many noble achievements attempted and sometimes achieved under the inspiration of the Jubilee traditions, but I do suggest that the theological foundations of many of these applications may need to be reviewed and clarified.[12]

In sum, this study calls for a rethinking of the Jubilee interpretations of texts in Luke-Acts, and particularly the Nazareth pericope. While the importance of this passage has long been recognized, there remains some disagreement as to how the text is best understood. This is due, in part, to the profundity and weightiness of the Isaianic message, which, though in one sense fulfilled in a Jewish synagogue many years ago, continues to inspire, confound, convict, and comfort many today.

---

12. Some of these applications (such as the calling of the church to care for the poor) are no doubt able to be sustained through other New Testament texts, and particularly those connected with the *basileia*. Others, such as the debt cancellation movement, might need to restrict some of their theological foundations to key Old Testament texts (such as Deut 15:1–11 and Lev 25:8–55).

Appendix 1
A History of Interpretation: The Jubilee in Luke-Acts

The application of Richard Hays's history of interpretation criterion for identifying Old Testament allusions required an examination of how the Jubilee has been interpreted in relation to Luke-Acts passages throughout the ages.[1] While the results of the examination are included in the body of the study above, the examination itself has been included here as an appendix. This assessment divides history into four periods: 1) the early church (the ante-Nicene, Nicene, and post-Nicene periods); 2) the Middle Ages (from the end of the post-Nicene period through to the start of the sixteenth century); 3) the early sixteenth century through to the mid-twentieth century; and, 4) recent interpretation (from the 1950s onwards). These divisions have been made since each period of time saw distinct developments in the interpretation of the Jubilee in Luke-Acts texts. This appendix will therefore address the history of interpretation of the Luke-Acts passages examined in chapters 5 and 6 above.[2] The second appendix explores the presence and absence of Jubilee language more widely within early church theology.

The Early Church Period

Addressing the interpretation of passages from Luke's Gospel in the early church is a difficult task, since Luke was not nearly so popular with the early

---

1. The Acts of the Apostles is included for the sake of completeness.

2. These passages will be treated together since so many of them have a history of interpretation that has no link with the Jubilee. While it could be argued that there should be a separate in-depth history of interpretation for each text, this is not necessary for the purposes of this study.

church fathers as the Gospels of Matthew and John.[3] In fact, there is only one work of significant length, John Chrysostom's *Homilies on the Acts of the Apostles*. Importantly, in the source materials that still exist, there is no reference to the Jubilee in any of the Lukan passages that have been examined in this study. That is, there is no early church author who recognized and affirmed any of the proposed allusions to the Jubilee in the Luke-Acts passages in chapters 5 and 6.[4] The only two passages in Luke-Acts which were linked to the Jubilee in the early church writings were Luke 9:14 and Acts 2:1–4. As will be discussed in the following appendix, it seems that this connection was made on the numerical significance of the number fifty, which seems to have been linked to the remission of sins by some Christian authors in the third century.

Regarding Luke 4:16–30, many early church authors recognized the significance of the passage; however, they never once referenced the Jubilee. Cyril of Alexandria, for example, wrote that the episode was designed that Jesus might "manifest Himself to the Israelites, and that the mystery of his incarnation should now shine forth to those who knew him not."[5] In accordance with the findings of this study, Cyril believed that the captives in the Isaianic text were spiritual captives[6] and viewed the "acceptable year of the Lord" as being "the joyful tidings of [Christ's] own advent . . . [the time when the gentiles gain] the Gospel message of salvation; by which they have been made partakers of the kingdom of heaven."[7] Similarly, Origen wrote that the captives in the Isaianic quotation were those who were under the bondage of sin with Satan as their ruling tyrant.[8] Thus, Jesus came to end spiritual oppression.[9] He also viewed a year acceptable to the Lord as "either one in which the proclamation of the Savior took place, or one in which the True lamb was offered for the sins of the world."[10] Another author who viewed the poor and oppressed in Luke 4:18–19 as those who were spiritually

---

3. Just, *Luke*, xvii. See also Bellinzoni, "Use of Luke," 59–61, 74–76 and Bovon, "Reception and Use," 395.

4. Origen referred to the Jubilee in relation to his discourse on the Lord's Prayer; however, his mentioning of the Jubilee was far removed from the suggested allusion in chapter 6. See Origen, "On Prayer," 145. All of Origen's references to the Jubilee (including the one in relation to the Lord's Prayer) are addressed in the next appendix ("The Early Church and the Jubilee").

5. Cyril of Alexandria. *St. Luke*, 1:58.

6. Cyril of Alexandria, *St. Luke*, 1:60–61.

7. Cyril of Alexandria, *St. Luke*, 1:61.

8. Origen, *Homilies*, 168–69.

9. Origen, *Homilies*, 168–69.

10. Origen, *Homilies*, 169.

oppressed was Eusebius.¹¹ He wrote that they were those "hampered by evil spirits, and bound for a long time like slaves by daemons. [Jesus] proclaimed forgiveness, inviting all to be free and to escape from the bonds of sin."¹² Thus, it seems the early church authors viewed the Isaianic quotation in Luke 4:18–19 as being a description of Jesus' ministry which centered on spiritual liberation, with the acceptable year of the Lord being equivalent to the time of salvation (that is, entrance into the *basileia* of God).

The Middle Ages

For the first eight hundred years of the Middle Ages, it seems that there was very little interest in the Jubilee. Indeed, there is only one passing mention of the Jubilee, made by the Venerable Bede when he described the heavenly kingdom mentioned in Acts 1:3 as a place of "true Jubilee rest."¹³ He was not, however, arguing that the text itself was an allusion to the Jubilee. Indeed, even in the Venerable Bede's commentary on Luke and St. Aquinas's *Catena Aurea* where he addressed the Gospel of Luke (and included a wide range of patristic commentaries and homilies from the previous centuries), there are no references to the Jubilee.¹⁴

The year 1300 CE, however, brought fresh attention to the biblical Jubilee when it was declared to be the first Christian Jubilee year, instituted by Pope Boniface VIII.¹⁵ The Bull *Antiquorum habet fida relatio* published by Pope Boniface VIII on February 22, 1300 detailed the aim of these Christian Jubilee years; they allow believers to receive "not only ample and copious, but the fullest pardon of all their sins."¹⁶ That is, Christian Jubilee Years were

---

11. Eusebius, *Proof of the Gospel*, 102.

12. Eusebius, *Proof of the Gospel*, 102. Eusebius did not address the meaning of the "acceptable year of the Lord."

13. Cited in Martin, *Acts*, 4.

14. Bede, *Complete Works* and Aquinas, *St. Luke*.

15. When Pope Boniface VIII instituted Christian Jubilees, he originally intended that they occur once every hundred years. In the early fourteenth century, however, there were many who were appealing to the pontiff for an earlier Jubilee. Clement VI, therefore, announced another Jubilee year in 1350. Since that time, Jubilee years have been declared at somewhat irregular intervals, though from 1450 to 1775 they occurred every twenty-five years. In total, there have been thirty Christian Jubilee years including 1300 CE. See Foley, *The Story of the Jubilee Years*, xiv and O'Grady, *Rome Reshaped*, 62–68.

16. O'Grady, *Rome Reshaped*, 61–62. For a summary of the conditions which must be met in order to receive this indulgence, see Thurston, *Holy Year*, 351.

considered to be an opportunity for all debts incurred by sins (already forgiven) to be canceled.[17]

The institution of Christian Jubilee years seemingly prompted strong interest in the biblical foundations of the Jubilee. In Erasmus's *Paraphrase on Luke*, for example, Erasmus recognized in Isaiah 61 an allusion to the year of Jubilee and therefore argued that Jesus' use of the quotation in Luke 4:18–19 represented a preaching of the true Jubilee of the Lord.[18] This true Jubilee was the time of everlasting rest and freedom, whereby all sins are forgiven and salvation is offered.[19] Thus, Jesus' preaching at Nazareth (Luke 4:16–30) represented a preaching of salvation, before the coming age of punishment and retribution.[20]

Erasmus therefore recognized Isaiah 61 as alluding to the Jubilee, and argued that Jesus himself used the text to preach about everlasting rest and freedom. His emphasis on freedom from sin resonates with the writings in the early church, many of which also presented the Isaianic quotation as emphasizing spiritual liberation from sin and Satan (see above). Erasmus did not, however, argue that Luke himself was concerned about the Jubilee.[21]

The Early Sixteenth Century through to the Mid-Twentieth Century

The interpretation that Isaiah 61 referred to the Jubilee, and therefore the historical Jesus was preaching a type of spiritual Jubilee in the Nazareth pericope, was continued by many commentators during the Reformation period. Johannes Brenz, for example, in *An Ecclesiasticall Exposition upon Saint Luke*, wrote that,

> this "spiritual" Jubilee [referred to in the Isaianic quotation in Luke 4:18–19] began first when Christ started preaching the gospel and continued not for a year only but forever . . . we were made captives of Satan through sin . . . but now Christ is come

17. Where the Jewish Jubilees focused on social reinstatement or reorganization, Christian Jubilees are decidedly spiritual in character. While some scholars have argued that Christian Jubilee years are a spiritualized continuation of the Hebrew Jubilee years, the distinct differences between the two are unmistakable. Foley, *The Story of the Jubilee Years*, xi.

18. Erasmus, *Paraphrase on Luke 1–10*, 145–46.

19. Erasmus, *Paraphrase on Luke 1–10*, 145–46.

20. Erasmus, *Paraphrase on Luke 1–10*, 147.

21. Admittedly, however, this may have been due to his hermeneutical methodology or the nature of the work he was writing (a paraphrase of Luke's Gospel).

and has made satisfaction for our sins. He has redeemed us from the power of Satan and has restored to us our former possession of Paradise.[22]

John Calvin was slightly more tentative. In relation to the same passage, he wrote that the reference to preaching "the acceptable year of the Lord" in Luke 4:19 *may* be an Isaianic reference to the Jubilee.[23] In any case, however, he nonetheless viewed the text as an allusion to the time of salvation which was manifested in Christ.[24] Others, such as Henry Bullinger, also wrote that the acceptable year was a reference to the Jubilee which is the time of salvation through Christ.[25]

Thus, the Reformers viewed the Jubilee as being a reference to the eternal redemption that comes from salvation. The captives are those who are under sin's dominion. Freedom occurs through faith in Christ. Jesus, it was argued, proclaimed a type of spiritual release (amongst other things) when he read from Isaiah 61 in Luke 4. Thus, in many ways, the Reformers were in line with Erasmus's interpretation of the Nazareth pericope; however, a rejection and strong criticism of the Catholic Jubilee years was developed during the Protestant Reformation. Importantly, there is no evidence that the Jubilee was linked with any other passage from Luke-Acts during the sixteenth century.

In the seventeenth century, there was a distinct development. In John Lightfoot's *Harmony on the Four Evangelists*, he argued that Luke 4:18–19 was not only an allusion to a spiritual year of Jubilee (which occurred at his death because "then there was redemption and restoring to a lost estate, and out of servitude, by his death") but also a year of Jubilee "in the proper and literal sense."[26] After a brief history of the Jewish Jubilee years, Lightfoot referred to an earlier work by the "most learned Mr. Broughton," who calculated that the final Jubilee year fell at the same time as the year of Jesus' death.[27] From Lightfoot's perspective, therefore, the quotation of Isaiah in the Nazareth pericope served two meanings: 1) that the final literal Jubilee year was to occur in the year of Christ's death; and, 2) that the preaching of the Gospel of freedom was beginning in Jesus' ministry.[28]

---

22. Cited in Marlorat, *Catholike and Ecclesiasticall Exposition*, 140.
23. Calvin, *Commentary*, 229–30.
24. Calvin, *Commentary*, 229–30.
25. Bullinger, *The Decades*, 267.
26. Lightfoot, *Whole Works*, 5:135.
27. Lightfoot, *Whole Works*, 5:135–36.
28. Lightfoot, *Whole Works*, 5:135–36.

Lightfoot's work is also significant because, while he didn't recognize any other allusions to the Jubilee in Luke's Gospel, he did argue that there were two other allusions in Acts. In relation to Acts 2:42–47, Lightfoot reiterated his calculations that the year was a literal Jubilee year.[29] Because of this, he argued that the background to the passage was that Jewish Christians, who were recovering their goods or land which had been sold or mortgaged, had learned of the kingdom of heaven, and they therefore pursued a "community of goods."[30] He also argued that the Synagogue of the Freedmen in Acts 6:9 was probably composed, at least in part, by those freed during the year of Jubilee.[31]

Despite Lightfoot's work, the dominant association between the Jubilee and Luke-Acts in the eighteenth, nineteenth, and the first half of the twentieth century remained centered on the Nazareth pericope. John Wesley, for example, writing in the eighteenth century, viewed the beneficiaries of the Isaiah 61:1–2 quotation in Luke 4:18 as those who were in a miserable spiritual state, and interpreted the acceptable year of the Lord as "plainly alluding to the year of Jubilee."[32] Similarly, in the nineteenth century, there were a number of commentators who saw an allusion to the year of Jubilee in Luke 4:18–19.[33] Most of these commentators saw Jesus' preaching from Isaiah as a declaration of the spiritual freedom and salvation that would come through his ministry.[34] That is, the text was viewed as having a strong connection with the *basileia* of God.[35] Significantly, however, there were also a number of Lukan commentators who didn't mention the Jubilee.[36]

29. Lightfoot, *Whole Works*, 8:75–76.
30. Lightfoot, *Whole Works*, 8:75–76.
31. Lightfoot, *Whole Works*, 8:414.
32. Wesley, *The New Testament*, 151. Matthew Henry, also writing in the eighteenth century, agreed with Wesley in viewing Luke 4:18–19 as an allusion to a spiritual Jubilee whereby the acceptable year of the Lord referred to the time of salvation. See Henry, *Commentary*, 5:360.
33. Spence and Lang, *St. Luke*, 109; Jamieson et al., *Commentary*, 103; Bliss, *Luke*, 84; Godet, *St. Luke*, 150; Farrar, *St Luke*, 103; Lenski, *St. Luke's Gospel*, 246–52; and Lindsay, *St. Luke*, 79.
34. The exception to this is the commentary by Jamieson, Fausset, and Brown, who seem to argue that the allusion to the Jubilee year in Luke 4:19 was a reference to Christ's healing ministry for physical maladies. See Jamieson et al., *Commentary*, 103.
35. See especially Farrar, who, in reference to Luke 4:19, argued that the original Jubilee was "only a type of the true Jubilee of Christ's kingdom," and Lindsay, who wrote that the same verse referred to the "entrance of the kingdom of the Messiah". Farrar, *St Luke*, 103 and Lindsay, *St. Luke*, 79.
36. Commentators of Luke's Gospel who didn't mention the Jubilee include: Foote, *Lectures*; Ward, *Saint Luke*; Stark, *Luke*; Thomson, *St Luke*; Goodwin, *S. Luke*; Schaff, *A Popular Commentary*; and Van Doren, *St Luke*.

By the early twentieth century, it seems that there were more commentators who ignored the suggested allusion to the Jubilee in Luke 4:18–19 than commentators who mentioned it.[37]

Thus, by the middle of the twentieth century, while there were some scholars who continued to view the Isaianic quotation in Luke 4:18–19 as an allusion to the Jubilee, it does not seem to have been considered to be of considerable importance. Moreover, it seems there were no commentators who argued that Luke specifically included the quotation to present Jesus as proclaiming a Jubilee year (in any sense) and Lightfoot's proposal about a literal Jubilee year occurring at the time of Jesus' death seems to have been largely forgotten.

The Jubilee in Recent Interpretation

While it seems that there were few (if any) scholars suggesting allusions to the Jubilee in Luke-Acts throughout the 1950s,[38] in 1961, André Trocmé wrote what would later be translated as *Jesus and the Nonviolent Revolution*, which would prove to have a profound effect on Jubilee interpretation. The book was popularized by John Howard Yoder in his work *The Politics of Jesus*, who, along with Trocmé, argued that Jesus' sermon at Nazareth in Luke 4 was in fact a call for the implementation of a genuine Jubilee year.[39] That is, according to Trocmé and Yoder, Jesus intended that debts be forgiven, lands revert back to the original owners (most likely the poor), prisoners be released, and that "the usurious system by which the ruling class prospered" be overthrown.[40] It was to be a profound social revolution. In contradistinction to Lightfoot, who had argued that the year of Jesus' death was an *actual* Jubilee year that would have been practiced by the Jews of the time, Trocmé instead argued that there is little evidence that the Jubilee was practiced,

---

Commentators of Acts who didn't mention the Jubilee include: Livermore, *Acts*; Wise, *Origin of Christianity*; McGarvey, *Acts*; Thomson, *Acts*; and Denton, *Acts*.

37. Commentators who mentioned the Jubilee in reference to Luke 4:18–19 include Hillard, *St. Luke*, 46 and Plummer, *St. Luke*, 121.

Others who didn't mention the Jubilee include: Findlay, *Acts*; McLaughlin, *Acts*; Clark, *Acts*; Furneaux, *Acts*; Creed, *St. Luke*; Steiner, *St. Luke*; and Manson, *Luke*.

38. While there were no doubt some references to the Jubilee in the 1950s, a demonstration of its perceived general lack of importance is seen in Dahunsi's ThD, which was entirely focused on the Nazareth pericope. While Dahunsi frequently referred to the *basileia* of God, he did not mention the Jubilee once throughout his entire dissertation. See Dahunsi, "Significance."

39. Trocmé, *Nonviolent Revolution*, 30 and Yoder, *Politics*, 32–33.

40. Trocmé, *Nonviolent Revolution*, 30 and Yoder, *Politics*, 32–33.

but that Jesus' Nazareth sermon was a radical call for the implementation of the lost Jewish institution.[41] Significantly, Trocmé and Yoder also identified a number of other Lukan texts which they viewed as containing Jubilary allusions.[42] Yoder's work is particularly significant, since it seems to present Luke himself as having a focus on the Jubilee.

After the publication of Yoder's work and the translation of Trocmé's book into English, there was an explosion of material relating the Jubilee to Luke-Acts, much of which was written in response to Yoder.[43] Indeed, the view that there is an allusion to the Jubilee in Luke 4 has become so popular that some scholars, such as Koet, argue that is now falls into the category of "general consensus."[44] Importantly, the vast majority of this literature only draws a connection between the Jubilee and the Nazareth pericope. There has not, however, been consensus as to the nature of the suggested Jubilee allusion in Luke 4. In very broad terms, it seems there are three major positions:[45]

1. The account represents the historical Jesus' declaration of Jubilee release;
2. The account details Luke's Jubilee programme; and
3. The account does not definitively demonstrate that either Jesus or Luke was referring to the Jubilee.

---

41. Trocmé, *Nonviolent Revolution*, 23–25.

42. Trocmé, *Nonviolent Revolution*, 26–38 and Yoder, *Politics*, 60–71.

43. See, for example, Bovon, *Lukas*, 1:205–15; Bacchiocchi, *From Sabbath to Sunday*, 16–19; Nolland, *Luke*, 1:197–203; Green, *Luke*, 214; Marshall, *Luke*, 184; Fitzmyer, *Luke (I–IX)*, 533; Stein, *Luke*, 157; Leifeld, "Luke," 867; Garland, *Luke*, 199–200, 208; Carroll, *Luke*, 111–15; Tiede, *Luke*, 107; Schweizer, *Good News*, 88–89; Brawley, *Luke-Acts and the Jews*, 20; Bock, *Luke*, 399, 405–6, 410; Kimball, "Jesus' Exposition," 103–10; Ringe, *Luke*, 65–71; Bruno, "Jesus is our Jubilee," 95–99; Hertig, "Jubilee Mission," 167–73, 176–77; Willoughby, "Concept of Jubilee," 48–55; Arias, "Mission and Liberation," 36–44; Johnson, *Luke*, 79; Pao and Schnabel, "Luke," 288–90; Wright, *Mission of God*, 301–2; Balentine, "He Unrolled the Scroll," 164; Smith, *Jesus Twofold Teaching*, 14–16; Matthey, "Luke 4:16–30," 3–11; Sloan, *Favorable Year*, 28–194; Blosser, "Jubilee," 64–153; Ringe, "Jubilee Proclamation," ii–iv, 1–296; Trites, *Luke*, 82; Heer, *Luke*, 78; Butler, *Luke*, 63; Evans, *Luke*, 75; Sanders, "Sins," 84–92; Ford, *My Enemy is My Guest*, 53–64; Barker, "The Time is Fulfilled," 23–26; and Strobel, "Ausrufung," 38–50.

44. See Koet, *Five Studies*, 25.

45. With regard to the first two categories, it is sometimes difficult to ascertain whether a particular scholar's work fits better into the first or second category. This is partly because when one talks about Jesus in Luke's Gospel, one is immediately talking about the Lukan Jesus. If is unclear as to whether a particular scholar's perspective better fits the first or second category, this study has generally opted to categorize them in the first category.

With regard to the first category, as mentioned above, there are those such as Trocmé who argue that Jesus called for the literal implementation of the lost Jewish institution.[46] Others agree that Jesus called for social and political reform but do not view his Nazareth sermon as a call for a literal Jubilee year.[47] Similarly, there are those who believe that the historical Jesus declared fulfillment of Jubilee promises in a physical tangible way (such as hope for the poor, oppressed, and imprisoned) but with less of an emphasis on social and political revolution.[48] Still others see Jesus' Nazareth declaration as a call for Jubilee release which encompassed spiritual release/salvation as well as physical, social, and possibly political reform.[49]

There are also those who indicate that it is likely (though not certain) that Jesus declared a Jubilee release. Within this group of scholars, there are some who argue that this release was from social, economic, and cultic injustices,[50] some who argue that Jesus called his followers to follow the Jubilee principle of debt cancellation,[51] some who argue that it was a picture of forgiveness and salvation,[52] and some who believe that Jesus declared a Jubilee release which encompassed spiritual release/salvation as well as social and/or political reform.[53] Within all of these categories, there are variations in thought as to how certain one can be of what the historical Jesus actually preached.

Within the second category, there is again significant variation in thought. There are some who argue that Luke presented Jesus' sermon at Nazareth as a declaration of Jubilee release which had both spiritual and physical aspects, and viewed the Jubilee as so central that he shaped much of the remainder of his writing (particularly his Gospel) according to Jubilary

---

46. Trocmé, *Nonviolent Revolution*, 30.

47. Rich, "Jesus and the Land Crisis," 155–57 and Hanks, *Third World*, 102–3.

48. Craddock, *Luke*, 62; Hollenbach, "Liberating Jesus," 154; Metzger, *Consumption and Wealth*, 30–31; Kinsler and Kinsler, *The Biblical Jubilee*, 103–6; and Baawobr, "Opening a Narrative Programme," 34.

49. White, "Jubilee," 10; Bruno, "Jesus is our Jubilee," 98; Arias, "Mission and Liberation," 45–48; Hoch, "The Year of Jubilee," 245–58; Wright, *Old Testament Ethics*, 205–6; Wright, *The Mission of God*, 301–2; Kimball, "Jesus' Exposition," 187–93; North, *The Biblical Jubilee*, 115–27; and Green, *Luke*, 212.

50. Carroll, *Luke*, 112.

51. Wright, *Victory of God*, 295.

52. Bock, *Luke*, 410; Hendriksen, *Luke*, 253–54; González, *Luke*, 64–65; Powell, *Luke's Thrilling Gospel*, 110; Trites, *Luke*, 82; Ryken, *Luke*, 168–77; Marshall, *Luke*, 184–85; and Bacchiocchi, *From Sabbath to Sunday*, 16–20.

53. Garland, *Luke*, 199–200; Ringe, *Luke*, 69–70; Esler, *Community and Gospel*, 181–82; Caird, *Luke*, 36; Baker, "The Jubilee and the Millennium Holy Years," 53–54; and Matthey, "Luke 4:16–30," 4–8.

theology.[54] Others also view the Nazareth pericope as a Lukan portrait of Jesus' declaring a Jubilee release in both a spiritual and physical sense, though they do not believe that the Jubilee has a central place throughout Luke-Acts.[55] Within both of these categories of thought there is variation as to how much one should emphasize the possible spiritual aspects of the Jubilee over and against the physical/social aspects. There are also some who argue that Luke believed Jesus' ministry began in an actual year of Jubilee, and so wanted to present the beginning of his ministry in that light.[56] Others see Luke as *probably* attaching Jubilary significance to the text; however, they remain uncertain.[57] Finally, there are some who argue that Luke portrayed Jesus as declaring a Jubilee release, though they do not explain the nature of the release.[58]

The third category of thought can again be subdivided into several categories. There are some scholars who argue that even though it is likely that the Isaianic text referred to the Jubilee, there is no evidence that either Luke or the historical Jesus were aware of the allusion.[59] Others are comfortable to say that it is possible that Luke or Jesus was aware of an allusion to the Jubilee, though this is not certain.[60] There are also other Lukan scholars who address the Nazareth pericope, yet evidently find the issue of the Jubilee so unimportant that they ignore it entirely.[61]

Thus, in sum, it seems that the relatively recent escalation in focus on the Jubilee in Luke-Acts (particularly in relation to the Nazareth pericope) occurred in large part in response and reaction to Trocmé's writings (popularized by Yoder). There is not, however, any consensus as to the presence,

---

54. Sloan, *Favorable Year*, 166–94 and Blosser, "Jubilee," 147–53.

55. Lieu, *The Gospel of Luke*, 32–33; Hertig, "Jubilee Mission," 176–77; Willoughby, "Concept of Jubilee," 51–55; Nolland, *Luke*, 1:197–98; Ford, *My Enemy is My Guest*, 54–56; and Leifeld, "Luke," 867.

56. Evans, *Luke*, 75.

57. Strauss, *The Davidic Messiah*, 221.

58. Wendel, *Scriptural Interpretation*, 239.

59. Rodgers, "Luke 4:16–30," 80; O'Brien, "Comparison," 438–40; Stein, *Luke*, 157; Edwards, *Luke*, 136–37; Parsons, *Luke*, 81; Prior, *Jesus the Liberator*, 139–41; and Pao and Schnabel, "Luke," 288–90. Some of these scholars do not explicitly state that Jesus or Luke was uninterested in the Jubilee; they only point out an allusion to the Jubilee within the Isaianic text.

60. Jeffrey, *Luke*, 70; Schweizer, *Good News*, 89; Tannehill, *Narrative Unity*, 68; Johnson, *Luke*, 81; and Klein, "The Sermon at Nazareth," 157. Klein, however, states that he believes it is extremely unlikely that Luke was aware of an allusion to the Jubilee.

61. Ellis, *Luke*, 14, 96–97; Geldenhuys, *Luke*, 167–68; Talbert, *Reading Luke*, 60; Vinson, *Luke*, 119–21; Morris, *St. Luke*, 126; Gooding, *According to Luke*, 81–84; and Mullins, *Luke*, 169–70.

extent, nature, or purpose of the suggested allusion/s to the Jubilee in the Nazareth pericope (or the entirety of Luke-Acts).

Summary of Findings

As has already been mentioned, there are a number weaknesses associated with the criterion of the history of interpretation, not least of which being that observations can only be based on those sources which have endured the ages. Nevertheless, the criterion provides some insight as to whether other readers, both critical and pre-critical, observed the same allusions as are suggested today.[62]

Regarding Luke 4:16–30, there were no early church authors who interpreted the text as having Jubilary allusions, which is highly significant given the programmatic importance of the text within Luke's two-part work. The first point at which authors seem to draw a connection between the Jubilee and the Nazareth pericope is after (and in response to) the institution of the first Catholic Jubilee year, declared in the year 1300 CE.[63] From that point onwards, there were many who saw Jesus' preaching from that text as a declaration of a spiritual Jubilee. In the seventeenth century, however, Lightfoot argued that the text was also significant because the year when the account occurred was an actual Jubilee year.[64] In the eighteenth, nineteenth, and early twentieth centuries, there remained some scholars who argued in favor of an allusion to the Jubilee in the Nazareth pericope; however, there was also a growing number who ignored proposed Jubilary connections. The publication and popularization of Trocmé's study, as reworked by Yoder, however, saw a greatly renewed interest in the suggested presence of Jubilary allusions. In particular, it saw the rise of those who now argue that Luke himself was keenly aware of the Jubilee institution and wrote the Nazareth account (in part) to describe Jesus' ministry of Jubilee release. There remains, however, little consensus as to whether or how one should connect the Nazareth pericope with the Jubilee. Thus, there is a long but patchy history of the Nazareth pericope being associated with the Jubilee; however, it is only very recently that some scholars have argued that Jesus and/or Luke were aware of, and intended, the connection between the Isaianic text and the Jubilee.[65]

62. Hays, *Echoes of Scripture*, 31.
63. Foley, *The Story of the Jubilee Years*, xiv.
64. Lightfoot, *Whole Works*, 5:135–36.
65. Though, admittedly, this is in part due to developments in hermeneutical methodologies.

Concerning the specific passages examined in chapter 6, there are generally very few authors throughout history who have supported the presence of Jubilee allusions. There were only two other references in Luke-Acts that were seen as having possible Jubilee allusions in the early church period (Luke 9:14; Acts 2:1-4), and there were no proposed Lukan Jubilary allusions in the Middle Ages.[66] There are three alleged allusions to the Jubilee in Acts (Acts 2:42-47; 4:32-37; 6:9) which were proposed during the seventeenth century, though each of these were only suggested by a single author. The remainder of the suggested Jubilee allusions in Luke-Acts have only been proposed in recent times and are only represented by a few scholars (some of them are only represented by a single scholar).[67]

In summary, it seems that the history of interpretation criterion does not support the presence of the suggested Jubilee allusions in Luke-Acts listed in chapter 6. Regarding the Nazareth pericope, there is a long history of interpretation, much of which has been largely reactionary (particularly in relation to the Catholic year of Jubilee and Trocmé's work). There are many who have seen an allusion in the Isaianic text, and many who have argued that Jesus may have declared a Jubilee release as a portrait of salvation. It is only recently, however, that there has been the range of views which

---

66. There is also only passing mention of the Jubilee by the Venerable Bede made in relation to Acts 1:3, though it seems he did not consider the text to be a Jubilary allusion *per se*.

67. The scholars who have referred to Jubilee allusions in Luke-Acts other than the Nazareth pericope are listed below:

1. Blosser, "Jubilee," 133-46 (Luke 1:46-55; 6:18-26, 34-36; 9:1-6; 11:1-4; 12:22-34; 14:12-24; 16:1-9, 19-31; 18:18-30; 19:1-10);
2. Ringe, "Jubilee Proclamation," 165-76, 180-243, 270-82 (Luke 5:17-26; 6:20-22; 7:18-23, 36-50; 11:4; 14:12-24; 16:19-31; 18:18-23; 19:1-10; Acts 10:34-43);
3. Sloan, *Favorable Year*, 123-28, 139-45 (Luke 6:20-26, 27-38; 11:2-4);
4. Hertig, "Jubilee Mission," 173-76 (Luke 1:46-55; 6:1-11; 14:12-24; 16:19-31);
5. Green, *Luke*, 116-19, 252, 548 (Luke 1:68-71; 6:1-11; 14:3-4);
6. Pao and Schnabel, "Luke," 266, 304 (Luke 2:3; 7:42-43);
7. Leifeld, "Luke," 888 (Luke 6:1-11);
8. Garland, *Luke*, 151 (Luke 3:1);
9. Tiede, *Luke*, 155 (Luke 7:18-23);
10. Edwards, *Luke*, 221-22 (Luke 7:24-30);
11. Pilgrim, *Good News to the Poor*, 138 (Luke 7:40-43);
12. Nolland, *Luke*, 1:357 (Luke 7:42);
13. Sanders, "Sins," 87 (Luke 7:42-43);
14. Kinsler and Kinsler, *The Biblical Jubilee*, 103-7, 141-43 (Luke 1:51-53; 7:18-23; 12:13-21; 14:7-14; Acts 2:1-4; 4:32-35);
15. Schürmann, *Das Lukasevangelium*, 76 (Luke 1:46-55); and,
16. Richard, "Now is the Time," 50-54 (Acts 2:1-47).

currently exists, including those who advocate that the Lukan tradition and/ or Luke himself viewed the Jubilee as a central element of the passage (and indeed, some who believe Luke viewed the Jubilee as a central element to his Gospel). That is, while there are many who have seen an allusion to the Jubilee in the Nazareth account, it is only relatively recently that the supposed Jubilee allusions in the Nazareth pericope have been seen structuring principles (a "manifesto") either for the ministry of the historical Jesus or for the whole Lukan corpus—and this despite the far more comprehensive and explicit use of the *basileia* of God throughout the Gospel account.

Appendix 2

The Early Church and the Jubilee

Concerning Hays's criteria for determining Old Testament allusions, one of the criticisms that has been leveled is that even though his methodology emphasizes the background of Old Testament and New Testament texts, it neglects the importance of early Christian sources, especially those subsequent to the writing of the New Testament.[1] Bates, for example, argues that one of the key questions that Hays ignores is how the Old Testament allusion in question was received in early Christianity *apart from* its proposed occurrence in the New Testament text.[2] He argues that if one is to assess intertextuality properly, one must examine all of the sociohistorical discourse that precedes, surrounds, and follows it.[3] In the case of this study, this would mean the inclusion of other Christian texts subsequent to the writing of Luke-Acts which address the Jubilee. That is, while the above appendix addressed the history of interpretation of specific suggested Lukan allusions to the Jubilee, it did not address other references to the Jubilee in the years directly after the Gospel of Luke was composed.[4] Thus, if one is to make a more conclusive determination regarding the presence and importance of interpretations of the Jubilee in the early church, a wider range of patristic material should be examined and not only in relation to Luke's Gospel. That is, did the idea of a Jubilee feature in early church ethics and theology? This appendix therefore addresses the wider possibility of references to the Jubilee in

---

1. Bates, "Beyond Hays's Echoes," 270.
2. Bates, "Beyond Hays's Echoes," 270.
3. Bates, "Beyond Hays's Echoes," 271.
4. The Testament of Levi hasn't been included in this chapter since it has been addressed in chapter 2.

the years directly after the Gospel of Luke was composed. If the Jubilee was understood in the patristic writings in a similar way to what has been proposed by those who see references to the Jubilee in Luke-Acts, this could provide evidence of a Jubilee tradition which supports Jubilary allusions. Conversely, if the wider sociohistorical discourse concerning the Jubilee in the early church has no relation to the proposed allusions in Luke-Acts, this will strengthen the case that Luke's text should not be read in connection to the Jubilee, as it will continue to highlight the level of discontinuity between the early church's understanding of the Jubilee and that which has been proposed in recent years.

Clement of Alexandria

The first obvious reference to the Jubilee in the early church was by Clement of Alexandria at the end of the second century.[5] In his *Stromateis*, he makes a passing reference to the Jubilee as "the chiefest rest."[6] It comes as part of a wider reference to the importance of knowledge, which Clement argued is essential for true perfection (alongside love).[7] His interest in the Jubilee seems to have been linked to its "seven-ness"; he also referred to the seven days of creation, the seven days of purification after becoming unclean, and the seven heavens.[8]

Clement's view of the Jubilee is dependent on the work of Philo, who also referred to the Jubilee in terms of rest in *On the Special Laws* (see chapter 2).[9] He did not relate the Jubilee to Jesus' ministry, nor does he give it any unique Christian meaning. Indeed, the brief nature of the reference suggests that the Jubilee held no special significance for Clement.

Hippolytus of Rome

It is not until the writings of Hippolytus of Rome and Origen of Alexandria in the early third century that one finds a distinctly Christian view of the Jubilee.[10] In Hippolytus's work *On the Psalms*, he argues that there are 150

---

5. O'Brien, "Comparison," 441.
6. Clement of Alexandria, *Strom.* 4.25 (*ANF* 2:438).
7. Clement of Alexandria, *Strom.* 4.25 (*ANF* 2:438).
8. Clement of Alexandria, *Strom.* 4.25 (*ANF* 2:438).
9. O'Brien, "Comparison," 441.
10. O'Brien, "Comparison," 441.

psalms because the number fifty is sacred.[11] According to Hippolytus, this is demonstrated by the days associated with the festival of Pentecost and the number of years in between Jubilee events.[12]

Hippolytus then wrote that there is a coming future assembly toward which both Pentecost and the Jubilee point.[13] This future event will seemingly be characterized by a state of release, as this is how the Jubilee and Pentecost are described.[14] Interestingly, Hippolytus wrote that while Pentecost is a clear symbol of the coming assembly, the Jubilee is merely a shadow of it.[15]

Hippolytus then went to write that the number fifty contains "seven sevens, or a Sabbath of Sabbaths" before referring to the significance of the fiftieth Psalm.[16] This Psalm, he believed, is "a prayer for the remission of sins, and a confession. For as, according to the Gospel, the fiftieth obtained remission, confirming thereby that understanding of the Jubilee, so he who offers up such petitions in full confession hopes to gain remission in no other number than the fiftieth."[17] Thus, it seems that Hippolytus associated the number fifty with the remission of sins. His reference to "the Gospel" is vague—there is no section of any Gospel which mentions the number fifty in connection with the remission of sins. Nor is there any explicit reference to Psalm 50 in the Gospels. It seems that Hippolytus was referring to the Gospel in terms of the good news of Jesus, contained in the Four Gospels, which achieved the remission of sins symbolized by the number fifty and spoken of in Psalm 50. His reference to the Jubilee demonstrates that he viewed it as a picture of the remission of sins. The Jubilee provisions (presumably including the announcement of the Day of Atonement, rest for the land, and the redemption of slaves and property) may therefore have been understood as addressing the sins of Israel.

Hippolytus therefore viewed the number fifty as being symbolic of the remission of sins, and he viewed the Jubilee as one of many expressions of this release. He also viewed the Jubilee as a shadow of a great future event which will be characterized by a great release.

---

11. Hippolytus, *Fr. Ps.* 1.3 (*ANF* 5:199).
12. Hippolytus, *Fr. Ps.* 1.3 (*ANF* 5:199).
13. Hippolytus, *Fr. Ps.* 1.3 (*ANF* 5:199).
14. Hippolytus, *Fr. Ps.* 1.3 (*ANF* 5:199).
15. Hippolytus, *Fr. Ps.* 1.3 (*ANF* 5:199).
16. Hippolytus, *Fr. Ps.* 1.4 (*ANF* 5:200).
17. Hippolytus, *Schol. Matt.* 1.4 (*ANF* 5:200).

Origen of Alexandria

Origen referred to the Jubilee on three separate occasions. In Origen's *Commentary on Matthew*, he connected it with the feeding of the five thousand.[18] He argued that Jesus' instruction to the crowd to sit in groups of hundreds or fifties (Mark 6:39–40; Luke 9:14) comes since,

> it was necessary that those who were to find rest in the food of Jesus should either be in the order of the hundred—the sacred number—which is consecrated to God, because of the unit, (in it) or in the order of the fifty—the number which embraces the remission of sins, in accordance with the mystery of the Jubilee which took place every fifty years, and of the feast at Pentecost.[19]

He therefore associated the Jubilee with rest in a similar way to Clement. He also agreed with Hippolytus in associating the Jubilee with Pentecost. As O'Brien has noted, it seems Origen made the connection based on the words πεντηκοστός and ἄφεσις, both of which only appear together in the Jubilee legislation in Leviticus 25 and in the account of the day of Pentecost in Acts 2.[20] Like Hippolytus, Origen viewed the number fifty as being symbolic of the remission of sins, and he used Pentecost and the Jubilee to demonstrate this.

Origen also referred to the Jubilee in his discourse on prayer.[21] He argued that the reference to "daily" or "today" in the Lord's Prayer ("Give us today our daily bread") is a reference to the entire present age.[22] He then argued that the references to particular days, months, seasons, and years for certain Old Testament feasts and assemblies can also be understood symbolically.[23] He briefly referred to the symbolic significance of the feast of unleavened bread, the Day of Atonement, and the Sabbatical years, before also mentioning "the so-called Jubilee, clearly to imagine whose nature even partially, or the true laws to be fulfilled in it, is for no one save Him who has contemplated the Father's counsel in reference to the order in all the ages according to His unsearchable judgments and His uninvestigable ways."[24] Thus, Origen believed that the Jubilee could be interpreted symbolically

---

18. Origen, *Comm. Matt.* 11.3 (*ANF* 9:433).
19. Origen, *Comm. Matt.* 11.3 (*ANF* 9:433).
20. O'Brien, "Comparison," 441.
21. Origen, "On Prayer," 145.
22. Origen, "On Prayer," 145.
23. Origen, "On Prayer," 145.
24. Origen, "On Prayer," 145.

(particularly with regard to the fifty years), though he did not elucidate how it should be understood.

Finally, Origen referred to the Jubilee in *De principiis* as part of his explanation of Philippians 1:23.[25] He stated that the reason why Paul wanted to depart and be with Christ was so that he might understand the purpose behind all things done on earth.[26] He lists many things (especially Jewish institutions from the Old Testament law) which he argues cannot be fully understood from an earthly perspective, including Jubilee years.[27] Thus, he effectively believed there was a deeper meaning to Jubilee years which cannot be understood.

As is evident above, there does not seem to be a close correlation between Origen's interpretation of the Jubilee in his commentary on Matthew's Gospel and his work on prayer. In both texts he used a spiritual hermeneutic consistent with his general system of exegesis; however, his emphases were entirely different.[28] The reference in *De principiis* demonstrated that he believed the Jubilee had a deeper meaning, though he seemingly wasn't sure about what it was. Overall, it seems that Origen was not particularly interested in the Jubilee. His chief purpose in referring to the Jubilee was to elucidate other truths.

The Fourth and Fifth Centuries

There are also a number of passing references to the Jubilee throughout the large corpus of literature of the Nicene and post-Nicene fathers:

1. Basil of Caesarea referred to the Jubilee as part of a wider explanation regarding why Cain should suffer sevenfold for his sins (Gen 4:15).[29] Basil argued that Scripture "continually assigns seven as the number of the remission of sins," and cited Sabbath years and Jubilee years as evidence (where Jubilee years are described as seven weeks of years).[30] In relation to the Jubilee, he argued that the resting of the land, remission of debts, and liberation of slaves effectively meant that life started over; the old life was completed.[31] Thus, Basil used the Jubilee

---

25. Origen, *Princ.* 2.11 (*ANF* 4:298).
26. Origen, *Princ.* 2.11 (*ANF* 4:298).
27. Origen, *Princ.* 2.11 (*ANF* 4:298).
28. Reno, "Origen and Spiritual Interpretation," 112–18.
29. Basil of Caesarea, *To Optimus the Bishop* 3 (*NPNF2* 8:297).
30. Basil of Caesarea, *To Optimus the Bishop* 3 (*NPNF2* 8:297–98).
31. Basil of Caesarea, *To Optimus the Bishop* 3 (*NPNF2* 8:298).

as an expression of the remission of sins, which was symbolized by the number seven.

2. Gregory of Nazianzus referred to the Jubilee in connection with the feast of Pentecost.[32] Like Basil of Caesarea, he also venerated the number seven; however, he focused on its mystical significance rather than its association with the remission of sins.[33] As part of his discourse on the number, he also referred to the importance of "Hebdomads of Hebdomads, alike in days and years. The Hebdomads of days give birth to Pentecost, a day called holy among them; and those of years to what they call the Jubilee, which also has a release of land, and a manumission of slaves, and a release of possessions bought."[34] This brief reference again underlines the Jubilee's numerical significance and the release with which it was associated. Unlike earlier writers, Gregory did not explicitly associate the Jubilee with the remission of sins.

3. In the *Apostolic Constitutions and Canons*, a prayer of thanksgiving is offered on behalf of God's provision for his people, which includes the appointment of the Jubilee.[35] It is listed alongside the Sabbath and Sabbath years, and is described as "the revolution of these . . . which is the fiftieth year for remission."[36]

4. John Chrysostom mentioned the Jubilee in reference to the righteous practices of the scribes and the Pharisees which are insufficient for entry into the kingdom of heaven (Matt 5:20).[37] His phraseology suggests that he understood the Jubilee as having been literally enacted; however, this also may be attributed to the polemical character of this section of his work.

5. The Gospel of Nicodemus refers to the memorial of Jesus as lasting until the Jubilee, which seems to be equated with the eschatological age which will last forever (though the reference is brief and quite unclear).[38]

6. Augustine briefly mentioned the Jubilee in his *Exposition on the Psalms* in reference to the lack of profit/gain made by the selling of

---

32. Gregory of Nazianzus, *On Pentecost* 2 (*NPNF*2 7:379).
33. Gregory of Nazianzus, *On Pentecost* 2 (*NPNF*2 7:379).
34. Gregory of Nazianzus, *On Pentecost* 2 (*NPNF*2 7:379).
35. *Apos. Con.* 36 (*ANF* 7:474).
36. *Apos. Con.* 36 (*ANF* 7:474).
37. Chrysostom, *Hom. Matt.* 64 (*NPNF*1 10:396).
38. *Gos. Nic.* 1:16 (*ANF* 8:425).

God's people in Psalm 44:12.[39] Augustine here used *jubilationibus*, which (at least in this text) he did not appear to link to the Jubilee of Leviticus 25.[40]

7. Another passing reference to the Jubilee is that by Jerome in his treatise *Against Jovinianus*. The Jubilee is mentioned as part of Jovinianus's claim, recorded by Jerome, that all who are saved will have equal reward, since,

> all Hebrews had the same Passover, the same Feast of Tabernacles, the same Sabbath, the same New Moons. In the seventh, the Sabbatical Year, all prisoners were released without distinction of persons, and in the year of Jubilee all debts were forgiven to all debtors, and he who had sold land returned to the inheritance of his fathers.[41]

Jerome then refutes Jovinianus's argument in the following paragraphs.[42] There is therefore no distinctly Christian meaning given to the Jubilee in Jerome's writings.

8. The final passing reference to the Jubilee is in Ambrose of Milan's second book, *On the Decease of His Brother Satyrus*, as part of his larger discourse on belief in the resurrection of the dead.[43] He mentions the Jubilee as part of his larger argument that the Sabbath in the law of Moses was a shadow of future rest.[44] Like other authors, Ambrose highlights the numerical significance of the Jubilee (even stating that the number of the Jubilee is sacred) and connects it closely with the number seven.[45]

Summary of Findings

When one considers the massive amount of literature the early church produced, it seems surprising that the Jubilee was mentioned so infrequently. This is particularly the case given the frequent mentions and the array of

---

39. Augustine, *Expositions* 44 (*NPNF2* 8:143).
40. Augustine, *Expositions* 44 (*NPNF2* 8:143).
41. Jerome, *Against Jovinianus* 2.18 (*NPNF2* 6:402–3).
42. Jerome, *Against Jovinianus* 2.18 (*NPNF2* 6:402–3).
43. Ambrose, *On the Decease* 2.108 (*NPNF2* 10:192).
44. Ambrose, *On the Decease* 2.108 (*NPNF2* 10:192).
45. Ambrose, *On the Decease* 2.108 (*NPNF2* 10:192).

interpretations of the Jubilee in the earlier Jewish Second Temple literature and the general Scriptural interpretive methods of the early church fathers, which valued every "jot and tittle" of the Old Testament.[46] It is clear, however, that the Jubilee did not exert any considerable influence on any early church writings.

The Jubilee's initial mention in Clement's writings was dependent on Philo's earlier work and showed no distinctly Christian interpretation. O'Brien argues that this is evidence that the early Christians only showed interest in the Jubilee "after inheriting late, second-Temple, Jewish writings on the subject."[47] It was not until Hippolytus and Origen that it was given a Christian meaning. Both authors argued that the principal importance of the Jubilee lay in its exemplification of the remission of sins associated with the number fifty. This meaning, however, was not endorsed by later writers in the fourth century, who mentioned the Jubilee infrequently and interpreted it in a variety of ways. It seems the most frequent interpretation in the fourth century was associating the Jubilee with the number seven, though it seems different authors made this connection for varying purposes. Thus, the Patristic understandings of the Jubilee are inconsistent with the more recent suggested Lukan references. Indeed, it seems there is no consistent understanding of the Jubilee which emerges from the early church material.

---

46. Visotzky, "Jots and Tittles," 264–67.
47. O'Brien, "Comparison," 442.

Bibliography

Aalen, S. "St. Luke's Gospel and the Last Chapters of 1 Enoch." *NTS* 13 (1966) 1–13.
Abogunrin, Samuel O. "Jesus' Sevenfold Programmatic Declaration at Nazareth: An Exegesis of Luke 4:15–30 from an African Perspective." *BThe* 1 (2003) 225–49.
Adeyemi, Femi. "What is the New Covenant 'Law' in Jeremiah 31:33?" *BSac* 163 (2006) 312–21.
Ahn, Yong-Sung. *The Reign of God and Rome in Luke's Passion Narrative: An East Asian Global Perspective*. Leiden: Brill, 2006.
Aland, Barbara, et al., eds. *The Greek New Testament*. 5th ed. Stuttgart: German Bible Society, 2014.
Alexander, Joseph A. *Commentary on the Prophecies of Isaiah*. Grand Rapids: Zondervan, 1970.
Allen, Leslie C. *Ezekiel 20–48*. WBC 29. Dallas: Word, 1990.
Andersen, F. I. "2 (Slavonic Apocalypse of) Enoch." In *OTP*, 1:91–221. 2nd ed. Peabody, MA: Hendrickson, 2011.
Anderson, Hugh. "Broadening Horizons: The Rejection at Nazareth Pericope of Luke 4.16–30 in Light of Recent Critical Trends." *Int* 18 (1964) 259–75.
Anderson, Richard H. "Theophilus: A Proposal." *EvQ* 69 (1997) 195–215.
The Ante-Nicene Fathers. Edited by Alexander Roberts and James Donaldson. 1885–1887. 10 vols. Repr. Peabody, MA: Hendrickson, 1994.
Aquinas, Thomas. *St. Luke*. Vol. 3 of *Catena Aurea: Commentary on the Four Gospels Collected out of the Works of the Fathers*, translated and edited by John Henry Newman. London: Parker, 1874.
Arias, Mortimer. "Mission and Liberation: The Jubilee; A Paradigm for Mission Today." *IRM* 73 (1984) 33–48.
Arnold, Bill T. "Luke's Characterizing Use of the Old Testament in the Book of Acts." In *History, Literature and Society in the Book of Acts*, edited by Ben Witherington, 300–323. Cambridge: Cambridge University Press, 1996.
Arnold, Elizabeth, and James McConnell. "Hijacked Humanity: A Postcolonial Reading of Luke 8:26–39." *Review and Expositor* 112 (2015) 591–606.
Aune, David E. *Apocalypticism, Prophecy and Magic in Early Christianity*. WUNT 199. Edited by Jörg Frey. Tübingen: Mohr Siebeck, 2006.
Aune, David E., et al. "Apocalypticism." In *DNTB* 45–58.
Baawobr, Richard K. "Opening a Narrative Programme: Luke 4:16–30 and the Black Bagr Narrative." *JSNT* 30 (2007) 29–53.

Bacchiocchi, Samuele. *From Sabbath to Sunday*. Rome: Pontifical Gregorian University Press, 1977.

Bailey, Kenneth E. *Jesus through Middle Eastern Eyes*. Downers Grove, IL: IVP Academic, 2008.

Baker, David L. "The Jubilee and the Millennium Holy Years in the Bible and Their Relevance Today." *Themelios* 24 (1998) 44–69.

Balentine, Samuel E. "He Unrolled the Scroll . . . and He Rolled up the Scroll and Gave it Back." *CrossCurrents* 2 (2009) 154–175.

Baltzer, Klaus. "Liberation from Debt Slavery after the Exile in Second Isaiah and Nehemiah." In *Ancient Israelite Religion: Essays in Honor of Frank Moore Cross*, edited by S. Dean McBride et al., 477–84. Philadelphia: Fortress, 1987.

Barker, Margaret. "The Time is Fulfilled: Jesus and the Jubilee." *SJT* 53 (2000) 22–32.

Barton, Stephen C. "Can We Identify the Gospel Audiences?" In *The Gospels for All Christians: Rethinking the Gospel Audiences*, edited by Richard Bauckham, 173–94. Grand Rapids: Eerdmans, 1998.

Bates, Matthew W. "Beyond Hays's Echoes of Scripture in the Letters of Paul: A Proposed Diachronic Intertextuality with Romans 10:16 as a Test Case." In *Paul and Scripture: Extending the Conversation*, edited by Christopher D. Stanley, 263–91. Atlanta: Society of Biblical Literature, 2012.

Bauer, Walter, et al., eds. *Greek-English Lexicon of the New Testament and Other Early Christian Literature*. 3rd ed. Chicago: University of Chicago Press, 2000.

Beale, G. K. *Handbook on the New Testament Use of the Old Testament*. Grand Rapids: Baker, 2012.

Beasley-Murray, G. R. *Jesus and the Kingdom of God*. Grand Rapids: Eerdmans, 1986.

Bede. *The Complete Works of Venerable Bede*. Edited by J. A. Giles. 8 vols. London: Whitaker, 1843–44.

Bellinzoni, Arthur J. "The Use of Luke in the Second Century." In *Literary Studies in Luke-Acts: Essays in Honor of Joseph B. Tyson*, edited by Richard P. Thompson et al., 59–76. Macon, GA: Mercer University Press, 1998.

Bergsma, John S. *The Jubilee from Leviticus to Qumran: A History of Interpretation*. VTSup 115. Boston: Brill, 2007.

———. "Once Again, the Jubilee, Every 49 or 50 Years?" *VT* 55 (2005) 121–25.

Betz, Otto. *Jesus, der Messias Israels: Aufsätze zur biblischen Theologie*. WUNT 42. Tübingen: Mohr, 1987.

Blenkinsopp, Joseph. *Isaiah 56–66*. AB 19B. New York: Doubleday, 2003.

Bliss, George R. *Commentary on the Gospel of Luke*. Philadelphia: American Baptist, 1884.

Block, Daniel I. *The Book of Ezekiel: Chapters 25–48*. NICOT. Grand Rapids: Eerdmans, 1998.

Blomberg, Craig. "A Response to G. R. Beasley-Murray on the Kingdom." *JETS* 35 (1992) 31–36.

Blosser, Donald W. "Jesus and the Jubilee: The Year of Jubilee and Its Significance in the Gospel of Luke." PhD diss., University of St. Andrews, 1979.

Bock, Darrell L. *Acts*. BECNT. Grand Rapids: Baker, 2007.

———. *Luke*. Edited by Moisés Silva. 2 vols. BECNT. Grand Rapids: Baker, 1994.

———. *Proclamation from Prophecy and Pattern*. JSNTSup 12. Sheffield: JSOT Press, 1987.

———. *A Theology of Luke and Acts*. Edited by Andreas J. Köstenberger. BTNT. Grand Rapids: Zondervan, 2012.
Boda, Mark J. "Figuring the Future: The Prophets and Messiah." In *The Messiah in the Old and New Testaments*, edited by Stanley E. Porter, 35–74. Grand Rapids: Eerdmans, 2007.
Bovon, François. *Das Evangelium nach Lukas*. 4 vols. EKKNT 3. Tübingen: Benziger, 1989.
———. *Luke the Theologian*. 2nd ed. Waco: Baylor University Press, 2006.
———. "The Reception and Use of the Gospel of Luke in the Second Century." In *Reading Luke: Interpretation, Reflection, Formation*, edited by Craig G. Bartholomew et al., 379–400. SHS 6. Grand Rapids: Zondervan, 2005.
Brawley, Robert L. "The God of Promises and the Jews in Luke-Acts." In *Literary Studies in Luke-Acts: Essays in Honor of Joseph B. Tyson*, edited by Richard P. Thompson et al., 279–96. Macon, GA: Mercer University Press, 1998.
———. *Luke-Acts and the Jews: Conflict, Apology, and Conciliation*. Atlanta: Scholars, 1987.
Brett, Mark. "Unequal Terms: A Postcolonial Approach to Isaiah 61." In *Biblical Interpretation and Method*, edited by Katharine J. Dell and Paul M. Joyce, 279–96. Oxford: Oxford University Press, 2013.
Brettler, Marc Zvi. *God is King: Understanding an Israelite Metaphor*. Edited by David J. A. Clines and Philip R. Davies. 2nd ed. JSOTSup 76. Sheffield: JSOT Press, 1989.
Bright, John. *The Kingdom of God*. Nashville: Abingdon, 1953.
Brodie, Thomas L. "Luke-Acts as an Imitation and Emulation of the Elijah-Elisha Narrative." In *New Views on Luke and Acts*, edited by Earl Richard, 78–85. Collegeville, MN: Liturgical, 1990.
Brooke, George J. *The Dead Sea Scrolls and the New Testament*. Minneapolis: Fortress, 2005.
Brown, Francis, et al. *A Hebrew and English Lexicon of the Old Testament*. Oxford: Clarendon, 1907.
Brueggemann, Walter. *Isaiah 40–66*. WesBC. Louisville, KY: Westminster John Knox, 1998.
Bruno, Christopher. "'Jesus Is Our Jubilee' . . . But How? The OT Background and Lukan Fulfillment of the Ethics of Jubilee." *JETS* 53 (2010) 81–101.
Bullinger, Heinrich. *The Decades of Henry Bullinger*. Edited by Thomas Harding. 5 vols. Cambridge: Cambridge University Press, 1849–1852.
Bullock, C. Hassell. *Encountering the Book of Psalms*. Grand Rapids: Baker Academic, 2001.
Bultmann, Rudolf. "ἀφίημι, ἄφεσις, παρίημι, πάρεσις." In *TDNT* 1:509–12.
Busse, Ulrich. *Das Nazareth-Manifest Jesu: Eine Einfürung in das lukanische Jesusbild nach Lk 4,16–30*. SBS 91. Stuttgart: Katholisches Bibelwerk, 1978.
———. *Die Wunder des Propheten Jesus: Die Rezeption, Komposition und Interpretation der Wundertradition im Evangelium des Lukas*. FB. Stuttgart: Katholisches Bibelwerk, 1977.
Butler, Trent C. *Luke*. Edited by Max Anders. HNTC. Nashville: Holman Reference, 2000.
Byrne, Brendan. *The Hospitality of God: A Reading of Luke's Gospel*. Collegeville, MN: Liturgical, 2000.
Caird, G. B. *The Gospel of St. Luke*. PenNTC. London: Penguin, 1963.

Calvin, John. *Commentary on a Harmony of the Evangelists, Matthew, Mark, and Luke*. Translated by William Pringle. 3 vols. Edinburgh: Calvin Translation Society, 1845.
Carey, Greg. *The Gospel according to Luke: All Flesh Shall See God's Salvation*. PGNT 3. Sheffield: Sheffield Phoenix, 2012.
Carroll, John T. *Luke: A Commentary*. Louisville, KY: Westminster John Knox, 2012.
———. *Response to the End of History: Eschatology and Situation in Luke-Acts*. SBLDS 92. Decatur, GA: Society of Biblical Literature, 1988.
Carroll, Robert P. *Jeremiah: A Commentary*. OTL. London: SCM, 1986.
Cassidy, Richard J. *Jesus, Politics, and Society*. New York: Orbis, 1983.
Catchpole, David R. "The Anointed One in Nazareth." In *From Jesus to John: Essays on Jesus and New Testament Christology in Honour of Marinus de Jonge*, edited by Martinus C. de Boer, 231–51. JSNTSup 84. Sheffield: JSOT Press, 1993.
Charles, R. H. *The Book of Jubilees or the Little Genesis*. London: Adam & Charles Black, 1902.
Charlesworth, James H. "From Messianology to Christology: Problems and Prospects." In *The Messiah: Developments in Earliest Judaism and Christianity*, edited by James H. Charlesworth, 3–35. Minneapolis: Fortress, 1992.
———. *The Old Testament Pseudepigrapha and the New Testament*. SNTSMS 54. Cambridge: Cambridge University Press, 1985.
Chilton, Bruce. "Announcement in *Nazara*: An Analysis of Luke 4:16–21." In *Gospel Perspectives: Studies of History and Tradition in the Four Gospels*, edited by R. T. France et al., 147-72. Gospel Perspectives 3. Sheffield: JSOT Press, 1981.
———. *The Glory of Israel: The Theology and Provenance of the Isaiah Targum*. JSOTSup 23. Sheffield: Sheffield Academic, 1983.
———. *God in Strength: Jesus' Announcement of the Kingdom*. TBS. Sheffield: JSOT Press, 1987.
———. *The Kingdom of God in the Teaching of Jesus*. IRT 5. Philadelphia: Fortress, 1984.
———. *Pure Kingdom: Jesus' Vision of God*. Grand Rapids: Eerdmans, 1996.
Cho, Youngmo. "Spirit and Kingdom in Luke-Acts: Proclamation as the Primary Role of the Spirit in Relation to the Kingdom of God in Luke-Acts." *AJPS* 6 (2003) 173–97.
Clark, George W. *The Acts of the Apostles*. 2nd ed. Philadelphia: American Baptist, 1917.
Clements, R. E. "The Messianic Hope in the Old Testament." *JSOT* 13 (1989) 3–19.
Clines, David J. A. *The Theme of the Pentateuch*. 2nd ed. JSOTSup 10. Sheffield: Sheffield Academic, 1997.
Cohen, Naomi G. "Philo and Midrash." *Judaism* 44 (1995) 196–207.
Cogan, Mordechai. *1 Kings*. AB 10. New York: Doubleday, 2000.
Collins, Adela Y., and John J. Collins. *King and Messiah as Son of God*. Grand Rapids: Eerdmans, 2008.
Collins, John J. *Apocalypticism in the Dead Sea Scrolls*. London: Routledge, 1997.
———. "A Herald of Good Tidings: Isaiah 61:1–3 and Its Actualization in the Dead Sea Scrolls." In *The Quest for Context and Meaning: Studies in Biblical Intertextuality in Honor of James A. Sanders*, edited by Craig A. Evans et al., 225–40. Leiden: Brill, 1997.

---. "The Kingdom of God in the Apocrypha and Pseudepigrapha." In *The Kingdom of God in 20th-century Interpretation*, edited by Wendell Willis, 81–96. Peabody, MA: Hendrickson, 1987.
---. *The Scepter and the Star*. 2nd ed. Grand Rapids: Eerdmans, 2010.
---. "The Works of the Messiah." *DSD* 1 (1994) 98–112.
Conzelmann, Hans. *The Theology of St. Luke*. Translated by Geoffrey Buswell. New York: Harper & Row, 1960.
Cook, Michael J. "Jesus at Nazareth's Synagogue: An Anti-Jewish Anachronism." *Shofar* 30 (2012) 133–35.
Cooper, Lamar E. "Qumran and the Messianic Hope." *CTR* 7 (2009) 63–80.
Craddock, Fred B. *Luke: Interpretation*. Louisville, KY: John Knox, 1990.
Creed, John Martin. *The Gospel according to St. Luke*. London: MacMillan, 1930.
Crockett, Larrimore C. "Luke 4:25–27 and Jewish–Gentile Relations in Luke-Acts." *JBL* 88 (1969) 177–83.
---. "The Old Testament in the Gospel of Luke, with Emphasis on the Interpretation of Isaiah 61:1–2." PhD diss., Brown University, 1966.
Cyril of Alexandria. *Commentary upon the Gospel according to St. Luke*. Translated by R. Payne Smith. 2 vols. TCLit. Oxford: Oxford University Press, 1859.
Dahunsi, Emanuel A. "The Significance of the Account of the Nazareth Episode in the Gospel of Luke." ThD diss., Southern Baptist Theological Seminary, 1957.
Dalman, Gustaf. "Heaven." In *JE* 6:298.
Danby, Herbert. *The Mishnah*. Translated by Herbert Danby. London: Oxford University Press, 1933.
Danker, Frederick W. *Luke*. 2nd ed. Proclamation Commentaries, edited by Gerhard Krodel. Philadelphia: Fortress, 1987.
Davies, Philip R. "Eschatology at Qumran." *JBL* 104 (1985) 39–55.
De Jonge, M., and A. S. Van Der Woude. "11Q Melchizedek and the New Testament." *NTS* 12 (1966) 301–26.
Delcor, M. "Melchizedek from Genesis to the Qumran Texts and the Epistle to the Hebrews." *JSJ* 2 (1971) 115–35.
Denton, W. *A Commentary on the Acts of the Apostles*. 2 vols. London: George Bell & Sons, 1874.
Dodd, C. H. *According to the Scriptures*. London: Nisbet, 1952.
Dowling, Elizabeth V. "Luke-Acts: Good News for Slaves?" *Pacifica* 24 (2011) 123–40.
Dumbrell, W. J. "The Davidic Covenant." *RTR* 39 (1980) 40–47.
Dyrness, William. *Themes in Old Testament Theology*. Downers Grove, IL: Paternoster, 1979.
Eaton, John H. *Kingship in the Psalms*. 2nd ed. TBS. Sheffield: JSOT Press, 1986.
Edwards, James R. *The Gospel according to Luke*. PilNTC, edited by D. A. Carson. Grand Rapids: Eerdmans, 2015.
Eichrodt, Walther. *Theology of the Old Testament*. Translated from the 6th German ed. by J. A. Baker. 2 vols. OTL. Philadelphia: Westminster, 1961.
Elias, Jacob W. "The Beginning of Jesus' Ministry in the Gospel of Luke." PhD diss., Toronto School of Theology, 1978.
---. "The Furious Climax in Nazareth (Luke 4:28–30)." In *The New Way of Jesus: Essays Presented to Howard Charles*, edited by William Klassen, 87–99. Newton, KS: Faith & Life, 1980.
Ellis, E. Earle. *The Gospel of Luke*. 2nd ed. NCB. Grand Rapids: Eerdmans, 1974.

———. *The Old Testament in Early Christianity*. Grand Rapids: Baker, 1992.

Eltester, Walther. "Israel im lukanischen Werk und die Nazarethperikope." In *Jesus in Nazareth*, 76–147. Berlin: Walter de Gruyter, 1972.

Epstein, Isidore, ed. *The Babylonian Talmud*. 36 vols. London: Soncino, 1935–1952.

Erasmus, Desiderius. *Paraphrase on Luke 1–10*. Translated and edited by Jane E. Phillips. Collected Works of Erasmus 47. Toronto: University of Toronto Press, 2016.

Esler, Philip Francis. *Community and Gospel in Luke-Acts*. SNTSMS. Cambridge: Cambridge University Press, 1987.

Eusebius. *The Proof of the Gospel*. Translated by W. J. Ferrar. 2 vols. TCLit. New York: SPCK, 1920.

Evans, Craig A. "The Function of the Elijah/Elisha Narratives." In *Luke and Scripture*, 70–83. Eugene, OR: Wipf & Stock, 2001.

———. "Inaugurating the Kingdom of God and Defeating the Kingdom of Satan." *BBR* 15 (2005) 49–75.

———. "Jesus and the Dead Sea Scrolls from Qumran Cave 4." In *Eschatology, Messianism and the Dead Sea Scrolls*, edited by Craig A. Evans and Peter W. Flint, 91–100. SDSSRL. Grand Rapids: Eerdmans, 1997.

———. *Luke*. Edited by W. Ward Gasque. UBCS. Grand Rapids: Baker, 1990.

———. "Mishna and Messiah 'In Context': Some Comments on Jacob Neusner's Proposals." *JBL* 112 (1993) 267–89.

———. "The Synoptic Gospels and the Dead Sea Scrolls." In *The Bible and the Dead Sea Scrolls*, edited by James H. Charlesworth, 75–96. SCO 3. Waco, TX: Baylor University Press, 2006.

Evans, Christopher F. *Saint Luke*. TPINTC. London: SCM, 1990.

Falcetta, Alessandro. *The Call of Nazareth: Form and Exegesis of Luke 4:16–30*. CahRB 53. Paris: Gabalda, 2003.

Farrar, F. W. *The Gospel according to St Luke*. Cambridge: Cambridge University Press, 1891.

Findlay, James Alexander. *The Acts of the Apostles: A Commentary*. London: Student Christian Movement, 1934.

Fitzmyer, Joseph A. *The Acts of the Apostles*. AB 31. New York: Doubleday, 1998.

———. "Further Light on Melchizedek from Qumran Cave 11." *JBL* 86 (1967) 25–41.

———. *The Gospel according to Luke (I–IX)*. AB 28. New York: Doubleday, 1981.

———. *The Gospel according to Luke (X–XXIV)*. AB 29. New York: Doubleday, 1985.

———. "The Role of the Spirit in Luke-Acts." In *The Unity of Luke-Acts*, edited by J. Verheyden, 165–84. BETL 142. Leuven: Leuven University Press, 1999.

———. "The Use of the Old Testament in Luke-Acts." In *SBL 1992 Seminar Papers*, edited by Eugene H. Lovering, 524–38. Atlanta: Scholars, 1992.

Flint, Peter. *The Dead Sea Scrolls*. Nashville: Abingdon, 2013.

Foley, Brian C. *The Story of the Jubilee Years, Later Called Holy Years 1300–1975*. Lancashire: T. Snape, 2000.

Foote, James. *Lectures on the Gospel according to Luke*. 2nd ed. Edinburgh: John Johnstone, 1849.

Forbes, Greg W., and Scott D. Harrower. *Raised from Obscurity: A Narratival and Theological Study of the Characterization of Women in Luke-Acts*. Eugene, OR: Pickwick, 2015.

France, R. T. *Jesus and the Old Testament*. Vancouver, BC: Regent College, 1998.

Freedman, H., and Maurice Simon, eds. *Midrash Rabbah*. 10 vols. London: Soncino, 1961.

Fried, Lisbeth S., and David N. Freedman. "Was the Jubilee Observed in Preexilic Judah?" In *Leviticus 23–27: A New Translation with Introduction and Commentary*, 2257–70. AB 3B. New York: Doubleday, 2001.

Friedrich, Gerhard. "εὐαγγελίζομαι." In *TDNT* 2:707–21.

Fuellenbach, John. *The Kingdom of God: The Message of Jesus Today*. New York: Orbis, 1995.

Furneaux, William Mordaunt. *The Acts of the Apostles*. Oxford: Clarendon, 1912.

Garland, David E. *Luke*. ZECNT. Grand Rapids: Zondervan, 2011.

Geldenhuys, J. Norval. *Commentary on the Gospel of Luke*. NLCNT. London: Marshall, Morgan & Scott, 1950.

Gerleman, G., "רצה." In *TLOT* 3:1259–61.

Glock, Albert. "Early Israel as the Kingdom of Yahweh: The Influence of Archaeological Evidence on the Reconstruction of Religion in Early Israel." *CTM* 41 (1970) 558–605.

Godet, F. *A Commentary on the Gospel of St. Luke*. New York: I. K. Funk, 1881.

Goldingay, John E. *Daniel*. WBC 30. Dallas: Word, 1989.

González, Justo. *Luke*. Belief. Louisville, KY: Westminster John Knox, 2010.

Gooding, David W. *According to Luke: A New Exposition of the Third Gospel*. Grand Rapids: Eerdmans, 1987.

Goodrich, John K. "Voluntary Debt Remission and the Parable of the Unjust Steward (Luke 16:1–13)." *JBL* 131 (2012) 547–566.

Goodwin, Harvey. *A Commentary on the Gospel of S. Luke*. Cambridge: Deighton, Bell, 1865.

Gottwald, Norman K. "Kingship in the Book of Psalms." In *The Oxford Handbook of the Psalms*, edited by William P. Brown, 437–44. Oxford: Oxford University Press, 2014.

Goulder, Michael D. *Luke: A New Paradigm*. 2 vols. JSNTSup 20. Sheffield: JSOT Press, 1989.

Grant, Jamie A. "The Psalms and the King." In *Interpreting the Psalms*, edited by David Firth and Philip Johnston, 101–118. Downers Grove, IL: InterVarsity, 2005.

Gray, John. *The Biblical Doctrine of the Reign of God*. Edinburgh: Clark, 1979.

Green, Joel B. "Good News to Whom? Jesus and the 'Poor' in the Gospel of Luke." In *Jesus of Nazareth*, edited by Joel B. Green et al., 59–74. Grand Rapids: Eerdmans, 1994.

———. *The Gospel of Luke*. NICNT, edited by Gordon D. Fee. Grand Rapids: Eerdmans, 1997.

———. "Internal Repetition in Luke-Acts." In *History, Literature and Society in the Book of Acts*, edited by Ben Witherington, 283–99. Cambridge: Cambridge University Press, 1996.

———. "'The Message of Salvation' in Luke-Acts." *ExAud* 5 (1989) 21–34.

———. *The Theology of the Gospel of Luke*. NTT, edited by James D. G. Dunn. New York: Cambridge University Press, 1995.

Gregory, Bradley C. "The Postexilic Exile in Third Isaiah: Isaiah 61:1–3 in Light of Second Temple Hermeneutics." *JBL* 126 (2007) 475–96.

Grundmann, Walter. *Das Evangelium nach Lukas*. 2nd ed. THKNT 3. Berlin: Evangelische, 1961.

Guelich, Robert A. *The Sermon on the Mount.* Waco, TX: Word, 1982.
Guilding, Aileen. *The Fourth Gospel and Jewish Worship.* Oxford: Clarendon, 1960.
Guillaume, Philippe. *Land, Credit and Crisis.* Sheffield: Equinox, 2012.
Gunkel, Hermann, and Joachim Begrich. *An Introduction to the Psalms.* Translated by James D. Nogalski. Mercer Library of Biblical Studies. Macon, GA: Mercer University Press, 1998.
Hahn, Scott W. "Kingdom and Church in Luke-Acts: From Davidic Christology to Kingdom Ecclesiology." In *Reading Luke: Interpretation, Reflection, Formation*, edited by Craig G. Bartholomew et al., 294–321. SHS 6. Grand Rapids: Zondervan, 2005.
Hanks, Thomas D. *God So Loved the Third World.* Translated by James C. Dekker. New York: Orbis, 1983.
Harbin, Michael A. "Jubilee and Social Justice." *JETS* 54 (2011) 685–99.
Harris, William V. *Ancient Literacy.* London: Harvard University Press, 1989.
Hartley, John E. *Leviticus.* WBC 4. Dallas: Word, 1992.
Hartsock, Chad. *Sight and Blindness in Luke-Acts.* Leiden: Brill, 2008.
Hays, Richard B. *The Conversion of the Imagination.* Grand Rapids: Eerdmans, 2005.
———. *Echoes of Scripture in the Gospels.* Waco, TX: Baylor University Press, 2016.
———. *Echoes of Scripture in the Letters of Paul.* New Haven: Yale University Press, 1989.
Heard, Warren. "Luke's Attitude toward the Rich and the Poor." *TJ* 9 (1988) 47–80.
Heer, Ken. *Luke.* WBCS. Indianapolis: Wesleyan, 2007.
Heinemann, J. "The Triennial Lectionary Cycle." *JJS* 19 (1968) 41–48.
Hendriksen, William. *New Testament Commentary: Luke.* Edinburgh: Banner of Truth Trust, 1979.
Henry, Matthew. *A Commentary on the Whole Bible.* 6 vols. London: Fleming H. Revell, 1930.
Hertig, Paul. "The Jubilee Mission of Jesus in the Gospel of Luke: Reversals of Fortunes." *Missiology* 26 (1998) 167–79.
Hilgert, Earle. "Central Issues in Contemporary Philo Studies." *BR* 23 (1978) 15–25.
Hill, David. "The Rejection of Jesus at Nazareth." *NovT* 13 (1971) 161–80.
Hillard, A. E. *The Gospel according to St. Luke.* 5th ed. London: Rivingtons, 1905.
Hoch, Brian. T. "The Year of Jubilee and Old Testament Ethics: A Test Case in Methodology." PhD diss., Durham University, 2010.
Hodgson, Robert. "The Testimony Hypothesis." *JBL* 98 (1979) 361–78.
Hoesl, Marcella. "The Kingdom: Preferential Option for the Poor." *Missiology* 10 (1982) 57–68.
Hoffman, Paul. "Vom Freudenboten zum Feuertäufer. Johannes der Täufer und Jesus von Nazareth in Q 7." In *Erinnerung an Jesus: Kontinuität und Diskontinuität in der neutestamentlichen Überlieferung*, edited by Ulrich Busse et al., 87–106. Göttingen: Vandenhoeck & Ruprecht, 2011.
Holladay, William L. *Jeremiah 1 and 2.* 2 vols. Hermeneia. Minneapolis: Fortress, 1989.
Hollenbach, Paul. "Liberating Jesus for Social Involvement." *BTB* 15 (1985) 151–57.
Horbury, William. *Jewish Messianism and the Cult of Christ.* London: SCM, 1998.
Horsley, Richard A. "Popular Messianic Movements around the Time of Jesus." *CBQ* 46 (1984) 471–95.

Horsley, Richard A., and John S. Hanson. *Bandits, Prophets, and Messiahs: Popular Movements in the Time of Jesus*. Edited by Adela Yarbro Collins and John J. Collins. New Voices in Biblical Studies. Minneapolis: Winston, 1985.
Houlden, J. L. "The Purpose of Luke." *JSNT* 6 (1984) 53–65.
Houston, Walter. "The Kingdom of God in Isaiah: Divine Power and Human Response." In *The Kingdom of God and Human Society: Essays by Members of the Scripture, Theology and Society Group*, edited by Robin Barbour, 28–41. Edinburgh: T & T Clark, 1993.
Jamieson, Robert, et al. *A Commentary, Critical and Explanatory, on the Old and New Testaments*. 2 vols. Hartford, CT: Scranton, 1871.
Jeffrey, David L. *Luke*. BTCB. Grand Rapids: Brazos, 2012.
Jeremias, Joachim. *Jesus' Promise to the Nations*. Translated by S. H. Hooke. London: SCM, 1958.
Johnson, Luke T. *The Gospel of Luke*. SP 3. Collegeville, MN: Liturgical Press, 1991.
Johnstone, William. "Hope of Jubilee: The Last Word in the Hebrew Bible." *EvQ* 72 (2000) 307–14.
Josephus. Translated by H. St. J. Thackeray et al. 10 vols. LCL. Cambridge, MA: Harvard University Press, 1926–1965.
Juel, Donald. *Messianic Exegesis: Christological Interpretation of the Old Testament in Early Christianity*. Philadelphia: Fortress, 1988.
Just, Arthur A., Jr., ed. *Luke*. ACCS, edited by Thomas C. Oden, New Testament 3. Downers Grove, IL: InterVarsity, 2003.
Kawashima, Robert S. "The Jubilee, Every 49 or 50 Years?" *VT* 53 (2003) 117–20.
Keck, Leander E. *The Gospel of Luke; The Gospel of John*. NIB 9. Nashville: Abingdon, 1995.
Kee, H. C. "Testaments of the Twelve Patriarchs." In *OTP* 1:775–828.
Keener, Craig S. *Acts: An Exegetical Commentary*. 4 vols. Grand Rapids: Baker, 2012.
Kilpatrick, G. D. "Luke 2,4–5 and Leviticus 25,10." *ZNW* 80 (1989) 264–65.
Kimball, Charles A. "Jesus' Exposition of Scripture in Luke 4:16–30." *Perspectives in Religious Studies* 21 (1994) 179–202.
———. *Jesus' Exposition of the Old Testament in Luke's Gospel*. JSNTSup 94. Sheffield: JSOT Press, 1994.
Kinsler, Ross, and Gloria Kinsler. *The Biblical Jubilee and the Struggle for Life*. New York: Orbis, 1999.
Kistemaker, Simon J. "The Structure of Luke's Gospel." *JETS* 25 (1982) 33–39.
Klein, Hans. *Das Lukasevangelium*. KEK 3. Göttingen: Vandenhoeck & Ruprecht, 2006.
Klein, William. "The Sermon at Nazareth (Luke 4:14–22)." In *Christian Freedom: Essays in Honor of Vernon C. Grounds*, edited by Kenneth W. M. Wozniak et al., 153–172. Lanham, MD: University Press of America, 1986.
Kloppenborg, John S. "Response to 'Riches, the Rich, and God's Judgment in 1 Enoch 92–105 and the Gospel according to Luke.'" In *George W. E. Nickelsburg in Perspective: An Ongoing Dialogue of Learning*, edited by Jacob Neusner et al., 572–85. 2 vols. SJSJ 80. Leiden: Brill, 2003.
Knight, Jonathan. *Luke's Gospel*. NTR. London: Routledge, 1998.
Knoppers, Gary N. "David's Relation to Moses: The Contexts, Content and Conditions of the Davidic Promises." In *King and Messiah in Israel and the Ancient Near East*, edited by John Day, 91–118. London: Bloomsbury, 2013.

Koch, Dietrich-Alex. *Die Schrift als Zeuge des Evangeliums*. BHT 69. Tübingen: J. C. B. Mohr, 1986.
Koch, Klaus. *The Rediscovery of Apocalyptic*. SBT 22. Naperville, IL: Allenson, 1970.
Kodell, Jerome. "Luke's Gospel in a Nutshell (Lk 4:16-30)." *BTB* 13 (1983) 16-18.
Koet, Bart J. *Five Studies on Interpretation of Scripture in Luke-Acts*. SNTA 14. Leuven: Leuven University Press, 1989.
———. "Isaiah in Luke-Acts." In *Isaiah in the New Testament*, edited by Steve Moyise and Maarten J. J. Menken, 79-100. London: T & T Clark, 2005.
Köhler, Ludwig. *Old Testament Theology*. Translated by A. S. Todd. 3rd ed. Philadelphia: Westminster, 1957.
Kraus, Hans-Joachim. *Theology of the Psalms*. Translated by Keith Crim. Minneapolis: Fortress, 1992.
Kratz, Reinhard G. "Das Alte Testament und die Texte vom Toten Meer." *ZAW* 125 (2013) 198-213.
Kuhn, Karl Allen. *The Kingdom according to Luke and Acts*. Grand Rapids: Baker, 2015.
Kvalbein, Hans. "The Wonders of the End-time Metaphoric Language in 4Q521 and the Interpretation of Matthew 11:5." *JSP* 9 (1998) 87-110.
Ladd, George E. "The Kingdom of God in 1 Enoch." *BSac* 110 (1952) 32-49.
———. "The Kingdom of God in the Jewish Apocryphal Literature." *BSac* 109 (1952) 164-74.
Lasine, Stuart. "Everything Belongs to Me: Holiness, Danger, and Divine Kingship in the Post-Genesis World." *JSOT* 35 (2010) 31-62.
Lattke, Michael. "On the Jewish Background of the Synoptic Concept 'The Kingdom of God.'" In *The Kingdom of God in the Teaching of Jesus*, edited by Bruce Chilton, 72-91. IRT 5. Philadelphia: Fortress, 1984.
Lauterbach, Jacob Z. *Mekhilta de-Rabbi Ishmael*. 2nd ed. 2 vols. Philadelphia: Jewish Publication Society, 2004.
Lee, David. *Luke's Stories of Jesus: Theological Reading of Gospel Narrative and the Legacy of Hans Frei*. JSNTSup 185. Sheffield: Sheffield Academic, 1999.
Leifeld, Walter L. "Luke." In *Matthew, Mark, Luke*, edited by Frank E. Gaebelein, 797-1059. EBC 8. Grand Rapids: Zondervan, 1984.
Leifeld, Walter L., and David W. Pao. "Luke." In *Luke-Acts*, 19-355. EBC, edited by Tremper Longman III and David E. Garland, rev. ed., vol. 10. Grand Rapids: Zondervan, 2007.
Lemche, Niels Peter. "The Manumission of Slaves: The Fallow Year, the Sabbatical Year, the Jobel Year." *VT* 26 (1976) 38-59.
Lenski, Richard C. H. *The Interpretation of St. Luke's Gospel*. Minneapolis: Augsburg, 1943.
Levine, Lee I. "The Nature and Origin of the Palestinian Synagogue Reconsidered." *JBL* 115 (1996) 425-48.
Levinson, Bernard M. "The Manumission of Hermeneutics: The Slave Laws of the Pentateuch as a Challenge to Contemporary Pentateuchal Theory." In *Congress Volume: Leiden, 2004*, edited by André Lemaire, 281-324. Leiden: Brill, 2006.
Lewy, Hildegard, and Julius Lewy. "The Origin of the Week and the Oldest West Asiatic Calendar." *Hebrew Union College Annual* 17 (1942-43) 1-152.
Lewy, Julius. "The Biblical Institution of Derôr in the Light of Akkadian Documents." *Eretz-Israel* 5 (1958) 21-31.
Lieu, Judith. *The Gospel of Luke*. Peterborough, England: Epworth, 1997.

Lightfoot, John. *The Whole Works of the Rev. John Lightfoot*. Edited by John Rogers Pitman. 13 vols. London: Dove, 1825.

Lindsay, Thomas M. *The Gospel according to St. Luke*. Edited by Marcus Dods and Alexander Whyte. 2 vols. Handbooks for Bible Classes and Private Students. New York: Scribner & Welford, 1887.

Litwak, Kenneth Duncan. "Echoes of Scripture? A Critical Survey of Recent Works on Paul's Use of the Old Testament." *CurBS* 6 (1998) 260–288.

———. *Echoes of Scripture in Luke-Acts*. JSNTSup 282. London: T & T Clark, 2005.

Livermore, Abiel A. *The Acts of the Apostles: With a Commentary*. Boston: James Monroe, 1844.

Longenecker, Bruce W. *Hearing the Silence: Jesus on the Edge and God in the Gap—Luke 4 in Narrative Perspective*. Eugene, OR: Cascade, 2012.

Lowery, Richard H. *Sabbath and Jubilee*. UBT. St. Louis: Chalice, 2000.

Lucas, Alec J. "Assessing Stanley E. Porter's Objections to Richard B. Hays's Notion of Metalepsis." *CBQ* 76 (2014) 93–111.

Luce, Harry K. *The Gospel according to St. Luke*. CGTC. Cambridge: Cambridge University Press, 1933.

Mack, Burton L. *The Lost Gospel: The Book of Q and Christian Origins*. New York: HarperCollins, 1993.

Mallen, Peter. *The Reading and Transformation of Isaiah in Luke-Acts*. LNTS 367. London: T & T Clark, 2008.

Manson, William. *The Gospel of Luke*. Edited by James Moffatt. MNTC. New York: Harper, 1930.

Marlorat, Augustin. *A Catholike and Ecclesiasticall Exposition of the Holy Gospell after S. Marke and Luke*. Translated by Thomas Tymme. London: Thomas Marsh, 1570.

Marshall, I. Howard. *The Gospel of Luke*. NIGTC. Grand Rapids: Paternoster, 1978.

———. *Luke: Historian & Theologian*. 3rd ed. Downers Grove, IL: InterVarsity, 1988.

———. *New Testament Theology*. Downers Grove, IL: InterVarsity, 2004.

Martin, Francis, ed. *Acts*. ACCS, edited by Thomas C. Oden, vol. 5. Downers Grove, IL: InterVarsity, 2003.

Martínez, Florentino García, and Eibert J. C. Tigchelaar. *The Dead Sea Scrolls: Study Edition*. 2 vols. New York: Brill, 1997.

Massyngbaerde Ford, Josephine. *My Enemy is My Guest: Jesus and Violence in Luke*. Eugene, OR: Wipf & Stock, 2010.

Matthey, Jacques. "Luke 4:16–30: The Spirit's Mission Manifesto, Jesus' Hermeneutics, and Luke's Editorial." *IRM* 89 (2000) 3–11.

Mays, James L. "The Language of the Reign of God." *Interpretation* 47 (1993) 117–26.

———. *The Lord Reigns: A Theological Handbook to the Psalms*. Louisville, KY: Westminster John Knox, 1994.

McComiskey, Douglas S. "Exile and Restoration from Exile in the Scriptural Quotations and Allusions of Jesus." *JETS* 53 (2010) 673–96.

McCracken, Victor. "The Interpretation of Scripture in Luke-Acts." *ResQ* 41 (1999) 193–210.

McGarvey, J. W. *A Commentary on Acts of Apostles*. Cincinnati: Wrightson, 1863.

McKay, Heather A. *Sabbath and Synagogue*. RGRW 122. New York: Brill, 1994.

McLaughlin, George A. *Commentary on the Acts of the Apostles*. Chicago: Christian Witness Company, 1915.

Meadowcroft, Tim. "Exploring the Dismal Swamp: The Identity of the Anointed One in Daniel 9:24–27." *JBL* 120 (2001) 429–49.
Méndez-Moratalla, Fernando. *The Paradigm of Conversion in Luke*. JSNTSup 252. London: T & T Clark, 2004.
Messner, Brian. "'In the Fifteenth Year' Reconsidered: A Study of Luke 3:1." *SCJ* 1 (1998) 201–11.
Metts, H. Leroy. "The Kingdom of God: Background and Development of a Complex Discourse Concept." *CTR* 1 (2004) 51–82.
Metzger, Bruce. *A Textual Commentary on the Greek New Testament*. 2nd ed. Stuttgart: Deutsche Bibelgesellschaft, 2001.
Metzger, James A. *Consumption and Wealth in Luke's Travel Narrative*. BibInt 88. Leiden: Brill, 2007.
Milgrom, Jacob. *Leviticus 23–27: A New Translation with Introduction and Commentary*. AB 3B. New York: Doubleday, 2000.
Miller, Merrill P. "The Function of Isaiah 61:1–2 in 11Q Melchizedek." *JBL* 88 (1969) 467–69.
Miller, Robert J. "Elijah, John, and Jesus in the Gospel of Luke." *NTS* 34 (1988) 611–22.
Miner, Daniel F. "A Suggested Reading for 11Q Melchizedek 17." *JSJ* 2 (1971) 144–48.
Morgenstern, Julian. "The Calendar of the Book of Jubilees, Its Origin and Its Character." *VT* 5 (1955) 34–76.
Morris, Leon. *The Gospel according to St. Luke*. London: InterVarsity, 1974.
Moscato, Mary A. "Current Theories Regarding the Audience of Luke-Acts." *CTM* 3 (1976) 355–61.
Mowinckel, Sigmund. *The Psalms in Israel's Worship*. Translated by Dafydd R. Ap-Thomas. 2 vols. Oxford: Blackwell, 1962.
Moyise, Steve. *The Old Testament in the New: An Introduction*. London: T & T Clark, 2001.
Müller, Mogens. "The Reception of the Old Testament in Matthew and Luke-Acts: From Interpretation to Proof from Scripture." *NovT* 43 (2001) 315–330.
Mullins, Michael. *The Gospel of Luke*. Chester Springs, PA: Dufour Editions, 2010.
Neirynck, Frans. "Q 6,20b–21; 7,22 and Isaiah 61." In *The Scriptures in the Gospels*, edited by Christopher M. Tuckett, 27–64. BETL 131. Leuven: Leuven University Press, 1997.
Neusner, Jacob. "Form and Meaning in Mishnah." *JAAR* 45 (1977) 27–54.
———. "From Scripture to Mishnah: The Origins of Mishnah's Fifth Division." *JBL* 98 (1979) 269–83.
———. "Messianic Themes in Formative Judaism." *JAAR* 52 (1984) 357–74.
———. "Mishnah and Messiah." In *Judaisms and Their Messiahs at the Turn of the Christian Era*, edited by Jacob Neusner et al., 265–82. Cambridge: Cambridge University Press, 1987.
The Nicene and Post-Nicene Fathers: First Series. Edited by Philip Schaff. 1886–1889. 14 vols. Reprint, Peabody, MA: Hendrickson, 1994.
The Nicene and Post-Nicene Fathers: Second Series. Edited by Philip Schaff and Henry Wace. 1890–1900. 14 vols. Reprint, Peabody, MA: Hendrickson, 1994.
Nickelsburg, George W. E. "Revisiting the Rich and the Poor in 1 Enoch 92–105 and the Gospel according to Luke." In *George W. E. Nickelsburg in Perspective: An Ongoing Dialogue of Learning*, edited by Jacob Neusner and Alan J. Avery-Peck, 2:547–71. SJSJ. Leiden: Brill, 2003.

---. "Riches, the Rich, and God's Judgment in 1 Enoch 92–105 and the Gospel according to Luke." In *George W. E. Nickelsburg in Perspective: An Ongoing Dialogue of Learning*, edited by Jacob Neusner and Alan J. Avery-Peck, 2:521–46. SJSJ. Leiden: Brill, 2003.
Noble, Lowell. "Ownership, Land, and Jubilee Justice." In *Making Housing Happen: Faith-based Affordable Housing Models*, edited by Jill S. Shook, 28–41. Eugene, OR: Cascade, 2010.
Nolland, John. "Classical and Rabbinic Parallels to 'Physician, Heal Yourself' (Lk 4:23)." *NovT* 21 (1979) 193–209.
---. "Impressed Unbelievers as Witnesses to Christ (Luke 4:22a)." *JBL* 98 (1979) 219–29.
---. *Luke*. WBC 35A–35C. Dallas: Thomas Nelson, 1989–1998.
Noorda, S. J. "'Cure yourself, Doctor!' (Luke 4:23): Classical Parallels to an Alleged Saying of Jesus." In *Logia: Les Paroles de Jésus—The Sayings of Jesus*, edited by J. Delobel, 459–67. BETL 59. Leuven: Leuven University Press, 1982.
North, Robert. *The Biblical Jubilee . . . after Fifty Years*. AnBib 145. Rome: Pontifical Bible Institute, 2000.
---. *Sociology of the Biblical Jubilee*. AnBib 4. Rome: Pontifical Bible Institute, 1954.
O'Brien, D. P. "A Comparison between Early Jewish and Early Christian Interpretations of the Jubilee Year." *StPatr* 34 (2001) 436–42.
Ó Fearghail, Fearghus. *The Introduction to Luke-Acts: A Study of the Role of Luke 1,1—4,44 in the Composition of Luke's Two-volume Work*. AnBib 126. Rome: Pontifical Bible Institute, 1991.
---. "Rejection in Nazareth: Lk 4 22." *ZNW* 75 (1984) 60–72.
O'Grady, Desmond. *Rome Reshaped: Jubilees 1300–2000*. New York: Continuum, 1999.
Origen of Alexandria. *Homilies on Luke*. Translated by Joseph T. Lienhard. The FC 94. Washington, DC: Catholic University of America Press, 1996.
---. "On Prayer." In *Origen: An Exhortation to Martyrdom, Prayer and Selected Works*, translated by Rowan A. Greer, 81–170. New York: Paulist, 1979.
O'Toole, Robert, "The Kingdom of God in Luke-Acts." In *The Kingdom of God in 20th-century Interpretation*, edited by Wendell Willis, 147–62. Peabody, MA: Hendrickson, 1987.
Pao, David W., and Eckhard J. Schnabel. "Luke." In *Commentary on the New Testament Use of the Old Testament*, edited by G. K. Beale and D. A. Carson, 251–414. Grand Rapids: Baker Academic, 2007.
Parsons, Mikeal C. *Luke*. Edited by Mikeal C. Parsons et al. Paideia. Grand Rapids: Baker, 2015.
Patrick, Dale. "The Kingdom of God in the Old Testament." In *The Kingdom of God in 20th-century Interpretation*, edited by Wendell Willis, 67–80. Peabody, MA: Hendrickson, 1987.
Paul, Shalom M. *Isaiah 40–66*. ECC. Grand Rapids: Eerdmans, 2012.
Perrin, Norman. *The Kingdom of God in the Teaching of Jesus*. London: SCM, 1963.
Petersen, Allan Rosengren. *The Royal God: Enthronement Festivals in Ancient Israel and Ugarit?* Edited by David J. A. Clines and Philip R. Davies. JSOTSup 259. Sheffield: Sheffield Academic, 1998.
Philo. Translated by F. H. Colson and G. H. Whitaker. 12 vols. LCL. Cambridge, MA: Harvard University Press, 1929–1962.

Pilgrim, Walter E. *Good News to the Poor: Wealth and Poverty in Luke-Acts.* Eugene, OR: Wipf & Stock, 2011.

Plummer, Alfred. *A Critical and Exegetical Commentary on the Gospel according to St. Luke.* 5th ed. ICC. Edinburgh: T & T Clark, 1922.

Poirier, John C. "Jesus as an Elijianic Figure in Luke 4:16–30." *CBQ* 71 (2009) 349–63.

Porter, Stanley E. "Allusions and Echoes." In *As It Is Written: Studying Paul's Use of Scripture*, edited by Stanley E. Porter and Christopher D. Stanley, 29–40. SBLSymS 50. Atlanta: Society of Biblical Literature, 2008.

———. "The Use of the Old Testament in the New Testament: A Brief Comment on Method and Terminology." In *Early Christian Interpretation of the Scriptures of Israel: Investigations and Proposals*, edited by Craig A. Evans and James A. Sanders, 79–96. JSNTSup 148. Sheffield: Sheffield Academic, 1997.

Powell, Ivor. *Luke's Thrilling Gospel.* Grand Rapids: Kregal, 1984.

Powell, Mark A. "Salvation in Luke-Acts." *WW* 12 (1992) 5–10.

Preuss, Horst D. *Old Testament Theology: Volume 1.* Translated by Leo G. Perdue. 2 vols. OTL. Louisville, KY: Westminster John Knox, 1995.

Prior, Michael. *Jesus the Liberator: Nazareth Liberation Theology (Luke 4:16–30).* TBS 26. Sheffield: Sheffield Academic, 1995.

Reicke, Bo. "Jesus in Nazareth—Luke 4:14–30." In *Das Wort und die Wörter: Festschrift Gerhard Friedrich zum 65. Geburtstag*, edited by Horst Balz and Siegfried Schulz, 47–55. Stuttgart: Kohlhammer, 1973.

Reimer, Ivoni Richter. "The Forgiveness of Debts in Matthew and Luke." In *God's Economy*, edited by Ross Kinsler and Gloria Kinsler, 152–68. New York: Orbis, 2005.

Reno, R. R. "Origen and Spiritual Interpretation." *ProEccl* 15 (2006) 108–26.

Rese, Martin. *Alttestamentliche Motive in der Christologie des Lukas.* Gütersloh: Gerd Mohn, 1969.

Rice, George E. "Luke 4:31–44: Release for the Captives." *AUSS* 20 (1982) 23–28.

———. "Luke 5:33—6:11: Release from Cultic Tradition." *AUSS* 20 (1982) 127–32.

———. "Luke's Thematic Use of the Call to Discipleship." *AUSS* 19 (1981) 51–58.

Rich, Mark. "Jesus and the Land Crisis." *ICJ* 2 (2002) 150–64.

Richard, Pablo. "Now is the Time to Proclaim the Biblical Jubilee." In *God's Economy*, edited by Ross Kinsler and Gloria Kinsler, 43–58. New York: Orbis, 2005.

Ringe, Sharon H. *Jesus, Liberation, and the Biblical Jubilee: Images for Ethics and Christology.* Eugene, OR: Wipf & Stock, 2004.

———. "The Jubilee Proclamation in the Ministry and Teaching of Jesus: A Tradition-critical Study in the Synoptic Gospels and Acts." PhD diss., Union Theological Seminary, 1981.

———. *Luke.* Edited by Patrick D. Miller and David L. Bartlett. WesBC. Louisville, KY: Westminster John Knox, 1995.

Ringgren, Helmer. "Behold Your King Comes." *VT* 24 (1974) 207–211.

Roberts, J. J. M. "The Enthronement of YHWH and David: The Abiding Theological Significance of the Kingship Language of the Psalms." *CBQ* 64 (2002) 675–86.

Rodgers, Margaret. "Luke 4:16–30—A Call for a Jubilee Year?" *RTR* 40 (1981) 72–82.

Rohrbaugh, Richard L. "Legitimate Sonship—A Test of Honour. A Social-Scientific Study of Luke 4:1–30." In *Modelling Early Christianity*, edited by Philip F. Esler, 183–97. London: Routledge, 1995.

Rowe, C. Kavin. *Early Narrative Christology: The Lord in the Gospel of Luke*. New York: Walter de Gruyter, 2006.
Rowland, Christopher. *The Open Heaven: A Study of the Apocalyptic in Judaism and Early Christianity*. London: SPCK, 1982.
Russell, David S. *The Method and Message of Jewish Apocalyptic*. OTL. London: SCM, 1964.
Ryken, Philip Graham. *Luke*. 2 vols. REC. Phillipsburg: P & R, 2009.
Sabourin, Leopold. *The Gospel according to St Luke: Introduction and Commentary*. Bandra, Bombay: St Paul Society, 1984.
Sacchi, Paolo. *Jewish Apocalyptic and Its History*. Edited by James H. Charlesworth and Lester L. Grabbe. Translated by William J. Short. JSPSup 20. Sheffield: Sheffield Academic, 1990.
Sanders, Jack T. *The Jews in Luke-Acts*. Philadelphia: Fortress, 1987.
―――. "The Prophetic Use of the Scriptures in Luke-Acts." In *Early Jewish and Christian Exegesis*, edited by Craig A. Evans et al., 191–98. Scholars Press Homage Series 10. Atlanta: Scholars, 1987.
Sanders, James A. "From Isaiah 61 to Luke 4." In *Luke and Scripture*, by Craig A. Evans and James A. Sanders, 46–69. Eugene, OR: Wipf & Stock, 2001.
―――. "Isaiah in Luke." In *Luke and Scripture*, by Craig A. Evans and James A. Sanders, 14–25. Eugene, OR: Wipf & Stock, 2001.
―――. "Sins, Debts and Jubilee Release." In *Luke and Scripture*, by Craig A. Evans and James A. Sanders, 84–92. Eugene, OR: Wipf & Stock, 1993.
Schaff, Philip. *A Popular Commentary on the New Testament*. 4 vols. New York: Scribner's, 1879.
Schiffman, L. H. "Messianic Figures and Ideas in the Qumran Scrolls." In *The Messiah: Developments in Earliest Judaism and Christianity*, edited by James H. Charlesworth, 116–29. Minneapolis: Fortress, 1992.
Schmidt, Karl Ludwig. *Der Rahmen der Geschichte Jesu*. Darmstadt: Wissenschaftliche Buchgesellschaft, 1969.
Schnabel, Eckhard J. *Acts*. ZECNT. Grand Rapids: Zondervan, 2012.
Schnackenburg, Rudolph. *God's Rule and Kingdom*. Translated by John Murray. Edinburgh: Nelson, 1963.
Schreck, C. J. "The Nazareth Pericope: Luke 4,16–30 in Recent Study." In *L'Evangile de Luc*, edited by F. Neirynck, 399–471. Leuven: Leuven University Press, 1989.
Schürmann, Heinz. *Das Lukasevangelium 1,1—9,50*. HTKNT 3. Freiburg: Herder, 1969.
―――. *Traditionsgeschichtliche Untersuchungen zu den synoptischen Evangelien*. KBANT 1. Düsseldorf: Patmos, 1968.
Schweizer, Eduard. *The Good News according to Luke*. Translated by David E. Green. London: SPCK, 1984.
Selman, Martin J. "The Kingdom of God in the Old Testament." *TynBul* 40 (1989) 161–83.
Shellard, Barbara. *New Light on Luke*. Edited by Stanley E. Porter. JSNTSup 215. London: Sheffield Academic, 2002.
Shepherd, Michael B. "Targums, the New Testament, and Biblical Theology of the Messiah." *JETS* 51 (2008) 45–58.
Shin, Gabriel K. *Die Ausrufung des endgültigen Jubeljahres durch Jesus in Nazaret: Eine historisch-kritische Studie zu Lk 4,16–30*. EUS 378. Bern: Peter Lang, 1989.

Siker, Jeffrey S. "'First to the Gentiles': Literary Analysis of Luke 4:16–30." *JBL* 111 (1992) 73–90.

Silva, Moisés. "ἀφίημι, ἄφεσις." In *NIDNTTE* 1:444–47.

Sloan, Robert B. *The Favorable Year of the Lord: A Study of Jubilary Theology in the Gospel of Luke*. Austin, TX: Scholars, 1977.

Smith, Barry D. *Jesus' Twofold Teaching about the Kingdom of God*. Sheffield: Sheffield Phoenix, 2009.

Spence, H. D. M., and John Marshall Lang. *St. Luke*. Edited by H. D. M. Spence and Joseph S. Exell. 2 vols. Pulpit Commentary. London: Funk & Wagnalls, 1907.

Spencer, Patrick E. *Rhetorical Texture and Narrative Trajectories of the Lukan Galilean Ministry Speeches*. LNTS. London: T & T Clark, 2007.

Spicq, Ceslas. *Theological Lexicon of the New Testament*. Translated and edited by James D. Ernest. 3 vols. Peabody, MA: Hendrickson, 1994.

Stanley, Christopher D. *Arguing with Scripture: The Rhetoric of Quotations in the Letters of Paul*. New York: T & T Clark, 2004.

―――. "Pearls before Swine." *NovT* 41 (1999)124–44.

Stark, James. *Commentary on the Gospel according to Luke*. 2 vols. London: Longmans, Green, Reader, and Dyer, 1866.

Steck, Odil H. "Der Rachetag in Jesaja LXI 2." *VT* 36 (1986) 323–38.

Stein, Robert H. *Luke*. NAC, edited by David S. Dockery, vol. 24. Nashville: Broadman, 1992.

Steiner, Rudolf. *Lectures on the Gospel of St. Luke*. Translated by D. S. Osmond. 1st ed. London: Rudolf Steiner, 1929.

Steinmann, Andrew E. "What Did David Understand about the Promises in the Davidic Covenant?" *BSac* 171 (2014) 19–29.

Strathearn, Gaye. "4Q521 and What it Might Mean for Q3–7." In *Bountiful Harvest: Essays in Honor of S. Kent Brown*, edited by Andrew C. Skinner et al., 395–424. Provo, UT: Brigham Young University, 2012.

Strauss, Mark L. *The Davidic Messiah in Luke-Acts*. JSNTSup 110. Sheffield: JSOT Press, 1995.

Strelan, Rick. *Luke the Priest*. Hampshire, England: Ashgate, 2008.

Strobel, August. "Die Ausrufung des Jobeljahres in der Nazareth-predigt Jesu; zur apokalyptischen Tradition Lc 4,16–30." In *Jesus in Nazareth*, edited by Erich Grässer, 38–50. Berlin: Walter de Gruyter, 1972.

―――. "Plädoyer für Lukas: Zur Stimmigkeit des chronistischen Rahmens von Lk 3.1." *NTS* 41 (1995) 466–69.

Talbert, Charles H. *Literary Patterns, Theological Themes and the Genre of Luke-Acts*. SBLMS 20. Missoula, MO: Scholars, 1974.

―――. *Reading Luke: A Literary and Theological Commentary*. Rev. ed. Macon, GA: Smyth & Helwys, 2002.

Tanenbaum, Marc H. "Holy Year 1975 and Its Origins in the Jewish New Year." *Jubilaeum* 7 (1974) 63–79.

Tannehill, Robert C. *Luke*. ANTC. Nashville: Abingdon, 1996.

―――. "The Mission of Jesus according to Luke IV 16–30." In *Jesus in Nazareth*, 51–75. Berlin: Walter de Gruyter, 1972.

―――. *The Narrative Unity of Luke-Acts: A Literary Interpretation*. Vol. 1. Philadelphia: Fortress, 1986–1990.

———. "What Kind of King? What Kind of Kingdom? A Study of Luke." *WW* 12 (1992) 17–22.
Thompson, Robin G. "Diaspora Jewish Freedmen: Stephen's Deadly Opponents." *BSac* 173 (2016) 166–81.
Thomson, James. *Exposition of the Acts of the Apostles, in a Series of Lectures*. London: Arthur Hall, Virtue, 1854.
———. *Exposition of the Gospel according to St Luke, in a Series of Lectures*. 2 vols. Edinburgh: Adam & Charles Black, 1849–50.
Thurston, Herbert. *The Holy Year of Jubilee: An Account of the History and Ceremonial of the Roman Jubilee*. 1900. Reprint, Montana: Kessinger, 2009.
Tiede, David L. *Luke*. ACNT. Minneapolis: Augsburg, 1988.
———. *Prophecy & History in Luke-Acts*. Philadelphia: Fortress, 1980.
Trites, Allison A. *The Gospel of Luke*. Edited by Philip W. Comfort. CBC 12. Wheaton, IL: Tyndale, 2006.
Trocmé, André. *Jesus and the Nonviolent Revolution*. Edited by Charles E. Moore. New York: Orbis, 2004.
Tuckett, Christopher. "The Christology of Luke-Acts." In *The Unity of Luke-Acts*, edited by J. Verheyden, 133–64. BETL 142. Leuven: Leuven University Press, 1999.
———. "Isaiah in Q." In *Isaiah in the New Testament*, edited by Steve Moyise and Maarten J. J. Menken, 51–61. London: T & T Clark, 2005.
———. "Luke 4,16–30, Isaiah and Q." In *Logia: Les Paroles de Jésus—The Sayings of Jesus*, edited by J. Delobel, 343–54. BETL 59. Leuven: University Press, 1982.
Turner, Max. *Power from on High: The Spirit in Israel's Restoration and Witness in Luke-Acts*. JPTSup 9. Sheffield: Sheffield Academic, 1996.
———. "The Sabbath, Sunday, and the Law in Luke/Acts." In *From Sabbath to Lord's Day: A Biblical, Historical, and Theological Investigation*, edited by D. A. Carson, 99–157. Eugene, OR: Wipf & Stock, 1999.
Van Doren, William H. *A Suggestive Commentary on the New Testament: St Luke*. 2 vols. London: R. D. Dickenson, 1867–69.
VanderKam, James C. *The Book of Jubilees*. Edited by Michael A. Knibb. Sheffield: Sheffield Academic, 2001.
Vinson, Richard B. *Luke*. SHBC 21. Macon, GA: Smyth & Helwys, 2008.
Violet, Bruno. "Zum rechten Verständnis der Nazareth-Perikope Lc 4 16–30." *ZNW* 37 (1938) 251–71.
Visotzky, Burton L. "Jots and Tittles: On Scriptural Interpretation in Rabbinic and Patristic Literatures." *Proof* 8 (1988) 257–69.
Viviano, Benedict T. "The Kingdom of God in the Qumran Literature." In *The Kingdom of God in 20th-century Interpretation*, edited by Wendell Willis, 97–107. Peabody, MA: Hendrickson, 1987.
———. *Trinity—Kingdom—Church*. NTOA 48. Göttingen: Vandenhoeck und Ruprecht, 2001.
Völkel, Martin. "Zur Deutung des 'Reiches Gottes' bei Lukas." *ZNW* 65 (1974) 57–70.
von Rad, Gerhard. "מֶלֶךְ and מַלְכוּת in the OT." In *TDNT* 1:565-71.
Wade, G. W. *The Book of the Prophet Isaiah*. 2nd ed. London: Methuen, 1929.
Waltke, Bruce K. *An Old Testament Theology*. Grand Rapids: Zondervan, 2007.
Ward, Monsignor Bernard. *The Holy Gospel according to Saint Luke*. London: Catholic Truth Society, 1897.
Watts, John D. W. *Isaiah 34–66*. Rev. ed. WBC 25. Nashville: Thomas Nelson, 2005.

Weatherly, Jon A. "The Jews in Luke-Acts." *TynBul* 40 (1989) 107–17.
Wendel, Susan J. *Scriptural Interpretation and Community Self-definition in Luke-Acts and the Writings of Justin Martyr.* NovTSup 139. Leiden: Brill, 2011.
Wenham, Gordon J. *The Book of Leviticus.* NICOT. Grand Rapids: Eerdmans, 1979.
———. *Exploring the Old Testament, Volume 1: The Pentateuch.* EBS. London: SPCK, 2003.
Wenham, John. "The Identification of Luke." *EvQ* 63 (1991) 3–44.
Wesley, John. *The New Testament with Explanatory Notes.* London: Nicholson, 1869.
Westermann, Claus. *Isaiah 40–66.* Translated by David M. G. Stalker. London: SCM, 1966.
White, James B. "Jubilee: The Basis for Social Action." *RJ* 21 (1971) 8–11.
Whybray, R. N. *Isaiah 40–66.* NCB. Grand Rapids: Eerdmans, 1975.
Willoughby, Robert. "The Concept of Jubilee and Luke 4:18–30." In *Mission and Meaning: Essays Presented to Peter Cotterell,* edited by Antony Billington et al., 41–55. Carlisle, England: Paternoster, 1995.
Wilson, Stephen G. *The Gentiles and the Gentile Mission in Luke-Acts.* SNTSMS 23. Cambridge: Cambridge University Press, 1973.
Wintermute, O. S. "Jubilees." In *OTP* 2:35–142.
Wise, Isaac M. *The Origin of Christianity and Commentary to the Acts of the Apostles.* Cincinnati: Bloch, 1868.
Wise, Michael, et al. *The Dead Sea Scrolls.* New York: HarperCollins, 1996.
Wright, Christopher J. H. *The Mission of God: Unlocking the Bible's Grand Narrative.* 2nd ed. Downers Grove, IL: InterVarsity, 2006.
———. *Old Testament Ethics for the People of God.* Rev. ed. Nottingham, UK: InterVarsity, 2004.
Wright, N. T. *Jesus and the Victory of God.* COQG 2. Minneapolis: Fortress, 1996.
———. *The New Testament and the People of God.* COQG 1. Minneapolis: Fortress, 1992.
Yoder, John H. *The Politics of Jesus.* 2nd ed. Grand Rapids: Eerdmans, 1994.
York, John O. *The Last Shall Be First: The Rhetoric of Reversal in Luke.* JSNTSup 46. Sheffield, England: JSOT Press, 1991.
Young, Edward J. *The Book of Isaiah.* 3 vols. Grand Rapids: Eerdmans, 1972.
Ziccardi, Constantino Antonio. *The Relationship of Jesus and the Kingdom of God according to Luke-Acts.* TGST 165. Rome: Pontifical Gregorian University Press, 2008

Scripture Index

Hebrew Bible/ Old Testament

Genesis

1	19
4:15	210
14:19	19
14:22	19
15:7	32
17:6	20
17:8	32
17:16	20
24:7	32
35:11	20
36:31	20

Exodus

6:4	32
14:8	19
15:18	19, 55
18:2	82
19:3-8	19
19:5	19
19:6	19, 59
20:4	19
21	33, 35
21:1-11	33-34, 69
21:2-11	34
22:25-26	33-34
22:25	181
23:10-11	33-34
23:11	81, 82
28:41	39
29:7	39
40:13-15	39

Leviticus

16:26	82, 87
16:34	87
20:24	32
25	30-33, 34, 35, 36, 37, 38, 40, 63, 67, 68, 71, 72, 82, 120, 152, 162, 163, 170, 174, 175, 176, 179, 180, 181, 182, 184, 209, 212
25:1-7	71
25:2	32
25:4-7	31
25:8-55	30-33, 192
25:8	68, 182
25:9-12	31
25:9-10	68
25:9	31, 62, 64
25:10	30, 31, 36, 37, 81, 82, 103, 134, 151, 177, 184
25:11-12	31
25:11	81
25:12	81, 152
25:13	31, 81, 103
25:14-17	40, 62, 71, 172
25:15	68

Leviticus (continued)

25:17	31
25:18–24	31, 62
25:19–22	31
25:21	63, 166
25:23–34	40, 62, 172
25:23	30
25:25–28	31
25:25	30
25:27	68
25:29–34	31
25:29	68
25:30	68, 81
25:31	81
25:32–33	68
25:33	81
25:34	68
25:35–55	36
25:35–38	34, 64, 180, 181
25:35–37	36
25:38	32, 33
25:39–55	31, 40
25:39–42	32
25:40	81
25:41	81
25:42	32, 33, 41
25:44–46	32
25:46	32
25:47–53	32
25:47	30
25:50	81
25:52	81
25:54	32, 81
25:55	33, 41
26:43–45	34
27	68, 72, 82
27:16–24	33
27:17	81
27:18	81
27:21	68, 81
27:22	68
27:23	81
27:24	81
27:26	68
27:28	68

Numbers

21:33–34	19
23:21	20
25:12	100
36:4	33, 40, 81

Deuteronomy

2:24	19
2:30	19
3:2–3	19
3:20	177
3:21	19
5:8	19
5:16	32
7:24	19
9:26	18
11:3	19
13:1–5	156
15	33–35, 63, 67, 170, 174, 181
15:1–18	34
15:1–11	174, 192
15:1–6	69
15:1	81, 82
15:2	81, 82, 103
15:3	81
15:7–11	69, 180
15:9	81
15:12–18	69
17:14–15	20
23:20	181
28:36	20
31:4	19
31:10	81, 82
32:6	28
33:5	20

Joshua

1:15	177
2:10	21
5:1	21

SCRIPTURE INDEX   235

6:2	21	18:28	20
8:1–2	21	19:10	39
10:30	21	22:16	82
10:42	21	23:1–2	39
24:28	177	23:5	29
24:33	177	24:18–25	20

Judges

1st Kings

3:8	20	1:24	39
3:10	21	5:1	39
3:12	20	8:66	177
4:2	20	11:14–21	20
4:23	21	11:29–39	20
		12:24	177
		14:14	20

1st Samuel

		17:1–2	16
		17:8–24	153, 155
2:10	18, 20	18–22	153
8–10	21	18	155
8:22	177	18:20–40	21
9:16	39	19:15	39
10:1	39	19:16	39
10:25	177	21:1–18	34
12:12	18	22:17	177
12:25	20	22:36	177
16:3	39		
16:13	39		

2nd Kings

2nd Samuel

		1	153
		4:18–37	21
2:7	39	5:1–19	154, 155
5:2	20	5:1–14	21
5:3	20	6:8–23	20
5:12	20	6:26–32	153, 155
5:17	39	15:5	20
6:19	177	17:7–8	20
7:1	20	18:15	16
7:5–16	21	19:32	20
7:13	21	23:25	20
7:14	29	24:20	20
7:16	21, 29		
8:11–14	20		
12:7	20, 39		

1st Chronicles

5:26	20
9:1	20
10:14	21
14:2	20
16:43	177
17:4–14	20, 21
17:12	21
17:13	29
17:14	18, 20, 21
18:6	20
28:4	20
28:5–7	20
28:5	18, 20
28:6	29
29:11	18, 20

2nd Chronicles

1:8–12	20
9:8	20
11:4	177
13:5–8	20
13:5	21
13:8	18, 20
17:5	20
18:16	177
20:29–30	20
25:22	177
31:1	177
36:20–23	40
36:23	21

Ezra

1:2	21
4:3	21
7:6	21
7:27	21

Nehemiah

2:8	21
5:1–13	34

Esther

2:18	82

Job

12:9–25	22
21:17–26	22
23:8–17	22
38:1—42:17	22

Psalms

2	23
2:2	23
2:6	23
2:7	23, 29
2:8–9	23
5	24
7	67
7:8–9	103
9:4	18
14:6	114
18	23
18:1–2	23
18:3	23
18:16–19	23
18:31–36	23
18:37–45	23
18:50	23
20	23
20:6–7	23
20:6	23
21	23
21:1–12	23
22:9	18
22:24	114
24	24
24:10	18
25:16	114
29:10	18
34:6	114
40:17	114
44:12	212
45	23
45:2	23

45:6	18	110:9	176
47	22	129:7	176
47:1–9	23	132	23
47:8	18, 22	132:10	23
50	208	132:18	23
69:29	114	144:1–11	23
72	23	144:1–2	23
72:1–2	23	145:11–13	18
80:16	47	146	30
82	67		
82:1-2	103		
82:3	114		

Proverbs

21:1	22

86:1	114		
88:15	114		
89	23		
89:19	23		
89:20	23		

Ecclesiastes

12:13	22

89:26	29		
89:27	23		
89:35–36	29		
89:38	23		
89:51	23		
93	22		

Isaiah

93:1	22, 58	1–39	25, 26
95–99	22	1–2	25
95	22	1:25–26	27
95:7–11	23	2:20	25
95:7–10	23	4:3–4	27
96:1–5	23	5:1–7	25
96:10–13	23	6	25
96:10	22, 23	6:1	18
97:1	22	6:5	18
97:2	23	6:9–11	43
97:6–7	23	9:6–7	25
97:10–12	23	10:1–2	25
98	22	10:20–25	25
98:3	23	11	64
98:9	23	11:1–5	25, 55
99:1–3	23	11:3–5	27
99:1	22	11:10–11	25
99:2–9	23	12	27
99:4	23	13–24	25
99:8	23	16:5	25
101	23	21:17–24	27
103:19	18	24:5	26
110	23	25:6–7	27
110:1–7	23	26:2	27
110:3	23		

Isaiah (continued)

27:1–6	25
28:5–6	27
29:18	165
32:15–16	27
33:17–24	27
33:22	18
34:8	38
35	105–06, 136
35:5	165
37:16–20	25
40–66	36
40–55	25, 28, 41
40:2	29
40:3–5	43, 145
40:9	56
40:12–20	25
41:21–22	27
42:1–4	38, 113
42:1–6	29
42:7	165
43:10	25
44	64
45:21–22	27
46:1–2	25
49	42
49:1–11	38, 113
49:1–7	29
49:6	43
49:7–13	92
49:8–13	36
49:8	26
49:22–26	27, 29
51:4–6	29
51:4–5	27
52	67
52:7–10	25
52:7	25, 56, 74, 103
52:10–11	27
53:7–8	43
53:12	43
54:10	26
55:3–4	25
55:3	26, 43
56–66	25, 38, 40, 42
56:3–4	27
57:13	100
57:15—58:14	137
57:15	100
58–59	42
58	30, 36–37, 41, 135, 136, 144, 159
58:1–12	36
58:2	36, 144
58:3–4	36
58:5	36, 136
58:6	36, 43, 81, 112, 116, 133, 134, 135, 136, 137, 144, 146
58:7	30
58:8	36, 37
58:9	36
58:10	30
59:21	26
60–62	42
60:4–16	27
60:12	25
61	5, 6, 7, 8, 9, 13, 30, 37–41, 42, 44, 83, 84, 86, 87, 89, 91, 99–123, 124, 131, 135, 136, 139, 140, 143, 145, 146, 147, 150, 153, 154, 155, 156, 159, 163, 164–67, 174, 177, 179, 185, 186, 188, 189, 190, 191, 196, 197
61:1–11	137
61:1–3	38, 36, 38, 40, 42, 43, 89, 102, 121, 176, 183
61:1–2	5, 8, 36, 43, 67, 99–123, 133, 140, 165, 189, 198
61:1	30, 39, 67, 81, 82, 100, 113, 114, 115, 116, 119, 136, 137, 146, 154, 165, 166
61:2	39, 67, 100, 107, 131, 136, 138, 146, 147, 149, 166
61:2–3	148
61:4–7	148
61:4–6	42

61:7	100
61:8	26, 30, 42
63:4	38, 176
63:16	28
64:8	28
66:1	18, 27
66:1–2a	43

Jeremiah

3:4	28
3:17	27
3:19	28
11:1–8	26
11:21–23	156
17:12	27
22:8–9	26
23:5–6	27
25:1–12	35
27:16	177
28:9	177
29:10	35
31:1–14	27
31:9	28
31:31–34	26
31:31–32	27
32:1–15	35
32:7–10	35
32:38–41	26
32:40	26
34:1–8	35, 41
34:8	37, 81, 82
34:15	37
34:17	37, 81
34:25	81
46:10	38
50:5	26

Lamentations

3:48	82

Ezekiel

1:26	18, 27
7:13–14	35
11:15–21	35
16:59	26
16:60	26
18:8	181
18:13	181
18:17	181
22:12	181
29:10	35
32:1–15	35
34:1–12	35
34:8–22	35
34:20–31	26
34:23–24	26
34:25	26
36:25–26	27
37:22–28	26
37:23–24	27
37:24–28	26
37:26	26
40:1	35
43:7	27
44:7	26
46:1–18	35
46:17	35, 37, 81
47:3	82

Daniel

2:31–44	26
2:44	18, 25
3:33	18
4:3	25, 26
4:17	25
4:25	25
4:31	18
4:32	25
4:34	25, 26
6:26	25
6:27	18
7:13–14	26
7:14–18	100, 109
7:14	18, 25

Daniel (continued)

7:18	18, 25, 26, 100
7:27	18, 25, 26
9	67
9:24–27	35, 67, 147, 174, 178
12:7	81

Hosea

2:14–15	27
2:18	26
6:7	26
8:1–6	26
14:4–5	28

Joel

1:20	82
4:18	82

Amos

9:11–12	27, 29

Obadiah

21	27, 57

Micah

3:8	39
4:13	27
7:8–17	27

Zephaniah

3:8–9	27
3:14–20	28
3:15	18

Haggai

1:9	177

Zechariah

8:20–21	27
14:9	27, 57
14:16–17	18

Malachi

1:6	28
2:10	28
3:1	100

New Testament

Matthew

4:13	129
5:3	100
5:20	211
5:21–48	79
6:1–6	79
6:12	170
6:16–18	79
11:5	104
13:53–58	126, 129, 130
13:54	129
13:55–56	129
13:57	129, 151, 152
15:32–39	184
17:24–27	79
19:29	90
23:13	79
26:28	86

Mark

1	126
1:4	86
1:14–15	126, 127, 159

SCRIPTURE INDEX 241

1:14	127	1:57	145
1:15	127, 146, 158	1:67	128
1:21–22	127	1:67–79	145
1:28	127	1:68–71	92, 204
1:45	127	1:68	176–77, 185
3:29	86	1:69–75	91
6:1–6	126, 129, 130	1:69	93
6:1	129	1:71	93
6:2	129	1:77	83, 86, 93, 98, 117, 136, 144
6:3	129, 148		
6:4	129, 151, 152	1:79	118
6:5	129	2:3–4	177–78
6:6	129	2:3	177, 204
6:12	93	2:6	145
6:39–40	209	2:10–11	92
7:1–23	79	2:10	113
8:1–10	184	2:13–14	64
9:5	79	2:21–22	145
10:1–12	79	2:21–24	145
10:29	90	2:24	129
10:51	79	2:25	128
12:28	79	2:27	128
		2:29–32	145
		2:30	93
Luke		2:32	79
		2:38	176
1–4	144, 158	2:41–42	145
1:1—4:44	132	3–4	159
1:2	107	3:1	178–79, 204
1:3–4	78	3:3	83, 86, 93, 98, 133, 136, 144
1:3	78		
1:14–55	163	3:4–6	43, 145
1:15	112, 128	3:6	93, 118
1:19	113	3:8	93
1:32–33	88, 91	3:16–18	92
1:32	88	3:18	113
1:35	112, 128, 140, 141, 145	3:19–20	127
		3:20	117
1:38	145	3:21–22	90
1:41–55	164	3:22	112, 128, 140, 141
1:41	128	3:38	79, 176
1:44–55	91	4:1	112, 128, 140, 141
1:46–56	145	4:2	141
1:46–55	96, 204	4:3–12	145
1:48	163	4:3	151
1:51–53	204	4:14–44	132, 159
1:52	114	4:14–30	3, 7, 9, 124, 125–26, 157, 159, 186

Luke (*continued*)

4:14–21	5
4:14–15	124, 126, 128, 157
4:14	112, 126, 128, 140, 141, 158
4:15	126, 157, 158
4:16–37	83
4:16–30	1, 2, 5, 99, 101, 104, 107, 110, 121, 124, 128, 129–157, 160, 165, 178, 182, 189, 190, 194, 196
4:16–22	156
4:16–19	6
4:16–17	138–40
4:16	129
4:17–20	129
4:17	24, 134
4:18–21	92, 101, 112, 128, 145
4:18–19	5, 14, 39, 43, 83, 95, 96, 103, 105–06, 107, 108, 110, 111, 112, 116, 117, 118, 131, 132–138, 140–45, 155, 159, 163, 164, 183, 189, 194, 196, 198, 199, 203
4:18	81, 83, 85, 86, 98, 112, 113, 114, 115, 118, 133, 135, 141, 143, 158, 183, 198
4:19	120, 133, 134, 145, 151, 159, 197, 198
4:20–30	145–57
4:21	102, 121, 122, 145, 146, 147, 150
4:22–30	156
4:22	129, 148, 149, 150, 151, 153
4:23–30	156
4:23–27	134
4:23–24	152, 154
4:23	134, 150, 151, 152
4:24–27	112, 129, 149
4:24	101, 120, 129, 144, 145, 151, 152, 153
4:25	154
4:25–27	101, 145, 152, 154, 155
4:27	134
4:28–30	101
4:28–29	109, 149, 150, 153, 156
4:28	129, 157
4:29–30	129
4:29	157
4:30	157
4:31–44	131
4:31–41	132
4:31–37	94, 117, 144, 157
4:38–40	115
4:39	83
4:40–43	91, 183
4:41–43	94
4:41	117
4:42	157
4:43–44	118
4:43	88, 90, 92, 113, 116, 133, 138, 141, 146, 150, 159
4:44	133, 157
5:1–32	131
5:8	143
5:11	83
5:12–25	115
5:15	183
5:17–26	143, 179–80, 185, 204
5:17–24	117
5:17	116
5:20	83
5:21	83
5:23	83, 93
5:24	83
5:27–32	115, 143
5:29–33	152
5:32	93
5:33–6:11	131
6:1–11	181–82, 204
6:1	152
6:6–10	115
6:6	157
6:9	93
6:13	139
6:17–20	110

SCRIPTURE INDEX 243

6:18–26	204	7:36–50	143, 167, 168, 169, 171, 185, 204
6:18–20	91	7:49–43	204
6:18–19	115	7:41	31, 170
6:18	116, 117, 183	7:42	204
6:19	116	7:42–43	169, 204
6:20–38	2	7:47	83
6:20–26	96, 99, 163, 163, 164, 165, 166, 167, 190, 204	7:48–49	117
		7:48	83
6:20–22	204	7:49	83
6:20–21	107	7:50	93
6:20	88, 95, 113, 114, 115, 145, 166	8:1–2	91, 92, 94, 117
		8:1	88, 90, 113, 118, 133
6:23	114	8:10	14, 88
6:25	166	8:12	93
6:27–38	180–81, 204	8:26–39	115, 117, 144
6:34–36	180, 204	8:36	93
6:39	118	8:39	133
6:42	83	8:43–46	115
6:49	47	8:47	116
7:1–10	115, 154	8:48	93
7:6	157	8:50	93
7:7	116	8:51	83
7:11–17	153, 154	9:1–6	182–83, 185, 190, 204
7:11	157	9:1–2	94
7:16	101, 112	9:2–6	92, 113
7:18–35	99, 101, 110, 165, 166, 167, 190	9:2	88, 91, 116, 118, 133
		9:6	91, 92, 113
7:18–23	85, 107, 121, 165, 190, 204	9:10–17	152
		9:11	88, 91, 116
7:20	166	9:14	31, 183–84, 194, 204, 209
7:21–28	94		
7:21–22	14, 83, 92, 105–06, 110, 112, 115, 118	9:22	101
		9:23–27	93
7:21	118, 166, 169	9:24	93
7:22–28	92, 113	9:27	88
7:22–23	182–83	9:31	29, 145
7:22	7, 104, 113, 114, 115, 146, 150, 153, 165, 166	9:33	79
		9:35	139
		9:36–37	152
7:23	150	9:37–43	117
7:24–30	204	9:39–42	116
7:24–28	153	9:42	116
7:27–28	14	9:46–48	96
7:27	153, 166	9:50	130
7:28	88, 90, 146	9:51	157
7:29–34	115	9:52	157
7:34	109	9:53	157

Luke (continued)

Reference	Pages
9:55–56	51
9:56	157
9:57	157
9:60	83, 88
9:62	88
10:1–16	116, 128
10:9	88, 91, 128, 183
10:11	88
10:13	93
10:21	112, 141
10:25	79
10:30	83
10:42	139
11:1–4	204
11:2–4	2, 167, 168, 169, 170, 171, 185, 204
11:2	89
11:4	83, 94, 143, 170, 204
11:13	141
11:14–16	117
11:16	151
11:20	88, 89
11:32	93
11:37	152
11:42	83
11:50–51	91
11:52	79
12:3	133
12:10–12	141
12:10	83, 143
12:13–21	115, 143, 163, 164, 204
12:16–21	46
12:20	91
12:22–34	172, 175, 176, 185, 190, 204
12:31–32	175
12:32	89
12:39	83
12:45–48	91
12:57–58	91
13:1–9	91
13:1–4	168
13:1	60
13:3	93
13:4	170
13:5	93
13:8	83
13:10–17	117, 157
13:10–13	115
13:18	88
13:20	88
13:22–30	91
13:23	93
13:28–29	88, 92
13:28	88, 91
13:29	88
13:32	117
13:33	112, 157
13:35	83
14:1–6	181–82
14:1–4	115
14:1	152
14:3–4	204
14:4	116
14:7–24	163, 164, 190
14:7–14	204
14:11	164
14:12–24	204
14:13	113, 115, 118
14:15–24	96
14:15	88
14:21	113, 115, 118
14:26	90
15	143
15:1	115
15:2	152
15:7	93
15:10	93
16:1–9	167, 168, 169, 171, 204
16:5	170
16:6	31
16:7	170
16:10–15	168
16:16	88, 89, 90, 92, 113
16:19–31	46, 61, 91, 96, 115, 143, 163, 164, 204
16:20	113, 115
16:22	113, 115
16:30	93
17:3	83, 93
17:4	83, 93

17:10	170	20:1	113
17:11–14	115	20:17	101
17:11	157	21:1–4	172, 173, 175, 176
17:15	116	21:3	113
17:19	93	21:5–38	90
17:20–37	14	21:6	83
17:20–35	93	21:22	51, 102, 138, 145
17:20	88	21:24	145
17:21	88	21:28–31	92
17:22–37	90	21:31	88
17:25	101	22–24	143
17:26–37	91	22–23	156
17:34	83	22:1	79, 83
17:35	83	22:7	79
18:3	51	22:16	88, 145
18:5	51	22:18	88
18:7	51, 138	22:22	157
18:8	51	22:24–27	96
18:13–14	96, 143	22:37	17, 43, 80, 145
18:15–30	96	22:51	116
18:16–17	96	22:64	151
18:16	83, 88	23:8	151
18:17	88, 102	23:34	83, 117
18:18–30	92, 172, 190, 204	23:35–37	151
18:18–25	143	23:35	93
18:18–23	172, 175, 176, 185, 204	23:37	93
		23:39	93
18:22	113	23:40–43	96
18:24	88, 175	23:42–43	92, 96
18:24–25	92	23:51	88, 96
18:25	88	24:19	101, 112
18:26	93	24:25–27	17, 80, 145
18:28	83	24:26–27	128
18:29–30	92	24:29	141
18:29	83, 88, 90, 175	24:31	118
18:31	17, 80	24:42	152
18:35–43	115, 118	24:44–47	17, 80, 145
18:41	79	24:44–45	128
18:42	93	24:47	83, 86, 93, 98, 117, 133, 136, 143
19:1–10	115, 172, 175, 176, 185, 204	24:49	141
19:8	113		
19:9	93		
19:10	93	**John**	
19:11–27	88		
19:11	88	4:44	151, 152
19:43–44	102, 138	7:53	177
19:44	83	16:32	177

Acts

1:1	78	8:22	83, 93
1:2	112	8:32–33	43
1:3	88, 195, 204	8:35	90, 92, 113
1:4	152	9:2	47
1:6	88	9:9–19	118
2:1–47	204	9:20	133
2:1–4	183–84, 194, 204	9:34	116
2:1–2	90	10:4–5	96
2:21	93	10:22	96
2:33a	91	10:23b–48	166
2:38	83, 93, 98, 136	10:25	96
2:40	93	10:34–48	92
2:42–47	172–76, 198, 204	10:34–43	4, 99, 101, 104, 110, 165, 167, 204
2:47	93	10:34	96
3:14	169	10:35	106, 120, 144, 151
3:19	93	10:36–38	154
3:22–23	137	10:36	92, 113, 166
3:22	101	10:37–38	7, 112
3:25	95	10:37	133, 166
4:9	93	10:38	83, 91, 111, 112, 113, 116, 133, 134
4:12	93	10:42	133, 166
4:26–27	113	10:43	83, 98, 136, 166
4:26	88	11:14	93
4:27	112, 113	11:18	93
4:29–30	91	11:20	90, 113
4:32–37	96, 172–76, 204	11:26	120
4:32–35	204	11:28–29	154
4:34	174	13	79
4:35	173	13:4–12	119
5:31	83, 93, 98, 136	13:20	31
5:42	90, 92, 113	13:24	93
6:9	184–85, 169, 204	13:26	93
7:15–16	47	13:32–48	92
7:23	47	13:32–33	89
7:24	51	13:32	92
7:25	93	13:34	43
7:30	47	13:38	83, 98, 136
7:37	101	13:46–48	93
7:49–50	43	13:47	93
7:53	47	14:3	149, 150
8:4–7	91, 94	14:7	113
8:4	113	14:9	93
8:5	133	14:15	92, 113
8:12–13	91	14:17	83
8:12	88, 92, 113	14:21	113
		14:22	88

15:1	93
15:11	93
15:21	133
15:35	113
16	117
16:10	113
16:17	93
16:30	93
16:31	93
17:7	88
17:18–34	92
17:18	92, 113
17:29	170
17:30–33	91
17:30	93
18:11	120
19:4	93
19:8	88
19:13	133
20:21	93
20:24	92, 149, 150
20:25	88, 118, 133
20:32	149, 150
22:6–13	118
24:3	78
24:5	78
24:24–25	91
25:11	169
25:16	169
26:13–18	118
26:17–18	119
26:18	83, 94, 98, 136
26:20	93
26:25	78
27	117
27:20	93
27:24	169
27:31	93
27:34	93
28:8	116
28:23–31	92
28:23	88
28:26–27	43
28:27	119, 134
28:28	79, 93
28:31	88, 118, 133
28:37	116

Romans

3:10–18	137

2nd Corinthians

1:21	113
6:16	137

Philippians

1:23	210

Hebrews

1:9	113

www.ingramcontent.com/pod-product-compliance
Lightning Source LLC
Chambersburg PA
CBHW050345230426
43663CB00010B/1998